RESPONSIVE TEACHING IN SCIENCE AND MATHEMATICS

Answering calls in recent reform documents to shape instruction in response to students' ideas while integrating key concepts and scientific and/or mathematical practices, this text presents the concept of responsive teaching, synthesizes existing research, and examines implications for both research and teaching. Case studies across the curriculum, from elementary school through adult education, illustrate the variety of forms this approach to instruction and learning can take, what is common among them, and how teachers and students experience them. The cases include intellectual products of students' work in responsive classrooms and address assessment methods and issues. Many of the cases are supplemented with online resources (www.studentsthinking.org/rtsm), including classroom video and extensive transcripts, providing readers with additional opportunities to immerse themselves in responsive classrooms and to see for themselves what these environments look and feel like.

Amy D. Robertson is a Research Assistant Professor in the Department of Physics at Seattle Pacific University, USA.

Rachel E. Scherr is a Senior Research Scientist in the Department of Physics at Seattle Pacific University, USA.

David Hammer is a Professor in the Departments of Education and Physics & Astronomy and the Center for Engineering Education and Outreach at Tufts University, USA.

Teaching and Learning in Science Series

Norman G. Lederman, Series Editor

Berry/Friedrichsen/Loughran
Re-examining Pedagogical Content Knowledge in Science Education

Taber
Student Thinking and Learning in Science: Perspectives on the Nature and Development of Learners' Ideas

Rennie/Venville/Wallace (Eds.)
Integrating Science, Technology, Engineering, and Mathematics: Issues, Reflections, and Ways Forward

Rosenblatt
Rethinking the Way We Teach Science: The Interplay of Content, Pedagogy, and the Nature of Science

Linder/Östman/Roberts/Wickman/Erickson/MacKinnon (Eds.)
Exploring the Landscape of Scientific Literacy

Abell/Appleton/Hanuscin
Designing and Teaching the Elementary Science Methods Course

Akerson (Ed.)
Interdisciplinary Language Arts and Science Instruction in Elementary Classrooms: Applying Research to Practice

Wickman
Aesthetic Experience in Science Education: Learning and Meaning-Making as Situated Talk and Action

Duschl & Bismack (editors)
Reconceptualizing STEM Education

Robertson/Scherr/Hammer
Responsive Teaching in Science and Mathematics

Visit www.routledge.com/education for additional information on titles in the Teaching and Learning in Science Series

RESPONSIVE TEACHING IN SCIENCE AND MATHEMATICS

Edited by Amy D. Robertson
Rachel E. Scherr
David Hammer

NEW YORK AND LONDON

First published 2016
by Routledge
605 Third Avenue, New York, NY 10017

and by Routledge
4 Park Square, Milton Park, Abingdon, Oxon, OX14 4RN

Routledge is an imprint of the Taylor & Francis Group, an informa business

© 2016 Taylor & Francis

The right of the editors Amy D. Robertson, Rachel E. Scherr, and David Hammer to be identified as the authors of the editorial material, and of the authors for their individual chapters, has been asserted in accordance with sections 77 and 78 of the Copyright, Designs and Patents Act 1988.

All rights reserved. No part of this book may be reprinted or reproduced or utilised in any form or by any electronic, mechanical, or other means, now known or hereafter invented, including photocopying and recording, or in any information storage or retrieval system, without permission in writing from the publishers.

Trademark notice: Product or corporate names may be trademarks or registered trademarks, and are used only for identification and explanation without intent to infringe.

Library of Congress Cataloging-in-Publication Data
   Responsive teaching in science and mathematics / by Amy D. Robertson, Rachel E. Scherr, David Hammer.
      pages cm. — (Teaching and learning in science series)
   Includes bibliographical references and index.
   1. Science—Study and teaching.   2. Mathematics—Study and teaching.   I. Robertson, Amy D., 1984–   II. Scherr, Rachel E.
III. Hammer, David.
   Q181.R4866 2016
   507.1—dc23
   2015013663

ISBN: 978-1-138-91698-2 (hbk)
ISBN: 978-1-138-91699-9 (pbk)
ISBN: 978-1-315-68930-2 (ebk)

Typeset in Bembo
by Apex CoVantage, LLC

CONTENTS

List of figures	vii
List of boxes	ix
List of tables	xi
Preface	xiii

1 What Is Responsive Teaching?   1
Amy D. Robertson, Leslie J. Atkins, Daniel M. Levin, and Jennifer Richards

2 A Review of the Research on Responsive Teaching in Science and Mathematics   36
Jennifer Richards and Amy D. Robertson

3 Examining the Products of Responsive Inquiry   56
Leslie J. Atkins and Brian W. Frank

4 Understanding Responsive Teaching and Curriculum From the Students' Perspective   85
Tiffany-Rose Sikorski

5 Navigating the Challenges of Teaching Responsively: An Insider's Perspective   105
April Cordero Maskiewicz

vi Contents

6 What Teachers Notice When They Notice Student Thinking: Teacher-Identified Purposes for Attending to Students' Mathematical Thinking 126
Adam A. Colestock and Miriam Gamoran Sherin

7 The Role Subject Matter Plays in Prospective Teachers' Responsive Teaching Practices in Elementary Math and Science 145
Janet E. Coffey and Ann R. Edwards

8 Attending to Students' Epistemic Affect 162
Lama Z. Jaber

9 Attention to Student Framing in Responsive Teaching 189
Jennifer Radoff and David Hammer

10 Methods to Assess Teacher Responsiveness *In Situ* 203
Jennifer Evarts Lineback

11 Documenting Variability Within Teacher Attention and Responsiveness to the Substance of Student Thinking 227
Amy D. Robertson, Jennifer Richards, Andrew Elby, and Janet Walkoe

Epilogue 249
David Hammer

List of Contributors 255
Author Index 259
Subject Index 265

FIGURES

1.1	Ofala's sense of what makes five odd: it has two groups of two and one left over	4
1.2	Representation that accompanies Ofala's explanation for why nine is odd	7
1.3	Representation that accompanies Ofala's explanation for why six is even	7
1.4	Illustration of Camille's discovery, from Hammer, *Discovery Learning and Discovery Teaching,* Cognition and Instruction, 1997, reprinted by permission of the publisher (Taylor & Francis Ltd, http://www.tandfonline.com)	8
1.5	Charging a pith ball with a neutral electrophorus, from Hammer, *Discovery Learning and Discovery Teaching*, Cognition and Instruction, 1997, reprinted by permission of the publisher (Taylor & Francis Ltd, http://www.tandfonline.com)	9
1.6	Two incoming light rays reflect diffusely from two points on the "R" and send multiple scattered light rays to the screen, at right	21
1.7	A diagram of light through an opening (L) and light through a translucent opening (R)	21
3.1	A central spot of light and "fuzzy edge"	60
3.2	The bouncing rays of light	61
3.3	Class consensus ideas	61
3.4	Modeling reflection from a parabolic mirror	62
3.5	Initial model of reflected light	63

viii Figures

3.6	A model of diffusely reflected light	63
3.7	A student models diffuse reflection as glowing light	64
3.8	Pac-Man pellets and potential well model of a Gaussian Gun	68
3.9	Force diagram of a box lifted at constant speed	72
4.1	Reconstruction of Ari's drawing	93
4.2	Reconstruction of Ari's water cycle diagram	95
4.3	Reconstruction of Leah's drawing	96
6.1	Individual teachers' attention to student thinking	138
6.2	Frequency with which tagged moments related to individual vs. group of students	139
6.3	Frequency with which tagged moments related to single point in time vs. extended period of time	140
8.1	Eric, on the right, and his tablemates	170
8.2	Eric mentions the floor stain	171
8.3	Eric gets frustrated	173
8.4	Eric smiles at Mr. James' praise	173
8.5	Eric raises his hand and Mr. James calls on him	175
8.6	Eric explains his idea about the water sinking down	175
8.7	Eric at a loss of words and Mr. James invites him to draw his idea on the board	176
8.8	Eric's first attempt to explain his idea with a drawing	178
8.9	Eric's second drawing attempt	180
9.1	Isaac and Jimmy's roller coaster	194
10.1	Redirection primary category codes	212
10.2	Focus redirection category codes	212
10.3	Mrs. Miller enacts a student's idea for an experimental design. The visual model includes an unopened water bottle placed into a clear plastic bag (quart-sized), which would then be sealed above the water bottle	222
11.1	Fine-grained breakdown of the focal episode. Numbers in parentheses refer to line numbers in transcript	232
11.2	Coarse-grained coherences in the focal episode	235

BOXES

3.1 *Five Laws of Energy Developed by Teachers in the Energy Project*   76
3.2 College Board physics objectives related to the work-energy theorem   79

TABLES

6.1	Teacher camera use	129
6.2	Approaches used by teachers for attending to student thinking	131
8.1	Timeline situating the episode	168
10.1	Classroom Excerpt A	206
10.2	Classroom Excerpt B	208
10.3	Classroom Excerpt C	213
10.4	Classroom Excerpt D	215
10.5	Mrs. Miller's redirections across three implementations of the water cycle module	218
10.6	Mrs. Miller's focus responsive redirections across three implementations of the water cycle module	218
10.7	Classroom Excerpt E	220
10.8	Classroom Excerpt F	221

PREFACE

Responsive teaching, at heart, celebrates the "having of wonderful ideas" (Duckworth, 2006). It stems from several foundational assumptions: that students come to classrooms with a wealth of productive knowledge and experience; that this wealth is too rich and diverse for teachers and curricula to know it in advance; and that students should learn to be the agents of their own learning. From these assumptions comes the stance that teaching begins with watching and listening. Responsive instruction foregrounds the substance of students' ideas, seeks out disciplinary connections within students' ideas, and adapts or builds instruction on the basis of students' ideas. Hammer, Goldberg, and Fargason (2012) write:

> A responsive approach . . . is to adapt and discover instructional objectives responsively to student thinking. The first part of a lesson elicits students' generative engagement around some provocative task or situation (or, perhaps, by discovering its spontaneous emergence). From there, the teacher's role is to support that engagement and attend to it—watch and listen to the students' thinking, form a sense of what they are doing, and in this way identify productive beginnings of scientific thinking. In this way, the teacher may select and pursue a more specific target, in a way that recognizes and builds on what students have begun.
>
> (p. 55)

Responsive teaching is increasingly the focus of teacher education and research. It responds to calls in recent science and mathematics reform documents (National Committee on Science Education Standards and Assessment, 1996; National Council of Teachers of Mathematics, 2000; National Research Council, 2012; Next Generation Science Standards, 2013) that instruction (i) integrate key

xiv Preface

concepts and scientific and/or mathematical practices and (ii) shape instruction on the basis of students' ideas. Ball (1993) describes this approach as both responsive to students and responsible to the discipline. Responsiveness

- enhances students' conceptual understanding (Carpenter, Fennema, Peterson, Chiang, & Loef, 1989; Empson & Jacobs, 2008; Fennema et al., 1996; Fennema, Franke, Carpenter, & Carey, 1993; Goldberg, 2012; Hiebert & Wearne, 1993; Kersting, Givvin, Sotelo, & Stigler, 2010; Pierson, 2008; Saxe, Gearhart, & Seltzer, 1999);
- promotes student agency and voice (Coffey, Hammer, Levin, & Grant, 2011; Gallas, 1995; Lemke, 1990; Levin, 2008); and
- promotes equitable participation by seeking to understand the ideas that all students—including those from culturally, linguistically, and socioeconomically diverse communities—bring to the classroom (Empson, 2003; Gallas, 1995; Hudicourt-Barnes, 2003; Michaels, 2005; Rosebery, Ogonowski, DiSchino, & Warren, 2010; Warren, Ballenger, Ogonowski, Rosebery, & Hudicourt-Barnes, 2001; Warren, Ogonowski, & Pothier, 2005).

For these reasons and others, the recent shift in attention toward practices of teaching—rather than skills—includes "attending and responding to student thinking" among "high leverage" or "ambitious" practices (Ball & Forzani, 2009; Lampert, Beasley, Ghousseini, Kazemi, & Franke, 2010; Lampert et al., 2013; Thompson, Windschitl, & Braaten, 2013; Windschitl, Thompson, Braaten, & Stroupe, 2012).

This book is for readers interested in the current state of research, including some of the pressing questions that future research may pursue. It grew out of our sense that responsive teaching is a key emerging area in science education, and that a number of researchers are beginning to make progress in documenting and understanding its instructional power. We began with a small conference held at Seattle Pacific University in 2013, with the goals of clarifying what our disciplines have to say about responsive teaching, envisioning future research directions and fostering inter-institutional collaborations. The conference involved presentations and video analysis sessions designed to bring out participants' diverse assumptions, as well as areas of consensus. Many of the participants traced their inspiration to similar sources, including classic studies by Ball (1993) and Goodwin (1994) and more contemporary work by Hammer and colleagues (Hammer, 1997; Hammer & van Zee, 2006). However, there were also substantial differences in the ways that various participants conceptualized responsiveness. Those similarities and differences are reflected in the chapters to follow.

The first two chapters introduce the idea of responsive teaching (Chapter 1) and synthesize existing research on teacher responsiveness in science and mathematics (Chapter 2). Chapters 3–11 unpack the substance of what teachers are doing as they respond to student thinking. These chapters address topics including

Preface **xv**

the intellectual products of students' work in responsive classrooms (Chapter 3), how teachers and students experience responsive teaching (Chapters 4–6), additional constructs that may enhance our study of responsive teaching—such as affect, framing, and pedagogical content knowledge (Chapters 7–9), and methods for and considerations in assessment (Chapters 10 and 11).

The particular contexts include a variety of grades and science disciplines. There are supplemental documents for many of the cases, including video and extensive transcripts, which we make available at http://www.studentsthinking. org/rtsm. These provide readers with additional opportunities to immerse themselves in responsive classrooms and to see for themselves what these environments look and feel like. We hope to bridge multiple communities—K–12 and university, research and practice—by drawing from examples across the curriculum and by examining implications for both research and teaching.

Finally, this book came to be because of the thoughtful contributions of many. To the teachers whose classrooms we studied, we thank you for making your incredible work visible to us and for the privilege of sharing it with the world. To the conference participants whose ideas and feedback brought this book to life—Carolina Alvarado, Leslie J. Atkins, Leema Berland, Jessica Bishop, Eleanor Close, Hunter G. Close, Janet E. Coffey, Luke Conlin, Abigail R. Daane, Sharon Fargason, Brian W. Frank, Fred Goldberg, Kara E. Gray, Paul Hutchison, Lama Z. Jaber, Matty Lau, Daniel M. Levin, Jennifer Evarts Lineback, Melissa J. Luna, April Cordero Maskiewicz, Sam McKagan, Jim Minstrell, Jennifer Radoff, Jennifer Richards, Rosemary S. Russ, Miriam Gamoran Sherin, Tiffany-Rose Sikorski, Chandra Turpen, Jessica Watkins, and Michael C. Wittmann—this book is yours as much as it is ours, and we feel privileged to be a part of your community. To Naomi Silverman, commissioning editor, and all the folks at Routledge involved in bringing this book to publication, and to Norman Lederman, Teaching and Learning in Science Series Editor—thank you for seeing the potential of our work, and thank you for seeing it through to publication. To the administrative team at Seattle Pacific University—Kathryn Houmiel and Leanna Aker—to whose copyediting eyes and logistical savvy we owe the consistency of our APA formatting, as well as the presence of coffee at our conference, thank you: your work is important to us. And finally, to the people whose gentle care and shared passions shepherded us through the day—Justin Robertson, Dale Hailey, and Lauren Hammer—thank you; we couldn't do this work without you.

Further Reading for Teachers and Teacher Educators

Ball, D.L. (1993). With an eye on the mathematical horizon: Dilemmas of teaching elementary school mathematics. *The Elementary School Journal, 93*(4), 373–397.

Bresser, R., & Fargason, S. (2013). *Becoming scientists: Inquiry-based teaching in diverse classrooms*. Portland, ME: Stenhouse Publishers.

xvi Preface

Chazan, D., & Ball, D.L. (1999). Beyond being told not to tell. *For the learning of mathematics, 19*(2), 2–10.

Elby, A., & Hammer, D. (2010). Epistemological resources and framing: A cognitive framework for helping teachers interpret and respond to their students' epistemologies. In L.D. Bendixon & F.C. Feucht (Eds.), *Personal epistemology in the classroom: Theory, research, and implications for practice* (pp. 409–434). Cambridge: Cambridge University Press.

Hammer, D. (1997). Discovery learning and discovery teaching. *Cognition and Instruction, 15*(4), 485–529.

Hammer, D., Goldberg, F., & Fargason, S. (2012). Responsive teaching and the beginnings of energy in a third grade classroom. *Review of Science, Mathematics, and ICT Education, 6*(1), 51–72.

Hammer, D., & van Zee, E. (2006). *Seeing the science in children's thinking: Case studies of student inquiry in physical science*. Portsmouth, NH: Heinemann.

Levin, D.M., Hammer, D., Elby, A., & Coffey, J. (2013). *Becoming a responsive science teacher: Focusing on student thinking in secondary science*. Arlington, VA: National Science Teachers Association Press.

Responsive Teaching in Science website [Online]: http://cipstrends.sdsu.edu/responsive teaching/

Russ, R.S., Coffey, J.E., Hammer, D., & Hutchison, P. (2009). Making classroom assessment more accountable to scientific reasoning: A case for attending to mechanistic thinking. *Science Education, 93*(5), 875–891.

SeanNumbers-Ofala. (2010). Mathematics Teaching and Learning to Teach, University of Michigan [Online]. http://hdl.handle.net/2027.42/65013

References

Ball, D.L. (1993). With an eye on the mathematical horizon: Dilemmas of teaching elementary school mathematics. *The Elementary School Journal, 93*(4), 373–397.

Ball, D.L., & Forzani, F.M. (2009). The work of teaching and the challenge for teacher education. *Journal of Teacher Education, 60*(5), 497–511.

Carpenter, T.P., Fennema, E., Peterson, P.L., Chiang, C.-P., & Loef, M. (1989). Using knowledge of children's mathematics thinking in classroom teaching: An experimental study. *American Educational Research Journal, 26*(4), 499–531.

Coffey, J.E., Hammer, D., Levin, D.M., & Grant, T. (2011). The missing disciplinary substance of formative assessment. *Journal of Research in Science Teaching, 48*(10), 1109–1136.

Duckworth, E. (2006). *"The having of wonderful ideas" and other essays on teaching and learning* (3rd ed.). New York, NY: Teachers College Press.

Empson, S.B. (2003). Low-performing students and teaching fractions for understanding: An interactional analysis. *Journal for Research in Mathematics Education, 34*(4), 305–343.

Empson, S.B., & Jacobs, V.R. (2008). Learning to listen to children's mathematics. In D. Tirosh & T. Wood (Eds.), *Tools and processes in mathematics teacher education* (pp. 257–281). The Netherlands: Sense Publishers.

Fennema, E., Carpenter, T.P., Franke, M.L., Levi, L., Jacobs, V.R., & Empson, S.B. (1996). A longitudinal study of learning to use children's thinking in mathematics instruction. *Journal for Research in Mathematics Education, 27*(4), 403–434.

Fennema, E., Franke, M.L., Carpenter, T.P., & Carey, D.A. (1993). Using children's mathematical knowledge in instruction. *American Educational Research Journal, 30*(3), 555–583.

Gallas, K. (1995). *Talking their way into science: Hearing children's questions and theories, responding with curricula*. New York, NY: Teachers College Press.

Goldberg, F. (2012). Responsive teaching and the emergence of energy ideas in third grade classrooms. Paper presented at the UW/SPU Speaker Series, Seattle, WA.

Goodwin, C. (1994). Professional vision. *American Anthropologist, 96*(3), 606–633.

Hammer, D. (1997). Discovery learning and discovery teaching. *Cognition and Instruction, 15*(4), 485–529.

Hammer, D., Goldberg, F., & Fargason, S. (2012). Responsive teaching and the beginnings of energy in a third grade classroom. *Review of Science, Mathematics, and ICT Education, 6*(1), 51–72.

Hammer, D., & van Zee, E. (2006). *Seeing the science in children's thinking: Case studies of student inquiry in physical science*. Portsmouth, NH: Heinemann.

Hiebert, J., & Wearne, D. (1993). Instructional tasks, classroom discourse, and students' learning in second-grade arithmetic. *American Educational Research Journal, 30*(2), 393–425.

Hudicourt-Barnes, J. (2003). The use of argumentation in Haitian Creole science classrooms. *Harvard Educational Review, 73*(1), 73–93.

Kersting, N.B., Givvin, K.B., Sotelo, F.L., & Stigler, J.W. (2010). Teachers' analyses of classroom video predict student learning of mathematics: Further explorations of a novel measure of teacher knowledge. *Journal of Teacher Education, 61*(1–2), 172–181.

Lampert, M., Beasley, H., Ghousseini, H., Kazemi, E., & Franke, M. (2010). Using designed instructional activities to enable novices to manage ambitious mathematics teaching. In M.K. Stein & L. Kucan (Eds.), *Instructional explanations in the disciplines* (pp. 129–141). New York, NY: Springer Science+Business Media.

Lampert, M., Franke, M.L., Kazemi, E., Ghousseini, H., Turrou, A.C., Beasley, H., . . . Crowe, K. (2013). Keeping it complex: Using rehearsals to support novice teacher learning of ambitious teaching. *Journal of Teacher Education, 64*(3), 226–243.

Lemke, J.L. (1990). *Talking science: Language, learning, and values*. Norwood, NJ: Ablex Publishing Corporation.

Levin, D.M. (2008). *What secondary science teachers pay attention to in the classroom: Situating teaching in institutional and social systems*. College Park, MD: University of Maryland.

Michaels, S. (2005). Can the intellectual affordances of working-class storytelling be leveraged in school? *Human Development, 48*, 136–145.

National Committee on Science Education Standards and Assessment, N.R.C. (1996). National Science Education Standards. Washington, D.C.: National Academy Press.

National Council of Teachers of Mathematics (2000). *Principles and standards for school mathematics*. Reston, VA: National Council of Teachers of Mathematics.

National Research Council (2012). *A framework for K-12 science education: Practices, crosscutting concepts, and core ideas*. Washington, D.C.: National Academies Press.

Next Generation Science Standards (2013). http://www.nextgenscience.org/next-generation-science-standards.

Pierson, J.L. (2008). *The relationship between patterns of classroom discourse and mathematics learning*. (Unpublished doctoral dissertation). University of Texas at Austin. Austin, TX.

Rosebery, A.S., Ogonowski, M., DiSchino, M., & Warren, B. (2010). "The coat traps all your body heat": Heterogeneity as fundamental to learning. *Journal of the Learning Sciences, 19*(3), 322–357.

Saxe, G.B., Gearhart, M., & Seltzer, M. (1999). Relations between classroom practices and student learning in the domain of fractions. *Cognition and Instruction, 17*(1), 1–24.

Thompson, J., Windschitl, M., & Braaten, M. (2013). Developing a theory of ambitious early-career teaching practice. *American Educational Research Journal, 50*(3), 574–615.

xviii Preface

Warren, B., Ballenger, C., Ogonowski, M., Rosebery, A.S., & Hudicourt-Barnes, J. (2001). Rethinking diversity in learning science: The logic of everyday sense-making. *Journal of Research in Science Teaching, 38*(5), 529–552.

Warren, B., Ogonowski, M., & Pothier, S. (2005). "Everyday" and "scientific": Rethinking dichotomies in modes of thinking in science learning. In R. Nemirovsky, A.S. Rosebery, J. Solomon, & B. Warren (Eds.), *Everyday matters in science and mathematics*. Mahwah, NJ: Lawrence Erlbaum Associates.

Windschitl, M., Thompson, J., Braaten, M., & Stroupe, D. (2012). Proposing a core set of instructional practices and tools for teachers of science. *Science Education, 96*(5), 878–903.

1
WHAT IS RESPONSIVE TEACHING?

Amy D. Robertson, Leslie J. Atkins, Daniel M. Levin, and Jennifer Richards

This book is about responsive teaching in science and mathematics. Before we explore nuances in the nature of responsive teaching, challenge common assumptions in the literature, and connect responsive teaching to other, relevant constructs—as do many of the chapters in this book—we first offer a rough sketch of what it is and what it looks like in practice. Our goal in doing so is not to make distinct analytical points or to add to the literature by challenging notions of responsive teaching; it is to give examples of responsive teaching and to show how each one instantiates this kind of instruction—to illustrate the phenomenon, so to speak, and to establish shared meaning for responsive teaching before we explore it together in the rest of the book.

Although different researchers, teachers, and teacher educators conceptualize, measure, and enact responsive teaching in distinct ways,[1] there are certain themes that recur across conceptualizations and instantiations. In particular, the literature highlights that responsive teaching involves:

(a) *Foregrounding the substance of students' ideas.* Responsive teaching involves attending to the meaning that students are making of their disciplinary experiences (Ball, 1993; Brodie, 2011; Carpenter, Fennema, Franke, Levi, & Empson, 2000; Coffey, Hammer, Levin, & Grant, 2011; Colestock & Linnenbringer, 2010; Duckworth, 2006; Gallas, 1995; Hammer, 1997; Hammer, Goldberg, & Fargason, 2012; Hammer & van Zee, 2006; Jacobs, Lamb, & Philipp, 2010; Lau, 2010; Levin, Hammer, Elby, & Coffey, 2012; Levin, 2008; Levin, Hammer, & Coffey, 2009; Pierson, 2008; Schifter, 2011; Sherin, Jacobs, & Philipp, 2011; Sherin & van Es, 2005, 2009; van Es & Sherin, 2008, 2010; Wallach & Even, 2005). It instantiates intellectual empathy, in that a primary aim of a teacher listening is to understand and be present to his

2 Amy D. Robertson et al.

or her students' thinking, rather than to evaluate or correct it. Teachers go beyond attending to whether or not students are sharing their ideas; they try to understand what students are saying, from the student's perspective.

(b) *Recognizing the disciplinary connections within students' ideas.* Responsive teaching is *disciplinary* in that the teacher listens for nascent connections between students' meanings and the discipline (Ball, 1993; Chazan & Ball, 1999; Gallas, 1995; Goldsmith & Seago, 2011; Hammer, 1997; Hammer et al., 2012; Hammer & van Zee, 2006; Hutchison & Hammer, 2010; Jacobs, Franke, Carpenter, Levi, & Battey, 2007; Jacobs et al., 2010; Levin et al., 2012; Russ, Coffey, Hammer, & Hutchison, 2009; Schifter, 2011; Sherin & van Es, 2005), including "disciplinary progenitors" (Harrer, Flood, & Wittmann, 2013) or "seeds of science" (Hammer & van Zee, 2006). These seeds may be, for example, the beginnings of canonical understanding, the instantiation of specific scientific practices, or the affective experiences that promote experiences of pleasure in doing science. They may include children's puzzlement over a phenomenon, their citing evidence to support an idea, their efforts toward precision, their using mechanistic reasoning (or the beginnings of it) to support their predictions or explanations, or their devising an informal experiment or suggesting an explanation; they could be the first flickers of scientific concepts, such as a sense of air as material, of living organisms as needing energy, or of energy as needing a source. In responsive teaching, the teacher "consider[s] the [discipline] in relation to the [students] and the [students] in relation to the [discipline]"(Ball, 1993, p. 394).

(c) *Taking up and pursuing the substance of student thinking.* Responsive teaching is *responsive* because it takes up and pursues the substance of student thinking (Ball, 1993; Carpenter, Fennema, Peterson, Chiang, & Loef, 1989; Colestock & Linnenbringer, 2010; Empson & Jacobs, 2008; Fennema et al., 1996; Fennema, Franke, Carpenter, & Carey, 1993; Gallas, 1995; Hammer, 1997; Hammer et al., 2012; Jacobs et al., 2010; Jacobs, Lamb, Philipp, & Shappelle, 2011; Lau, 2010; Levin et al., 2012; Lineback, 2014; Maskiewicz & Winters, 2012; Pierson, 2008; Russ et al., 2009; Schifter, 2011; Sherin & van Es, 2005). The short-term and, in some cases, long-term direction that the classroom activity takes emerges from the students themselves and from the connections that teachers and, in some cases, students make between students' reasoning and the discipline. Teachers may, for example, invite students to assess one another's ideas, draw connections between students' ideas themselves, encourage students to design and conduct experiments to test their ideas, or plan entire units of inquiry that take up a student's question.

This kind of teaching is grounded in an empirically and theoretically supported expectation that students' intuitive thinking about science is productive and resourceful (diSessa, 1993; Hammer, 1996, 2000; Hammer, Elby, Scherr, & Redish, 2005; Hammer et al., 2012; Hammer & van Zee, 2006; May, Hammer, & Roy, 2006; Smith III, diSessa, & Roschelle, 1993):

What Is Responsive Teaching? **3**

. . . this approach presumes—in fact it builds from—a view that children are richly endowed with resources for understanding and learning about the physical world: Engage children in a generative activity, and there will be productive beginnings to discover and support.

(Hammer et al., 2012, p. 55)

Responsive teaching serves multiple instructional goals, such as fostering productive scientific discourse and argumentation, promoting participation in scientific practices, and enhancing students' conceptual understanding. See Chapter 2 for more on the benefits of responsive teaching.

It may be tempting to interpret these three characteristics as a checklist of sorts—a set of actions that cultivate or constitute responsive teaching. We suspect, instead, that responsive teaching grows out of and is grounded in a stance toward students and their ideas rather than through any particular structure of activities, and we caution readers against viewing this list as prescriptive. Likewise, highlighting these three may suggest that they are distinct acts in a performance—e.g., that the teacher may follow a routine of first eliciting ideas, then seeking out connections, etc.—when they are far more integrated in practice, as the examples below show. Finally, it may be tempting to think that these three characteristics cover the space of "responsive teaching moves"—that is, that these and only these activities will be at play in a responsive classroom. In reality, teachers balance a range of instructional goals, and they select and foreground ideas and activities for a variety of reasons, not always because of their substance and connection to disciplinary ideas and practices (e.g., a teacher may foreground an idea offered by a student who has spoken up for the first time in order to encourage that student's participation in class discussions).

In the remainder of this chapter, we will explore what responsive teaching looks like in detail. First, we will use seminal examples from the literature to illustrate what we mean above by (a), (b), and (c), and then we will offer several classroom examples of responsive teaching across the curriculum, from K–12 to university science instruction. We show that responsive teaching takes different forms in different contexts—that teachers can recognize a variety of disciplinary opportunities within their students' thinking, from opportunities to distinguish between experimental variables (Ann), to opportunities to pursue mechanistic thinking (Jenny), to opportunities to clarify what is meant by specific scientific language (Leslie and Irene), to opportunities to capitalize on students' intuitive notions of force (David). We show that teachers take these opportunities up in diverse ways, including planning experiments to test students' ideas (Ann), proposing that students investigate a student-generated number group (Ball), allowing students' emergent ideas to influence the direction of classroom inquiry (many), and designing homework (Leslie and Irene) or clicker questions (David) on the basis of student thinking. We encourage our readers to sample from our examples according to their own purposes; one certainly need not read all six to get a feel for what we mean by responsive teaching.

Clarifying the Characteristics of Responsive Teaching: Seminal Examples From the Literature

The "Sean numbers" example from Ball's "With an Eye on the Mathematical Horizon: Dilemmas of Teaching Elementary School Mathematics" (Ball, 1993) and the unit on electrostatics described in Hammer's "Discovery Learning and Discovery Teaching" (Hammer, 1997) are two seminal, first-hand accounts of responsive teaching. In this section, we look to Ball and Hammer to clarify the three characteristics of responsive teaching articulated in the introduction: foregrounding the substance of students' disciplinary ideas, recognizing the disciplinary connections within students' ideas, and taking up or pursuing the substance of students' ideas.

Responsive Teaching in Elementary Mathematics: Excerpts From Ball (1993)[2]

In "With an Eye on the Mathematical Horizon: Dilemmas of Teaching Elementary School Mathematics," Ball describes an example from her third-grade classroom in which students discuss what it means for a number to be even or odd. Sean, a student in the class, presents his idea that six is both odd and even, because it is made up of three (odd) groups of two (even).[3] Mei and Ofala disagree with Sean. Mei argues that if six is both odd and even, so is ten, and Sean agrees with her—according to his definition, ten is both odd and even. Mei objects on the grounds that if

> you keep on going *on* like that, . . . maybe we'll end up with *all* numbers are odd and even! Then it won't make sense that all numbers should be odd and even, because if all numbers were odd and even, we wouldn't be even *having* this discussion!
>
> (p. 386)

Ofala also objects to Sean's idea, on the basis of her sense of what makes a number even or odd: "even numbers have two in them, . . . and also *odd* numbers have two in them—except they have *one left*" (pg. 386), as in her drawing, replicated in Figure 1.1 below.

FIGURE 1.1 Ofala's sense of what makes five odd: it has two groups of two and one left over.

Despite Mei's, Ofala's, and another student's—Riba's—protests, Ball tells us that Sean "persisted with this idea that some numbers could be both even and odd" (p. 386). She describes the dilemma she faced in deciding whether or not to encourage Sean and his classmates to explore patterns with "Sean numbers" as they also searched for patterns with even and odd numbers. On the one hand, she worried that doing so would confuse students, since the idea of "Sean numbers" is "nonstandard knowledge" and may therefore "interfere with the required 'conventional' understandings of even and odd numbers" (p. 387). On the other hand, exploring these numbers "ha[d] the potential to enhance what kids [were] thinking about 'definition' and its role, nature, and purpose in mathematical activity and discourse" and to "prepare the children for subsequent encounters with primes, multiples, and squares" (p. 387). Ultimately, Ball chose to "legitimize" the pursuit of "Sean numbers."

Foregrounding the Substance of Students' Ideas

Throughout this example, Ball foregrounds the substance of Sean's, Mei's, and Ofala's mathematical ideas. In her writing, she describes each idea in detail; in the transcript, she attends to what Sean is saying by asking him whether Mei's paraphrase of his idea is accurate, asking him, "Is that what you are saying, Sean?" (p. 386). In doing so, she maintains a stance of curiosity and openness toward what Sean *means*; she does not evaluate his idea against a predetermined instructional goal but instead seeks to make sense of his thinking. In the transcript that accompanies the online video of this discussion, she asks similar questions of other students, such as, "What are you trying to say?" (p. 4), "So, are you saying all numbers are odd then?" (p. 3), and "Why would that work?" (p. 4).

In addition, the *students'* attention to the ideas of their peers—and to the embedded mathematics within these ideas—reinforces our sense that Ball consistently attends to and highlights students' mathematical thinking. For example, after Sean presents his sense that six is both even and odd, Mei first revoices his idea— "I think I know what he is saying . . . I think what he's saying is that you have three groups of two. And three is an odd number so six can be an odd number *and* an even number." (p. 386)—and then challenges it with her own thinking, arguing that one possible consequence is that *all* numbers would then be called both odd and even, which doesn't make sense to her. We suspect that this culture of peer responsiveness is at least in part initiated and sustained by the *teacher's* attention to and curiosity about students' mathematical ideas, and to her promoting this attention among her students. Regularly throughout the transcript of this extended interaction (see video online), Ball incites her students to listen to one another ("Can we listen to her one more time? Say again one more time what you're saying the definition is of an odd number." (p. 5)), to seek to understand one another ("Just a second, Sean. Let's make sure people understand what she's suggesting."), to help one another out ("Could somebody help us out with this?" (p. 2)), to try on one another's ideas ("Who thinks they could come up and try a number on

6 Amy D. Robertson et al.

the board using her definition ... " (p. 5)), and to assess whether or not they agree ("Okay, do other people agree with him? Mei, you disagree with him?" (p. 3)).

Recognizing the Disciplinary Connections Within Students' Ideas

Throughout her reflection on the "Sean numbers" example, Ball consistently highlights the disciplinary connections within (and disciplinary potential of) her students' ideas. For example, she recognizes that Ofala's definition of odd numbers—that they "have two in them—except they have *one left*" (p. 386)— is "in essence, the formal mathematical definition of an odd number: $2k + 1$" (p. 386). She not only *sees* these connections between Ofala's reasoning and the discipline; Ball also calls out the mathematics in what she is saying and doing in the course of instruction (see p. 4 of online transcript):

Ofala: [describing how she knows that nine is an odd number:] This two together, this two together, this two together, and this two together [drawing Figure 1.2]. There's one left. And even numbers like six [drawing Figure 1.3], you can't get anything in the middle. There isn't one left.

Ball: So you're saying the even numbers are the ones where you can group them all by twos, and the odd ones are the ones where you end up with one left over?

Mei: Yeah, I think I agree.

Sean: But, if six is an even number, then how come there's three here and there's not one left out?

Ofala: Because, even numbers are like things like this. They have—even numbers have two in them, and also odd numbers have two in them, except they have one left.

Mei: Yeah.

Ball: Okay, so, Ofala, you're—you actually are suggesting a definition. I think. Let's have everybody hear that one more time.

In this excerpt, Ball first revoices the implicit definition that Ofala is using—even numbers can be grouped by twos, and odd numbers have one left over—and then observes *that* she is proposing a definition for odd and even numbers. In addition, Ball sees the disciplinary potential in "Sean numbers" for fostering disciplinary practices around the role of definition and "its purpose in mathematical activity and discourse" (p. 387). She describes her experience of connecting students' ideas to the discipline more generally, writing:

> To do this productively, I must understand the specific mathematical content and its uses, bases, and history, as well as be actively ready to learn more about it through the eyes and experiences of my students ... I must consider the mathematics in relation to the children and the children in relation to

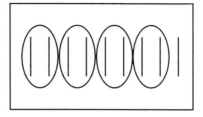

FIGURE 1.2 Representation that accompanies Ofala's explanation for why nine is odd.

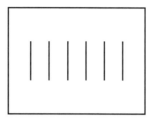

FIGURE 1.3 Representation that accompanies Ofala's explanation for why six is even.

the mathematics. My ears and eyes must search the world around us, the discipline of mathematics, and the world of the child with both mathematical and child filters.

(p. 394)

Ball also sees disciplinary connections *between* students' mathematical ideas, nourishing the seeds of mathematical discourse within her classroom community. For example, she coordinates Sean's proposal with Mei's concern about its generality and with Ofala's objection that it did not satisfy her definition of odd numbers. Just after Mei presents her argument ("if you keep on going *on* like that . . ."), Ball turns to the class and asks, "Are people following this disagreement? This is an important thing that I didn't even realize we were disagreeing about. So it's important to see if we can try to figure this out" (p. 4). This is when Ofala jumps in, and Ball consistently redirects the class' attention back to the substance of what Ofala is presenting, inviting them to understand her definition and then try it out themselves.

Taking Up and Pursuing the Substance of Students' Ideas

The ideas that emerge as Ball's students "wor[k] with patterns with odd and even numbers" (p. 385) shape the short- and long-term direction that the class takes. In the moment, Ball maintained a focus on Sean's definition and on Mei's and Ofala's counterarguments, inviting her students to assess one another's ideas for their mathematical sensibility and consistency. When Ofala presents her definition for odd numbers, she encourages students to "tr[y] some experiments with it, with numbers that they expected to work because they already knew them to be odd" (p. 386), again inviting students to seek consistency between Ofala's definition and their existing knowledge about odd numbers. In the longer term, Ball takes up "Sean numbers," suggesting that her students explore patterns with Sean numbers as they did so with odd and even numbers.

Responsive Teaching in High School Physics: Example From Hammer (1997)

In "Discovery Learning and Discovery Teaching," Hammer describes a series of events that unfold in his high school physics course, beginning with "Camille's discovery." Camille notices that if she brings a neutral electrophorus[4] near a charged foam plate and then touches the electrophorus with her finger, the foam plate lifts off the table, as shown in Figure 1.4. (We explore the science of this electrostatic phenomenon in endnote 4—and we do the same for other phenomena introduced throughout this chapter for those who wish to read further.) Hammer names this phenomenon "the Marino phenomenon" after Camille, and the class goes on to explain it over the next several days. Amelia, Ning, and Joanne propose the "HAM theory," a three-part charge separation model: (1) "charge is not created but separated"; (2) "the charges involved are the positive nuclei and negative electrons that ... make up atoms"; and (3) "different materials have different tendencies to accept or give up electrons" (p. 509). Ning uses the HAM theory to explain the Marino phenomenon in terms of induced polarization: she argues that when the electrophorus is brought near the negatively charged foam plate, "negative charge is repelled toward the top of the electrophorus, and positive charge is attracted to the bottom" (p. 509). Negative charges leave the plate via the finger that touches the top, and the electrophorus is left with a net positive charge, which would then attract the negatively charged foam plate. Several students—including Steve, Susan, Bruce, and Sean—object to Ning's explanation, arguing that "the electrophorus could [not] be charged one way on top and another way on the bottom" (p. 510).

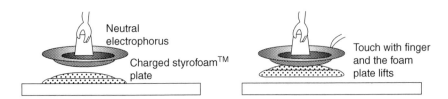

FIGURE 1.4 Illustration of Camille's discovery, from Hammer, *Discovery Learning and Discovery Teaching*, Cognition and Instruction, 1997, reprinted by permission of the publisher (Taylor & Francis Ltd, http://www.tandfonline.com).

The "HAM authors['] and adherents['] ... account of the Marino phenomenon" (p. 510) (i.e., induced polarization) is reinforced by an experiment that Hammer conducts at his students' suggestion. In the course of this experiment, Hammer shows his students that a pith ball is charged by a neutral electrophorus and then repels from the foil-covered straw when the foam plate is near, but "settles back" when Hammer moves the foam plate away.

While the "HAM adherents" explain the pith ball's behavior in terms of induced polarization, Steve, Susan, Bruce, and Sean articulate their own explanation that the pith ball is charged by its proximity to the foam plate—the electrophorus acts as a "conduit of charge." Other students offer additional explanations, including that a "spark" jumps between the electrophorus and the foam plate (Susan), or that the behavior is caused by an "aura" or "force field" (Bruce) (pp. 510–511).

Neutral electrophorus with foil covered straw, touching a pith ball

Charged foam plate

Bring the charged foam plate close to the electrophorus and the pith ball repeats away from the fell covered straw

Remove the foam plate, and the repulsion stops

FIGURE 1.5 Charging a pith ball with a neutral electrophorus, from Hammer, *Discovery Learning and Discovery Teaching*, Cognition and Instruction, 1997, reprinted by permission of the publisher (Taylor & Francis Ltd, http://www.tandfonline.com).

10 Amy D. Robertson et al.

The class then "drew depictions of the competing accounts" (p. 511)—the HAM charge-separation model and the charging-by-proximity model—on the blackboard. Toward the end of the class period, Hammer tells us, the students identify a "serious problem with the latter: If the charges were moving through the electrophorus to charge the pith ball, the electrophorus and foam plate would have the same charge and thus should repel each other" (p. 512), but they know, from the Marino phenomenon and other experiments, that they attract.

Ning then suggests an experiment that she feels will confirm the HAM theory: rather than touching the top of the electrophorus, which presumably had a negative charge, she suggests they touch the bottom (presumed to be positively charged). Doing so would *add* negative charge to the neutral electrophorus, resulting in a net negative charge, and the foam plate would be repelled. Hammer does the experiment, which produces results inconsistent with Ning's prediction; they end the class period with Hammer's comment that "[they] would need to think further about this experiment and that [they] had not resolved the debate between the HAM and proximity explanations" (p. 512). The quiz the students take the next day asks them to defend their position in the debate, to address counterarguments, and to design an experiment that would distinguish between the two theories.

Foregrounding the Substance of Students' Ideas

Throughout this example, Hammer maintains a focus on the substance of his students' scientific ideas and practices. He describes in detail the students' observations (e.g., the Marino phenomenon), explanations (e.g., the HAM theory and the charging-by-proximity model), and proposals for experiments (e.g., Ning's suggestion that he touch the bottom—rather than the top—of the electrophorus), seeking to preserve the meaning they were making as they try to understand the Marino phenomenon and other investigations of charge. He invites students to bring their own models to bear on these investigations, and he seeks to understand how the authors of each model would make sense of new phenomena they observed (e.g., how (i) the HAM theory adherents and (ii) the charging-by-proximity adherents make sense of the pith ball's behavior as the foam plate is brought close to the neutral electrophorus in Figure 1.5). He notices when students are making connections between phenomena—such as when Susan suggested that a "spark" jumps between the foam plate and the electrophorus, the way that "a charge can 'jump' across the 'small space to another nerve' in a synapse" (p. 510).

Recognizing the Disciplinary Connections Within Students' Ideas

As he foregrounds the substance of students' ideas, Hammer calls attention to the "seeds" of disciplinary ideas and practices embedded therein. For example, he sees in Camille's discovery of the Marino phenomenon opportunities for students to participate in science as a socially constructed endeavor ("it was another opportunity to show the students that their discoveries mattered" (p. 508)), to see observation and exploration as central to scientific progress, and to build connections to physicists' notions of induced polarization and charging by induction. He sees Steve's, Susan's, Bruce's, and Sean's original questions about the HAM theory in terms of a reasonable, disciplinary alternative—they thought "charge [was] a property of the object as a whole, so they were troubled by an account of different parts of the electrophorus having different charges" (p. 510). He weighs the epistemological and conceptual affordances and constraints of Susan's, Sean's, Greg's, and Bruce's use of terminology (e.g., that the behavior of the pith ball when the foam plate is brought near the electrophorus is because of a "spark," a "current," an "aura," or a "force field"): he was "pleased that these students were looking for connections and ideas from other phenomena" but was "daunted by the very different notions they were expressing about charge and current" (p. 511). He searched for the scientific "beginnings," wondering "whether some of what they were saying might serve as seed for the physicist's concepts of an electric field or an electric potential" (p. 511).

Taking Up and Pursuing the Substance of Students' Ideas

Over the course of these several days, Hammer "elevate[s]" his students' ideas "to the level of curriculum" (p. 513), adapting his instruction as specific ideas and proposals for experiments emerge. Students' ideas and observations form the basis of the inquiry that takes place in both the short- and long-term. Hammer deviates from the intended order of the worksheets his students are completing to pursue explanations for the Marino phenomenon, and two competing theories surface that the class then investigates, seeking to accumulate evidence and counterevidence for each one. As they go, Hammer invites students to conduct experiments that test their ideas (e.g., Ning's suggestion to touch the bottom of the electrophorus rather than the top). In all of this, he promotes classroom practice that mirrors that of science: students are encouraged to explore their observations, to explain what they see in terms of models, to consider competing models and counterarguments, and to reconcile inconsistencies between their models and their observations.

Illustrating Responsive Teaching Across the Curriculum: Examples From K–12 and University Classrooms

Now that we have used examples of responsive teaching from the literature to illustrate what we mean by foregrounding the substance of students' ideas, recognizing disciplinary connections within students' ideas, and taking up and pursuing the substance of these ideas, we turn to more recent examples from K–12 and university science classrooms, gleaned from research and professional development projects in which we have been involved. In doing so, we aim to showcase a diversity of ways in which responsive teaching is enacted while continuing to illustrate its central characteristics.

12 Amy D. Robertson et al.

Responsive Teaching in Elementary Science: Example From Ann's 5th-grade Discussion of Magnetism

The following example comes from the classroom of a 5th-grade teacher, Ann, who participated in a professional development project that engaged teachers—and, by proxy, their students—in drawing on their own experiences to construct causal explanations of scientific phenomena. This example highlights a teacher's recognition of an emergent opportunity to engage students in disambiguating variables, an important practice for clarifying and making progress on the specific questions they are seeking to answer. This example also represents a large-scale adaptation from the intended lesson, which was originally focused on preparing for a test.

Example From Ann's class

Ann's 5th-grade class is approaching a statewide standardized test that requires students to define force as a push or a pull and to identify different types of forces (e.g., gravity and magnetism). To initiate a review conversation, Ann poses a question about magnetism, raised previously by a student: "Can magnets work underwater?" Although she indicates that the class cannot spend much time on the "whys of magnetism," she encourages students to think about the question and to consider how it relates to forces.

Students talk in groups at their tables about whether or not magnets work underwater, and Ann pulls them together for a whole-class discussion. (See http://www.studentsthinking.org/rtsm for a full transcript of the discussion.) The discussion quickly evolves into a back-and-forth about some of the "whys" that Ann initially tried to minimize. Some students argue that the magnets are going to try to connect under water, as on land, depending on how strong they are, whereas other students argue that the pressure of the water will prevent them from sticking together. As the discussion continues, Ann recognizes that some students are thinking of different scenarios than the one she originally imagined:

Caroline[5]: The force of the water when it pushes it down, like the, um, force pushes, pushes, pushes it down, it probably, um, won't, like, stick together because all the pressure, all the water-

Ann: The pressure from the water is going to be—overcome the magnetism?

Caroline: Yeah, so I say no, but Wendy says yes.

(Many students start contributing; Ann reminds them to be active listeners.)

Ann: Um, Allan, why do you say no?

Allan: Because, just like Elena said, there's too much force on them for them to stick together.

Ann: The water pressure is too much?

Allan: Yeah because sometimes if the waves are strong, the magnets will separate and fall apart.

What Is Responsive Teaching?   **13**

Student: What if it's just a little bit of water?
Ann: Okay, so that's just what I was going to ask you . . .

Ann indicates that she was thinking of testing the magnets in small containers of water, rather than the bigger bodies of water she hears Caroline and Allan talking about. Allan changes his mind because "there's only a little bit of space in that cup" but also makes a bid to try it out in a pool. Ann considers using the sink before pausing for a question from Kimmy:

Kimmy: Are you all, are you saying that—it's based on—the force is based on the amount of space the water has in the ()?
Ann: Well—Allan and Caroline, you want to answer Kimmy's question?
Caroline: Well, () in the cup, um, there's not enough water because the magnets are going to be like right next to each other because of the cup. But say if we put it in the sink, they'll probably be far away, so all the pressure from the water will probably keep them apart. And basically it's about how much water and how much space ().

Several students suggest ways to tweak Ann's setup so the magnets are farther apart. Ann indicates they can try the experiment in a variety of ways, but she also seeks to draw students' attention to the fact that they are now considering two variables in their explanations—the presence or absence of water, and the distance between the magnets. She gets two magnets and holds them progressively closer to each other until they finally click, showing that they have to be relatively close together to attract, even in the air:

Ann: So what we're sort of trying to figure out is—two things. First of all, will they work at all in water? But then Caroline, you guys have sort of also brought up the whole idea of how close they have to be.

The class spends the rest of the period talking about why it would be harder for magnets to work underwater (e.g., water is "stronger than air," in that we can walk through air but have to push through water when we swim), trying various ways to test whether magnets work underwater, and discussing students' findings. They only return to an explicit discussion of forces in the last five minutes of class.

How This Example Instantiates Responsive Teaching

The conversation in Ann's class reflects the three characteristics of responsive teaching articulated earlier in the chapter, intertwined in the flow of classroom practice. Throughout the discussion, Ann listens to and revoices students' ideas, often in a questioning tone to invite student feedback (e.g., "The water pressure is too much?"). She also keeps track of how students' ideas and questions relate to one another and facilitates students' direct talk with each other when appropriate,

14 Amy D. Robertson et al.

as in the case of Kimmy's question ("Allan and Caroline, you want to answer Kimmy's question?").

As Ann attends to the substance of students' reasoning, she recognizes particular disciplinary connections and adapts her instruction responsively at several scales. For instance, Ann notes distinct variables inherent in students' thinking (water and distance) and seeks to engage students in the scientific practice of disambiguating variables in the course of their joint exploration (Ford, 2005). This emergent objective represents a larger-scale adaptation to Ann's original plan for the day—to review forces for the upcoming test. Other adaptations are smaller-scale in nature (e.g., allowing students to alter her planned experimental setup).

In an informal interview after class, Ann reflects on the larger-scale adaptation as creating tension for her. She notes the strong tension she feels between pursuing questions that the class finds interesting and making sure her students are prepared for the standardized test. While she foregrounds test preparation in subsequent lessons, the class returns to the question of whether magnets work underwater after the test and engages in a week-long inquiry that expands from whether magnets work underwater to whether *anything* can block magnetism (Richards, Johnson, & Nyeggen, 2015).

Responsive Teaching in High School Biology: Example From Jenny's 10th-Grade Class Discussion of Diffusion and Osmosis[6]

The following example comes from Jenny's 10th-grade biology class. Jenny participated in a professional development project that focused on supporting secondary science teachers in developing practices of attending and responding to students' ideas and reasoning. This example in particular highlights how a teacher attends to and leverages students' nascent mechanistic ideas[7] as she supports them in constructing an understanding of a biological phenomenon. As in the case of Ann, the example is situated within certain institutional constraints—Jenny is accountable to high-stakes standardized tests and standardized curricula—and so illustrates some of the pressing instructional tensions that teachers navigate as they are responsive to their students.

Example From Jenny's Class

In this example, Jenny shows her students a stanza from Samuel Taylor Coleridge's poem "The Rime of the Ancient Mariner"[8] and asks them to explain what they think the following two lines mean:

> *Water, water everywhere and all the boards did shrink*
> *Water, water everywhere, nor any drop to drink*

The high school biology curriculum guide used in Jenny's district suggests this activity and places it after students have studied processes of diffusion and osmosis, intending to give students an opportunity to apply their understanding of osmosis and associated vocabulary (e.g., hypertonic and hypotonic solutions[9]) to their interpretation of the poem. Jenny's students have already explored diffusion, but instead of having the discussion when the curriculum guide suggests, Jenny decides to explore how her students reason about the mechanisms at work before they have been formally introduced to osmosis and related terminology. She sees this as a valuable opportunity to understand and leverage students' thinking in order to build their understanding.

At the beginning of the lesson, Jenny projects the two lines from "The Rime of the Ancient Mariner" on the screen. She tells the students that the lines are from a poem, written from the perspective of a man lost at sea, and she asks them to write what they think the poem means in their notebooks. After they have written quietly for a few minutes, Jenny asks them to share their interpretations with the rest of the class.

As the conversation begins, students immediately recognize that the sailor cannot drink the salt water of the ocean. As Andrew says, "I think it's some guy that's stranded in the middle of the ocean, and he's stuck on one little board, and he can't drink the water because it has salt in it." Jenny picks up on Andrew's idea:

Jenny: The salt water—why can't we drink the salt water?

Toan: Because of the salt.

Jenny: So what does the salt do?

Hawaney: It makes you more thirsty. It dehydrates you.

Grace: I think the salt absorbs the water.

Jenny: So salt absorbs water? The way . . . a sponge absorbs water?

Brian: It doesn't like get rid of it, but it gets . . . enough of it . . .

Rachel: Isn't it like so your body can't use it? . . . Like it's still there but it's in a form that your body can't use.

Jenny: So maybe it alters the water—is that what you're saying?

Rachel: I mean, I guess it would be some kind of chemical process where it wouldn't exactly be water any more. It would be like a form that your body couldn't use.

Here, Jenny revoices Grace's idea that salt absorbs water and works to understand more specifically *how* Grace thinks this occurs (e.g., similar to how a sponge absorbs water). Similarly, she revoices Rachel's idea that the salt makes it "so your body can't use [the water]" and checks to make sure she understands Rachel's meaning.

As the conversation continues, Jenny asks the students to consider the first part of the stanza, "Water, water everywhere and all the boards did shrink."

16 Amy D. Robertson et al.

Jenny: So—why would they shrink?

Brian: Oh!

Rachel: Well, I know that um if you take a drum that's too tight, and you put water on it, or sometimes you like hold it like over a fire, then it'll tighten, so I think like maybe if it evaporates . . . (trails off)

Jenny: If . . . the water evaporates . . . then . . .?

Rachel: Maybe because the molecules come together and get in the way somehow.

Metzy: Like a sponge.

Jenny: Okay . . . why would the water evaporate?

Jenny picks up on Rachel's idea, based on her personal experience, for why something wet might shrink. She presses Rachel to explain what would happen if the water evaporates and then, a turn later, why the water would evaporate. Through Jenny's pressing Rachel to articulate what happens when the water evaporates and why the water evaporates in the first place, the mechanism for shrinking within Rachel's idea becomes clearer: the water molecules that were originally in the wood leave, and the wood molecules then get closer together, shrinking the board.

With Rachel's idea clarified, Jenny reflects it back to the rest of the class, asking them whether it makes sense. When some students say that it does not, Jenny again breaks Rachel's response into two parts, first asking whether they agree that there is water in the wood. Andrew asserts that that there is water in the wood so long as "it just came off a tree or something." Shortly after this, Brian synthesizes the class discussion up to this point:

Brian: Okay. So the tree-so wood comes from trees . . . and the tree, and trees need water in order to uh survive, when you cut the tree down and make the uh, wood, there's still water left inside of it, but when you put it in salt water the salt water will evaporate the actual water inside of it.

Here Brian identifies the entities ("actual water" and "salt water") and activity ("evaporation," in this case referring generally to the process by which the water leaves the wood) that could be used to form a mechanistic explanation (Russ et al., 2009). After a short clarification from Moyatu—who points out that wood typically *absorbs* water—Jenny returns to Brian's claim, revoices it, and then asks, "Why would salt water evaporate water?"

The conversation proceeds for several minutes with the students proposing multiple different explanations for why the water will evaporate from the wood, including that water is the "universal solvent" and is dissolving the wood (such that the board shrinks) and that the water inside the tree combines with salt and "the tree would just not want it." Each time a student offers a new explanation, Jenny revoices it, and often she asks the rest of the class what they think. When Tina presents her claim that the tree "would not want" the water, Jenny presses back, pointing out that the tree is not only taking in water, and asking what else the tree is doing. Several students argue that the tree also expels water, and Jenny once again challenges them to articulate a mechanism. Tilson suggests "osmosis," and Jenny asks him to say what he means; he answers that "water moves from [a] high-density place to a low-density place." The students take this up, offering examples of both osmosis and diffusion, and Jenny asks them whether these mechanisms "come into play here."

Students begin to make connections between osmosis and the scenario under consideration (e.g., Rachel considers the concentration of oxygen in the salt versus fresh water), as well as continue to offer explanations for why the water might evaporate from the wood (e.g., Metzy posits that "it's gonna go through the water cycle thing"). Jenny takes up the mechanism in Rachel's idea—that oxygen moves from high to low concentration—and again asks the students how it "applies here." Haja and Grace begin to argue that there is a higher concentration of water in the board than in the ocean, with Grace explaining that "the water in the ocean is a mixture of NaCl and H_2O but the water in the board is just H_2O so that's a higher concentration." Brian sums this up, saying:

Brian: So if you took like a—if you took like a drop of salt water and compared it to a drop of just regular water, there'd be more of the regular water in the regular water because there's also salt in the salt water so the salt water has a lower concentration of water since it's mixed with the salt, so the water molecules would move to the outside of the board where there's a lower concentration.

They go on to consider together how the mechanism by which water leaves the *board* is analogous to the process by which one's body dehydrates, connecting "all the boards did shrink" and "not a drop to drink" in the original poem.

How This Example Instantiates Responsive Teaching

Throughout this example, we see Jenny's efforts to foreground her students' thinking and to try to understand their meaning rather than evaluating or correcting it. For example, she attends to Grace's idea that salt absorbs water and to Rachel's idea that salt water is in a form the body cannot use, and she attempts to understand both students' meaning. Her response to Rachel's idea leads Rachel to draw on her knowledge of the disciplinary core idea of a chemical process changing the nature of a substance (NGSS Lead States, 2013).

Jenny also elicits students' mechanistic thinking—for example, when she presses Grace to explain *how* salt absorbs water—and recognizes the nascent mechanistic reasoning in what her students are saying. In picking up on Rachel's drum example, Jenny supports Rachel in instantiating the disciplinary practice of constructing plausible mechanistic accounts for phenomena (both in Rachel's

18 Amy D. Robertson et al.

own past experience and in the "thought experiment" invoked by the poem). An interview with Jenny after class supports this interpretation of Jenny's questions to Rachel. When asked what she thought about Rachel's idea, Jenny said:

Jenny: I think what she's saying there is she knows that the drum head is going to shrink in that process so the boards are going to shrink . . . and to me that's the mechanism [she has] available . . . to explain why some things can get smaller. Evaporation means that it's going to go away and therefore it's going to get smaller.

The drum exchange also illustrates how Jenny adapts instruction on the basis of her students' ideas. While Jenny did not expect the idea of evaporation to come up in this conversation geared toward diffusion and osmosis, she takes up Rachel's idea and follows it, using it as a starting point for further exploration. Rather than Jenny pointing out that the phenomenon suggested by the poem is not evaporation but instead osmosis, she makes space for the *idea* of osmosis to *emerge* from the class' consideration of what would make the water evaporate.

Responsive Teaching in Pre-service Elementary Teacher Education: Example From Leslie and Irene's Undergraduate Course Developing Ideas About Blurriness

In this section, we provide an extended example from a university course, *Scientific Inquiry*, that is structured to be wholly responsive: the content and direction of the course proceeds from students' ideas, investigations, and conversations. It is a course for undergraduate pre-service elementary teachers at California State University, Chico, co-taught by a biologist (Irene) and a physicist (Leslie). Unlike other courses offered in the major, this course is designed to address the "inquiry" standards from the last iteration of the California State Science Standards (California State Bureau of Education, 1998) by engaging students in the practices of science as they model complex phenomena (e.g., an eye, a pinhole theater, the tides, or the pitch from a glass of water when struck with a fork). The explicit lack of any predetermined content to be covered allows for increased attention to students' reasoning, a focus on students' own language, and an emergent curriculum.

Extended Example From Leslie and Irene's Class

In the example below, students have already dissected an eye and are now collaborating in four-person groups on questions related to how the eye works. Some groups are using lenses, curious about how the lens of the eye affects images we see; others are constructing a model of the eye, beginning with a hole in a box; still others are paying careful attention to patterns in visual phenomena (e.g., they find that they cannot focus on objects that are too close to their faces).

Early on, it became clear to the instructors that all groups had, in one way or another, been examining "crisp" and "blurry" images, so they ask the six groups to share an example of "blurriness" with the class. They anticipate that a whole-class conversation around these observations might help students identify ways in which their investigations are illustrating similar or different phenomena. Where the ideas are similar, an understanding of how images are constructed (whether it's with a pinhole, lens, or eye) might emerge. Where the ideas are different, students might gain more precision in what is meant by "focused" and "blurry" images, and how those differ from related ideas, like low-resolution images.

In response to Leslie's and Irene's request for an example of "blurriness,"[10] the groups offer the following six observations:

1. Hold your finger really close to your eye. You cannot focus on it; it's blurry.
2. Stare straight ahead at some writing, you cannot read things in your peripheral vision; they're blurry.
3. Look at the image made by a large pinhole camera. It is blurry.
4. Shine a Maglite on an object. The shadow cast by this object is not blurry, but you can make it seem blurry if you give that object a "ragged edge."
5. Shine light through a cut-out "R" shape that is covered with a translucent paper (a light post-it note). It will appear blurry, but if there is no paper then it is not blurry.
6. Stare at an image and then close your eyes. The afterimage (the hazy negative you see with your eyes closed) has a blurry "edge."

Noticing that few groups have developed detailed explanations for *why* these phenomena appear blurry, the instructors begin the conversation by asking students, quite simply, "So what is blurriness?"

In the transcript below, groups begin to describe—and progressively explain—the six observations, articulating that the location of an image on the retina matters, referring to a model for the reflection of light that they had previously discussed in class, and then connecting that model to the phenomena of blurry and focused images (see video at http://www.studentsthinking.org/rtsm):

Amanda: We kind of talked about we did this thing with like peripheral vision ... when [light] comes in, you know, straight in, the lens is directing it and it comes to a center spot. And we were talking about peripheral vision how it's like more unfocused and maybe that's because the light from those—from, y'know this area over here [in the periphery] is coming in at like angles so the lens can't like focus it right to the middle as well, and we talked about how there's that little spot on the back and we think—of the retina whatever it's called.

Breanna: The fovea [central part of the retina].

Amber: And we were thinking maybe that has to do with like how you focus, like focus on images 'cause when you're looking straight at

20 Amy D. Robertson et al.

something that light that's coming into your lens is directed back to that center spot—

Breanna: Or closer to the center spot.

Irene: Let me see—you're saying that the peripheral vision is more blurry and fuzzy. It's not as crisp because it's [the light from the object is] not hitting towards the center of your retina.

Amanda: Yeah.

Here the group is articulating an idea that is not obvious to most students—that images are not simply out there in the world to be seen, but that the eye must somehow direct (if not construct/project) that image onto the retina. However, the group offers no mechanism by which the peripheral image is blurry.

The group that originally proposed that light coming through a cut-out **L** projects a crisp **L** on the wall and that light coming through a translucent **R** projects a fuzzy blob of light (observation (5), see previously) speaks up immediately after Amanda, Amber, and Breanna. Caitlin offers a mechanistic description, linking what happens to the light rays with the blurriness of the image:

Caitlin: We were talking about with the **R** that we couldn't see it was like spread out because it kooshes [leaves the **R** in all directions][11] off of the post-it. And so [the light is] like spread out—but then with like the **L** through the aluminum it doesn't koosh so it's crisp.

Irene: How would you—like, could you draw that or do you have a way of like representing that or another way of thinking of it.

Caitlin: I don't know—do you? [Laughter.]

The reasoning presented here suggests a nascent model of blurriness—the **R** image is blurry because the light "kooshes" off the post-it note, spreading out in all directions (as in Figure 1.6), while the **L** image does not "koosh." Caitlin does not elaborate on why the "spread out" light is blurry.

At this point Leslie sketches the two masks (**L** & **R**) on the board (Figure 1.7). Students describe the light rays, and Leslie draws the rays and notes the phrases they use on her diagram: the light rays that leave the **L** do not overlap; with the **L** there is just one ray landing in each place on the screen, so it is dim; the rays leaving the **R** go in many directions; these rays will hit the screen "all over;" the rays are "fragmented" by the **R**; they "spread out" and "overlap" at the screen.

The ideas are still quite tentative, offered as suggestions, and students describe characteristics that might matter but do not yet link these ideas to why the image might be blurry. When a student suggests that the **L** should be brighter because the rays do not fragment, Breanna offers what seems like a counterargument—that fragmenting light makes for "too much" light reaching any one spot. Students seem to be conflating "too much"—which suggests that the intensity of the light causes the blurriness—with "too many"—which suggests that rays from too many

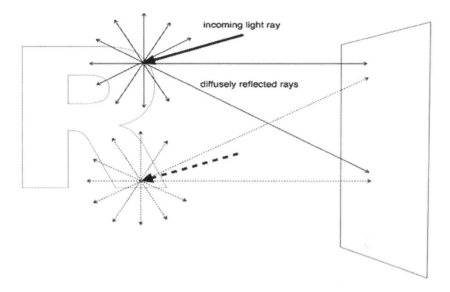

FIGURE 1.6 Two incoming light rays reflect diffusely from two points on the "R" and send multiple scattered light rays to the screen, at right.

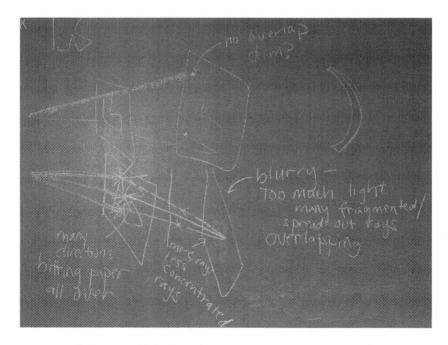

FIGURE 1.7 A diagram of light through an opening (L) and light through a translucent opening (R).

22 Amy D. Robertson et al.

places cause the blurriness. As Breanna elaborates her ideas, she takes up the latter, clarifying that rays from multiple different points on the translucent **R** overlap on the screen:

Breanna: But I think that that would kind of be the opposite [that the **R** should be brighter]. Because, um, this, the top one [the **L** drawn on the board in Fig. 1.6] there's no overlapping. It might be more dim. And then the bottom one if there's overlapping it would be brighter.

Leslie: And you say it's dim because just one ray got here [for the **L**] while in this one [the **R**] it will fragment and send many rays here? (writes on board)

Breanna: Yeah. What I think is there's so many little fragmented rays, they're going many different directions that's why it's going blurry.

Leslie: So because they went many directions from here (points to translucent **R**)—

Breanna: And they're hitting the paper all over. There might be a lot of them but they're hitting so many spots on the paper that it doesn't make a crisp image.

Breanna's description of why the **R** is blurry—rays "fragment" upon striking the **R** shape (the "kooshing" that Caitlin calls our attention to), and those fragmented rays are projected to many spots on the paper—is consistent with scientific descriptions. Moreover, it suggests that a "focused" or "crisp" image would be one in which rays do not fragment, or, if they do, they are somehow brought back together.

Within this conversation about blurriness, Leslie and Irene recognize some students productively modeling light rays as they seek to describe blurriness, and they use that as the foundation of a homework assignment that asked students to create their own diagrams and explanations for the blurry **R** that Caitlin's group had created. After students completed the assignment, the class met in small groups to create whiteboards of their work and then discussed the whiteboards as a class. Students quickly reached consensus around the idea of blurriness. As Breanna summarizes, "Overlapping rays from multiple origins . . . will cause an image to be blurry." The direction that the remainder of the unit took emerged from connections that students made between this definition and their original observations, and between other phenomena of interest. They came to consensus on a final description of focus: "All the rays from an originating point come back together in the same spot on the retina."

How This Example Instantiates Responsive Teaching

Throughout this extended example, Leslie and Irene enact responsive teaching that weaves together the three characteristics articulated in the introduction to this chapter. When Irene revoices Amber's, Amanda's, and Breanna's ideas—and later, when Leslie diagrams at the board—they do so based on the students' ideas and descriptions, foregrounding the students' explanations rather than the instructor's expertise. While the instructors notice whether or not the examples students offer fit a canonical understanding of focused and blurry images—which is certainly one way to seek out connections between students' ideas and the discipline—their primary task is to recognize disciplinary *opportunities* in those ideas. They see in these ideas opportunities for rich scientific conversations in which students model phenomena, and they imagine ways to support students in moving from a cataloging of things that are "hazy" in appearance towards a more nuanced view that determines whether or not these phenomena are governed by similar mechanisms. The homework assignment that Irene and Leslie ultimately ask students to complete focuses on using their own ideas and diagrams to explain the observation made by one of the student groups, requiring *students* to attend to and make sense of one another's thinking, and to do so in a way that preserves and highlights their own (individual) ideas. In addition, this assignment capitalizes on and extends the productive mechanistic reasoning inherent in Caitlin's and Breanna's explanation for blurriness.

We often think of responsive teaching as adapting instruction to address students' ideas: a preplanned lesson meets with an unexpected question or idea, and the instructor takes up and pursues this idea instead of continuing with the lesson as planned. The nature of this *Scientific Inquiry* class means that describing it as "*adapting* instruction on the basis of students' ideas" is a bit misleading; student ideas *determine* the instructional sequence. Although the instructors plan in advance, generally meeting for an hour after class to discuss students' ideas and a sequence of activities for the next day, the plans are loose and designed to take up and pursue students' scientific ideas. In this extended example, Leslie and Irene recognized a theme—blurriness—among the students' explorations, and this observation prompted them to ask students to share an example of blurriness. The nature of the examples that students shared—more focused on the ways to produce the phenomenon than on explanations of blurry images—inspired Leslie and Irene to press students to articulate *what blurriness is*. Students' own explanations for the images they had been exploring became the grounds for collective representation and negotiation of blurriness.

Trying for Responsiveness in a University Physics Lecture: Example From David's Introductory Physics Course Discussion of Forces[12]

Unlike the example above, where the content of the course is largely driven by students' ideas, David has been trying to incorporate responsiveness in a class with very clear content objectives—a large introductory physics lecture. In doing so, he has faced a number of challenges. Goals of "covering content" make it difficult to spend time listening to students' reasoning. Students take the course for many different reasons and as part of many different programs, which makes it important

24 Amy D. Robertson et al.

to stay with the planned syllabus. Another difficulty is the number of students: David has had as many as 180, and at some institutions, introductory courses have several times more than that. It is only possible to hear directly from a fraction of the students, those who speak up or whom the instructor can hear while students work in groups. Another means of hearing from the class as a whole is through "clickers"—instructors pose multiple-choice questions and students click in their answers (Dufresne, Gerace, Leonard, Mestre, & Wenk, 1996; Mazur, 1997).

While it is not possible in lecture settings to follow students' thinking in the ways we show in the other examples in this chapter, there is room for responsiveness in smaller ways in the flow and substance of a lecture session, such as we illustrate here. It can also happen in somewhat larger-scale ways, such as with homework or exam problems that pick up on reasoning that arose from students.

Example From David's Class

The following example (available at http://www.studentsthinking.org/rtsm) is from David's calculus-based introductory physics course at Tufts University. About 75 students enrolled in the course. During the first lecture of the course, David poses a short series of questions about striking a bowling ball or a basketball to get it moving. Students laugh at the idea of his using his foot—kicking the bowling ball would hurt! So he uses a heavy rubber mallet, and when he poses the question, a significant majority predict that if he swung the mallet "in the same way"—that is, raising it to the same height and trying to make the same motion—the basketball would move much faster than the bowling ball. Several students explain that the bowling ball has more mass, so the same force would have a smaller effect.

Another question asks students to compare the force by the mallet on the ball to the force by the ball on the mallet. Most of the students have taken high school physics, and most answer that these would be equal in strength.[13] David then puts up a slide asking, "Was the force by the mallet on the bowling ball equal to the force by the mallet on the basketball?"[14] Almost all students say "yes."

David uses the opportunity to point out a contradiction: that would mean that the force by the bowling ball on the mallet would be the same strength as the force by the basketball on the mallet. But everyone knows it would hurt to kick a bowling ball! Doesn't that mean kicking a bowling ball exerts a greater force on your toe?

The class discusses this for several minutes, but David leaves the question unresolved and assigns it as part of their problem set due the following week (see http://www.studentsthinking.org/rtsm for a copy of the homework question). One week later, just after the students hand in their assignment, David poses the question again. Ninety-one percent still answer yes, the mallet exerts the same magnitude force on the bowling ball as on the basketball. David asks students to explain why they voted as they did. Emma is the first to volunteer; she explains that "it's the same force, except the basketball has very little mass, so it accelerates a lot. And the bowling ball has a lot of mass, so it doesn't really accelerate." David responds by reiterating her reasoning, to her satisfaction, "if you give the same force . . . but one has a much smaller mass, the acceleration will be much larger." But he challenges it:

David: So that would help me understand that if the forces are the same, this is why the basketball shoots out so fast. But what I want to know is, if the forces are the same, why does it hurt my toe, to hit one, how do I account for that?

Emma: Because, if you [pause] your foot isn't going to accelerate as much [kicking the basketball].

He and Emma have a brief exchange to clarify that she is saying his foot would not accelerate as quickly on kicking the basketball. Taylor agrees:

Taylor: Basically it takes your foot a shorter time to come to rest when it hits the bowling ball than when it hits the basketball. It's, like, more of an abrupt coming to rest.

Immediately following, Taylor goes on to compare the situation to a person jumping off a building onto a trampoline, saying that it takes more time for the person to come to rest.

David: That sounds like, would I be correct to say that my foot has a higher acceleration, kicking the bowling ball?

Taylor: Yes.

David: I would be correct to say that.

Taylor: Or it has the same, but it just [inaudible]

David: Well, all right, so you said it's a more abrupt stop for the foot, and 'more abrupt stop' sounds like higher acceleration. Mary?

Mary: It takes more force for the bowling ball to overcome friction, it takes more force to accelerate. But you're kicking each, the basketball and the bowling ball with the same force it's going to hurt your foot more with the bowling ball because it takes more force to push the bowling ball versus pushing the basketball. And that's why it hurts.

David: Oh, I see. More of the force goes into my foot when kicking the bowling ball. [to Shivani] Go ahead.

Shivani: I just want to add that the bowling ball has so much mass that it doesn't change shape upon the impact. So when you kick it, a very small surface area of your foot gets injured.

David: Oh, it's a small surface area of my toe, and it gets more spread out for the basketball.

26 Amy D. Robertson et al.

Another student says "something similar," and then David calls on "one more" saying he had a question he wanted to ask. Nikhil gives "a counterargument" to Shivani's reasoning.

Nikhil: If you had a basketball that had the same hardness, and like the same flexibility as the bowling ball, but it had less mass, it would still hurt less.
David: So if I had a light, stiff basketball that doesn't dent at all.
Nikhil: Yeah.

After Nikhil presents his argument, David constructs a new clicker question, repeating Taylor's reasoning.

David: When I go to kick the bowling ball, my foot stops more abruptly. My question back to you is . . . is it correct to say that my foot's acceleration is higher?

He rephrases the question to focus on the mallet, "because I like my feet," and the poll shows 59% say yes, the mallet has a higher acceleration when it hits the bowling ball than when it hits the basketball. With 59% not a very strong majority, he suggests students talk in groups to try to sort it out. After a couple of minutes (omitted from the video) he polls again to find 72% now say yes, a more abrupt stop means a higher acceleration.

In the discussion that followed, Maayan explains that the acceleration must be the same across the two balls, because it was a "premise of the question" that the force is the same, and by Newton's Second Law the acceleration must be the same too. David had been thinking of this connection too, which showed a new version of the contradiction: if the total force on the mallet is the same, its acceleration must be the same, but the mallet seems to stop more abruptly when it hits the bowling ball.

How This Example Instantiates Responsive Teaching

In modest ways, this example illustrates David's foregrounding of student ideas. He does so on aggregate, via clicker questions, and on smaller scales in his request that students offer arguments to support their answers and in his revoicing the reasoning that they give. For example, when Shivani argues that "when you kick it [the bowling ball], a very small surface area of your foot gets injured," David does not evaluate her response but reflects her meaning back to her, saying, "Oh, it's a small surface area of my toe, and it gets more spread out for the basketball."

David's in-the-moment choices reflect his sense of disciplinary potential in students' thinking, with respect to conceptual substance as well as disciplinary engagement. Shivani's argument, for example, that the force for the bowling ball is more concentrated in "a very small surface area of your foot," and Nikhil's response, showed both students working toward sensible, coherent mechanistic understanding. They were "doing physics," and doing it well. Moreover, the number of students interested to speak up, and the class's animated conversations when they broke into groups, reflected aspects of disciplinary engagement that David hoped to cultivate.

In addition, David's initial choice of question—kicking a bowling ball and a basketball with your foot—reflects his *anticipation*, both of students' conceptual resources for understanding physical phenomena and of their likely epistemological stances toward physics. He had found this to be an effective "launching question" (Hammer et al., 2012), in that it taps into students' productive knowledge about physical phenomena. At the same time, he expects that this kind of question will violate students' expectations at the start of his course about what the course will entail. That is, David chose a question that would allow him to be responsive in a way that a more traditionally posed physics question (e.g., "a force applied to a more massive object") would not.

Finally, this example shows David taking up and pursuing his students' thinking, including in his spending more time on the topic than he had planned and in his using student reasoning to shape the flow of the discussion from that point forward. The students' sense that the mallet stops more abruptly gave David his next clicker question, and it helped that 72% of the students agreed that "stopping more abruptly" meant "higher acceleration."

Discussion

In this chapter, we have shown that the form that responsive teaching takes can vary across contexts; that teachers can recognize a variety of disciplinary opportunities in what their students say and do—from mechanistic thinking, to the beginnings of canonical understanding, to nascent scientific practices; and that teachers may take up their students' ideas in different ways, from planning experiments to test a student's idea, to proposing that students investigate patterns in "Sean numbers," to allowing students' emergent ideas to dictate the direction of the class's inquiry. Despite this variation, we have articulated three characteristics that help us understand what it is that responsive classrooms have in common: they foreground the substance of students' disciplinary ideas, recognize the disciplinary connections within students' ideas, and take up and pursue the substance of students' ideas.

As we look across the classroom cases presented above, we also notice some similarities and differences in the time-scales over which the teacher is responsive, in the constraints and competing goals that the teachers experience as they attempt to be responsive, in the knowledge that is entailed in teaching responsively, and in the classroom cultures that are displayed in these examples. Here we briefly discuss these themes before closing the chapter.

28 Amy D. Robertson et al.

Time-Scales: Responsive Teaching in the Long- and Short-Term

Responsive teaching may entail adapting instruction in-the-moment and responding on the microscale to students' ideas as they emerge. In some cases it may also involve elevating students' ideas to the level of the curriculum, such that students' questions and observations frame and guide an entire unit of instruction.

At the grain size of moment-by-moment responsiveness, Ball invites students to experiment with Ofala's definition of odd numbers; Hammer tries experiments that his students suggest; Ann recognizes that her students are talking about two different variables that may affect the behavior of magnets; Jenny presses Grace to articulate a mechanism for how water absorbs salt; Leslie and Irene connect students' definitions of blurriness to one another; and David authors clicker questions on the spot that are based on the ideas he hears in his lecture. In some cases, this moment-by-moment responsiveness is accompanied by longer-term responsiveness. Ball chooses to elevate "Sean numbers" to the same level as even and odd numbers in her students' explorations of number patterns; a multi-day investigation of induced polarization in Hammer's high school physics course is initiated by Camille's discovery of the "Marino phenomenon;" Ann plans a unit around the questions and nascent experiments that emerge in the magnetism discussion; and the *idea* to pursue blurriness as a phenomenon—and the resulting direction of the students' inquiry in Leslie and Irene's class—emerged from the natural direction taken by students' investigations of how the eye works. That each of these is an example of responsive teaching suggests that it is possible to have both responsive *moments* and responsive *units;* it happens at multiple grain sizes.

Competing Goals: Responsive Teaching and "Instructional Tensions"

Ball's (Ball, 1993) and Hammer's (Hammer, 1997) first-hand accounts (and others', e.g., Chazan & Schnepp, 2002; Levin, 2008; Levin et al., 2009; Maskiewicz, this volume) illuminate the tensions that teachers often feel when students offer ideas that are both canonically incorrect *and* productive toward other instructional goals (e.g., building a mathematical or scientific community), or, more generally, when there are competing goals at play. Hammer (1997) defines this as the "instructional tension":

> For the purposes of this article, I adopt this description of the instructional tension, which I suggest is both genuine and legitimate: It is legitimate for me to want students to understand that some materials conduct electricity and others do not; it is also legitimate for me to want students to explore phenomena, design experiments, and invent their own explanations. Ultimately, I know, these two agendas should not conflict; they are both aspects of the same overall goal that the students develop scientific understanding.

But what I hope will happen ultimately is of little help in this moment, as I try to decide how to respond.

(p. 488)

This tension may take the form of feeling torn between two seemingly-in-conflict instructional agendas, as in the quote above; other times, it may take the form of discerning whether one is really listening to and understanding students' ideas without projecting one's own (or the canonical) meaning onto what they have said; still other times it may take the form of balancing or coordinating the myriad ideas that students put forth.

These "instructional tensions" are at the heart of responsive teaching; they are a natural consequence of seeking to embody a practice that "is, at once, honest to mathematics and honoring of children" (Ball, 1993, p. 394) and that enacts an expansive vision of "content"—one that includes and strives for more than canonical correctness. Ball suggests that teachers must *embrace,* rather than try to *resolve,* such "pedagogical dilemmas," and that doing so empowers teachers to really *listen* to their students.

The teachers in our examples likewise experienced such instructional tensions. Ann was faced with a decision between foregrounding students' ideas about the magnetism question and reviewing particular canonical content (in this case, forces) for the upcoming standardized test. She articulated both sides of this tension in a conversation after class—she felt a sense of "commitment to the kids that I don't want them to see something on the test that we've never even talked about," yet she preferred and ultimately chose to honor students' demonstrated interest in the magnetism discussion. Similarly, Jenny teaches in a high-stakes testing environment, where teachers are accountable for students' passing scores on an exam that is required for graduation. As a result, her content goals are never far from her mind, and they must be balanced with her attention to students' thinking. Thus Jenny occasionally tries to guide her students to the canonical answer. For example, after allowing the conversation to proceed with the term "evaporation" for a while, Jenny asks students to recall what they learned about diffusion, and the language of the possible mechanism shifts from evaporation to what students remember about diffusion. David likewise acknowledges the many constraints imposed by the nature of his lecture course: expected content coverage, large numbers of students, and a need to stick to the syllabus.

In spite of these tensions and constraints, teachers in these courses both value and instructionally prioritize students' ideas, and students experience their ideas as meaningful to the teacher and central to the construction of their own understandings. For example, as the discussion in Jenny's class comes to a close, Haja asks her, "Do you have your own analysis on this?," suggesting that she believes that the consensus they have come to has been directed by *their* (rather than Jenny's) understandings.

30 Amy D. Robertson et al.

Knowledge: Intellectual Demands of Responsive Teaching

These examples also highlight the role that knowledge of the discipline plays in responsive teaching. Hammer (1997) argues that "this view of the coordination of inquiry and traditional content places substantial intellectual demands on the teacher" (p. 517). For example, locating "a substantive connection" between (i) physicists' conceptions of charge, electric fields, and/or electric potential and (ii) Susan's notion of a "spark" or Bruce's notion of "aura" or "force field"; understanding how adherents of two competing theories are making sense of a new experiment in the moment; recognizing the conceptual and epistemological potential of Camille's discovery of the "Marino phenomenon"; and figuring out why Ning's experiment didn't work all drew on Hammer's extensive knowledge of the content and practices of the discipline. Not only this, Hammer (and others) must *coordinate* the many different ideas—as well as multiple, often competing, goals—as he listens for the science in students' thinking.

Likewise, we see that Ann brings her knowledge of experimental design to bear on her teasing out Caroline's conflation of the variables of distance and environment; Jenny presses Grace to explore the mechanism underlying the "absorption" of salt by water, knowing that the pursuit of mechanistic reasoning is central to science; Leslie and Irene tease apart which of their students' accounts of blurriness offer *descriptions* and which ones offer *explanations;* and David recognizes that "stopping more abruptly" implies a higher acceleration of his foot. Thus each of these teachers brings his or her knowledge of both the content and the practices of science to bear as he or she recognizes and seeks to build on the "seeds of science" in their students' ideas, embodying a practice that is "both responsive to students and responsible to [the discipline]" (Ball, 1993, p. 396).

Classroom Culture: Responsiveness to Nascent Practices of Responsiveness Among Students

Although we have focused on what makes *teaching* responsive, we notice that across our examples *students* are also listening, responding to, and building on one another's ideas. For example, Mei revoices Sean's idea and then challenges its generality; and Amanda, Amber, and Breanna collaboratively share out their explanation for blurriness, building on and adding to one another's contributions. We suspect that responsive teaching is often embedded in responsive *classrooms* (Bresser & Fargason, 2013) and that in such classrooms teachers model and reinforce responsiveness to the substance of scientific ideas.

Conclusion

In this chapter, we have articulated three actions that the literature often highlights as characteristic of responsive teaching, and we have illustrated what responsive

What Is Responsive Teaching? **31**

teaching looks like across examples from the literature and from K–12 and university science classrooms. These examples illuminate the diversity of forms that responsive teaching can take, and they showcase that it occurs across multiple timescales, is intellectually demanding, and is often embedded in a classroom culture of responsiveness, and that when teachers instantiate it, they often experience an "instructional tension." We hope that in immersing themselves in these examples—in getting a glimpse of responsive teaching in action—our readers are better prepared to engage with the scholarship in the remainder of this book.

Acknowledgments

The authors gratefully acknowledge the support of NSF grant numbers ESI 0455711, DRL 0822342, DUE 0837508, EHR/DUE 0831970, DRL 1140785, and DRL 0733613. We also wish to thank Abigail R. Daane, David Hammer, and Rachel E. Scherr for their thoughtful feedback.

Notes

1 See Chapter 2 for a detailed discussion of several different conceptualizations of responsive teaching and for an overview of some of the reasons that research and teaching communities value responsive teaching.
2 Content reproduced with permission from Mathematics Teaching and Learning to Teach, University of Michigan. (2010). In SeanNumbers-Ofala [Online]. Available: http://hdl.handle.net/2027.42/65013.
3 To view video of this discussion, see the following link: http://deepblue.lib.umich.edu/handle/2027.42/65013.
4 Generally speaking, an electrophorus is an object (usually a capacitor) that can be charged by induction. In this case, the electrophorus is "charged by induction" when it is brought near the negatively charged Styrofoam plate: the positive charges in the electrophorus are attracted to the Styrofoam plate, and the negative charges in the electrophorus are repelled from the plate. The result is that the negative charges move toward the top of the electrophorus, and the positive charges move toward the bottom, closer to the Styrofoam. When the finger touches the electrophorus, some of the negative charges leave—in part because the negative charges near the finger are repelled from the other negative charges that have accumulated near the top of the electrophorus—and the electrophorus thus obtains a net positive charge. The electrostatic force between the electrophorus and foam plate (a function of the net charges on each one) increases, and the Styrofoam plate is attracted toward the electrophorus, lifting it off the table.
5 All students' names are pseudonyms.
6 Full transcript of this example is published in Levin, Hammer, Elby, & Coffey, 2012, and can be downloaded at http://www.nsta.org/publications/press/extras/responsive.aspx.
7 We adopt Russ et al.'s (2009) criteria for mechanistic reasoning: mechanistic explanations specify the "activities" (the components that "produce change") and the "entities" (the "things that engage in those activities"), and they "describe how each stage of the mechanism progresses to the next stage" (called "chaining," p. 880). Russ et al. say that mechanistic reasoning "involves more than just reasoning about causality itself—it is

32 Amy D. Robertson et al.

more than identifying the 'X' that causes 'Y' to happen." It "also requires that students think about *how* 'X' brings about 'Y'" (p. 881). For example, a mechanistic explanation for why the pressure of a gas increases as temperature does would consider that pressure is caused by the collisions of the particles of a gas with the walls of its container and would describe how increasing the temperature would increase the frequency and intensity of those collisions. The *beginnings* of mechanistic reasoning might include connecting entities and activities or causal sensemaking.

8   The full poem can be found easily on the Internet. A good hardcopy version with commentary and illustrations is cited here: Coleridge, S.T. (2008). *The Rime of the Ancient Mariner*. Edison, NJ: Chartwell Books.

9   In a hypertonic solution, solute concentration is higher on the outside of a membrane (e.g., a cell membrane). In a hypotonic solution, the solute concentration is higher on the inside.

10 To briefly summarize how a blurry image is formed, we explain observation (5). A light ray reflecting off of any point on a translucent **R** is scattered in all directions (see Figure 1.6). When these rays fall on a screen (as shown in the diagram) or a retina, they will not project a "crisp" or "focused" image, but will overlap with rays that reflect off of other points on the object. However, if a pinhole (an opaque surface with a tiny opening) is inserted between the object and the screen, a clear, upside-down image will be created because only "one" ray from each spot on the object reaches the screen. A lens creates a crisp image by bending rays such that the rays that scattered from one point are brought back together on the screen (creating a clear and bright image). The eye, with its lens and pinhole-like pupil, employs both mechanisms to project a clear image on the retina lining the back of the eye. When the pinhole is large (such that more than one ray from each spot on the object reaches the screen) or the screen/retina is not at the ideal location, the image will appear blurry. In our peripheral vision, the receptors are so far apart that we cannot see fine details, regardless of whether or not the image projected on the retina is blurry.

11 In earlier conversations, the class modeled light rays leaving an object in all directions, similar to the pattern of rubber strands from a koosh ball.

12 Special thanks to David Hammer for providing detailed notes, on the basis of which this section was written.

13 Newton's Third Law says they must be equal: all forces come in equal and opposite pairs, by object A on object B and by object B on object A.

14 The force by the mallet on the bowling ball, hitting at the same speed, is larger than the force by the mallet on the basketball. One way to see this is to think of kicking the two balls, which is part of this discussion—kicking a bowling ball hurts! Another way to see it is to focus on the mallet. It is moving at the same speed, just before it hits either ball. When it hits the basketball, it slows down, but it keeps moving forward. When the mallet hits the bowling ball, on the other hand, it comes to an abrupt stop; it even bounces backward a little. So the bowling ball has a much stronger effect on the mallet's motion. In more formal terms, the mallet has a larger acceleration, hitting the bowling ball, which means there's a larger force on it—and the force by the ball on the mallet must be equal and opposite to the force by the mallet on the ball.

References

Ball, D.L. (1993). With an eye on the mathematical horizon: Dilemmas of teaching elementary school mathematics. *The Elementary School Journal, 93,* 373–397.

Bresser, R., & Fargason, S. (2013). *Becoming scientists: Inquiry-based teaching in diverse classrooms, grades 3–5*. Portland, ME: Stenhouse Publishers.

Brodie, K. (2011). Working with learners' mathematical thinking: Towards a language of description for changing pedagogy. *Teaching and Teacher Education, 27*, 174–186.

California State Board of Education. (1998). *Science content standards for California public schools*. Sacramento, CA: California Department of Education Press.

Carpenter, T.P., Fennema, E., Franke, M.L., Levi, L., & Empson, S.B. (2000). *Cognitively Guided Instruction: A research-based teacher professional development program for elementary school mathematics*. Madison, WI: NCISLA, Wisconsin Center for Education Research, University of Wisconsin.

Carpenter, T.P., Fennema, E., Peterson, P.L., Chiang, C.-P., & Loef, M. (1989). Using knowledge of children's mathematics thinking in classroom teaching: An experimental study. *American Educational Research Journal, 26*(4), 499–531.

Chazan, D., & Ball, D.L. (1999). Beyond being told not to tell. *For the Learning of Mathematics, 19,* 2–10.

Chazan, D., & Schnepp, M. (2002). Methods, goals, beliefs, commitments, and manner in teaching: Dialogue against a calculus backdrop. *Social Constructivist Teaching, 9,* 171–195.

Coffey, J.E., Hammer, D., Levin, D.M., & Grant, T. (2011). The missing disciplinary substance of formative assessment. *Journal of Research in Science Teaching, 48,* 1109–1136.

Colestock, A., & Linnenbringer, T. (2010). Selective archiving as a tool for supporting mathematics teacher inquiry and exploring teachers' sensemaking of students' mathematical thinking. Paper presented at the Annual Meeting of the American Educational Research Association, Denver, CO.

diSessa, A.A. (1993). Toward an epistemology of physics. *Cognition and Instruction, 10,* 105–225.

Duckworth, E. (2006). *"The having of wonderful ideas" and other essays on teaching and learning* (3rd ed.). New York, NY: Teachers College Press.

Dufresne, R.J., Gerace, W.J., Leonard, W.J., Mestre, J.P., & Wenk, L. (1996). Classtalk: A classroom communication system for active learning. *Journal of Computing in Higher Education, 7,* 3–47.

Empson, S.B., & Jacobs, V.R. (2008). Learning to listen to children's mathematics. In D. Tirosh & T. Wood (Eds.), *Tools and processes in mathematics teacher education* (pp. 257–281). The Netherlands: Sense Publishers.

Fennema, E., Carpenter, T.P., Franke, M.L., Levi, L., Jacobs, V.R., & Empson, S.B. (1996). A longitudinal study of learning to use children's thinking in mathematics instruction. *Journal for Research in Mathematics Education, 27,* 403–434.

Fennema, E., Franke, M.L., Carpenter, T.P., & Carey, D.A. (1993). Using children's mathematical knowledge in instruction. *American Educational Research Journal, 30,* 555–583.

Ford, M.J. (2005). The game, the pieces, and the players: Generative resources from two instructional portrayals of experimentation. *Journal of the Learning Sciences, 14,* 449–487.

Gallas, K. (1995). *Talking their way into science: Hearing children's questions and theories, responding with curricula*. New York, NY: Teachers College Press.

Goldsmith, L.T., & Seago, N. (2011). Using classroom artifacts to focus teachers' noticing: Affordances and opportunities. In M.G. Sherin, V.R. Jacobs, & R.A. Philipp (Eds.), *Mathematics teacher noticing: Seeing through teachers' eyes* (pp. 169–187). New York, NY: Routledge.

Hammer, D. (1996). More than misconceptions: Multiple perspectives on student knowledge and reasoning, and an appropriate role for education research. *American Journal of Physics, 64,* 1316–1325.

34 Amy D. Robertson et al.

Hammer, D. (1997). Discovery learning and discovery teaching. *Cognition and Instruction, 15,* 485–529.

Hammer, D. (2000). Student resources for learning introductory physics. *American Journal of Physics, 68,* S52-S59.

Hammer, D., Elby, A., Scherr, R.E., & Redish, E.F. (2005). Resources, framing, and transfer. In J.P. Mestre (Ed.), *Transfer of learning from a modern multidisciplinary perspective* (pp. 89–119). USA: Information Age Publishing, Inc.

Hammer, D., Goldberg, F., & Fargason, S. (2012). Responsive teaching and the beginnings of energy in a third grade classroom. *Review of Science, Mathematics, and ICT Education, 6,* 51–72.

Hammer, D., & van Zee, E. (2006). *Seeing the science in children's thinking: Case studies of student inquiry in physical science.* Portsmouth, NH: Heinemann.

Harrer, B.W., Flood, V.J., & Wittmann, M.C. (2013). Productive resources in students' ideas about energy: An alternative analysis of Watts' original interview transcripts. *Physical Review Special Topics—Physics Education Research, 9,* 023101.

Hutchison, P., & Hammer, D. (2010). Attending to student epistemological framing in a science classroom. *Science Education, 94,* 506–524.

Jacobs, V.R., Franke, M.L., Carpenter, T.P., Levi, L., & Battey, D. (2007). Professional development focused on children's algebraic reasoning in elementary school. *Journal for Research in Mathematics Education, 38,* 258–288.

Jacobs, V.R., Lamb, L.L.C., & Philipp, R.A. (2010). Professional noticing of children's mathematical thinking. *Journal for Research in Mathematics Education, 41,* 169–202.

Jacobs, V.R., Lamb, L.L.C., Philipp, R.A., & Shappelle, B.P. (2011). Deciding how to respond on the basis of children's understandings. In M.G. Sherin, V.R. Jacobs, & R.A. Philipp (Eds.), *Mathematics teacher noticing: Seeing through teachers' eyes* (pp. 97–116). New York, NY: Routledge.

Lau, M. (2010). *Understanding the dynamics of teacher attention: Examples of how high school physics and physical science teachers attend to student ideas* (Unpublished doctoral dissertation). College Park, MD: University of Maryland.

Levin, D.M. (2008). *What secondary science teachers pay attention to in the classroom: Situating teaching in institutional and social systems* (Unpublished doctoral dissertation). University of Maryland. College Park, MD.

Levin, D.M., Hammer, D., & Coffey, J.E. (2009). Novice teachers' attention to student thinking. *Journal of Teacher Education, 60,* 142–154.

Levin, D.M., Hammer, D., Elby, A., & Coffey, J. (2012). *Becoming a responsive science teacher: Focusing on student thinking in secondary science.* Arlington, VA: National Science Teachers Association Press.

Lineback, J.E. (2014). The redirection: An indicator of how teachers respond to student thinking. *Journal of the Learning Sciences,* 1–42.

Maskiewicz, A.C., & Winters, V.A. (2012). Understanding the co-construction of inquiry practices: A case study of a responsive teaching environment. *Journal of Research in Science Teaching, 49,* 429–464.

May, D.B., Hammer, D., & Roy, P. (2006). Children's analogical reasoning in a third-grade science discussion. *Science Education, 90,* 316–330.

Mazur, E. (1997). *Peer instruction.* Upper Saddle River, NJ: Prentice Hall.

NGSS Lead States. (2013). *Next Generation Science Standards: For states, by states.* Washington, D.C.: The National Academies Press.

Pierson, J.L. (2008). *The relationship between patterns of classroom discourse and mathematics learning* (Unpublished doctoral dissertation). University of Texas at Austin. Austin, TX.

Richards, J., Johnson, A., & Nyeggen, C.G. (2015). Inquiry-based science and the Next Generation Science Standards: A magnetic attraction. *Science and Children, 52,* 54–58.

Russ, R.S., Coffey, J.E., Hammer, D., & Hutchison, P. (2009). Making classroom assessment more accountable to scientific reasoning: A case for attending to mechanistic reasoning. *Science Education, 93,* 875–891.

Schifter, D. (2011). Examining the behavior of operations: Noticing early algebraic ideas. In M.G. Sherin, V.R. Jacobs, & R.A. Philipp (Eds.), *Mathematics teacher noticing: Seeing through teachers' eyes* (pp. 204–220). New York, NY: Routledge.

Sherin, M.G., Jacobs, V.R., & Philipp, R.A. (2011). *Mathematics teacher noticing: Seeing through teachers' eyes.* New York, NY: Routledge.

Sherin, M.G., & van Es, E.A. (2005). Using video to support teachers' ability to notice classroom interactions. *Journal of Technology and Teacher Education, 13,* 475–491.

Sherin, M.G., & van Es, E.A. (2009). Effects of video club participation on teachers' professional vision. *Journal of Teacher Education, 60,* 20–37.

Smith III, J.P., diSessa, A.A., & Roschelle, J. (1993). Misconceptions reconceived: A constructivist analysis of knowledge in transition. *The Journal of the Learning Sciences, 3,* 115–163.

van Es, E.A., & Sherin, M.G. (2008). Mathematics teachers' "learning to notice" in the context of a video club. *Teaching and Teacher Education, 24,* 244–276.

van Es, E.A., & Sherin, M.G. (2010). The influence of video clubs on teachers' thinking and practice. *Journal of Mathematics Teacher Education, 13,* 155–176.

Wallach, T., & Even, R. (2005). Hearing students: The complexity of understanding what they are saying, showing, and doing. *Journal of Mathematics Teacher Education, 8,* 393–417.

2

A REVIEW OF THE RESEARCH ON RESPONSIVE TEACHING IN SCIENCE AND MATHEMATICS

Jennifer Richards and Amy D. Robertson

In this chapter, we provide an overview of existing literature related to responsive teaching. We begin by emphasizing that responsive teaching is not a new idea. It has roots in Dewey's (1997) focus on educative experiences, where educators scout ahead "to see in what direction an experience is heading" (p. 38) and assess its potential for growth toward particular ends in interaction with "what is actually going on in the minds of those who are learning" (p. 39). It resonates with Bruner's (2003) notion that students have productive intuitions for disciplinary learning, such that any subject can be taught, in some authentic form, to any student at any age by working with both his or her intuitions and the fundamental structures of the discipline.

What is newer is an emphasis on how these principles play out in particular disciplinary and pedagogical contexts. This chapter explores several well-documented and frequently cited subsets of literature that share a central focus on teachers' practices of attending to the substance of students' ideas and adapting instruction in light of what they notice—what we describe in this book as "responsive teaching." Looking across these subsets, certain commonalities emerge, as articulated in Chapter 1:

- Responsive teaching foregrounds attention to the substance of students' ideas.
- Responsive teaching recognizes disciplinary connections within those ideas.
- Responsive teaching takes up and pursues students' ideas.

Each subset of literature also has its own unique characteristics, however, which we turn our attention to here. We begin by describing each subset of literature, with an eye toward how it characterizes responsive teaching. We then highlight affordances of responsive teaching that scholars have posed either theoretically or empirically. Finally, we look across the subsets of literature, this time to draw out distinctions and to open questions that may shape the field's work on responsive teaching moving forward.

Depictions of "Responsive Teaching" in the Literature

In this section, we provide an overview of different subsets of literature that center on teachers' practices of attending and responding to student thinking in science and mathematics. We do not claim that this review is exhaustive; rather, we intend for it to serve as an introduction to some of the better-documented and better-cited efforts in the field. We begin with a close look at one of the earliest efforts to help teachers adapt their mathematics instruction in response to what students say and do, Cognitively Guided Instruction (CGI). We then review the "mathematics teacher noticing" literature and its connection to responsive teaching before turning to two distinct approaches that scholars have used in studying responsive teaching. We call the first of these approaches the "discursive" approach; these papers focus on the kinds of talk that comprise responsive interactions between teachers and students. The second approach, representing a substantial fraction of the work in responsive teaching to date, uses in-depth case studies to unpack the nature of responsive teaching, including the tensions teachers experience while seeking to respect their students' ideas *and* to be responsible to their disciplines.

Cognitively Guided Instruction (CGI)

One early and well-documented effort to support teachers in grounding their instruction in the substance of students' mathematical thinking is the Cognitively Guided Instruction (CGI) program (Carpenter, Fennema, & Franke, 1996; Carpenter, Fennema, Franke, Levi, & Empson, 2000; Carpenter, Fennema, Peterson, Chiang, & Loef, 1989; Fennema et al., 1996; Fennema, Franke, Carpenter, & Carey, 1993; Franke, Carpenter, Fennema, Ansell, & Behrend, 1998; Franke, Carpenter, Levi, & Fennema, 2001; Franke & Kazemi, 2001). Drawing on research on children's conceptual development in specific content areas like addition and subtraction, researchers developed "an organized set of frameworks that delineated the key problems in the domain of mathematics and the strategies children would use to solve them" (Franke & Kazemi, 2001, p. 103).[1] The program aimed in part to familiarize teachers with these principled frameworks and the progressions that children often follow to develop more sophisticated understandings. Researchers expected that teachers would use the frameworks as they worked with individual students, both to support their interpretation of students' strategies and to decide on problems—more sophisticated either numerically or strategically—that would move their thinking forward (Fennema et al., 1993; Franke et al., 1998):

The CGI analysis provides a basis for selecting critical problems and for understanding what students' responses imply about their mathematical understanding. Because the framework is highly principled, it is possible to select a few key problems that will show what a student knows, and responses to individual problems fit together to provide a coherent profile of the strategies a student uses.

(Carpenter et al., 1996, p. 14)

What researchers found was that CGI teachers conceptualized and took up the frameworks in different ways. Some teachers used the frameworks as the researchers originally expected—as templates for assessing the strategies students were using and selecting appropriate next problems (Carpenter et al., 2000). For other teachers, the frameworks served as the basis for teachers' *own* developing models of student thinking. Rather than treating the frameworks as static templates, these teachers "continually reflect[ed] back on, modif[ied], adapt[ed], and expand[ed] their models in light of what they hear[d] from their students" (Carpenter et al., 2000, p. 5). Franke et al. (1998) describe this reflection and adaptation as the basis of generative growth for teachers.

Studies of the effectiveness of the CGI approach cite positive teacher outcomes. For example, an early study (Carpenter et al., 1989) found that CGI teachers listened more closely to the range of strategies students used to solve problems than did control teachers. In fact, the principled, research-based CGI frameworks oriented teachers to particular kinds of things to "listen for" in student thinking and ways to build on students' current understandings toward increasingly sophisticated mathematics. As one exemplar CGI teacher, Ms. J, described:

As a teacher you have to be a supreme listener to kids, and not only do you learn to just listen, but then you learn what to listen for and what might be some possible next steps you might want to take.

(Fennema et al., 1993, p. 580)

CGI teachers also more accurately predicted which problems their students would be able to solve, as measured by "the match between [the teacher's] predictions for [which strategies] each target student [would use to solve particular problems] and that student's actual response" (Carpenter et al., 1989, p. 511), suggesting that they came to know individual students' problem-solving approaches in detail.

Mathematics Teacher Noticing

Other work in mathematics education has focused not on how teachers make sense of research-based frameworks of student thinking but on how the teachers themselves distill key features of students' mathematical thinking from a chaotic, complex instructional environment (Colestock & Linnenbringer, 2010; Gold-smith & Seago, 2011; Jacobs, Franke, Carpenter, Levi, & Battey, 2007; Jacobs, Lamb, & Philipp, 2010; Jacobs, Lamb, Philipp, & Shappelle, 2011; Schifter, 2011; Sherin & Star, 2011; Sherin, Jacobs, & Philipp, 2011; Sherin, Russ, & Colestock, 2011; Sherin & van Es, 2005, 2009; van Es, 2011; van Es & Sherin, 2008, 2010; Walkoe, 2013).[2] Noticing students' mathematical thinking is framed as a skill or set of skills that can be learned; for instance, Jacobs et al. (2010) reported differences in the noticing skills of teachers that were related to the amount of time the teachers had spent in noticing-related professional development and that were not accounted for by years of teaching experience. Increased skill in noticing students' mathematical thinking is generally characterized by move-ment from superficial evaluation of students' ideas to detailed, evidence-based interpretation of their meanings and consideration of how their ideas connect to broader issues of mathematics learning and teaching (e.g., Sherin & van Es, 2005; van Es, 2011).

Much of the existing literature on mathematics teacher noticing has taken place in the context of professional development settings, in which teachers inter-act with classroom video (Sherin & Han, 2004; Sherin & van Es, 2005, 2009; van Es, 2011; van Es & Sherin, 2008, 2010) or student artifacts (Goldsmith & Seago, 2011; Jacobs et al., 2011). Some recent work has moved into the classroom setting (e.g., Sherin & van Es, 2009; van Es & Sherin, 2010) and has noted a relationship between increased noticing in the professional development setting and increased noticing or responsiveness while teaching, suggesting some degree of transfer-ability. However, the authors also highlight substantial variability in the classroom setting, with teachers sometimes taking up students' ideas as objects of inquiry and sometimes not.

What counts as evidence of noticing students' mathematical thinking dif-fers somewhat amongst mathematics teacher noticing researchers. For example, Sherin and van Es (2009) coded observations of classroom interactions on the basis of whether they displayed confirming or disconfirming evidence of teacher attention to student mathematical thinking. Confirming evidence included teach-ers acknowledging that students were presenting ideas or teachers tagging ideas as interesting, but did not always require the teacher to put the mathematical sub-stance of the ideas on display. In contrast, Jacobs et al. (2010) attended explicitly to whether teachers noticed the "mathematically significant details, such as how children counted, used tools or drawings to represent quantities, or decomposed numbers" (p. 183). This distinction may be due partly to the differing contexts in play (in-the-moment instruction in Sherin and van Es (2009) versus written reflection in Jacobs et al. (2010)) and may also be linked to Jacobs and colleagues' prior involvement with the CGI project, which focused on the details of students' problem-solving strategies.

Researchers who study teacher noticing might not consider them-selves to be studying responsive teaching, in part due to a debate about what noticing involves. Generally, researchers have divided noticing into three separate processes—noticing, interpreting, and responding—and argue about whether these processes are nested or separable (Colestock & Linnenbringer, 2010; Jacobs et al., 2010; Jacobs et al., 2011; Sherin, Jacobs, et al., 2011; Sherin, Russ, et al., 2011). Some authors argue that noticing is the most fundamental process; others argue that noticing and interpreting are inseparably connected but that a response follows from these two; and others argue that the three are so deeply entangled that they cannot be meaningfully separated.[3] Regardless, noticing researchers agree that noticing and making sense of student thinking are important precursors to teaching responsively and are a worthy aim of teacher development.

Discursive Studies of Responsive Teaching

Similar to Sherin and van Es's (2009) efforts to identify teacher noticing during instruction, several researchers studying responsive teaching take a discursive approach to defining and evaluating such teaching in classroom interactions (Brodie, 2011; Lineback, 2014; Pierson, 2008). This approach grows out of a larger body of literature on classroom discourse and the functions and meanings of particular markers in the flow of talk. For instance, researchers build on previously defined discourse moves such as "revoicing" (O'Connor & Michaels, 1993) and the "reflective toss" (van Zee & Minstrell, 1997) in considering what teachers do to keep the focus on students' ideas in the classroom.

In particular, the detailed schemes laid out in Lineback's (2014) and Pierson's (2008) research point to how they conceptualize and identify responsive teaching. Pierson defined categories of discourse moves that represent low responsiveness, medium responsiveness, and two different kinds of high responsiveness. Low, Medium, and High I responsiveness differ in the extent to which teachers' responses connect to what students have said, but all three focus (at least to an extent) on correctness and on the teacher's thinking and objectives. High II responsiveness is distinct in maintaining a primary focus on *students'* ideas and sense-making. Lineback's scheme highlights a particular kind of moment in the flow of classroom activity—when the teacher redirects the students' activity or the focus of the conversation. Similar to Pierson's scheme, Lineback considers whether a given redirection is tied to students' ideas that came before (i.e., whether the new activity is "grounded in, and therefore responsive to . . . students' comments" (p. 23)). She also considers *how* the redirection is tied to students' previous ideas—the most responsive redirections are ones in which students are invited to consider one another's ideas in more depth. As seen in these two schemes, the discursive focus moves beyond whether a teacher is attending and responding to student thinking or not (e.g., Sherin and van Es's (2009) confirming or disconfirming evidence) to consider the nature of that responsiveness—how teachers are attending and responding to students' ideas, with implications for how well teachers are doing so.

There are several shared assumptions underlying a discursive approach to responsive teaching. First, there is a sense that learning occurs through discourse, so a critical part of supporting student learning is supporting students' opportunities to voice and interact with their own ideas. As Lineback (2014) noted, "The more students talk about mathematics, the more they are likely to learn about the nature and discipline of mathematics" (p. 3); Brodie's (2011) notion of giving a learner "a chance to articulate and hence deepen her thinking" (p. 181) communicates a similar sense that thinking may become richer through expression. Second, the cited papers share an assumption that what students are saying and doing is linked to their teachers' prior moves. Pierson (2008) highlighted this relationship as follows:

> By encouraging students to verbalize their thinking and provide explanations of their ideas, discursive moves with high levels of responsiveness . . . can support coherence and clarity in thinking, help the speaker plan and regulate a course of action, encourage the organization and integration of new ideas into prior experience, and expose errors in reasoning.
>
> (p. 34)

In other words, moves high in responsiveness on the part of the teacher can support students in articulating and explaining their own thinking, putting it on display for themselves and others to clarify and assess.

There are also researchers who make use of the discourse markers described above to demarcate boundaries of cases of responsive teaching, but whose work does not necessarily align with the assumptions articulated above. For instance, in her dissertation work, Lau (2010) defined discursive evidence of attending and not attending to student thinking. She used these categories of evidence to delineate instances of each in teachers' classroom practice, with the aim of studying the identified instances in more depth. Similarly, Richards's (2013) dissertation drew on evidence from the cited discourse studies to define cases in which teachers were relatively stably focused on students' ideas, analyzing what supported this focus in each case. Such case study research foregrounds the nature and dynamics of responsive teaching—what it entails, how it feels, what supports or constrains it, etc.—and is the subject of the next section.

Case Studies of Responsive Teaching

The responsive teaching case study literature can roughly be divided into two subsets: (1) first-hand practitioner accounts of responsive teaching and (2) researchers' analyses of examples of responsive teaching. We begin by reviewing numerous first-hand accounts (Ball, 1993; Chazan & Ball, 1999; Chazan & Schnepp, 2002; Hammer, 1997; Hutchison & Hammer, 2010; Lampert, 1990; Rosebery & Warren, 1998) that provide a detailed look inside responsive teaching from the perspective

42 Jennifer Richards and Amy D. Robertson

of the teacher. These accounts foreground important characteristics of the *nature* of responsive teaching, highlighting that it is (a) active and intentional, (b) highly contextualized, and (c) tension filled.

First, practitioner accounts of responsive teaching depict teachers playing active roles in shaping the conversations that take place (Ball, 1993; Chazan & Ball, 1999; Hammer, 1997; Hutchison & Hammer, 2010; Lampert, 1990). Responsive teaching is filled with continual decision points in which teachers must decide how to connect what they are hearing from students and their own instructional goals. For instance, Hutchison (Hutchison & Hammer, 2010) describes a moment in his physics class in which students were considering what makes some objects float. The class had posed both weight and density as options, and one student, Katie, indicated that there might be a linear relationship between weight and density. Hutchison decided to introduce a mathematical definition of density as weight/volume and describes why this choice seemed productive to him in the moment:

> The moment seemed instructionally ripe, both conceptually and episte-mologically . . . In the discussion among students that immediately pre-ceded this, many students were using the words "weight" and "heavy" when talking about the relevant features of objects with respect to floating and sinking. Just before I wrote down the equation, Katie argued that when "weight" is added to a floating cup its "density" must somehow increase. I meant to build from the students' reasoning, and so I chose to use the word they had been using. I also think of "weight" as a more everyday, common-sense word than "mass," and I thought using weight would help maintain the commonsense feel of the class discussion up to that point.
>
> (Hutchison & Hammer, p. 516)

As evidenced, Hutchison made an active move that was responsive to what students had been discussing, the ways in which they were discussing their ideas, and how he hoped to support their continued scientific work. Lampert's (1990) discussion of her role in a fifth-grade mathematics class depicts a similar level of active participation: "I assumed the role of manager of the discussion and some-times participated in the argument, refuting a student's assertion" (p. 50), indicat-ing that she not only facilitated, but also added her own voice to the conversation at key moments.

The example from Hutchison and Hammer (2010) also illustrates our second point—responsive teaching is highly contextualized (Chazan & Ball, 1999; Cha-zan & Schnepp, 2002; Hammer, 1997). Hutchison's decision to define density as weight/volume was made in a particular moment with particular features that Hutchison took into consideration. As he noted, his "choice of 'weight' rather than 'mass' was not premeditated; that is, [he] did not walk into the class that day thinking [he] would define density in this way" (Hutchison & Hammer, 2010, p. 516). Rather, he considered the immediate context and made a choice about how to move forward. Chazan and Ball (1999) describe similar dynamics at play in their mathematics classrooms, ultimately arguing for a pragmatic approach to responsive teaching "in which teacher moves are selected and invented in response to the situation at hand, to the particulars of the child, group or class and to the needs of the mathematics" (p. 7).

Third, practitioner accounts often make explicit some of the tensions associated with responsive teaching (Ball, 1993; Chazan & Schnepp, 2002; Rosebery & Warren, 1998). Ball (1993) describes several dilemmas that arose as she attempted to teach third-grade mathematics in a way that "respects the integrity both of mathematics as a discipline *and* of children as mathematical thinkers" (p. 376), such as what to do when a student's novel mathematical definition diverged from canonical views of even and odd numbers. Others raise similar concerns about how to manage these—at least at times—competing goals. For example, Schnepp (Chazan & Schnepp, 2002) describes two ways of taking up students' ideas in his advanced placement calculus course and the tensions he feels with respect to each:

> When I am mainly listening and assessing, the process is extremely time consuming and students may not be learning the mathematical facts and methods that I am supposed to cover. But, students *are* being challenged to be intellectually independent and to think about why they believe something should be considered true in mathematics . . . When I am more active in discussions of student exploration, my contributions can bring their ideas closer to standard ideas in the curriculum. But, if I become too active, students will quickly apply pressure for me to just tell them how to do it.
>
> (p. 179)

These first-person examples highlight some of the considerations and difficulties that come into play as teachers attend and respond to the substance of student thinking.

Researchers have also used case studies to unpack what influences responsive teaching (Lau, 2010; Levin, 2008; Levin, Hammer, & Coffey, 2009; Maskiewicz & Winters, 2010, 2012; Richards, 2013; Russ & Luna, 2013; Wallach & Even, 2005). These findings in many ways parallel the findings above and connect responsive teaching to other constructs in the literature. For instance, in Schnepp's (Chazan & Schnepp, 2002) quote above, he highlights what he is "supposed to cover" as an important consideration in his teaching. Levin's (2008) dissertation work on responsive teaching in science classrooms also highlights the salience of curricular coverage for teachers, along with other institutional priorities that serve to constrain responsiveness (e.g., work environments that draw attention to other issues, like classroom management). Several case studies tie responsive teaching to the construct of *framing* (Lau, 2010; Levin, 2008; Levin et al., 2009; Maskiewicz & Winters, 2010; Russ & Luna, 2013), indicating that whether and how teachers attend and respond to student thinking is interrelated with what they think is

44 Jennifer Richards and Amy D. Robertson

"going on" in the classroom at any given time. Other cases tie responsive teaching to teachers' *content knowledge* in various ways (Richards, 2013; Wallach & Even, 2005). Wallach and Even noted that a teacher, Ruth, heard her students' solutions through her own understanding of a posed math problem. Richards noted a similar relationship between one teacher's (Mr. S's) changing understanding of what constitutes a satisfactory scientific explanation and the nature of his presses on students' ideas in class discussions. Another teacher (Ms. L) was more likely to pursue students' ideas in a responsive manner when she did *not* know the answer to the question they were grappling with and could thus inquire alongside them.

In summary, the diverse body of case studies provides in-depth analyses of the nature and dynamics of responsive teaching. We see the insights from first-hand accounts of responsive teaching as a particularly important contribution from this subset of literature, adding to our understanding of responsive teaching from within.

Posited Affordances of Responsive Teaching

The subsets of literature described above, as well as other pieces related to responsive teaching, posit affordances associated with attention and responsiveness to the substance of student thinking. In this section, we address several in turn.

Responsive Teaching Treats Student Thinking as Resourceful and Is Consistent with Constructivist Learning Theory

In responsive teaching, teachers start from the assumption that the ideas students bring to the table are *sensible* and *productive*, and they seek to engage with and refine these ideas (Ball, 1993; Carpenter et al., 1996; Duckworth, 2006; Hammer, Goldberg, & Fargason, 2012; Hammer & van Zee, 2006; Rosebery & Warren, 1998). For instance, Hammer, Goldberg, and Fargason write:

> . . . this approach presumes—in fact it builds from—a view that children are richly endowed with resources for understanding and learning about the physical world: Engage children in a generative activity, and there will be productive beginnings to discover and support.
>
> (p. 55)

By valuing and seeking to build from students' existing knowledge, researchers have argued that responsive teaching is theoretically consistent with constructivism (Levin, Hammer, Elby, & Coffey, 2013; Pierson, 2008).

Responsive Teaching May Promote More Equitable Participation

Teaching that treats students as capable sense-makers, with productive resources and experiences to bring to bear in the classroom, can promote equitable participation (e.g., Empson, 2003; Gallas, 1995; Hudicourt-Barnes, 2003; Michaels, 2005; Rosebery, Ogonowski, DiSchino, & Warren, 2010; Warren, Ballenger, Ogonowski, Rosebery, & Hudicourt-Barnes, 2001; Warren, Ogonowski, & Pothier, 2005). The authors cited here specifically describe or call for teaching that attends to and builds on the resources that students from culturally, linguistically, and socioeconomically diverse communities bring to the classroom, and they demonstrate how these resources are continuous with disciplinary ideas and practices. For instance, Michaels (2005) reflects on working-class children's narrative practices, which rely heavily on justifications derived from everyday experiences. She describes how these practices may be seen as "intellectual affordance[s] for working-class children in learning science—their trust in their own experience as evidence and their willingness to rely on it in making sense out of abstract or counterintuitive scientific concepts" (p. 140). Teachers' recognition and support of such diverse entry points may provide an "in" for students who are often marginalized in traditional classroom discourse.

Responsive Teaching Is a Means of Formative Assessment

Literature on formative assessment (e.g., Black & Wiliam, 1998; Erickson, 2007) describes teachers' use of the information that they glean from formal and informal classroom assessments to inform their instructional decisions. Responsive teaching is a means of such formative assessment (as argued by Empson & Jacobs, 2008; Levin et al., 2013; Pierson, 2008), as it attends to student thinking and adapts instruction in both the short and long term to support and build on students' developing understandings. However, responsive teaching is distinct from other forms of formative assessment in its particular attention to the *substance* of student thinking (Coffey, Hammer, Levin, & Grant, 2011)—the meaning that students are making within their disciplinary experiences—and in its stance toward that thinking as productive and resourceful. Teachers primarily listen to students in order to *build* on their thinking, rather than to correct it.

Responsive Teaching Fosters Enhanced Student Conceptual Understanding

Likely related to its alignment with constructivism and processes of formative assessment (an empirically established means of improving student understanding—see Black & Wiliam, 1998), responsive teaching promotes enhanced student conceptual understanding (Carpenter et al., 1989; Empson & Jacobs, 2008; Fennema et al., 1993; Fennema et al., 1996; Goldberg, 2012; Hiebert & Wearne, 1993; Kersting, Givvin, Sotelo, & Stigler, 2010; Pierson, 2008; Saxe, Gearhart, & Seltzer, 1999). For example, Fennema et al. (1996) found that gains in students' mathematics achievement co-occurred with shifts in teachers' responsiveness to their students' mathematical thinking. Studies have also found higher gains in student performance in responsive classrooms than in more traditional classrooms (e.g., Empson & Jacobs, 2008; Goldberg, 2012; Pierson, 2008).

46 Jennifer Richards and Amy D. Robertson

Responsive Teaching Provides Rich Opportunities For Students to Engage In Disciplinary Thinking and Practices

In addition to conceptual understanding, researchers have demonstrated that responsive teaching opens space for students to engage in important kinds of disciplinary thinking and practices (Ball, 1993; Coffey et al., 2011; Hammer et al., 2012; Hutchison & Hammer, 2010; Richards, 2013; Schifter, 2011). Students in responsive classrooms engage in explanation-building, argumentation, and authentic assessment of one another's ideas, all central aspects of what it means to do science or mathematics. Further, as *teachers* attend to student activity in such contexts, they may capitalize on the "beginnings" of disciplinary ideas and practices in student talk and action. For instance, when Sean proposes that six is both even and odd in Ball's third-grade mathematics classroom, Ball sees an opportunity (in both Sean's proposition and the debate that ensues) for her students to explore the role of mathematical definitions and their "nature and purpose in mathematical activity and discourse" (p. 387). Throughout the "Sean numbers" episode, Ball invites students to evaluate one another's thinking and to try on their peers' definitions of even and odd numbers. By distributing authority for the construction and assessment of ideas and by elevating nascent scientific and mathematical practices that emerge in the flow of classroom activity, responsive teaching brings students closer to the heart of what it means to *do* science or mathematics.

Responsive Teaching Promotes Teacher Learning and Development

Finally, teachers' knowledge, values, and practices shift as they engage with the substance of students' disciplinary ideas (Carpenter et al., 1989; Empson & Jacobs, 2008; Fennema et al., 1996; Franke et al., 1998; Franke & Kazemi, 2001; Gallas, 1995; Philipp, Thanheiser, & Clement, 2002; Rosebery & Warren, 1998; Sherin & van Es, 2009). For instance, Fennema et al. describe a feedback loop among teachers in the CGI project between their practice and their attention to student thinking:

> As the teachers saw that their students were capable of inventing strategies and doing more than they had anticipated, they increasingly made problem solving a greater part of their instruction; the children increasingly solved harder problems and reported their thinking; the teachers listened and understood children's thinking better; and so it continued.
>
> (p. 431)

In listening to their students, teachers learned that students are capable of sophisticated mathematics, gained knowledge about student thinking, and shifted their classroom practice to provide more opportunities for independent problem-solving. Making sense of students' ideas can also help teachers enhance their own content understandings (Philipp et al., 2002; Rosebery & Warren, 1998).

Future Directions for Work on Responsive Teaching

Based on the content of reform-oriented science and mathematics education standards (e.g., NGA Center and CCSSO, 2010; NGSS Lead States, 2013) and on the burgeoning discussion about ambitious teaching and high-leverage practices (e.g., Lampert et al., 2013; Thompson, Windschitl, & Braaten, 2013; Windschitl, Thompson, Braaten, & Stroupe, 2012), we anticipate that responsive teaching will continue to be a focus of research and teacher development efforts. In this final section, we look across the subsets of literature to draw out distinctions and to open questions that may shape this future work. Some of the questions we raise are more clearly research questions, whereas others are more about matters of design and implementation of learning environments for teachers. However, these sorts of questions tend to overlap and shed light on each other in practice, and as such, we do not make clear delineations between them here. We simply point to them as issues worth further consideration and pursuit. Throughout we orient the reader to the chapters in the remainder of this edited collection and ways that they can further the discussion on several of these issues.

Are There Particular Moves that Characterize Responsive Teaching?

The literature we have reviewed differs with respect to whether specific teacher moves are characteristic of responsive teaching or whether responsive teaching by its very nature is more amorphous. Generally, the mathematics teacher–noticing literature, the discursive studies, and some case studies articulate teacher moves or stances that are indicative of responsive teaching, and use these to identify and in some cases rank examples of responsive teaching. The noticing literature and the case studies draw on such moves and stances as probable evidence that a teacher is attending and responding to student thinking, whereas the discursive studies largely *define* responsive teaching by specific actions the teacher takes. Lineback (Chapter 10, this volume) extends this conversation by explicitly considering the affordances and limitations of three such methods that may be used to assess teachers' responsiveness *in situ* in the classroom.

Other case studies of responsive teaching have called this approach into question. As highlighted previously, Chazan and Ball (1999) explicitly challenge the practice of defining specific sets of teacher moves, arguing instead that teachers necessarily select and invent moves in response to the situation at hand when they are being responsive. For instance, Hutchison's (Hutchison & Hammer, 2010) insertion of a mathematical expression for density would be considered a less responsive move according to the discourse frameworks, but his reflection indicates how it was responsive to his interpretation of students' ideas and framings at the time. Maskiewicz (Chapter 5, this volume) provides an insider's perspective on the highly contextual decision points she navigated as she taught responsively in a professional development setting.

These variations pose a challenge for researchers, particularly with respect to describing progress in responsive teaching. Some researchers have highlighted shifts in the frequency or presence of certain moves or markers as progress (e.g., Lineback, 2014; Pierson, 2008; Sherin & van Es, 2009), but this approach is complicated by the role of context noted previously, as well as the variability in teachers' responsiveness highlighted by several authors (e.g., Lau, 2010; Maskiewicz & Winters, 2012). Robertson et al. (Chapter 11, this volume) explicitly model responsive teaching as a multifaceted, nested phenomenon, touching on the implications of variability in teacher responsiveness for notions of progress. Furthermore, Maskiewicz and Winters's (2012) case study of one teacher's classroom practice describes the variability in her responsiveness as a function of differing contributions from students, highlighting an additional consideration that was the source of much discussion during our conference—should we primarily consider the *teacher* in determining responsiveness, or should we focus on the *students*?

How Do Students Participate in and Perceive Responsiveness?

The literature on teacher responsiveness has mostly focused on the teacher's role in attending and responding to students' ideas. However, on close inspection of the classroom dialogue reported in accounts of responsive teaching (e.g., Ball, 1993; Hammer, 1997; Lampert, 1990; Lineback, 2014), we notice that students are also attending and responding to one another's ideas. It is this kind of authentic engagement between students that breaks the mold of the traditional IRE discourse pattern (Mehan, 1979) and motivates us to ask, "How do students participate in and perceive responsiveness?"

Thus far, the thread of peer responsiveness has been the focus of few studies (see, for instance, Alvarado, Daane, Scherr, & Zavala, 2014, which examines peer responsiveness among in-service K–12 teachers in a teaching seminar). Future work could examine the nature and impact of peer responsiveness, as well as how teachers and students co-construct a responsive classroom culture. A related line of inquiry could be further exploration of how students experience responsive teaching and peer responsiveness; Chazan and Ball (1999) call for "ways of probing the sense that different students make of varied teacher moves" (p. 9), and several recent efforts explore students' perspectives on responsive classroom environments (Jaber, 2014; Robertson et al., 2014). Sikorski (Chapter 4, this volume) further explores this issue.

What Are "Ways in" to Responsive Teaching?

The literature on responsive teaching has also considered a variety of ways in which teachers may be introduced to and supported in pursuing practices of responsive teaching. We conceptualize these as "ways in" to responsive teaching and explore different approaches here.

One way of thinking about "ways in" to the practices of responsive teaching is to look for the "seeds" of responsive teaching that recur within and across subsets of literature. For instance, if we look at how different literatures define and describe expertise in responsive teaching, there are productive beginnings that could be noticed and supported. Expertise in CGI might begin with a teacher noticing patterns in the ways that children solve problems, or noticing varying degrees of sophistication within one strategy for solving addition problems. One "seed" of expert mathematics-teacher noticing might be marshaling evidence to support generalizations about teaching and learning, and one "seed" of expert responsiveness, as defined by the discourse literature, may be acknowledging that teacher moves matter for student talk and learning. Expert responsiveness in the sense described by case studies may begin with teachers recognizing that "one size does not fit all"—that responsive teaching must necessarily be tailored to specific aims, individuals, and settings.

If we look for personal resources that are brought to bear in responsive teaching, we notice that the literature repeatedly points to the knowledge, dispositions, and motivations entailed. Case studies of responsiveness (e.g., Ball, 1993; Hammer, 1997; Lampert, 1990; Paley, 1986; Richards, 2013; Rodgers, 2002; Rosebery & Warren, 1998) show teachers expressing care for and curiosity about their students, in both disciplinary and more holistic ways, and providing authentic disciplinary experiences for their students because of the joy they themselves feel when they engage in math or science. These implicit themes may represent natural "ways in" that could be capitalized on and connected to the practices of responsive teaching. Future work could explore additional reasons that teachers engage with student thinking (for a contribution to this line of work, see Colestock & Sherin, Chapter 6, this volume) and how "seeds" of responsive teaching can be connected to practices of responsive teaching in the ways that responsive teaching connects the seeds of science or math to disciplinary ideas and practices.

A second way of thinking about "ways in" is to consider the approaches researchers and teacher educators use to induct teachers into the practices of responsive teaching. Similar to the discussion of "seeds" above, we find that approaches vary according to what researchers and teacher educators think responsive teaching *is* and what they think it requires: a set of skills requiring specialized training, a set of classroom moves, and/or the embodiment of particular orientations toward student thinking. For instance, to support teachers in framing students' ideas as sensible and productive, some researchers regularly use videotaped classroom interactions and invite teachers to focus on the meaning students are making and the disciplinary connections embedded in their contributions, assuming that teachers have productive resources for doing so (Hammer & van Zee, 2006; Levin et al., 2013). Other researchers make use of videotaped classroom interactions to promote productive orientations toward student thinking *and* to develop teachers' specialized skills in noticing students' ideas, assuming that these are not a natural

50 Jennifer Richards and Amy D. Robertson

outgrowth of being observant or of teaching experience (e.g., Jacobs et al., 2010; Sherin, Jacobs, & Philipp, 2011)

Researchers have also developed tools for teachers to use during instruction or as they plan for instruction—again, matching their conceptualizations of responsive teaching. These range from the series of research-based frameworks on problems and solution strategies in CGI, to particular talk moves and strategies teachers can use to elicit and take up student thinking in the classroom (Fraivillig, Murphy, & Fuson, 1999; Michaels & O'Connor, 2012; Minstrell, Anderson, & Li, 2011; Stein, Engle, Smith, & Hughes, 2008; Thompson et al., 2013; Windschitl et al., 2012), to launching questions designed to spark scientific discussion and to generate mechanistic thinking (Hammer et al., 2012; Thompson et al., 2013; Windschitl et al., 2012). Generally, much work remains to be done in understanding how teachers take up, apply, and/or adapt the various "ways in" to responsive teaching described in this section.

What Constructs and Contextual Considerations Can Enhance the Study of Responsive Teaching?

Finally, researchers have brought a variety of constructs to bear on their understandings of responsive teaching. As described above, the literature repeatedly points to specific types of knowledge and dispositions brought to bear in responsive teaching—conceptual and epistemological knowledge, care for students as disciplinary learners and people, joy in mathematical and scientific inquiry, etc. Additional contributions in this volume include Coffey's and Edwards's (Chapter 7) analysis of how prospective elementary school teachers' orientations toward the disciplines of math and science influenced their responsiveness, and Jaber's (Chapter 8) focus on an additional disciplinary dimension of student talk and action to which teachers may attend—students' epistemic affect.

Another central construct in the responsive teaching literature is framing. Described as the teacher's sense of "what is going on here," framing has been used to explain variation in teacher attention and responsiveness within and across teachers (Lau, 2010; Levin et al., 2009; Maskiewicz & Winters, 2010; Russ & Luna, 2013). Radoff and Hammer (Chapter 9, this volume) add to this body of work by considering how a teacher's attention to her *students'* framing affected her responsiveness. The construct of framing also draws attention to contextual considerations in teaching, including the larger structures and systems within which teachers work. Research has demonstrated that such systems may have priorities and visions of teaching that draw attention away from student thinking (Levin, 2008; Thompson et al., 2013). In their chapter, Atkins and Frank (Chapter 3, this volume) consider how the variable but sophisticated products that emerge as a result of responsive inquiry in their classrooms differ from the canon, and the challenges that these distinctions pose for responsive teaching at scale. We anticipate that further research will continue to flesh out the relationships between these constructs/contextual considerations and responsive teaching, as well as identify other relevant constructs and contextual considerations that can be brought to bear on our understanding of teacher responsiveness.

Acknowledgments

Many thanks to Leslie J. Atkins, David Hammer, Rachel E. Scherr, Tiffany-Rose Sikorski, and Mark Windschitl for constructive, critical feedback on this chapter, and to Chandra Turpen for ideas at the outline stage.

Notes

1 These frameworks are detailed and domain specific. For instance, addition and subtraction are broken down into four basic classes based on the action or relation that students need to complete or consider. Each class can be further decomposed on the basis of which quantity is unknown, and the quantities themselves can be changed in the moment to enhance or diminish the difficulty of the problem.

2 For the purposes of this literature review, we chose to focus on the noticing literature that draws particular attention to students' mathematical thinking. Other literature that characterizes the myriad foci of teachers' attention is not included.

3 Jacobs et al. (2011) offer empirical support for the relationship between noticing and responding. In their study, K–12 teachers watched video of a kindergartener solving a mathematics problem and then wrote down (a) how they might respond to the student and (b) what the student actually did as he solved the problem. The authors found that almost all of the teachers whose hypothetical response [(a)] was tied to the student's mathematical understanding also provided evidence of attending to his problem-solving strategy [(b)]. However, the reverse did not hold: only a subset of the teachers who attended to his problem-solving strategy [(b)] decided how to respond on the basis of it [(a)]. Responding to the student's thinking was coupled with noticing, but the reverse was not necessarily true.

References

Alvarado, C., Daane, A.R., Scherr, R.E., & Zavala, G. (2014). Responsiveness among peers leads to productive disciplinary engagement. In P.V. Englehardt, A.D. Churukian & D.L. Jones (Eds.), *2013 Physics Education Research Conference Proceedings* (pp. 57–60). Melville, NY: AIP Press.

Ball, D.L. (1993). With an eye on the mathematical horizon: Dilemmas of teaching elementary school mathematics. *The Elementary School Journal, 93*(4), 373–397.

Black, P., & Wiliam, D. (1998). Assessment and classroom learning. *Assessment in Education, 5*(1), 7–74.

Brodie, K. (2011). Working with learners' mathematical thinking: Towards a language of description for changing pedagogy. *Teaching and Teacher Education, 27,* 174–186.

Bruner, J.B. (2003). *The process of education.* Cambridge, MA: Harvard University Press.

Carpenter, T.P., Fennema, E., & Franke, M.L. (1996). Cognitively Guided Instruction: A knowledge base for reform in primary mathematics instruction. *The Elementary School Journal, 97*(1), 3–20.

52 Jennifer Richards and Amy D. Robertson

Carpenter, T.P., Fennema, E., Franke, M.L., Levi, L., & Empson, S.B. (2000). *Cognitively Guided Instruction: A research-based teacher professional development program for elementary school mathematics.* Madison, WI: NCISLA, Wisconsin Center for Education Research, University of Wisconsin.

Carpenter, T.P., Fennema, E., Peterson, P.L., Chiang, C.-P., & Loef, M. (1989). Using knowledge of children's mathematics thinking in classroom teaching: An experimental study. *American Educational Research Journal, 26*(4), 499–531.

Chazan, D., & Ball, D.L. (1999). Beyond being told not to tell. *For the Learning of Mathematics, 19*(2), 2–10.

Chazan, D., & Schnepp, M. (2002). Methods, goals, beliefs, commitments, and manner in teaching: Dialogue against a calculus backdrop. *Social Constructivist Teaching, 9,* 171–195.

Coffey, J.E., Hammer, D., Levin, D.M., & Grant, T. (2011). The missing disciplinary substance of formative assessment. *Journal of Research in Science Teaching, 48*(10), 1109–1136.

Colestock, A., & Linnenbringer, T. (2010). *Selective archiving as a tool for supporting mathematics teacher inquiry and exploring teachers' sensemaking of students' mathematical thinking.* Paper presented at the Annual Meeting of the American Educational Research Association, Denver, CO.

Dewey, J. (1997). *Experience and education* (1st Touchstone ed.). New York, NY: Touchstone.

Duckworth, E. (2006). *"The having of wonderful ideas" and other essays on teaching and learning* (3rd ed.). New York, NY: Teachers College Press.

Empson, S.B. (2003). Low-performing students and teaching fractions for understanding: An interactional analysis. *Journal for Research in Mathematics Education, 34*(4), 305–343.

Empson, S.B., & Jacobs, V.R. (2008). Learning to listen to children's mathematics. In D. Tirosh & T. Wood (Eds.), *Tools and processes in mathematics teacher education* (pp. 257–281). The Netherlands: Sense Publishers.

Erickson, F. (2007). Some thoughts on "proximal" formative assessment of student learning. *Yearbook of the National Society for the Study of Education, 106*(1), 186–216.

Fennema, E., Carpenter, T.P., Franke, M.L., Levi, L., Jacobs, V.R., & Empson, S.B. (1996). A longitudinal study of learning to use children's thinking in mathematics instruction. *Journal for Research in Mathematics Education, 27*(4), 403–434.

Fennema, E., Franke, M.L., Carpenter, T.P., & Carey, D.A. (1993). Using children's mathematical knowledge in instruction. *American Educational Research Journal, 30*(3), 555–583.

Fraivillig, J.L., Murphy, L.A., & Fuson, K.C. (1999). Advancing children's mathematical thinking in Everyday Mathematics classrooms. *Journal for Research in Mathematics Education, 30*(2), 148–170.

Franke, M.L., Carpenter, T., Fennema, E., Ansell, E., & Behrend, J. (1998). Understanding teachers' self-sustaining, generative change in the context of professional development. *Teaching and Teacher Education, 14*(1), 67–80.

Franke, M.L., Carpenter, T.P., Levi, L., & Fennema, E. (2001). Capturing teachers' generative change: A follow-up study of professional development in mathematics. *American Educational Research Journal, 38*(3), 653–689.

Franke, M.L., & Kazemi, E. (2001). Learning to teach mathematics: Focus on student thinking. *Theory Into Practice, 40*(2), 102–109.

Gallas, K. (1995). *Talking their way into science: Hearing children's questions and theories, responding with curricula.* New York, NY: Teachers College Press.

Goldberg, F. (2012). *Responsive teaching and the emergence of energy ideas in third grade classrooms.* Paper presented at the UW/SPU Speaker Series, Seattle, WA.

Goldsmith, L.T., & Seago, N. (2011). Using classroom artifacts to focus teachers' noticing: Affordances and opportunities. In M.G. Sherin, V.R. Jacobs & R.A. Philipp (Eds.),

Mathematics teacher noticing: Seeing through teachers' eyes (pp. 169–187). New York, NY: Routledge.

Hammer, D. (1997). Discovery learning and discovery teaching. *Cognition and Instruction, 15*(4), 485–529.

Hammer, D., Goldberg, F., & Fargason, S. (2012). Responsive teaching and the beginnings of energy in a third grade classroom. *Review of Science, Mathematics, and ICT Education, 6*(1), 51–72.

Hammer, D., & van Zee, E. (2006). *Seeing the science in children's thinking: Case studies of student inquiry in physical science.* Portsmouth, NH: Heinemann.

Hiebert, J., & Wearne, D. (1993). Instructional tasks, classroom discourse, and students' learning in second-grade arithmetic. *American Educational Research Journal, 30*(2), 393–425.

Hudicourt-Barnes, J. (2003). The use of argumentation in Haitian Creole science classrooms. *Harvard Educational Review, 73*(1), 73–93.

Hutchison, P., & Hammer, D. (2010). Attending to student epistemological framing in a science classroom. *Science Education, 94,* 506–524.

Jaber, L.Z. (2014). *Affective dynamics of student disciplinary engagement in science* (Doctoral dissertation). Tufts University, Boston, MA.

Jacobs, V.R., Franke, M.L., Carpenter, T.P., Levi, L., & Battey, D. (2007). Professional development focused on children's algebraic reasoning in elementary school. *Journal for Research in Mathematics Education, 38*(3), 258–288.

Jacobs, V.R., Lamb, L.L.C., & Philipp, R.A. (2010). Professional noticing of children's mathematical thinking. *Journal for Research in Mathematics Education, 41*(2), 169–202.

Jacobs, V.R., Lamb, L.L.C., Philipp, R.A., & Shappelle, B.P. (2011). Deciding how to respond on the basis of children's understandings. In M.G. Sherin, V.R. Jacobs & R.A. Philipp (Eds.), *Mathematics teacher noticing: Seeing through teachers' eyes* (pp. 97–116). New York, NY: Routledge.

Kersting, N.B., Givvin, K.B., Sotelo, F.L., & Stigler, J.W. (2010). Teachers' analyses of classroom video predict student learning of mathematics: Further explorations of a novel measure of teacher knowledge. *Journal of Teacher Education, 61*(1–2), 172–181.

Lampert, M. (1990). When the problem is not the question and the solution is not the answer: Mathematical knowing and teaching. *American Educational Research Journal, 27*(1), 29–63.

Lampert, M., Franke, M.L., Kazemi, E., Ghousseini, H., Turrou, A.C., Beasley, H., . . . Crowe, K. (2013). Keeping it complex: Using rehearsals to support novice teacher learning of ambitious teaching. *Journal of Teacher Education, 64*(3), 226–243.

Lau, M. (2010). *Understanding the dynamics of teacher attention: Examples of how high school physics and physical science teachers attend to student ideas* (Doctoral dissertation). University of Maryland at College Park, College Park, MD.

Levin, D.M. (2008). *What secondary science teachers pay attention to in the classroom: Situating teaching in institutional and social systems* (Doctoral dissertation). University of Maryland at College Park, College Park, MD.

Levin, D.M., Hammer, D., & Coffey, J.E. (2009). Novice teachers' attention to student thinking. *Journal of Teacher Education, 60*(2), 142–154.

Levin, D., Hammer, D., Elby, A., & Coffey, J. (2013). *Becoming a responsive science teacher: Focusing on student thinking in secondary science.* Arlington, VA: National Science Teachers Association Press.

Lineback, J.E. (2014). The redirection: An indicator of how teachers respond to student thinking. *Journal of the Learning Sciences,* 1–42.

Maskiewicz, A.C., & Winters, V. (2010). *Interpreting elementary science teacher responsiveness through epistemological framing.* Paper presented at the 9th International Conference of the Learning Sciences, Chicago, IL.

Maskiewicz, A.C., & Winters, V.A. (2012). Understanding the co-construction of inquiry practices: A case study of a responsive teaching environment. *Journal of Research in Science Teaching, 49*(4), 429–464.

Mehan, H. (1979). *Learning lessons: Social organization in the classroom.* Cambridge, MA: Harvard University Press.

Michaels, S. (2005). Can the intellectual affordances of working-class storytelling be leveraged in school? *Human Development, 48,* 136–145.

Michaels, S., & O'Connor, C. (2012). *Talk science primer.* Cambridge, MA: TERC.

Minstrell, J., Anderson, R., & Li, M. (2011). *Building on learner thinking: A framework for assessment in instruction.* Commissioned paper for the Committee on Highly Successful STEM Schools or Programs for K–12 STEM Education: A Workshop. Washington, DC: Board on Science Education.

NGA Center (National Governors Association Center for Best Practices) and CCSSO (Council of Chief State School Officers). (2010). *Common core state standards for mathematics.* Washington, DC: NGA Center and CCSSO.

NGSS Lead States. (2013). *Next generation science standards: For states, by states.* Washington, DC: National Academies Press.

O'Connor, M.C., & Michaels, S. (1993). Aligning academic task and participation status through revoicing: Analysis of a classroom discourse strategy. *Anthropology & Education Quarterly, 24*(4), 318–335.

Paley, V.G. (1986). On listening to what the children say. *Harvard Educational Review, 56*(2), 122–131.

Philipp, R.A., Thanheiser, E., & Clement, L. (2002). The role of a children's mathematical thinking experience in the preparation of prospective elementary school teachers. *International Journal of Educational Research, 37,* 195–210.

Pierson, J.L. (2008). *The relationship between patterns of classroom discourse and mathematics learning* (Doctoral dissertation). University of Texas at Austin, Austin, TX.

Richards, J. (2013). *Exploring what stabilizes teachers' attention and responsiveness to the substance of students' scientific thinking in the classroom* (Doctoral dissertation). University of Maryland at College Park, College Park, MD.

Robertson, A.D., Eppard, E.P., Goodhew, L.M., Maaske, E.L., Sabo, H.C., Stewart, F.C., . . . Wenzinger, S.T. (2014, Summer). Being a Seattle Pacific University Learning Assistant: A transformative experience of listening and being heard. In B.A. Lindsey (Ed.), *American Physical Society Forum on Education Newsletter:* American Physical Society.

Rodgers, C.R. (2002). Voices inside schools—Seeing student learning: Teacher change and the role of reflection. *Harvard Educational Review, 72*(2), 230–253.

Rosebery, A.S., Ogonowski, M., DiSchino, M., & Warren, B. (2010). "The coat traps all your body heat": Heterogeneity as fundamental to learning. *Journal of the Learning Sciences, 19*(3), 322–357.

Rosebery, A.S., & Warren, B. (1998). *Boats, balloons and classroom video: Science teaching as inquiry.* Portsmouth, NH: Heinemann.

Russ, R.S., & Luna, M.J. (2013). Inferring teacher epistemological framing from local patterns in teacher noticing. *Journal of Research in Science Teaching, 50*(3), 284–314.

Saxe, G.B., Gearhart, M., & Seltzer, M. (1999). Relations between classroom practices and student learning in the domain of fractions. *Cognition and Instruction, 17*(1), 1–24.

Schifter, D. (2011). Examining the behavior of operations: Noticing early algebraic ideas. In M.G. Sherin, V.R. Jacobs & R.A. Philipp (Eds.), *Mathematics teacher noticing: Seeing through teachers' eyes* (pp. 204–220). New York, NY: Routledge.

Sherin, B., & Star, J.R. (2011). Reflections on the study of teacher noticing. In M.G. Sherin, V.R. Jacobs & R.A. Philipp (Eds.), *Mathematics teacher noticing: Seeing through teachers' eyes* (pp. 66–78). New York, NY: Routledge.

Sherin, M.G., & Han, S.Y. (2004). Teacher learning in the context of a video club. *Teaching and Teacher Education, 20,* 163–183.

Sherin, M.G., Jacobs, V.R., & Philipp, R.A. (2011). *Mathematics teacher noticing: Seeing through teachers' eyes.* New York, NY: Routledge.

Sherin, M.G., Russ, R.S., & Colestock, A.A. (2011). Accessing mathematics teachers' in-the-moment noticing. In M.G. Sherin, V.R. Jacobs & R.A. Philipp (Eds.), *Mathematics teacher noticing: Seeing through teachers' eyes* (pp. 79–94). New York, NY: Routledge.

Sherin, M.G., & van Es, E.A. (2005). Using video to support teachers' ability to notice classroom interactions. *Journal of Technology and Teacher Education, 13*(3), 475–491.

Sherin, M.G., & van Es, E.A. (2009). Effects of video club participation on teachers' professional vision. *Journal of Teacher Education, 60*(1), 20–37.

Stein, M.K., Engle, R.A., Smith, M.S., & Hughes, E.K. (2008). Orchestrating productive mathematical discussions: Five practices for helping teachers move beyond show and tell. *Mathematical Thinking and Learning, 10,* 313–340.

Thompson, J., Windschitl, M., & Braaten, M. (2013). Developing a theory of ambitious early-career teaching practice. *American Educational Research Journal, 50*(3), 574–615.

van Es, E. (2011). A framework for learning to notice student thinking. In M.G. Sherin, V.R. Jacobs & R.A. Philipp (Eds.), *Mathematics teacher noticing: Seeing through teachers' eyes* (pp. 134–151). New York, NY: Routledge.

van Es, E.A., & Sherin, M.G. (2008). Mathematics teachers' "learning to notice" in the context of a video club. *Teaching and Teacher Education, 24,* 244–276.

van Es, E.A., & Sherin, M.G. (2010). The influence of video clubs on teachers' thinking and practice. *Journal of Mathematics Teacher Education, 13,* 155–176.

van Zee, E., & Minstrell, J. (1997). Using questioning to guide student thinking. *Journal of the Learning Sciences, 6*(2), 227–269.

Walkoe, J.D.K. (2013). *Investigating teacher noticing of student algebraic thinking* (Doctoral dissertation). Northwestern University, Evanston, IL.

Wallach, T., & Even, R. (2005). Hearing students: The complexity of understanding what they are saying, showing, and doing. *Journal of Mathematics Teacher Education, 8,* 393–417.

Warren, B., Ballenger, C., Ogonowski, M., Rosebery, A.S., & Hudicourt-Barnes, J. (2001). Rethinking diversity in learning science: The logic of everyday sense-making. *Journal of Research in Science Teaching, 38*(5), 529–552.

Warren, B., Ogonowski, M., & Pothier, S. (2005). "Everyday" and "scientific": Rethinking dichotomies in modes of thinking in science learning. In R. Nemirovsky, A.S. Rosebery, J. Solomon & B. Warren (Eds.), *Everyday matters in science and mathematics.* Mahwah, NJ: Lawrence Erlbaum Associates.

Windschitl, M., Thompson, J., Braaten, M., & Stroupe, D. (2012). Proposing a core set of instructional practices and tools for teachers of science. *Science Education, 96,* 878–903.

3

EXAMINING THE PRODUCTS OF RESPONSIVE INQUIRY

Leslie J. Atkins and Brian W. Frank

Many definitions of scientific inquiry emphasize *activities*—for example, the National Science Education Standards (NSES) defines inquiry as "ways in which scientists study the natural world and propose explanations;" the National Research Council (NRC) lists five actions students take when engaging in inquiry (e.g., "engages in scientifically oriented questions," "formulates explanations from evidence," etc.). These definitions lend themselves to curriculum and instruction that foreground activities, ensuring that students are looking at data, formulating explanations, constructing experiments, etc. In contrast, we view inquiry as a process of refining ideas, and *scientific* inquiry as the more specific practice of refining ideas about natural phenomena as to be increasingly coherent and mechanistic (Hammer & van Zee, 2006). Unlike definitions of inquiry that foreground activities, definitions that foreground *ideas* suggest that in order to successfully engage a class of students in scientific inquiry, an instructor or curriculum must attend and respond to the substance of students' ideas. Our interest, as instructors and researchers, lies in responsiveness in the service of inquiry, that is, responsiveness in service of developing students' own ideas.

The authors of this chapter are instructors in courses that fit such a description of "responsive scientific inquiry," including *Student-Generated Scientific Inquiry* (Salter & Atkins, 2013), a pre-service course on light and color for elementary teachers; *Advanced Inquiry*, an upper division physics course for pre-service (middle school) teachers (Atkins et al., 2014); and *Energy Two*, a professional development course for high school teachers in the Energy Project (Close, DeWater, Close, Scherr, & McKagan, 2010; Scherr et al., 2012a; Scherr et al., 2012b; Scherr et al., 2013). These courses largely forgo textbooks and worksheets and focus on developing students' own ideas. Consistent with descriptions from Hammer, Goldberg, and Fargason (2012), the courses begin by engaging students

The Products of Responsive Inquiry **57**

in phenomena and are shaped by ways in which instructors identify and build on their thinking.

Among the roles that we as instructors play in such courses is that of a "responsive guide," ensuring "that, by whatever routes the class explores, the students eventually make their way to key landmarks" (Hammer, Goldberg, & Farguson, 2012, p. 69). The literature on responsive teaching, particularly in science, has emphasized identifying and taking up the "productive beginnings" of science in students' ideas: what scientific substance can we find in students' ideas, and what possible "routes" do those ideas suggest? This chapter extends that work by describing the "routes" and the "landmarks:" what are the products that result from responsive teaching and how they are reached?

In our courses, we find that while there are regularities in both student ideas and classroom dynamics (e.g., Sherin, Azevedo, & diSessa, 2005), a consequence of responsive inquiry is the idiosyncratic nature of student inquiries that emerge (e.g., Maskiewicz & Winters, 2012). When we intend to "cover" similar sets of topics from one class to the next, we find that the final products of those inquiries can vary from year to year; students often reach target ideas in unanticipated ways; and the products themselves can be difficult to compare to one other and even to the canon. The investigations and the resulting products bear the thumbprints of the individual students: their ideas and backgrounds shape the inquiry and its outcome, and, we believe, this is key to sustaining student engagement over weeks of intense inquiry and is consistent with scientific practice. Idiosyncrasies in the products of students' inquiry present tensions for instructors and researchers when considering the broader role that fully responsive teaching might play in courses with precisely defined content objectives and standardized assessments, and in classrooms that must coordinate curricula across multiple classes and grades.

We present in this chapter several examples of these intellectual products of our responsive science teaching courses—what are arguably the "content objectives," "key landmarks," or "targets" that are generated. These products take the form of explicit, class-negotiated conceptual objects: a set of "laws," terminology and definitions, and representational conventions. These cases are selected to meet two goals: first, they illustrate how a stance of responsiveness promotes the development of rigorous scientific ideas; second, these products highlight three characteristics of the products of responsive teaching—characteristics that expose tensions instructors may face and raise questions for responsive teaching, particularly regarding efforts to standardize instruction and assessment. These characteristics are:

1. The products exhibit variation from class to class;
2. The products exhibit variation from the canon; and
3. The products are locally meaningful, but may be difficult to assess outside of the context of the classroom in which they were developed.

Variation From Class to Class: Models of Diffuse Reflection

The Class Context

The examples in this section are taken from two different semesters of the *Scientific Inquiry* course for pre-service elementary school teachers at CSU, Chico. The class is a group of 24 junior and senior undergraduate "Liberal Studies" majors, the majority of whom plan to enter a multiple subjects credential program after graduation. The class meets five hours a week with one or two faculty, depending on the semester. (The first author is one faculty member.) All classes are video-taped, field notes are kept, and student work is photographed.

Scientific Inquiry is a responsively taught course that engages students in crafting and investigating their own scientific questions, beginning with a phenomena or puzzle that the instructors introduce. The primary topics of the course are typically light, color, and the eye; these topics are chosen because they are interdisciplinary, not covered in other courses, and easily investigated with simple materials. Students spend much of their time working in small groups as "research teams"—defining their own questions, designing empirical investigations, developing models and representations of their ideas, and sharing their findings and developing theories with the class. Whole-class discussion, writing assignments, and peer review are used to help students articulate and refine their ideas and to work toward consensus in how they conceptualize and engage in representational practices (e.g., Salter & Atkins, 2013).

Students, usually starting with observations of pinhole cameras, work to craft explanations over a period of 4–5 weeks. In this process, students have generated rules for how light travels. In our experience, it is typical for these rules to be, for the most part, easily relatable to the canon. Students, for example, tend to develop models in which light moves out in all directions from a source, travels in straight lines, reflects off surfaces, and must enter the eye in order to be seen. There is, however, variation in the process by which students arrive at those conclusions, including the questions and investigations that frame their pursuits and, consequently, variation in how students articulate their ideas, especially in terms of the theoretical constructs students invent to make sense of their observations.

Class Activity

In this section, we illustrate this variation by describing two different instantiations of student ideas about "diffuse reflection": the critical idea of how light reflects off of everyday (non-mirror-like) objects. In doing so, we aim to highlight both the variation in student models and the ways in which these idiosyncrasies reflect differences in the nature of the pursuits students undertook along the way.

Briefly, the main idea developed in each of the episodes below is this: when a light ray strikes a surface, some of the light is absorbed and some reflected. Diffuse

The Products of Responsive Inquiry **59**

reflection occurs when the ray is reflected off in multiple directions, rather than reflecting off at one angle (as happens when a ray of light strikes a mirror, which is termed specular reflection). This reflection accounts for why multiple people can see an object: rays reflect off in all directions to reach all viewers.

The brief narratives below describe these pursuits. The discussions and investigations mentioned span several days, if not weeks, of class. A thread is provided, connecting ideas in a causal story to highlight the key questions, investigations, and models that led to the final products we would like to consider. In the moment-to-moment interactions in the class, however, the discussions and investigations seemed far less orderly and goal oriented than the descriptions would have one believe; the ideas were often engaged with and reconsidered over many weeks, and not all students' ideas and pursuits are described.

Episode 1: Every Reflection Is a Combination of Specular and Diffuse

The Spring 2010 semester began by considering a beam of light from a flashlight. The instructors imagined that, over the course of their investigations, students would recognize that light has to enter your eye to see it and that what appears to be a "light beam" is actually light reflecting off of small particles in the path of the beam. As described below, this initial prompt led to a range of ideas about light, including descriptions of diffuse reflection. Though the anticipated outcome was never explicitly addressed, students did arrive at a sophisticated and canonical understanding of reflection.

Shortly after introducing our prompt, one group of students became curious about the ability to see a beam of light from casino spotlights near their homes but not from the flashlights in our classroom. Models students used to explain this discrepancy represented the light from flashlights as "ricocheting" off the walls, interfering with the original rays of light so that there was no beam to be seen; whereas outside, they argued, a light beam can travel without being disturbed.

In discussing these ideas, one group became interested in describing the process by which the *beam* of light is created: does the flashlight funnel light rays, not unlike gathering sticks in a bundle so that they all align? Or does the flashlight block light rays, so that those headed in directions other than straight out of the tube are blocked from traveling? As the class took up this question (quickly determining the rays were blocked), one group of students observed a "fuzzy edge" to the light projected by the beam (see Figure 3.1). There were two competing ideas to explain this "fuzziness": light "bends" around the corner of the tube or light "bounces" along the tube as it travels.

Students quickly determined that the light is not only blocked by the tube (a scientist would describe it as being absorbed), but is "bouncing" (reflecting) down the tube to create the "fuzzy edge." Understanding these bouncing rays became

60 Leslie J. Atkins and Brian W. Frank

FIGURE 3.1 A central spot of light and "fuzzy edge."

a central concern to the class (for more detail, see Atkins & Salter, 2011). Implicit in the definition and representations was the idea that light reflects off the wall in one particular direction (see Figure 3.2). (Note that this model of light reflecting from the walls of the tube is not scientifically correct; the light should reflect diffusely—in all directions—as students will later determine.)

Groups defined and pursued questions related to the nature of these rays in small teams. Some measured the intensity of reflected light relative to the incoming light using simple luxmeters. Another group attempted to differentiate rays that bounced once from those that bounced twice. Others examined whether or not light reflecting from white paper is absorbed.

Ultimately the class constructed a model in which a light ray incident on paper is reflected in all directions (described by students as a "koosh" because of its similarity to a "koosh ball"), while a light ray incident on shiny objects (like a mirror) is *still* reflected in all directions, but in one direction more than all others. In addition, they found that much of the light that hits a mirror is absorbed. While perhaps surprising, a student notes that this makes sense because "metal slides heat up in the sun."

These ideas were discussed as a class, and our consensus diagrams and descriptions are shown in an image from one student's notebook (see Figure 3.3).

Not only has this student (and the class) developed sophisticated and generative models of reflection, but these models exist in a rich ecology of ideas related to

The Products of Responsive Inquiry 61

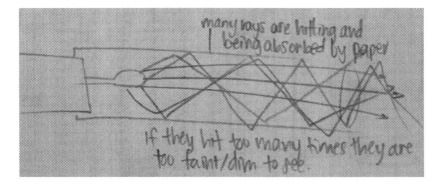

FIGURE 3.2 The bouncing rays of light.

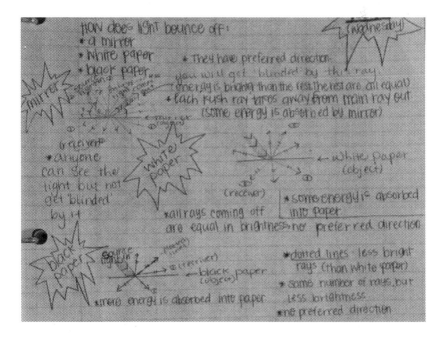

FIGURE 3.3 Class consensus ideas.

reflection. For example, some kinds of reflections are described "blinding," other kinds allow "anyone" to see the light; energy is absorbed into the objects when it is reflected (more so for black than for white); and she has developed conventions for illustrating her ideas—thicker lines for more intense light, and hash-marks to illustrate when rays are equal intensity. Moreover, these ideas were developed in scientific ways—through an iterative progression of questions, observations, models, and argumentation.

Episode 2: Every Surface Is Glowing

During the Spring 2011 semester, students also developed a model of diffuse reflection. However, the ideas unfolded in a markedly different trajectory.

Using the same Maglite flashlights to generate a spot of light, students did not attend to the beam, but noticed that the spot has a dark center and that the size of this central dark spot varies as you unscrew the cap (essentially moving the lightbulb in and out). Students worked to model this, developing rules for light reflecting from mirrored surfaces and curved mirrored surfaces. Figure 3.4 shows student models of the reflector, with the bulb "in" and close to the reflector (at left) and the bulb "out" (at right). In these models, the rays travel out from the bulb in all directions and reflect at angles equal to the angle of incident light. (In the diagrams, red rays are those that did not reflect.) The absence of light rays in the middle explains the dark spot.

We concluded our first unit on light without ever broaching the subject of diffuse reflection. When we began our second unit of inquiry, pinhole theaters (a simple box with a pinhole on one side and a screen on the other where an inverted image is visible), the students incorrectly extended their model of reflection off of mirrors to reflection off of surfaces more generally. They modeled light as reflecting off of *surfaces* at an angle equal to the angle of incident light (true for mirrors, but not other surfaces). However, this model raised a troubling question for the class: how is it that every point on the object seems to be sending a ray into the pinhole?

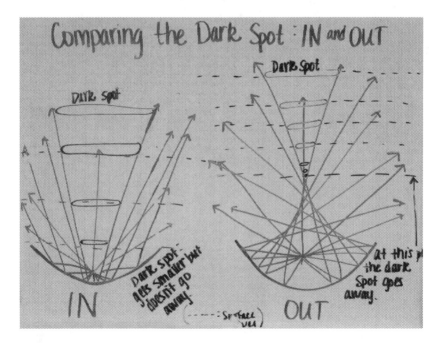

FIGURE 3.4 Modeling reflection from a parabolic mirror.

The Products of Responsive Inquiry   **63**

One model that resolved this involved imagining multiple "bounces" of light in a "lumpy" real world, where there would almost always be a path that light could take such that any given point would have a ray reflecting into the pinhole to project an image. For example, as shown in Figure 3.5, students show a ray of light from the sun reflecting off of a flower, then a rock, and then the tree before entering the pinhole. Each reflection is still following the earlier model (in which rays reflect off at equal angles):

This model was challenged, however, by concerns that such a model would still give us "patchy" images, and that with indoor lighting it would be too dim to be seen after one "bounce" of light.

As an alternative model, another group suggested ("what we want to think") that light "goes out in all directions when it hits a surface" (see Figure 3.6).

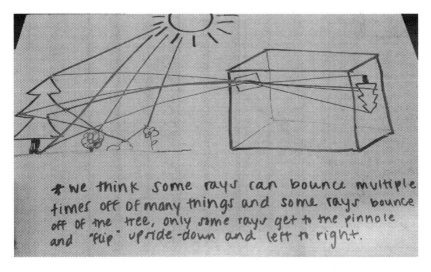

FIGURE 3.5 Initial model of reflected light.

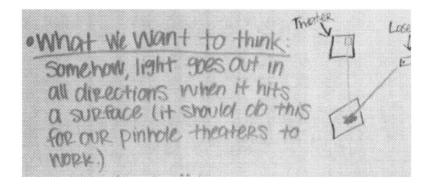

FIGURE 3.6 A model of diffusely reflected light.

Darcy noted that she was uncomfortable with this idea but could not articulate why. Alyssa commented that such a model suggests that there is little difference between a "glowing" object and a reflecting object—in both cases, light would be emanating in all directions from an object, whether it is a source of light or simply reflecting light.[1] Pointing to the chair, Alyssa noted that it does not seem to be glowing:

Alyssa: Like, say that's what we think [light going out in all directions]. Wouldn't we be seeing it as like, a shiny brown? Like it'd be—look like the desk was kind of lit up. Like in the cartoons where the—like—they get an idea and the light bulb's kind of like, fuzzy? So wouldn't the desk be all *fuzzy* brown? And the chair would be all *fuzzy* yellow? Not just yellow and brown? It wouldn't just—you know what I mean?
Leslie: Like, it would be almost a glowing neon yellow chair.
Alyssa: Exactly. And nothing's, like, *glowing* when you look at it.

Figure 3.7 shows another student, Janeal, responding by poking a Maglite bulb through a piece of paper (creating a point on the paper that is glowing white). She compares that glow to the glow created when a laser beam reflects off of the paper (the reflected red dot does look like the somewhat "fuzzy" glow of a bulb) and argues that both are examples of "glowing" (which she describes by vocalizing an angelic sounding "aaaah"), contrasting this with specular reflection (which she describes by vocalizing 'bullet' noises: "ptew! ptew!"):

Janeal: If you bring it (the laser pointer) close enough to the object (the paper) you have like the 'aaaah.' So I think there *is* a 'aaaaah,' and that's reaching all of our eyes.

FIGURE 3.7 A student models diffuse reflection as glowing light.

The Products of Responsive Inquiry **65**

Leslie followed up by asking if this means that objects like the chair that Alyssa mentioned is glowing, and Sarah ultimately distinguishes "reflection" (what scientists would call specular reflection) from "fragmentation" (that is, diffusely reflected light):

Sarah: But like I think what we think is happening is kind of like what Darcy is saying—like, we don't see the light rays coming from the light but it's obvious—but the room is obviously lit up. But I wouldn't say that the room is like, glowing like—we're not all glowing. But the light rays are still there and like they're still hitting off of every one of us. And they're still hitting off the desks. But it's fragmenting versus reflecting.

Sarah continues to describe that objects in the room don't appear to be glowing only because they are in a well-lit room, whereas in a dark room with a "legit spotlight," the chair would seem to glow. She takes issue with calling this "fragmentation" of light a "reflection"—and is unsure whether or not it is "glowing," but agrees that the rays leave both a light and a non-shiny object in the same way. The instructor (Leslie) compares Sarah's "spotlight" on a chair to the light off of the moon, which seems to glow in the night sky even though it is only reflecting light.

Ultimately the class describes light reflecting off of "non-shiny things," taking into account the range of ideas that led to this consensus:

When light hits a non-shiny thing . . . (1) some light is absorbed—the colors we *don't* see are absorbed, (2) some will bounce off of multiple things—but not too much (including the paper in the pinhole), (3) some will head into the pinhole, (4) light that *does* leave the object fragments and goes off in all directions—similar to a "candle," (5) when light fragments it's weaker.

Again, and consistent with descriptions of responsive teaching, these ideas are constructed in scientific ways: students model the reflection of light, apply that model in a new context, debate its implications, and refine their models accordingly. And, again, their conclusions are deeply scientific: like the first class, they note, correctly, that some light is absorbed—and go further in relating this to the color of the object. Like the first class, they also correctly recognize that light will reflect off in all directions, which they describe as a "fragmentation" of the original ray—and, again, they go further in describing how this is similar to light that leaves a source. They correctly address that light might reflect off of several objects before reaching a final destination, and they note that this reflected light is weaker.

Products of Responsive Inquiry

For the classes described above, students developed models of diffuse reflection that—in some fashion or another—appropriately modeled light reflecting from

66 Leslie J. Atkins and Brian W. Frank

an object. In each class, however, this model addressed the very particular concerns that were raised by the students that semester:

1. In the first semester, where students began discussing diffuse reflection by noticing a "fuzzy edge" to a beam of light, this model included the idea that—for all reflections—some light is absorbed and some light is reflected off in all directions. This helped us account for the dim, "fuzzy" nature of the bouncing rays.
2. In the second semester, students developed this model in the context of pinhole cameras. Because students were troubled by the similarity between sources of light, which send rays out in all directions, and objects, which also send reflected rays out in all directions, our model of reflected light explicitly addressed the fact that such reflections were modeled identically to the light emitted from a candle. This addressed students' questions about whether or not objects are "glowing."

The Role of Responsiveness

Identifying elements of responsive inquiry in these classroom episodes is relatively straightforward: students' ideas, observations and experiences are attended to and form the core of the curriculum. Students and instructors can be seen attending to and responding to the contributions of each other. Anticipated directions are not always achieved, but one can see clear progress towards coherent, mechanistic descriptions of scientific phenomena. The models they develop stem from the observations they make and the questions that these observations pose. In this way, the "productive beginnings" of science become sophisticated products of scientific inquiry through responsive instruction.

Variation From the Canon: Pac-Man Pellets

The Class Context

This next example comes from the *Advanced Inquiry* course for pre-service foundational science (middle school) teachers at CSU, Chico. The semester discussed here was a very small class of four; only one student had previously taken a traditional college-level physics class. The other three had taken one semester of *Physical Science and Everyday Thinking* (PSET) (Goldberg, Robinson, Otero, Kruse, & Thompson, 2008). We met for five hours a week in a lab classroom. The class was not videotaped, and the narrative below is reconstructed from field notes and snapshots taken during class.

Class Activity

The class began by asking students to graph and describe the motion of falling objects. Whereas some students in the class were familiar with the statement that

The Products of Responsive Inquiry **67**

acceleration due to gravity is 9.8 m/s^2, it was not trivial to interpret this correctly. Ultimately, students described the motion associated with constant acceleration by saying that an object changes its speed by a set amount (9.8 m/s) every second that it falls. Such a description is consistent with canonical physics ideas and was an imagined outcome of these early conversations in the class.

Once this description of constant acceleration was constructed we began looking at what happens every *meter* that an object falls. For the instructor, this topic was motivated by Galileo's interest in whether constant acceleration should describe a constant change in velocity for every unit of *time* or for every unit of *distance* and a hope that students would begin to consider how the taken-for-granted constructs in physics were once contested. Again, the students struggled initially, but, instead of simply finding that speed does not increase linearly with the distance traveled, students found that a falling object gains $19.6 \text{ m}^2/\text{s}^2$ of speed-squared for every meter that it falls. This description is consistent with physics (consistent with energy conservation and gravitational energy near the surface of the Earth), but not a common way of conceptualizing motion.

The class discussed what to make of this. In particular, we wondered how to make sense of a quantity like "speed-squared." A similar conversation regarding what "distance-per-second-squared" meant had led to insights about 9.8 m/s^2, and we sought a similar understanding of $19.6 \text{ m}^2/\text{s}^2$. (Unlike 9.8 m/s^2, the instructor did not have an imagined outcome in mind for this quantity.) During the conversation, one student turned away, sketching notes on his whiteboard and after some time re-entered the conversation, claiming that it is as if there were little "pellets-of-speed-squared" distributed through space—similar to the way the "Pac-Man" arcade game distributes pellets at regular interval through the maze. Every meter of elevation contained a chunk of "speed squared" that an object would acquire as it traversed that meter. Although this representation did not address how to make sense of the quantity "speed squared," it led students to make the following statements:

> Energy is distributed in space, not time. Like Pac-Man moving through the maze. Gravitational potential energy (GPE) must not be in the object—it's in the space between objects.

> Something about the physical space is more relevant than the time.

> If you were going to say that energy were in one place or the other—if it were in *space* or *time*—you'd say it was located in space.

Reiterating these ideas, my field notes indicate:

> I loved this idea and compared it to working for an hourly wage . . . as I moved through time I could picture myself, every minute, picking up another nickel. So money, when you work for an hourly wage, is evenly

distributed in time. So we're finding that something is evenly distributed in space for falling objects. And those Pac-Man pellets that we pick up each meter ... don't give Pac-Man a certain amount of speed—they give Pac-Man a certain amount of "speed-squared." "BUT WHY?" the class asks! "I DON'T KNOW!" the teacher answers!

This idea—"pellets" distributed in space that will give objects a set amount of speed-squared as they go by—was generative and used throughout the semester. As we described a Gaussian gun (ferromagnetic ball bearings near a magnet), students employed the "Pac-Man pellet" representation. As the ball traverses space it "consumes" the pellets, acquiring speed-squared. While pellets are evenly distributed near the Earth's surface (every meter gets a "pellet")—consistent with the observation that the gravitational force does not appreciably depend on height near the earth's surface—the pellets were closer together when close to a magnet (the force of a magnet is considerably stronger when closer to the magnet). The figure below (see Figure 3.8) shows a preliminary sketch of pellet-distribution near a magnet that students constructed to represent magnetic potential energy in both a "Pac-Man pellet" representation and a gravitational/height representation.

Products of Responsive Inquiry

The conceptual products of this inquiry include:

1. As an object falls near the surface of the Earth, it gains 19.6 m^2/s^2 of "speed squared" every meter.
2. This suggests that we can represent "speed squared" as located in space above the earth.

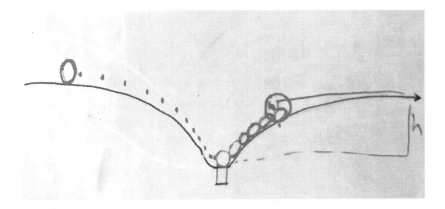

FIGURE 3.8 Pac-Man pellets and potential well model of a Gaussian Gun.

The Products of Responsive Inquiry **69**

This representation has clear parallels to canonical descriptions of potential energy: a Pac-Man pellet can be interpreted as a quantum of potential energy stored in the field between two interacting objects. It is linked to the canonical representation of 'potential wells' (as shown in the above diagram), in which the steepness of the well and the density of pellets are related. It is related to the idea of equipotential lines (a line representing a region in space in which an object is at the same "altitude" relative to an interacting body, and the distance between lines represent a uniform change in altitude). And the relationship between kinetic energy (which varies with speed-squared) and these pellets is consistent with the relationship between change in kinetic energy and gravitational potential energy near earth's surface: mgh $= \Delta(\frac{1}{2}mv^2)$.

The Role of Responsiveness

The ideas and the representation of those ideas were not anticipated in advance and, though consistent with established physics, represent a novel contribution. Furthermore, the *pursuit* of these ideas and representations was also not anticipated: the class—driven by the ideas of one student in particular, but taken up and extended by the instructor and class—was "involved in constructing and implementing a radically new, wider and more complex object and concept for their activity" (Engeström & Sannino, 2010). That is, not only the product of the inquiry but also the inquiry itself is unanticipated: what kind of problem we are pursuing and what kinds of outcomes will constitute progress towards solving that problem. The "problem" posed by the instructor—understanding how to interpret the fact that a constant amount of *speed squared* is gained for every meter an object falls—was ultimately dropped in favor of understanding how to interpret the fact that a constant amount of speed squared is gained *for every meter* an object falls. That is, the students' interests shifted our attention from one aspect of the quantity to another. In this way, the inquiry is responsive inquiry, in which the instructor and students respond to the scientific substance of students' own ideas in service of developing and refining those ideas.

From the instructor's point of view, these products—though unanticipated—represent desired outcomes for responsive inquiry: as a class we generated a problem to solve and crafted a generative solution to that problem that is consistent with the physics canon.

As an instructor with a long history of teaching about energy, the connections between this representation and the canon were readily apparent as they arose during instruction, even if they were unanticipated in advance. It was easy to imagine, in the moment, that the "Pac-Man pellet" representation would be generative. As an instructor, I (L.J.A.) was able to envision how describing and diagramming Pac-Man pellets would be fruitful. For example, one of the most interesting questions that emerged was this: as a ball rolls away from a magnet and "poops Pac-Man pellets," will it "poop" an infinite number of pellets or not? Put

70 Leslie J. Atkins and Brian W. Frank

another way, if the slope of the "well" is always positive, does this mean that the well is infinitely high? This question connects to questions of escape velocity, of calculus, and why you can set a "zero" of potential energy for objects sufficiently far apart. That is to say, whereas the products of our inquiry are not always easily aligned with the canon, the ideas may nonetheless be scientifically meaningful and generative.

In the next section, we examine additional idiosyncratic descriptions of energy—ones that are equally powerful, generative ideas—but which were harder to connect to the canon.

Locally Meaningful: The Laws of Energy

The Class Context

The Energy Project is a two-week summer institute for in-service science teachers. The class described here is from "Energy Two," a course for returning secondary science teachers in their second summer with the program. The summer class meets for six hours a day for two weeks, during which time a team of researchers collected video data of the class's activities.

Nine in-service teachers representing a range of scientific disciplines participated in the class, which was facilitated by two instructors (including the first author). During their time with the summer institute, the participants constructed representations of energy (Scherr et al., 2012b), debated forms of energy (McKagan, Scherr, Close, & Close, 2012), found regularities in those representations, and summarized those to construct a set of statements that relate energy and forces.

Below we provide a brief overview of the representations that participants used, the relationship between these representations and investigations, and the development of the "laws of energy" that they generated.

Class Activities

A more complete description of this course and its approach to energy instruction can be found in Close, et al., 2010, and Scherr, et al., 2012a, 2012b, and 2013. Briefly, they describe instruction as one in which "the focus . . . shifts from the learning of specific concepts within the broad theme of energy to the gradual regimentation of the interplay between learners' observation, thinking, graphic representation, and communication . . . The learning of specific energy content . . . becomes more learner-directed and unpredictable, though at no apparent cost to its extent" (p. 9). Much of the work happens in small groups, who then summarize their work and present it to the larger class, where consensus-building conversations refine their ideas. There are, then, both the short-time-scale conceptual products (e.g., a way of representing the energy dynamics of a particular

The Products of Responsive Inquiry **71**

phenomenon) and the longer-time-scale products consisting of consensus statements that seek to summarize understandings across a range of discussions, products, and ideas.

Representing Energy Dynamics with Energy Theater

In the instructional sequence that follows, the class is engaged in doing that latter work of building consensus statements regarding energy and forces. Key to interpreting this conversation is understanding a unique representational learning activity, "Energy Theater," that the in-service teachers used (Daane, Wells & Scherr, 2014; Scherr, Close, Close & Vokos, 2012b). The activity is a way of representing energy dynamics—including *type* of energy present, *where* that energy is located, and *how* the energy changes—in a scenario. The participants use their bodies in Energy Theater to represent a "unit of energy," using signs to indicate the form of their energy and walking between marked spaces on the floor to represent transfers of energy between objects. It typically takes many participants coordinating their actions to represent the energy dynamics of a given situation.

For our purposes, it is important to note that this conceptualization of energy is strikingly different from how energy is typically presented. Following a particular "unit" of energy through a scenario is not a common way of considering energy transfers and transformations. This alone makes it hard to interpret the class ideas and to see how they correspond to more common descriptions of energy.

Relating Forces and Energy Through Their Representations

One goal that the instructors had in mind for the summer course was addressing the work-energy theorem. The two instructors imagined that this would involve linking the teachers' energy representations with diagrams that represent forces on objects and considering the connection between the two (for example, in the diagram, Figure 3.9, F_{EB} connotes the force by the Earth on the block).

The instructors began pursuing this objective by having the class revisit an Energy Theater for a box being lifted at a constant speed, then creating a force diagram for the scenario, and seeking relationships between the forces and energies. A snapshot from the whiteboard is shown in Figure 3.9. The diagram is preliminary; readers will note that one force is drawn twice and that there are missing forces on the hand. The F_{EB} arrow on the hand is not accurate; it should read F_{EH}. The focus in the conversation that follows is on the F_{HB} and F_{BH} forces and their role in energy transfers.

After having engaged in this activity and a range of "Energy Theaters" to represent multiple phenomena, including some of students' own choosing, we asked them to create some "possibly true statements about energy."

72 Leslie J. Atkins and Brian W. Frank

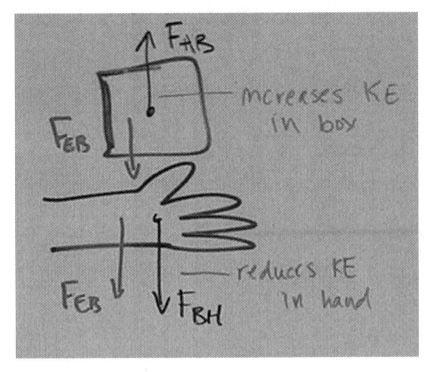

FIGURE 3.9 Force diagram of a box lifted at constant speed.

Episode 1

The class split into two groups. One became engaged in a conversation surrounding microscopic processes and made no progress on candidate statements, while another developed a set of what they called "possible true statements about energy, ignoring thermal." These statements were:

1. Energy transfers result in motion.
2. Motion is important to transfers and transformations.
3. If contact forces result in motion, there is a transfer of energy.
4. If non-contact forces like gravity and magnetic result in motion, there's a transformation of energy.
5. Gravity/magnetic can't transfer energy.

The ensuing conversation addressed each statement in turn, focusing on the following questions: (1) Is the statement clear enough to agree or disagree with? and (2) Does everyone agree with the statement?

Leslie: The first one I notice—it's not energy transfers *can* result in motion, they *do*. And when you say—I guess my question would be—when you say "results in motion"—results in *causing* motion? *Changing* motion?

The Products of Responsive Inquiry **73**

This question is significant: "work" (as physics defines it) happens when a force is involved in a displacement. Whereas the teachers do not explicitly refer to "work," their questions—is the motion or change in motion important? Is it causal?—indicate that they are carefully grappling with questions relating to how to characterize what, ultimately, physics characterizes as "work."

The teachers engage with the question of whether what is relevant is *motion, position, changes in motion,* or *changes in position.* As part of this effort, Doug brings the conversation back to the question of whether or not energy transfers result in changes in velocity, referencing the lifted box (see Figure 3.9) to suggest that, even for objects that seem to move at a constant speed, the sequence of energy transfers is such that the object first gains kinetic energy (speeds up), and then that energy is transformed into potential (so it slows back down). Ultimately, he will argue that the first sentence can be rewritten "energy transfers result in a change in velocity"—a statement that will be further refined to say "when forces transfer energy, they transfer kinetic energy."

Dan counters that this may be an artifact of our representation: we treat these steps sequentially in Energy Theater (energy enters the box and then transforms), but they may be simultaneous:

Dan: I don't see that necessarily being true. If you have that motion. So when we're thinking of our blocks or our Energy Theater units we're thinking about this happens [KE transfers in] then that happens [KE turns to PE]—it doesn't just keep on—I think that the two things can be happening simultaneously.

The conversation continues, and ultimately Doug agrees with Dan: the net kinetic energy that an object has (and so the motion of the object) will not necessarily change when energy is transferred to that object. Nancy notes that this is easier to represent in Energy Theater than in other representations. Following her comment, Leslie returns to their original statement to see if there is a better way of phrasing these ideas; Stamatis suggests language consistent with the teachers' conversation, "certain forces, when they transfer energy, they transfer kinetic energy." Nancy considers that idea:

Nancy: "When. When forces transfer energy it's kinetic energy" . . . So are we saying the only kind of energy that can be transferred is kinetic energy? Is that what that says?
Doug: Yes that's what I'm thinking.
Nancy: And you know what I sort of like about that is that when we're talking about thermal energy—and that's kind of what happens. You're transferring the kinetic energy from the particles going faster to the particles going slower.

Stamatis asks the group if this statement is consistent with the first group's intent. Everyone agrees and we take a break for lunch with the new statement on the board "When forces transfer energy, they transfer kinetic energy."

The next episode begins after returning from the lunch break.

74 Leslie J. Atkins and Brian W. Frank

Episode 2

In this episode, we begin with the second statement: "Motion is important to transfers and transformations." We identify two different interpretations of this statement—one, that "motion" might refer to the presence of kinetic energy, and two, that an object must be moving for transfers and transformations of energy to take place.

Rita: I think that what we meant by it was that it seems to always be involved no matter if it is what was being transferred or what it was being transformed from or transformed to—like, all of the different combinations that we have written down include kinetic energy. So we didn't go from like chemical to gravitational. We went through kinetic energy to get to gravitational. And I think that's what we meant. I think that's what we meant by "involved in" as well.

Leslie: So you're—would it be the same thing to say that every transfer and transformation—like you never flipped [changed your symbol in Energy Theater] or walked [changed your position in Energy Theater] without at one point being a KE?

Boris: You never flipped or—

Leslie: Or walk from one object to another. You never transformed or transferred without at least at one point being a KE.

Nancy: Being kinetic energy.

Leslie: [To Rita] So you—in your rephrasing you didn't use 'motion' you used 'kinetic energy.' It seems like *kinetic energy* is important to or involved in. I couldn't think of a transfer or a transformation that didn't involving KE.

Nancy: We were not able to.

Rita turns to Ron, recognizing that this idea is not the same as their conversations that developed the statement, where motion, not kinetic energy, was the important consideration:

Ron: . . . the object was moving for something to change. So not necessarily kinetic energy—just motion. Yeah.

Nancy: Well I'm actually wondering if maybe I'm not more comfortable with this substitution of kinetic energy for the word motion which is—was that—that's what I heard you say.

At this point, Leslie suggests that these are not two competing ideas, but two separate statements to be considered:

Leslie: I see two different ideas. One is that this idea that kinetic energy showed up for every transfer and transformation. And the second idea is: I never

The Products of Responsive Inquiry **75**

transformed or transferred with it moving—without there being some kind of displacement too.

Nancy briefly raises a question, confusing the lack of a change in kinetic energy with a lack of kinetic energy. Once resolved, Leslie returns to the two questions, referring back to an earlier conversation about pressing against a puck that isn't moving and one that is:

Leslie: . . . what I heard from Ron is that—you're saying there's something else about motion, too—there's something about the fact that—and I'm going back to the example of the puck when the puck is still and the forces are applied we didn't transfer energy. The puck is moving the forces are applied *did* [transfer energy]. So the motion matters not only because kinetic energy was transferred, but because it told me whether or not anything was transferred. These are two different questions.

Turning to the board, Leslie summarizes the two ideas by rewriting the second point ("Motion is important to transfers and transformations") to highlight the two ideas: one—voiced by Rita—replaces the word motion with "kinetic energy" and notes that it is important because it is always present; the second idea—Ron's original intent—is that motion is important because only when objects are in motion can energy transfers take place (the phrase "and/or transforms" is also added later). The consensus statement as written is "KE is present in all transfers and transformations. Motion helps us figure out if a force transfers energy." Below the teachers negotiate the addition of one more phrase, so that the final statement is "KE is present in all transfers and transformations. Motion helps us figure out if a force transfers and/or transforms energy."

Nancy: Do you want to put "transformed" in there too?
Ron: I want to put transformed in there, too.
Leslie: Where?
Ron: In the second one.
Leslie: So: "motion helps us figure out the force transfers and/or." Do you feel like this is getting at, Ron, your concern—what you didn't like about the first one that's different—
Ron: Well I just think the first one was totally different than what I was thinking. I mean I like the first one to think about. But the—the second one is what I was originally thinking.
Leslie: So let's tackle them in turn.

Boris, Nancy, Rita, and Ron quickly agree with the first statement. Tina and Doug think through two separate scenarios to examine whether or not they agree with the first statement—a cup moving at a constant rate and a puck on

76 Leslie J. Atkins and Brian W. Frank

a spring (moving between gravitational and spring potential energy, but with motion—and kinetic energy—required to make that transition):

Tina: No, in other words (referring to the scenario on the board in Figure 3.9)—I push up. The cup's pushing down, we have the forces are balanced, yet it has to have kinetic energy. . . .

Doug: . . . if I take the puck and I flip it on the side and now I set it on the spring. I have two forces, one is the force of gravity the other is the force of the spring. As I release the puck—gravity is now able to transition into the spring, but it can't—that force of gravity—or that energy of gravity can't pass into the spring unless it does what?

?: Moves.

Doug: Moves. Which means you need a kinetic energy to transition into the spring. . . . I think that totally speaks to what you're point was—Number 1. Which is why I like it.

Boris: I just don't understand the second one.

Leslie: Okay—let's agree or disagree with the first one—and so far, I think everyone is a thumbs up. [All show thumbs up.]

Leslie: So we have two laws for energy!

Voices: Yay! Woo hoo!

Products of Responsive Inquiry

After the conclusion of the episode described above, the conversation progresses by shifting attention to Boris's concern regarding the next statement: "Motion helps us figure out if a force transfers energy." Ultimately this phrase becomes the more precise statement: "A force on an object in the direction of motion increases kinetic energy. A force on an object opposite the direction of motion decreases kinetic energy." Through negotiations similar to those above, which continue for several more hours of instruction, with frequent references back to our representations and scenarios, the class ultimately endorsed the following "laws of energy."

Box 3.1. Five Laws of Energy Developed by Teachers in the Energy Project

1. When forces transfer energy, they transfer kinetic energy.
2. Kinetic energy is present in all transfers and transformations (potential energy always transforms into or from kinetic energy).
3. A force on an object in the direction of motion increases kinetic energy. A force on an object opposite the direction of motion decreases kinetic energy.

The Products of Responsive Inquiry **77**

4. Transfers of energy are due to contact forces. Transformations of energy are due to non-contact forces.
5. Forces transfer or transform energy proportional to their magnitude.

And these laws were subject to the following specified conditions:

i. Interactions in which there are no changes in thermal energy.
ii. We do not consider microscopic interactions.

These ideas are consistent with the work-energy theorem, which quantifies the relationship between forces and changes in kinetic energy. A lengthier discussion of the relationship between the ideas above and canonical descriptions of the work-energy theorem is provided in the "Challenges" section hereafter.

Responsiveness of Instruction

Not only are the instructors attending to the ideas of the participants, but the participants themselves are also attending and responding to one another's ideas. The interactions are richly responsive, and a range of intentions and ideas are integrated in establishing the set of laws.

These final products were strongly shaped by the instructors. The sustained effort to relate forces and energy was an articulated goal of instruction, and the pursuit of that goal began when Leslie asked students to consider the hand raising a box and noting that it seems plausible to say that the hand somehow is responsible for giving the box energy. In addition, the development of broader, "possibly true statements" was also a goal set by the instructors.

However, the unfolding and the outcome of this work—the questions that the participants sought to resolve and the particular structure of the laws they constructed—is clearly jointly constructed, with the participants' ideas strongly shaping the questions and the products of our inquiry.

Challenges

Above, we presented the conceptual products that arise in responsively taught science courses. As noted, these products were chosen to highlight three characteristics of the products of responsive inquiry: they may vary from one class to the next; they may vary from the canon; and they may be locally meaningful but difficult to interpret outside of the context of their development.

These characteristics are reassuring: we would not expect actual scientific discoveries to develop in a single, logical pathway, independent of the context in which they arose. And so, in a class that seeks to engage students in doing science as

78 Leslie J. Atkins and Brian W. Frank

they construct their own scientific ideas, we might anticipate this kind of variation. That is, such characteristics suggest that students' work mirrors that of scientists.

These characteristics, however, also present challenges—particularly when we consider that our courses are often part of a sequence and must meet specified standards, that our students are required to pass assessments with very particular representations, or that an instructor needs to recognize the background of the scientific content in these ideas. Below these challenges are discussed in the context of the examples introduced previously.

Variation From Class to Class: Challenges for Curriculum and Assessment

When considering the two episodes in which students arrived at models of diffuse reflection, it seems relatively straightforward to see how their ideas related to the scientific concept of diffuse reflection. In this regard, we might note that concerns about whether students had really learned "diffuse reflection" and other important ideas about light are minimal. This confirms the notion that responsive teaching is an approach that can unite both "inquiry" and "content" goals: when students engage in deeply scientific work with skilled faculty, they can develop canonical scientific concepts.

Nonetheless, we anticipate challenges when taking such an approach to scale. Assessment alone proves challenging: in the classes described above, we write exam questions anew each term to match the language and ideas of the students. Educating administration and assessors on how to understand and assess responsive teaching is not a minor task; it is hard to imagine how it might happen in our current K–12 climate. Promoting a style of instruction that requires idiosyncratic and context-dependent evaluation seems to go against current trends, where pre-determined standards, learning progressions, and standardized assessments are the norm.

Variation From the Canon: Challenges for Assessment

Similarly, when considering the "Pac-Man pellets" model of potential energy in light of the California State Science Standards (Grade 9–12, Physics) that these students will be asked to teach in their future careers, it is hard to definitively say that the standards concerning energy–arguably desired outcomes–were reached. The product the students generated—a novel model of potential energy as distributed in space—is certainly not explicit in the Standards; nor can they be clearly linked to standardized tests. With looming licensure exams, this is not a trivial concern for these students: knowing how to "solve problems" means using mathematical formulas to find numerical solutions—not to generate and employ a novel representation. It is also unlikely that these representations would be built on in future courses, where the novel representations would not be part of the instructor's repertoire.

Locally Meaningful: Challenges of Assessment

One of the challenges for evaluating the "content" of responsively developed ideas lies in how difficult it can be to connect these ideas to canonical ideas. During instruction, the "five laws" from the Energy Project appeared to be consistent with canonical physics, but the connection to the work-energy theorem was not obvious to the instructor (L.J.A.). Upon reflection, those connections became clear, but in the moment we simply knew that the class had generated connections between force and energy that seemed plausible given the range of scenarios we had examined.

Even after recognizing the connection to more typical descriptions of the work-energy theorem, explaining these laws and their connection to the canon is not simple. Doing so requires explaining representational conventions, so that phrases like "transfer kinetic energy" make sense. That is, these laws do not claim that kinetic energy decreases at the same rate that potential energy increases, but that the energy itself transforms from one form to another. Another representational choice—locating potential energy in an object—is not necessary (indeed, the *Advanced Inquiry* class modified that with the Pac-Man pellets); it is the convention that this group uses. And finally, evaluating the relationship to the canon also requires explaining the limitations of the laws. Here, the group has limited their laws to instances in which thermal energy is not relevant.

There is a more subtle concern with evaluating the products of this inquiry. Hammer, Goldberg, and Fargason, writing on energy instruction, note that "understanding the concept of energy means, in part, understanding what kind of idea it is and what kind of intellectual pursuit it supports" (p. 52). In a typical introductory physics class, the work-energy theorem generally supports a pursuit of quantitative problem-solving. For example, the College Board sets the following objectives for instruction in AP Physics C: Mechanics.

Box 3.2. College Board Physics Objectives Related to the Work-Energy Theorem

C. Work, energy, power

1. Work and the work-energy theorem

   a. Students should understand the definition of work, including when it is positive, negative, or zero, so they can
      i. Calculate the work done by a specified constant force on an object that undergoes a specified displacement.
      ii. Relate the work done by a force to the area under a graph of force as a function of position, and calculate this work in the case where the force is a linear function of position.

>   iii. Use integration to calculate the work performed by a force F(x) on an object that undergoes a specified displacement in one dimension.
>   iv. Use the scalar product operation to calculate the work performed by a specified constant force F on an object that undergoes a displacement in a plane.
>
> b. Students should understand and be able to apply the work-energy theorem, so they can:
>   i. Calculate the change in kinetic energy or speed that results from performing a specified amount of work on an object.
>   ii. Calculate the work performed by the net force, or by each of the forces that make up the net force, on an object that undergoes a specified change in speed or kinetic energy.
>   iii. Apply the theorem to determine the change in an object's kinetic energy and speed that results from the application of specified forces, or to determine the force that is required in order to bring an object to rest in a specified distance.

That is, in most physics courses, the work-energy theorem is introduced as a mathematically derived consequence. Understanding "work" and its role in describing the relationship between force and energy is generative not for the role it plays in tracking energy flows and examining patterns and regularities in those transfers and transformations. Rather, it is useful in that it allows one to "calculate the work done," "relate the work done . . . to the area under a graph," "calculate the change in kinetic energy," and "determine the force that is required in order to bring an object to rest."

The laws developed in Energy Two, on the other hand, were not developed to support quantitative problem-solving. The intellectual pursuit that generated these statements was characterizing regularities in energy transfers and transformations across a range of settings and developing clear consensus statements that summarized our work. More broadly, our goal was to investigate the mechanisms of energy transfers and transformations. In this way, the laws developed in Energy Two serve entirely different goals from traditional descriptions of the work-energy theorem. They cannot be evaluated in the ways suggested by the College Board; or, if evaluated in such ways, they would be found lacking.

A solution would lie in radically reconsidering the kinds of statements that become "standards" and "objectives" for courses, and (or) reimagining how we might measure proximity to canonical ideas. And this is the core challenge that we believe the 5 Laws episode highlights: The products of responsive teaching are necessarily linked to the kinds of pursuits and questions raised by students and supported by instructors. As such, these products—we suspect—cannot be clearly aligned with predetermined standards in simple, easily assessed ways.

Discussion

We began this chapter by noting how different definitions of inquiry can either foreground the activities undertaken by students or foreground the development of ideas. Responsive science teaching, it has been argued, offers an approach that makes it possible for instructors to coordinate both inquiry and content objectives. Pursuing these two objectives is not without its tensions and challenges (e.g., Hammer, 1997; Ball, 1993). These include the oft-noted claim that students productively engaged in authentic inquiry may arrive at conclusions that are odds with conclusions established by the scientific community; they may make sense of unanticipated data (Hammer, 1997); or they may develop ideas that are at odds with fundamental principles (May, Hammer, & Roy, 2006). Guiding students responsively is a challenge as well: practices of noticing and interpreting the substance of student ideas is complex, requiring not only the individual knowledge, skills, and dispositions of teachers, but communities and infrastructures that supports teachers in that work (Levin, Hammer, & Coffey, 2009). What we add to this conversation is the following: when such tensions are navigated and challenges are met, students can effectively engage in productive scientific inquiry and generate profoundly scientific content—and yet uncertainty concerning the nature of what has been learned still remains. Such uncertainties and tensions are part of the fabric of responsive teaching as we define it and, although not problematic in many regards, raise critical challenges when imagining responsive teaching as a widespread pedagogical approach.

In seeing our own students' ideas as simultaneously idiosyncratic and scientific, we see connections to recent work on desettling (Bang, Warren, Rosebery, & Medin, 2012), in that it entails "imagining multivoiced meanings of core phenomena as open territory for sense-making in the science classroom, similar to the kinds of meaning-making opportunities that are available to scientists in the field" (p. 308). In our classrooms, such open-ness to sense-making has often meant that both teachers and students are "learners [who] learn something that is not yet there," and who create new activity, knowledge, and skills in a setting where "nobody knows exactly what needs to be learned" (Engeström & Sannino, 2010). In its most modest forms, we see students as developing ideas about light that only vary slightly from each other and from the canon, but that nonetheless emerge from nuanced inquiries that make it difficult to completely disentangle them from the pursuits in which they arose. Even these minor idiosyncrasies, we believe, may present a challenge for widespread adoption of responsive inquiry instruction.

Engeström and Sannino, speaking on studies of expansive learning, note that this view of what learners undertake differs from acquisition and participation metaphors in which learners might be understood to primarily take up or move into competencies that already exist. Instead, it is proposed that *expansion* serves a more apt metaphor to capture learning in which knowledge, culture, and practices are created or transformed, not merely preserved or transmitted. When students

82 Leslie J. Atkins and Brian W. Frank

are allowed to shape their intellectual pursuits, the particular concepts that are a product of these pursuits may coalesce in ways that are quite different from the cannon (e.g., "Pac-Man pellets"); and while it may be the case that we can recognize connections to the canon (e.g., as a representational practice that supports conceptualizations of potential energy as distributed in space), as the intellectual demands in even recognizing connections to the canon increases, the challenges for curriculum, instruction, and assessment broaden.

For us, novel departure from the canon is evidenced most clearly in the development of the Five Laws of Energy, in which in-service teachers "recreate" the work-energy theorem in a new way. Their laws address what are arguably unique scientific questions—questions that were shaped by both instructors and students—about causality and energy transfers and transformations. The products resulting from that inquiry are strikingly absent from most energy instruction, and perhaps from most other intellectual pursuits in which the concept of energy has relevance. The Energy Project, then, does not seem to merely be engaging in-service teachers in recapitulating existing scientific pursuits and established practices; but, together with these in-service teachers, the Energy Project is *creating* a kind of practice with respect to energy and new concepts that support that practice. In doing so, the products of that pursuit, while not entirely inconsistent with the work-energy theorem in its usual guise, are nonetheless new and are not likely be assessed using the traditional metrics of "understanding" the work-energy theorem.

In reflecting on these cases, we are left with the prospect that responsive instruction will necessarily be *expansive*. Canonical scientific ideas are transformed through emerging practices. While the Energy Project represents a striking example, we believe this may be characteristic of the reflexive nature inherent to responsive instruction. In some regards, this claim we are making is not new; the conflict between "content" and "inquiry" and the tensions of responsive teaching have been articulated before. Our intention is to illustrate, by examining what may be perceived as "best-case scenarios"—instruction that can be clearly identified as responsive scientific inquiry, in which student ideas and questions are pursued in deeply scientific ways, and where the products of that instruction are consistent with canonical ideas—that these products nonetheless pose challenges. We think it is critical to be clear that instruction that transforms (and does not merely recapitulate) both scientific ideas and practices will not be easily assessed and built on in typical schooling.

Acknowledgments

This work was funded by grants to Leslie J. Atkins by the National Science Foundation (#0837058, #1140785) and to Brian W. Frank (#1140784). We are grateful to the Energy Project, particularly Rachel Scherr and Stamatis Vokos; to student research assistants Andrew Lerner, Tony deCasper, Rachel Boyd, and Vanessa

Quevedo; and to co-instructors Irene Salter and Kim Jaxon. We also thank the organizers of the conference, and the reviewers of this chapter, in particular Fred Goldberg, Matty Lau, Amy Robertson, Rachel Scherr, and Tiffany Sikorski.

Note

1 Scientifically speaking, this idea is correct: both a source of light and a non-shiny object that we see send light rays out in all directions. However, because the object will absorb some light, it will never be as bright as the source and so will not appear to "glow." An exception—when a reflector of light seems to glow—occurs in some cases when source of light is not visible—for example, the moon.

References

Atkins, L.J., Erstad, C., Gudeman, P., McGowan, J., Mulhern, K., Prader, K., . . . & Timmons, A. (2014). Animating energy: Stop-motion animation and energy tracking representations. *The Physics Teacher, 52*(3), 152–156.

Atkins, L.J. & Salter, I.Y. (2011). "What's a fourth? What's a fifth? What's the point?": Constructing definitions in scientific inquiry. *EARLI Annual Conference*, Exeter, UK.

Ball, D.L. (1993). With an eye on the mathematical horizon: Dilemmas of teaching elementary school mathematics. *Elementary School Journal, 93*, 373–397.

Bang, M., Warren, B., Rosebery, A.S., & Medin, D. (2012). Desettling expectations in science education. *Human Development, 55*, 285–301.

Close, H.G., DeWater, L.S., Close, E.W., Scherr, R.E., & McKagan, S.B. (2010). Using The Algebra Project method to regiment discourse in an energy course for teachers, *AIP Conf. Proc.* 1289, 9.

Daane, A.R., Wells, L., & Scherr, R.E. (2014). Energy Theater. *The Physics Teacher, 52*(5), 291–294.

Engeström, Y., & Sannino, A. (2010). Studies of expansive learning: Foundations, findings and future challenges. *Educational Research Review, 5*, 1–24.

Goldberg, F., Robinson, S., Otero, V., Kruse, R., & Thompson, N. (2008). *Physical science and everyday thinking, 2nd ed. It's about time.* Armonk, NY: Herff Jones Education Division.

Hammer, D. (1997). Discovery learning and discovery teaching. *Cognition and Instruction, 15*(4), 485–529.

Hammer, D., Goldberg, F., & Fargason, S. (2012). Responsive teaching and the beginnings of energy in a third grade classroom. *Review of Science, Mathematics and ICT Education, 6*(1), 51–72.

Hammer, D., & van Zee, E. (2006). *Seeing the science in children's thinking: Case studies of student inquiry in physical science* (Book and DVD). Portsmouth, NH: Heinemann.

Levin, D., Hammer, D., & Coffey, J. (2009). Novice teachers' attention to student thinking. *Journal of Teacher Education, 60*(2), 142–154.

Maskiewicz, A.C., & Winters, V.A. (2012). Understanding the co-construction of inquiry practices: A case study of a responsive teaching environment. *Journal of Research in Science Teaching, 49*, 429–464.

May, D.B., Hammer, D., & Roy, P. (2006). Children's analogical reasoning in a 3rd-grade science discussion. *Science Education, 90*(2), 316–330.

McKagan, S.B., Scherr, R.E., Close, E.W., & Close, H.G. (2012). Criteria for creating and categorizing forms of energy. In N.S. Rebello, P.V. Engelhardt, & C. Singh (Eds.), *AIP Conference Proceedings-American Institute of Physics* (pp. 279–282). Melville, NY: AIP Press.

Salter, I.Y., & Atkins, L.J. (2013). Student-generated scientific inquiry for elementary education undergraduates: Course development, outcomes and implications. *Journal of Science Teacher Education, 24*(1), 157–177.

Scherr, R.E., Close, H.G., McKagan, S.B., & Vokos, S. (2012a). Representing energy. I. Representing a substance ontology for energy. *Physical Review Special Topics-Physics Education Research, 8*(2), 020114.

Scherr, R.E., Close, H.G., Close, E.W., & Vokos, S. (2012b). Representing energy. II. Energy tracking representations. *Physical Review Special Topics–Physics Education Research, 8*(2), 020115.

Scherr, R.E., Close, H.G., Close, E.W., Flood, V.J., McKagan, S.B., Robertson, A.D., Seeley, L., Wittmann, M.C., & Vokos, S. (2013). Negotiating energy dynamics through embodied action in a materially structured environment. *Physical Review Special Topics–Physics Education Research, 9*(2), 020105.

Sherin, B., Azevedo, F.S., & diSessa, A. (2005). Exploration zones: A framework for describing the emergent structure of learning activities. In R. Nemirovsky, A.S. Rosebery, B. Warren, & J. Solomon (Eds.), *Everyday matters in science and mathematics: Studies of complex classroom events* (pp. 329–366). Mahwah, NJ: Lawrence Erlbaum.

4

UNDERSTANDING RESPONSIVE TEACHING AND CURRICULUM FROM THE STUDENTS' PERSPECTIVE

Tiffany-Rose Sikorski

Only ten days stand between Ms. H's fifth-grade class and summer vacation, and yet her students listen with intensity as she formulates her next science question. "Stop and turn to your groups," she says, "cuz I'm gonna write down the ideas you just had, cuz I can't be in two places at once. And I want you to talk about, how did we go from a puddle, the rainwater, all of the sudden to discussing weather?"

Ms. H pauses for half a second, but the class remains silent, waiting for the signal. She continues, "How did we switch gears. Where are these connections? What's going on in your head right now as they're talking about these ideas? At your table. Go."

The group of four students closest to the video camera leisurely begin the conversation. Leah sits upright and leans forward, trying to see something over on the other side of the room. Ari sits to her left, and as usual is the first to speak. He begins, "I think this kinda started because we have so many questions that we wanted to find out more about how . . . why that puddle disappeared."

Our research team began videotaping Leah's and Ari's class six weeks prior, on the day that Ms. H first posed to her students what came to be known as the puddle question. The puddle question was the opening to a responsive curriculum unit on the water cycle. The question asked students to consider what might have happened to a hypothetical puddle of water that disappears over the course of a day. Ideas flowed freely on Day 1: "it evaporated" (Nick); "the puddles . . . got absorbed into the ground because of the grass" (Lisa); "it could have gone down like a drain or something" (Michael); "maybe I think the puddles evaporated from the sun's rays and became a cloud full of moisture" (James).

After the opening question, the class wove through a series of discussions and experiments to test their ideas, trying to figure out how factors like the amount

86 Tiffany-Rose Sikorski

of water, water temperature, and air temperature may have affected the puddle's disappearance. By the last day of the module, students were asking questions about weather, cloud formation, and the difference between snow and sleet. *How did the class get from the puddle question to wondering about weather?* That was Ms. H's question, and mine too, as I tried to understand how students made sense of their winding lines of inquiry.

Ms. H's question created an opportune moment for gathering evidence about how Leah, Ari, John, and Molly experienced the responsive water cycle unit. The remainder of this chapter makes the case that if the science education community wishes to refine the craft of responsiveness and also broaden its sphere of influence, we must follow Ms. H's example and pay closer attention to how responsive teaching looks and feels from the students' perspective.

Organization of the Chapter

This chapter explores how students perceive responsive science teaching. For simplicity, two facets of students' perspective are highlighted: first, their sense of agency, and second, their sense of the flow of the activities, topics, and conversations.

The chapter begins with a brief review of agency and flow in responsiveness literature. The review argues that although responsive teaching clearly values students' sense of agency and flow, few studies have addressed these constructs explicitly. An extended example from Ms. H's class follows the literature review to illustrate important differences in how students may experience agency and flow in responsive classrooms and to highlight analytic tools for making these constructs an explicit focus of research.

Finally, the chapter concludes with implications, and the argument that closer attention to the student perspective matters for responsiveness literature and, perhaps more importantly, for improving the quality of curriculum sequencing debates within the broader science education community.

Agency and Flow in Responsiveness Literature

Evidence of productive disciplinary engagement in responsive classrooms abounds (Ball, 1993; Duckworth, 2001; Engle & Conant, 2002; Gallas, 1995; Hammer, 1997; Hammer & Van Zee, 2006; Levin, Hammer, Elby, & Coffey, 2013; Rosebery & Warren, 1998). Studies of responsive teaching have documented learners of all ages seeking mechanism, checking for consistency between theory and observation, challenging their peers with counterexamples, refining models and analogies, and engaging in every other aspect of inquiry considered essential to science learning in standards documents (Achieve, 2012). Responsive teaching clearly provides opportunities for students to *do science*.

In contrast, the evidence base for students' sense of agency in responsive teaching is developing, as is an understanding of how students perceive the flow of activities, topics, and ideas. Despite their implicit importance in responsiveness literature, agency and flow are rarely the explicit focus of responsive teaching analyses. Illustrative case studies suggest that, at least for some students, responsive teaching empowers students to shape the direction of their inquiry. But there are also signs in existing data that for some students responsive curriculum does not engender a sense of agency or flow so much as a sense of disempowered frustration or confusion.

Agency

In theory, responsive teaching, which puts student thinking front and center, should help students feel that their ideas are worthy of consideration, that they play a valuable role in creating and assessing ideas, and that their ideas drive decisions about where to go next in class. Responsive literature uses many terms for this collective set of learning goals related to students' authority over ideas: inquiry voice (Lindfors, 1999), voice (Gallas, 1995), agency (Engle & Conant, 2002), intellectual agency (Hammer, Goldberg, & Fargason, 2012), and epistemic agency (Hutchison & Hammer, 2010). For simplicity, I use the term agency henceforth.

Student agency can be a goal in and of itself. Duckworth (2001) explains, "If there is any basic principle in my teaching, it's that people are to feel free to express their thoughts about what is going on and why, and that those thoughts are to be taken seriously" (p. 19). Making space for students' ideas to be heard is a recurrent theme in responsive literature. "Classrooms are increasingly about voice," Lindfors (1999) explains, "about *having* it, about *using* it" (p. 67).

Student agency can also be viewed as a means to epistemological learning goals. In responsive classrooms, students "participate in the formation, assessment, and elaboration of concepts", in contrast to students' traditional roles of "following instructions to get points" or "trying to find out the correct information" (Levin, Hammer, Elby, & Coffey, 2013, pp. 8, 32). But in order for students to come to appreciate the criteria used to develop and evaluate ideas in the discipline—an epistemic goal—they must recognize their own role in developing and assessing those ideas (Coffey, Hammer, Levin, & Grant, 2011).

When making claims about student agency in a classroom, it is important to know something about the students' perspective, i.e., how the classroom looks and feels from the students' point of view. That students can share, argue about, and refine their ideas does not necessarily mean students see the classroom as centered on and shaped by *their* ideas, *their* voices.

Jaber (2014) offers the exemplary case of Sandra, an elementary student who shared ideas and asked questions while participating in responsive curricula in her fourth- and fifth-grade science classes. For example, during a class discussion about clouds, Sandra says:

88 Tiffany-Rose Sikorski

> I actually have a question for Andrew . . . I don't really understand what you're saying. May- maybe I'm not hearing this right but to me you're saying that, that some of that water evaporates into the cloud and some of it just- [shifted her gaze away from Andrew to an empty space].
>
> (p. 59)

According to Jaber, evidence for agency (Scardamalia, 2002) in this line includes Sandra's willingness to make space in the conversation to ask a question of her peer, and also her sense that she can "evaluat[e] her own understanding" of Andrew's idea (Jaber, 2014, p. 61). However, to support these claims about agency, it helps to have more information about Sandra's point of view. To that end, Jaber conducted a stimulated recall interview with Sandra on the focal exchange with Andrew. Jaber makes an important distinction between evidence of agency in the classroom data (what Sandra does) and evidence of agency in interviews (what Sandra says about her experience). In the interview, Sandra described her experience in the responsive science curriculum as a time when the students could "take the reins", raise many questions, and share ideas:

> Having kids gather around in a circle and talking about- and in the beginning giving couple of ideas in there and then just step back and let them take it on from there, let them take the reins . . . the teacher starts it and then let the kids do it. . . . Because it's great to have some ideas out there and to have fun with it! I remember the fourth and fifth grades, those are the best science years I've ever had because I just had fun. Both teachers just bring in a couple of ideas and just let you take it on from there. So it was FUN!
>
> (p. 72)

The interview illustrates that Sandra was asking questions of her own accord, that she felt the teacher giving power over to the students, and moreover that she enjoyed the experience. Sandra's case is a compelling example of how responsive teaching can support agency for some students.

Duckworth (2001) also provides data that addresses student agency. After the conclusion of an eight-week responsive unit on the topic of density, Duckworth asked her teacher-learners to write short reflective papers about what they learned. Excerpts from these papers are available in the postscript to Duckworth's account of the module. Two excerpts, from classmates Jacques and Evelyne, illustrate how what feels like agency to one student can feel like disempowerment to another. According to Jacques:

> Each Tuesday evening, all propositions, good or bad, right or wrong, could be made, and never was any value judgment brought to bear on them. Everyone had the occasion to have wonderful ideas and to be proud of them. To the point (please forgive me if this appears somewhat presumptuous) that

I currently have the very validating feeling of having myself discovered the principle of floating.

(p. 38)

In contrast, Evelyne writes:

... when Jacques has a wonderful idea, it certainly was that for him and maybe for others (cf. Henri) but for me it was the coup de grâce ... Henri tried to help me out, but no matter how much he explained to me, made me drawings, and repeated in different forms, nothing was internalized. I seemed to understand for the moment, but when I have to re-explain it, I get muddled and nothing is coherent anymore ...

(p. 36)

Evelyne's account highlights Jacques' ownership of ideas, Henri's authority, and her struggle to access peers' ideas, but lacks evidence of her own ideas or voice. She was not discouraged by the experience, but rather left feeling "very deeply the need to know what [she wants] to" (p. 36).

Though these cases seemed to depict a static notion of agency, something a student experiences or does not, responsiveness literature also includes examples of contextual variation in agency. Hutchison and Hammer (2010), for example, found that in some moments pre-service teachers exercised agency during their inquiry into density, but in other instances seemed to fall into the typical science classroom game of citing authoritative knowledge and seeking definitive answers. The authors support these claims about agency on the basis of how students introduce and work with ideas in class (p. 140). However, making such claims solely based on what students do and say in class is fraught with challenges. Students' refusal to take up the game of responsive teaching, for example, may be an act of agency rather than a failure to exercise agency.

Flow

Designers of pre-sequenced curriculum take very seriously the idea of coherence, or storyline, or *flow*. In simple terms, flow refers to the way that topics, ideas, and activities unfold at multiple time scales in a curriculum (Kuipers, Viechnicki, Massoud, & Wright, 2009; Roth & Givvin, 2008). Just as one might consider flow in a movie script, a book plot, or in the organization of this chapter, curriculum can also be thought of as flowing.[1]

Unlike traditional curriculum, a responsive curriculum's storyline or flow is not planned in advance. Instead, a responsive curriculum is more like a *Choose Your Own Adventure* story[2], where what comes next depends in large part on the ideas and questions that students raise in the moment. Some of these possible menu items are anticipated in advance; others are generated on the spot by the teacher. The flow (or lack thereof) is therefore dynamic and emergent.

90 Tiffany-Rose Sikorski

Responsiveness literature has carefully documented flow from the teacher's perspective, for example:

> . . . I started a class discussion to have students share, contest, and further develop their arguments. The conversation took off! So many students had so many ideas to share that it was a challenge to keep track of it all. During the class, I felt like I had a hard time following all the arguments . . .
>
> (Ms. Henson's reflection on *The Owl and the Snakes (1)*;
> in Levin et al., 2013, p. 57)

> Somehow they [students] switched to talking about skin color and how skin changes color when it's in the sunlight, when it's been exposed to sunlight for a certain amount of time. And they talked about tans and sunburns. And to me that was interesting because it was, it had come out of a plant conversation. And in my mind I made the connection between melanin and chlorophyll . . .
>
> (Ms. Finnerty's reflection on plant growth discussion;
> in Ballenger, 1998, p. 67)

Teacher reflections can be an important professional development tool (Duckworth, 1987; Hammer & van Zee, 2006; Levin et al., 2013; Rosebery & Warren, 1998) and provide valuable information for researchers who study responsive classrooms. But they are not substitutes for student-generated commentary and reflection, which are noticeably absent in responsiveness literature. Duckworth (2001), Dennis (1998), and van Zee, Hammer, Bell, Roy, and Peter (2005) are three examples of studies that do contain learner commentaries. However, all three studies feature *teacher-learners* reflecting on their experience in a responsive unit, and not K–12 students.

The question of how students make sense of the flow is of particular importance in responsive classrooms because responsiveness hinges on students coming to see science as deriving from and shaped by their ideas. We must explore how students think next moves are chosen, by whom, and for what purposes.[3] These questions are precisely what makes Ms. H's question in the opening episode of the chapter so important:

> . . . how did we go from a puddle, the rainwater, all of the sudden to discussing weather? How did we switch gears. Where are these connections? What's going on in your head right now as they're talking about these ideas?

One way to interpret Ms. H's question is as follows: Tell the *story* of how we got from talking about puddles to talking about weather. The next section illustrates how Ms. H's "connecting question" opens up access to the students' perspective and to questions of agency and flow.

A Glimpse into the Students' Perspective

Context of the Clip

Ms. H's fifth-grade class began Day 1 of "puddle unit", formally titled the water cycle module, with the following question:

> Suppose that one night, it rains. Lots and lots of rain. When you arrive at school, you notice that there are puddles of rainwater in the parking lot. But when you go home, you notice that the puddles are gone. What happened to the rainwater?

The class worked on the puddle question for a total of nine two-hour-long lessons, spread out over one month. Ms. H was responsive during the unit, in that she "decided where to go next," a phrase she used often in her course, based on students' ideas and questions. As aforementioned, her class moved from talking about puddles and what happened to the rainwater on Day 1 to discussing weather, cloud formation, and what causes rain on Day 9. A detailed account of the unit is available in both Maskiewicz and Winters (2012) and Sikorski (2012).

On Day 9, Ms. H asks students to students to retrace their steps and explain how they got from the puddle question to talking about weather. The focal group discusses the question for approximately ten minutes. Two questions frame the analysis of their discussion:

1. *Flow:*   How does the focal group describe the sequence of ideas, topics and/ or events in the module?
2. *Agency:*   To whom do students attribute the origin of those ideas, topics, and/ or events?

The analysis that follows is not a comprehensive case of the focal group's experience in the module, but rather an opportunistic glimpse.

Walk-Through of the Clip

The clip starts at the opening scene in the introduction of the chapter, when Ms. H poses the aforementioned "connecting question" to the class:

> Ms. H: Stop and turn to your groups, cuz I'm gonna write down the ideas you just had, cuz I can't be in two places at once. And I want you to talk

92 Tiffany-Rose Sikorski

about, how did we go from a puddle, the rainwater, all of the sudden to discussing weather? How did we switch gears. Where are these connections? What's going on in your head right now as they're talking about these ideas? At your table. Go.

The focal group of Ari, John, Molly, and Leah immediately identify questions, experiments, and causality as central components of their stories. In the transcript, double hashtags indicate overlapping speech, forward slashes indicate "false starts or abandoned language" (Varelas et al., 2008, p. 93), hyphens indicate interruptions of turn, and asterisks mark inaudible words or phrases.

1. *Ari:*   I think this kinda started because we have so many questions that we wanted to find out more about how // why that puddle disappeared.
2. *John:*   Like we start exploring one thing, then we test an experiment, ## then it brings up another one. ##
3. *Molly:*   ## Like what affects it, like ##
4. *Ari:*   Yeah, it's like—
5. *Molly:*   Why it happens. And then it goes to another thing, why *that* happens [hitting hand on desk]. And then it goes to another thing, why *that* happens [hitting hand on desk].
6. *Ari:*   Yeah, because like, it's a question. Well, does the w // does the water (★★★) affect it. Then, when that and also it just kind of // then all the sudden you're like, wait, why does weather (★★★) affect it? Then you keep moving along from // like, this is where you started right here. [Ari draws a quick sketch on his folder; see Figure 4.1] Puddle. And then you went to here [pointing to his sketch], to here, to here, to here, and now right here.
7. *Ari:*   What? [to Leah]
8. *Molly:*   ## Yes. ##
9. *Leah:*   [looking at Ari's paper] ## That kinda makes sense. ##

In lines 1–9, the students begin to construct a synergistic account of their experience in the unit. They confirm each other's contributions with "yeah," "yes," and "that kinda makes sense" (4, 6, 8, 9). They utilize and repeat a shared speech pattern "why . . . then . . . why . . . then" (2, 5, 6). The students repeat and take up each other's vocabulary ("like" in lines 2, 3, 4 and "affect" in lines 5, 6). These linguistic markers suggest that the students are constructing a story together, as opposed to individually (see Coates, 1995).

Following Ari's initial contribution that everything started with their questions about the puddle, the group successively refines their account. John adds that their questions led to experiments, which led to more questions. Molly further clarifies that the purpose of the experiments was to look for causal chains, or in her language, to find "why *that* happens" and "what affects it." Ari adds to Molly's idea, filling in particular causal chains they were trying to build, i.e. "how does water (★★★) affect it, why does weather affect it."

Curriculum from the Students' Perspective   93

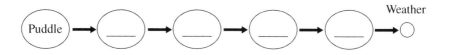

FIGURE 4.1 Reconstruction of Ari's drawing.

At line 6, Ari draws an impromptu sketch on the back of his folder (see Figure 4.1). His drawing depicts the idea that the students got from the puddle question to talking about weather via a chain of questions. Leah, noticing that Ari drew on the back of his folder, goes and gets some notepaper after line 9. Molly also gets up from the table. While the two girls are gone, Ari and John continue the discussion, reconfirming their sense that the path through the puddle unit was a series of seemingly endless questions and experiments.

10. *Ari:* But I think all have something to do with the puddle, in a way.
11. *John:* So it just starts with a simple question. We test it. Then that testing leads to another question which leads to another question
12. *Ari:* Yeah
13. *John:* which leads to another question
14. *Ari:* But it was <worth it>
15. *John:* and it keeps going and going and going and going and going.
16. *Ari:* Till finally you're really really really really tired of writing more than you'd like (★★★. ★★★).
17. *Ari:* I mean a question that we had // I (★★★) that it was really different answers to the questions. It was so simple that it was kind of hard in a way.
    [Molly and Leah return, with blank paper in hand that they distribute to each group member. Ms. H's students regularly keep track of their ideas on white boards or paper, as evidenced in Ari's line 16.]
18. *John:* Mhm.
19. *Ari:* It made you think more. Cuz like more than like (★★★) all you have to do is like . . .

In line 10, Ari suggests that the puddle question was not only a starting point for the inquiry, but also a sort of orienting question that everything else relates back to. Both Ari and John note that the initial question was simple, but also generative, leading to many different answers. And in lines 16 and 19 Ari notes that sometimes the line of questioning grew tiring, but made him "think more." Ari's precise language in line 14 is unclear and noted accordingly.

In lines 1–19, Leah, Ari, John, and Molly seem to agree that at the puddle module was a set of questions and experiments aimed at uncovering causal relationships between variables related to evaporation, and not just a collection of disconnected topics or activities. Also important, John and Ari indicate they were

94 Tiffany-Rose Sikorski

the agents of the questioning ("a question that we had"), and that their experiments were a source of questions.

But a shift occurs at line 19, as Ari gets increasingly tongue-tied and caught up in his words. John looks at Ari and listens patiently, but also yawns and forcefully opens his eyes as if falling asleep. Finally, at line 20, John jumps with a transitional "okay" and firm tone, suggesting that he is ready to get the group back on track to answer Ms. H's prompt:

20. *John:* Okay, so it started with the puddle of rainwater. Then we decided to test if more or less water evaporated faster. We found out that less did. Then we tested . . . with the containers over it to make sure it was evaporating.
21. *Leah:* Here [holding up her folder]
22. *John:* Then . . .
23. *Leah:* Look through all my papers, or yours.
24. *John:* Huh?
25. *Leah:* [holding up her folder] Look through all the papers and see
26. *Ms. H:* Uh voice levels at your tables please.
27. *John:* [whispering] Wait, no, and then . . . . we did that experiment with the
28. *Ari:* We have ten days of school left.
29. *Leah:* What?
30. *Ari:* Ten days of school left. Well not ten of school but ten days till we're finished here. [Ari re-draws Figure 4.1 on the paper that Leah handed out]

Starting with line 20, the synergy of the discussion breaks. Students stop confirming each other's responses and instead verbally indicate confusion or mismatch in the conversation (24, 27, 29). The storylines diverge. John tries to fill in specifics of the experiments they conducted during the module. Leah points out that the notes and papers they have been keeping all this time might be useful ("Look through all the papers and see"), but John declines and attempts to refocus. He leans forward, places his head in his hands, and closes his eyes, clearly concentrating on remembering the key events of the unit.

31. *John:* Okay, so um . . .
32. *Leah:* Four days till my birthday.
33. *John:* Then we did um, we tested the the hotter one and then the colder one. The one that was heated by the beverage warmer.
34. *Molly:* I like the beverage warmer.
35. *John:* And then we went to those three room temperature, 10 seconds in a microwave, 20 seconds in a microwave, and the 20 seconds evaporated last and the room temperature evaporated first. Then we put water with ice in it with um water without ice, and the one with ice evaporated faster. Which led us to that colder water evaporates faster.

John's developing story explains the purpose of each experiment, and how one experiment led to the next. The first experiment was to test whether "more or

Curriculum from the Students' Perspective

less water evaporated faster." After seeing that less water evaporates faster, then the students made sure that the water was actually evaporating. (They put a container over the puddles to "catch" the evaporating water.) Next, the students tested whether hot or cold water evaporates faster. They repeated the experiment using three puddles: one with the water at room temperature, one with water heated for 10 seconds, and one with water heated for 20 seconds. The puddle of room temperature water evaporated first. Then they repeated the experiment again, using regular water and ice water, and came to the unexpected finding that "colder water evaporates faster." Curiously, John stops here, and never explicitly connects the final experiment back to the question of weather. In this segment, John also introduces a passive construction, "which led us to," as if the experiment itself guides the students to a conclusion.

After John finishes his story, the focal group writes quietly for almost three minutes. Ari and Leah's drawings are visible to the camera, and they illustrate some important differences in how the students sequence the topics in their storyline. As previously shown, Ari draws "puddle" connected to a series of undefined topics, and ending with "weather." Underneath that, he draws a diagram of the water cycle (see line 36 and Figure 4.2). Under the diagram, he writes, "We started with the puddle but we moved on because of curiosity & more questions."

Leah, on the other hand, starts her drawing with the ocean, then to puddle, to lake, and back to puddle. Her chain resembles a version of the water cycle, as shown in Figure 4.3. Underneath, she writes: "Water starts in the ocean, then <goes> evaporates into the air, then into rain droplets, then into a different form of water." Whereas Ari views the sequence of topics and activities as a chain of questions driven by the students' curiosity and perhaps headed toward the water cycle, Leah seems to view the sequence of topics as moving through different components of the water cycle.

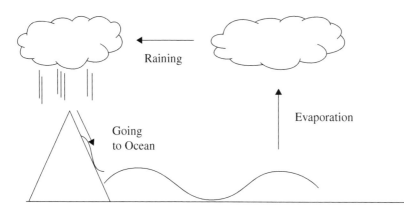

FIGURE 4.2 Reconstruction of Ari's water cycle diagram.

96 Tiffany-Rose Sikorski

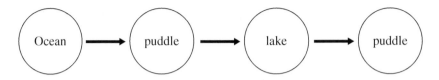

FIGURE 4.3 Reconstruction of Leah's drawing.

After the three minutes of silent work, Ari announces that he is done writing, and the groups' conversation about how they got from the puddle question to the weather question comes to a close:

36. *Ari:* I kind of drew a small diagram of the weather, I mean of the water cycle. [30-second pause; more quiet from the group]
37. *Ari:* Anyway, so . . . if we have a chance to do something today, I think we could probably research more about the water cycle, if we have time today. [students write and draw]
38. *Molly:* Done!
39. *Leah:* What did you do for this?
40. *Molly:* I wrote about how we got to weather. Like she just told us to do. You mean what I wrote?
41. *Molly:* Okay, now I'm done.
42. *Ari:* So, what should we do?
43. *Leah:* She hasn't asked us. I think we should research.

When Ari does reference the water cycle in lines 36 and 37, he marks the topic as an area for future research, rather than a topic that holds their prior work together. He makes a note on his paper next to the water cycle drawing: "If we have time, study water cycle." Another difference in Leah's and Ari's perspective on the responsive unit shows up in lines 36–43. When Ari completes his writing, he immediately starts thinking about where to go next. He suggests that the students could research the water cycle, and distinguishes the water cycle from the topic of weather (36). Leah echoes Ari's recommendation that the next step involve "research," but notes that Ms. H has not asked yet for next moves. For Leah, what comes in the sequence next depends on Ms. H's directions, echoing Molly's point: "I wrote about how we got to weather. Like she just told us to do."

Summary of Findings

Flow: How Does the Focal Group Describe the Sequence of Ideas, Topics and/or Events in the Module?

John, Molly, and Ari describe the unit as a seemingly endless line of questioning and/or experimenting. However, students seem to have differing senses about the origin of their questions, the specific content of those questions and experiments, and how they felt about the endless line of questions in the module. Ari experiences the module as being driven by the class's curiosity and questions, with everything relating back to the puddle question. John's storyline contains a linear chain of experiments, testing ideas, and generating new questions to test, apparently driven by the students' interest and also the phenomenon itself.

Students' responses also differ in the degree to which they specify the topics and activities in the sequence. John fills in his storyline with the purpose and key finding of each experiment, but on the other hand never actually connects his storyline back to the topic of weather. Ari marks the puddle and weather questions as the two ends of a line of inquiry, but leaves the entire middle of the story blank. Ari may have different expectations than John about what counts as a sufficiently detailed prompt, or he may actually be remembering the sequence differently, in order or salience of events. Leah draws a chain that starts with puddle and ends with weather, but omits any mention of experiments.

Students identify "water cycle" as an overarching or key topic within the sequence. Many of the students in Ms. H's class, including Leah, explicitly used the phrase water cycle or drew a diagram resembling the water cycle on their papers, suggesting that the idea played an important role in how students were making sense of their experience in the responsive module. Ari identified the water cycle as an area for further exploration. John's story is an exception: He does not reference the water cycle at all during his remembering of the chain of experiments his group conducted during the module. Despite the name of the module, the fact that so many students refer to the water cycle in their responses to Ms. H's connecting prompt is surprising. The module starts out with the puddle question and went from there; a lecture on the "water cycle" or mapping ideas to the "water cycle" did not occur. In the approximately fourteen pages of chart paper that Ms. H used to keep track of students' questions and ideas over the course of the module, the phrase water cycle appeared only once. However, it was circled and highlighted for emphasis.

Ms. H's perspective may simultaneously shape and serve as secondary evidence of the students' perspective. At the start of Day 9, Ms. H provides a detailed recapitulation of the students' questions and comments over the course of the module. A very small snippet of that recap was as follows:

> . . . So, and John over here decided the other day to say, "Well wait a minute. Every time we ask a question, we keep going all the sudden we're asking more questions and we have more things to think about. . . . Colder temperatures. Why all the sudden is it colder by the water? Is any of this having to do with this water quote unquote cycle?

By marking the students' ideas about the water cycle and endless line of questioning in her storyline, she may have reinforced their inclusion in the students' responses to the connecting prompt later on Day 9.

Agency: To Whom Do Students Attribute the Origin of Those Ideas, Topics, and/or Events?

Students attribute the origin of their questions to themselves, the class, and to Ms. H. For example, Ari indicates that the questions arose primarily from the class's "curiosity." But, Leah, here and in other unpublished analyses, characterizes the questions as prompted by Ms. H's directions (see Sikorski, 2012). Leah's statements at least open up the possibility that for some students responsive teaching still feels heavily teacher-directed.

Another facet of agency involves attribution or ownership of ideas. An asymmetry exists between Ms. H's indexing of ideas in her storylines and students' indexing of ideas on Day 9. Consider another portion of Ms. H's recap of events, which she shares while visiting a small group during "how did we get from a puddle to weather" question:

> But didn't we just start talking about // Chuck started wondering about // we were wondering about the clouds that were at the ocean. And we started talking about air temperature and humi the humidity and ground temperature and how do these things all affect it and all the sudden Candice started talking about well weather moves from the Pacific Ocean towards us. And then we started talking about where is weather?

Ms. H's account attributes ideas to Chuck and Candice, two students who were sitting at other tables. In doing so, Ms. H marks students as owners of ideas, and she apparently indexes the flow of class according to the ideas that students raise. Yet in the student storylines presented here, names are notably missing. In some cases, students absolve themselves completely from the trajectory of the conversation, putting the agency with the phenomenon itself: "It turned into a weather conversation." In other cases, students mark question and ideas as theirs: "We had so many questions." Occasionally, Ms. H is referenced as the source of the question or activity, i.e., "I wrote about weather just liked she told us to do." The students are capable of keeping track of each other's ideas, and often do so during class discussions. The lack of indexing here may suggest that some students do not actually view the responsive water cycle unit as driven by their ideas. Or it may be that students index ideas according to speaker locally, but do not see it as necessary to index ideas according to speaker when giving a more global account of how the class moved from one topic to another.

Making Claims About the Student's Perspective

As discussed in the literature review, studies of responsiveness closely attend to students' discourse (including gestures, expressions, and generated artifacts) as they make sense of a phenomenon. These analyses are exogenous (Stevens, 2010) in that researchers observe what the students are doing, compare that work to the practices and aims of professional science, and formulate claims about students' productive disciplinary engagement, but without necessarily or explicitly attending to the students' point of view on the matter.[4]

The multifaceted question of how responsive teaching looks and feels from the students' perspective involves many related constructs, i.e., agency, flow, epistemology, voice, ownership, affect, identity, and more. One task for future work will be to develop a theoretical framework that appropriately captures the many dimensions of students' perspective. As a candidate conceptual framework, narrative coherence encompasses how "students make sense about a curriculum—the text itself, the roles intended for them, the phenomena under investigation, and their teachers actions" (Kuipers, Viechnicki, Massoud, & Wright, 2009, p. 248). Within this framework, disciplinary engagement can be thought of as the substance of the text, epistemology as the rules by which the text is spontaneously generated and refined, and agency as students' roles in authoring that text.

How does one gather and interpret high-quality evidence of students' perspectives? The claims presented in the chapter are grounded in a relatively small slice of data from the water cycle module. Ms. H explicitly asks students to construct a storyline with a start (the puddle question) and an end (the weather). Students' descriptions of how they got from the puddle question to the weather question revealed some striking similarities and differences in how students made sense of water cycle unit. These storylines are reconstructions shaped by students' experiences in the unit, but also possibly by their interpretation of Ms. H's prompt and its purpose, their peers' responses, etc. Thus, care must be taken in recognizing that differences in students' responses to connecting prompts like the one Ms. H posed may result from any one or a confluence of these factors.

Student interviews are another high quality source of evidence. Interviews allow students to comment on the salient features of the module, how next moves for the unit were decided, and how they felt about the sharing of ideas in class. I became interested in the focal group's perspective on the unit years after the episode was collected, too late to go back and interview students. In retrospect, I would have liked to ask all four students but especially Leah about her experience in the unit, what ideas she shared, and how those ideas were taken up. I would have liked to ask Ari what he meant by "researching the water cycle" and Molly how she felt about the endless line of questioning. Again, care must be taken in analyses of these interviews, to recognize the dynamics of the interview itself and the reconstructive nature of memory (Bartlett, 1932/1995; Russ, Lee, & Sherin, 2012).

As the glimpse into Ms. H's classroom shows, classroom video and artifacts can still be mined purposefully to gain a deeper understanding of the students' experience. Many teachers who practice responsiveness, including Ms. H, begin each day with a "this is where we left off yesterday" conversation. When students participate in these conversations, they engage in a retelling of the previous day.

They may point out salient questions, topics, lines of inquiry, and key conclusions, or even disagree about events on days prior. They may attribute ideas, or not. Transitions, as viewed by the teacher or researcher, are also useful places to look for evidence. Students may point out a line of questioning as irrelevant or off-task; or they may suggest what they see as a natural next step in their inquiry, as Ari did when he suggested researching the water cycle. Student affect in class and in interviews can act as a marker of discontinuity or flow (Czikszentmihalyi, 1990; Festinger, 1957). At the end of Day 9, for example, Ms. H asked students to share their final thoughts about the unit. A student named Andrew said: "It makes your mind // it makes your mind really start to work . . . and it makes you have a lot of questions." Another student, Sam, was not so positive: "Well, like, when I ask a question, you [Ms. H] go, 'I don't know. You tell me.' And then it's like [pretends to poke himself in the eye]." Sam's statement is a tangle of affect and agency; he expresses frustration with Ms. H's insistence that he answer his own questions.

Additional techniques for accessing students' subjective experience in school are discussed in Erickson et al. (2008) and Cook-Sather (2009). The analyses presented here avoid language that suggests there is a correct account of how the class got from talking about the puddle to talking about weather. While certain details of storylines can be confirmed or refuted—for example, the order that John's group conducted the experiments or ideas that Ms. H attributes to students—there is no single storyline characterizing the water cycle curriculum as it played out in Ms. H's class. The students, Ms. H, and the author all made sense of the unit in different ways, and, further, we reconstruct those accounts continuously. Thus, a reasonable outcome of studying the students' perspective in a responsive curriculum would be identification of key patterns, differences, and salient features of students' storylines, including a discussion of how next moves are selected, by whom, and for what purpose.

Implications

Responsive educators and researchers are interested in student thinking, but to date have not taken up the task of explicitly studying students' perspective on agency and flow in responsive teaching. Attention to the students' perspective in responsive teaching will push the community forward in two important ways: by situating responsive teaching within the broader discussion about curriculum sequencing in science education, and by spurring more systematic empirical work to document the impact of responsive teaching on all learners.

Larger trends in science curriculum development are towards increasingly predetermined sequences. The 1999 TIMSS video study found that U.S. science lessons consist of engaging activities and topics, but lack a strong content storyline to hold the activities together or to help students build deeper understanding of concepts (Roth & Givvin, 2008). Since the release of the TIMSS findings, teams

Curriculum from the Students' Perspective **101**

from the Biological Sciences Curriculum Study, Project 2061, Weizmann Institute for Science, and many other institutions have developed pre-sequenced curriculum materials that clearly lay out storylines for a particular topic or concept. In many cases, the sequences are somewhat flexible and allow teachers to adapt the storyline to their students' thinking. In extreme cases, these pre-sequenced curricula are the antithesis of responsive teaching and leave little room for teachers to deviate from the script to follow student ideas.

In both responsive and pre-sequenced curriculum, there is the goal of helping students build some sort of flow or continuity, but the nature of that continuity and how it is constructed differs. Proponents of a pre-sequenced approach argue that students see science as disconnected facts because the typical science course presents topics in precisely that way. Teachers may select topics and activities that appeal to students' interests, but the sequence does not build up into any larger unifying ideas in science. From this perspective, the priority for curricular reform is to create a sequence that allows students to recognize and utilize relationships between scientific knowledge (Fortus & Krajcik, 2013).

Proponents of responsive curriculum suggest that students' disconnected experience in science results primarily from science being treated as a body of knowledge to acquire, rather than a way of making sense of the world. Teaching practices and students' epistemological ideas related to science are linked (Smith, Maclin, Houghton, & Hennessey, 2000). Thus, the priority for curriculum reform from this perspective is to open up opportunities for students to build ideas collaboratively and to revise those ideas over time using epistemic criteria central to science such as causality, consistency, clarity, and intelligibility. The sequence of activities and topics emerges as students try to refine their ideas and as the class decides, *What might we do next in order to test, clarify, or further elaborate our ideas?* If we help students build on and refine their thinking collaboratively, then they will start seeing science as Einstein did—"nothing more than the refinement of everyday thinking" (as cited in van Zee, Hammer, Bell, Roy, & Peter, 2005). Further, responsive curricula allow for multiple storylines, rather than just one.

It would be naïve to try to end the debate between responsive and pre-sequenced curriculum, to seek in vain a single approach that works for all students, at all times, for all learning goals. Yet, there is room to improve the empirical rigor of the curriculum sequencing debates. While most curriculum designers presume that their sequences, whether emergent or predetermined, will make sense to students, few studies actually include empirical evidence to confirm (or refute) that assumption. Empirical validation of instructional sequences typically involves interviewing or surveying students pre- and post-instruction to establish shifts in their conceptual understanding, nature of science views, or motivation and affect towards science (Méheut, 2004), but not students' sense of agency or flow.[5]

The responsive teaching community can help shift these debates in a more productive direction by pushing for better empirical evidence and analysis of students' perspectives in both forms of curriculum. The responsive teaching community has developed tools for listening closely to students. These tools need to be marshaled in new ways so that we attend not only to the substance of student thinking and reasoning about natural phenomena, but also to how responsive teaching and curriculum looks and feels from the student's perspective.

Acknowledgments

Portions of this chapter originally appeared in Sikorski, T. (2012). *Developing an alternative perspective on coherence seeking in science classrooms.* Unpublished doctoral dissertation, University of Maryland, College Park, MD. Earlier versions of these arguments were presented at the 2013 Science Teaching Responsiveness Conference in Seattle, WA, and at the 2012 National Association for Research in Science Teaching Annual Conference in Indianapolis, IN.

The author thanks Editors Amy Robertson and Rachel Scherr for extremely helpful comments on prior versions of this chapter. As well, Matty Lau, Paul Hutchison, The George Washington University DBER Group, and University of Maryland Physics Education Research Group provided valuable insights on the data presented in this chapter. Finally, the author thanks Ms. H and her fifth-grade class of 2009.

This material is based on work supported by the National Science Foundation under Grant No. "Learning Progressions for Scientific Inquiry: A Model Implementation in the Context of Energy" NSF DRL 0732233. Any opinions, findings and conclusions, or recommendations expressed in this material are those of the author and do not necessarily reflect the views of the National Science Foundation.

Notes

1 Czikszentmihalyi (1990) uses *flow* to refer to a specific psychological experience characterized by intense yet effortless focus, a sort of special case that might be discovered through considering students' sense of flow of the activities, topics, and conversations in science class.
2 Thank you to Jennifer Lineback for the analogy.
3 van Zee, Hammer, Bell, Roy, & Peter (2005) demonstrate how co-writing a joint reconstruction of an inquiry experience can be used as a tool for accessing facilitators' and learners' perspectives.
4 However, Engle & Conant (2002) do use markers of metacognitive awareness as evidence of productive disciplinary engagement.
5 See Muller, Jain, Loesser, & Irby (2008) for an important exception.

References

Achieve, Inc. (2012). Next Generation Science Standards, 2nd draft. Retrieved from http:// www.nextgenscience.org/next-generation-science-standards

Ball, D. (1993). With an eye on the mathematical horizon: Dilemmas of teaching elementary school mathematics. *The Elementary School Journal, 9*(4), 373–397.

Ballenger, C. (1998). Three teachers' perspectives on knowing in science. In A. Rosebery & B. Warren (Eds.), *Boats, balloons, and classroom video: Science teaching as inquiry* (pp. 61–72). Portsmouth, NH: Heinemann.

Bartlett, F.C. (1932/1995). *Remembering: A study in experimental and social psychology.* Cambridge, UK: The University Press.

Coates, J. (1995). The negotiation of coherence in face-to-face interaction: Some examples from the extreme bounds. In M.A. Gernsbacher & T. Givon, (Eds.), *Coherence in spontaneous text* (pp. 41–58). Philadelphia, PA: John Benjamins.

Coffey, J.E., Hammer, D., Levin, D.M., & Grant, T. (2011). The missing disciplinary substance of formative assessment. *Journal of Research in Science Teaching, 48*(10), 1109–1136.

Cook-Sather, A. (2009). *Learning from the student's perspective: A sourcebook for effective teaching.* Boulder, CO: Paradigm.

Czikszentmihalyi, M. (1990). *Flow: The psychology of optimal experience.* New York, NY: HarperCollins.

Dennis, E. (1998). Floating balloons, floating theories. In A. Rosebery & B. Warren (Eds.), *Boats, balloons, and classroom video: Science teaching as inquiry* (pp. 13–24). Portsmouth, NH: Heinemann.

Duckworth, E. (1987). The virtues of not knowing. In E. Duckworth (Ed.), *"The having of wonderful ideas" and other essays on teaching and learning* (pp. 64–69). New York, NY: Teachers College Press.

Duckworth, E. (2001). *Tell me more: Listening to learners explain.* New York, NY: Teachers College Press.

Engle, R., & Conant, F. (2002). Guiding principles for fostering productive disciplinary engagement: Explaining an emergent argument in a community of learners classroom. *Cognition and Instruction, 20*(4), 399–483.

Erickson, F., Bagrodia, R., Cook-Sather, A., Espinoza, M., Jurow, S., Shultz, J., & Spencer, J. (2008). Students' experience of school curriculum: The everyday circumstances of granting and withholding assent to learn. In F.M. Connelly, M.F. He, & J. Phillion (Eds.), *The SAGE handbook of curriculum and instruction* (pp. 198–219). Thousand Oaks, CA: SAGE Publications.

Festinger, L. (1957). *A theory of cognitive dissonance.* Stanford, CA: Stanford University Press.

Fortus, D., & Krajcik, J. (2013). Curriculum coherence and learning progressions. In B. Fraser, C. McRobbie, & K. Tobin (Eds.), *Second international handbook of science education* (pp. 783–798). Dordrecht, The Netherlands: Springer Verlag.

Gallas, K. (1995). *Talking their way into science: Hearing children's questions and theories, responding with curriculum.* New York, NY: Teachers College Press.

Hammer, D. (1997). Discovery teaching, discovery learning. *Cognition & Instruction, 15*(4), 485–529.

Hammer, D., Goldberg, F., & Fargason, S. (2012). Responsive teaching and the beginnings of energy in a third grade classroom. *Review of Science, Mathematics and ICT Education, 6*(1), 51–72.

Hammer, D., & van Zee, E.H. (2006). *Seeing the science in children's thinking: Case studies of student inquiry in physical science.* Portsmouth, NH: Heinemann.

Hutchison, P., & Hammer, D. (2010). Attending to student epistemological framing in a science classroom. *Science Education, 94*(3), 506–524.

Jaber, L. (2014). *Affective dynamics of students' disciplinary engagement in science.* Unpublished doctoral dissertation, Tufts University, Boston, MA.

Kuipers, J., Viechnicki, G.B., Massoud, L.A., & Wright, L.J. (2009). Science, culture, and equity in curriculum: An ethnographic approach to the study of a highly-rated curriculum unit. In K. Bruna & K. Gomez (Eds.), *The work of language in multicultural classrooms* (pp. 241–268). New York, NY: Routledge.

Levin, D., Hammer, D., Elby, A., & Coffey, J. (2013). *Becoming a responsive science teacher: Focusing on student thinking in secondary science.* Arlington, VA: NSTA Press.

Lindfors, J.W. (1999). *Children's inquiry: Using language to make sense of the world.* New York, NY: Teachers College Press.

Maskiewicz, A., & Winters, V. (2012). Understanding the co-construction of inquiry practices: A case study of a responsive teaching environment. *Journal of Research in Science Teaching, 49*(4), 429–464.

Méheut, M. (2004). Teaching-learning sequences: Aims and tools for science education research. *International Journal of Science Education, 26*(5), 515–535.

Muller, J., Jain, S., Loeser, H., & Irby, D. (2008). Lessons learned about integrating a medical school curriculum: Perceptions of students, faculty and curriculum leaders. *Medical Education, 42,* 778–785.

Rosebery, A.S., & Warren, B. (Eds.) (1998). *Boats, balloons and classroom video: Science teaching as inquiry.* Portsmouth, NH: Heinemann.

Roth, K., & Givvin, K. (2008). Implications for math and science instruction from the TIMSS 1999 Video Study. *Principal Leadership,* 22–27.

Russ, R., Lee, V., & Sherin, B. (2012). Framing in cognitive clinical interviews: Cues and interpretations. *Science Education, 96*(4), 573–599.

Scardamalia, M. (2002). Collective cognitive responsibility for the advancement of knowledge. In B. Smith (Ed.), *Liberal education in a knowledge society* (pp. 67–98). Chicago: Open Court.

Sikorski, T.R.J. (2012). *Developing an alternative perspective on coherence seeking in science classrooms.* Unpublished doctoral dissertation, University of Maryland, College Park, MD.

Smith, C.L., Maclin, D., Houghton, C., & Hennessey, M.G. (2000). Sixth-grade students' epistemologies of science: The impact of school science experiences on epistemological development. *Cognition and Instruction, 18,* 349–422.

Stevens, R. (2010). Learning as a members' phenomenon: Toward an ethnographically adequate science of learning. *National Society for the Study of Education, 109*(1), 82–97.

van Zee, E., Hammer. D., Bell, M., Roy, P., & Peter, J. (2005). Learning and teaching as inquiry: A case study of elementary school teachers' investigations of light. *Science Education, 89*(6), 1007–1042.

Varelas, M., Pappas, C., Kane, J., Arsenault, A., Hankes, J., & Cowan, B. (2008). Urban primary-grade children think and talk science: Curricular and instructional practices that nurture participation and argumentation. *Science Education, 92,* 65–95.

5

NAVIGATING THE CHALLENGES OF TEACHING RESPONSIVELY

An Insider's Perspective

April Cordero Maskiewicz

With the current emphasis on student-centered instruction, we have learned to minimize "telling" in our classrooms, but in many cases we have replaced it with questions and discussions that masquerade as an exploration of ideas (Lindfors, 1999). We often inquire in ways that only reveal what the students already know about the content or that elicit the target ideas that we want students to learn (Coffey, Hammer, & Levin, 2011). In essence, the shift from lecturing to questioning has mainly been a superficial change because our philosophical position about our role as teachers has not shifted. We still see ourselves as "knower" and deliverer-of-information, and pedagogical success continues to be measured by student attainment of specific content goals.

Yet in a responsive classroom, the teacher's role is to listen to and identify ways to build upon *students'* thinking—cultivate it—to advance students' scientific knowledge. Several years ago, I became intrigued with what it could mean for student ideas to have a significant voice in my biology classroom, to practice *responsive teaching* with student ideas influencing the path of instruction. Putting my students' thinking in the foreground meant shifting my focus from what "I wanted them to know" to what they were actually saying and thinking. During this time I have come to understand my new role in this environment as one of participant/learner, where students' ideas become the objects of inquiry instead of the disciplinary concepts described in textbooks and standards. This shift, however, is much easier to write about than to enact. As I gave careful consideration to my students' ideas, I had to relinquish a significant amount of control over topics of discussion and investigation, as well as the schedule—what the class would be doing the next day or even later that hour.

106 April Cordero Maskiewicz

The purpose of this chapter is to reflect on some of the challenges of teaching responsively when scientific inquiry is the goal. In this environment the ideas offered by students are numerous, and the paths one can pursue are limitless, and, consequently, tensions arise for the teacher as instructional decisions have to be made. In this self-study I describe these tensions as I practiced responsive teaching during a two-week professional development science workshop. Although the learners were practicing elementary teachers, the uncertainties and challenges I experienced are consistent with those described by other responsive practitioners working with elementary and high school students (Ball, 1993; Gallas, 1995; Hammer, 1997; van Zee & Minstrell, 1997). My explicit focus on the challenges of promoting mechanistic thinking in scientific inquiry adds to these self-reflection accounts.

Setting the Stage: Scientific Inquiry and Mechanistic Explanations

One objective for science class is to help learners recognize the value of mechanistic explanations. The thought is that students should attempt to explain how things happen (whether or not their ideas are correct), and teachers should recognize and promote those efforts in service of scientific inquiry (Chinn & Maholtra, 2002; Hammer, Russ, Mikeska, & Scherr, 2008; Russ, Scherr, Hammer, & Mikeska, 2008). According to Russ et al. (2008), what counts as mechanistic and thus valuable for scientific explanation and inquiry are accounts that (a) are non-teleological, (b) causal, (c) built from experience, and (d) describe underlying or relevant structure. In other words, mechanistic explanations provide "a causal account for why something happens in the way it does" (Reiser et al., 2001, p. 276).

I define scientific inquiry as *the pursuit of coherent, mechanistic accounts of natural phenomena* (Hammer et al., 2008); it is something that students are "doing" as they pursue an explanation for an intriguing phenomenon. This definition aligns with the Next Generation Science Standards (Achieve, Inc., 2013), which state that students should engage in the enterprise of science as a whole: "the wondering, investigating, questioning, data collecting and analyzing" (p. 1, Appendix H).

Scientific inquiry—as I defined it—is best facilitated through responsive teaching, and thus inquiry and responsiveness are complementary. As teachers elicit and respond to students' ideas and reasoning, learners come to understand the science classroom as a place to wonder about how things work, to draw on personal experiences to develop explanations, and to consider and debate each other's ideas in pursuit of the best account of a phenomenon. In this environment, explanations that are consistent and account for multiple observations will emerge as "better" explanations. As such, the pursuit of coherent, mechanistic explanations becomes a characteristic of the responsive classroom.

The Practitioner's Perspective

A precedent exists for reflecting on one's teaching practice and acknowledging the challenges of changing one's pedagogy in order to generate insight and knowledge of specific teaching practices (Ball, 1993; Gallas, 1995; Hammer, 1997; Lampert, 1985; Lampert & Ball, 1998; van Zee, 2000). Some of these self-studies articulate the tensions involved in genuine, extended attention to the substance of student reasoning (Ball, 1993), and common to these self-studies are the instructors' emphasis on creating a *responsive community* in which students do the majority of the intellectual work as they listen, respond to, and challenge each other's ideas.

In this chapter I build on these practitioners' reflections about being responsive to student ideas by adding my own experiences and struggles with when to step in and how to guide the learning while maintaining responsiveness in a class where scientific inquiry is the primary goal. I don't claim to provide an ideal model of how to teach responsively or to offer a comprehensive discussion of the advantages and disadvantages of responsive teaching. Rather, I offer an insider's perspective of the tensions I experienced when I practiced responsive teaching, and I reflect on the decisions I made. My hope is that this reflection illuminates the challenges of teaching responsively, not because they can be resolved or eliminated, but rather because we (as instructors that teach responsively) need to learn to expect these tensions if we are going to invite and honor students' thinking in the classroom. I negotiated the challenges of facilitating inquiry responsively by prioritizing some activities (e.g. the "doing" of science) over others (e.g. covering the disciplinary core content) and came to peace with the tensions I experienced.

Context for This Self-Study

Overall Project

The professional development (PD) workshop in which the teachers in this chapter participated was part of an NSF-funded project to, in part, help teachers learn to facilitate scientific inquiry.[1] The goal for the PD workshops was to (a) engage teachers in scientific inquiry and (b) help them recognize and promote *students'* productive engagement in inquiry. Often inquiry is included in curricula as an "add-on" activity, but this PD project took inquiry as a central objective, with both the teacher and learners bringing scientific curiosities and understandings to class so that the community could examine and debate the merits of those ideas and extend their own understanding. The project spanned three years and included one- or two-week workshops each summer and biweekly teacher meetings during the school year. Several 15–20 hour modular curricular materials were developed by our research group to provide teachers with a context with which to explore and promote responsive teaching through science inquiry (see http://cipstrends.sdsu.edu/responsiveteaching/).

108 April Cordero Maskiewicz

The Summer 2 Workshop

The workshop that provides the context for this chapter spanned two weeks and took place during the second summer of the three-year PD project. Fourteen practicing third- through sixth-grade teachers from a large school district in southern California participated in morning "science talks," designed to model responsive teaching through science inquiry, and afternoon discussions of classroom video, often taken from their own classrooms, where children's scientific reasoning was on display. This second summer built upon the scientific inquiry the teachers had previously engaged in (Summer 1 and during the biweekly meetings during the previous school year).

Composting and decomposition provided the context for the two-and-a-half to three-hour morning science talks in Summer 2. As the teachers engaged in this sustained inquiry, their own ideas were validated, taken up, and extended by their peers. My intent was that as participants involved others in their sense-making about how or why something works, they would begin to see themselves and their peers as curious, creative scientists. The overarching PD goal was that over the course of three years, as the teachers participated in discourse with others to make connections, provide support, question, clarify, generalize, and refine explanations, they would discover that science *is* inquiry. We hoped these experiences would help them approach their own science instruction in the same way.

Prior to the start of the workshop, I developed two specific objectives for the morning science talks.

> *Objective 1*: Participants would "take up" (become intrigued by and invested in) the phenomena of what occurs in a compost pile as things change and seem to disappear.
>
> *Objective 2*: Participants would develop a tangible, mechanistic model of the process of decomposition.

Objective 1 intentionally contrasts with the common expectation the classroom learner has of trying to discern the response the teacher is looking for, or simply doing the task the teacher told him or her to do without being intellectually invested in it. Rather, my desire was for the participants to become intrinsically interested in making sense of and developing their own models for what happens during decomposition. Evidence that I had achieved this objective would be revealed by the types of ideas and questions proposed by the participants, as well as their involvement in the discussions.

For Objective 2, I hoped that by reflecting on their own and their peers' ideas, experiences, and reasoning, the participants would have the opportunity to refine their accounts of decomposition. Achieving Objective 2 would mean that the participants arrived at a meaningful, mechanistic, mutually agreed upon explanation of the phenomenon of decomposition, which might not necessarily be scientifically accurate.

As I pursued my two objectives for the summer workshop, I navigated a variety of challenges, which revolved around how to be responsive to ideas while still influencing the direction of inquiry. I use examples in this chapter to explore three of these challenges: (1) the challenge of fostering mechanistic reasoning, (2) the challenge of balancing facilitation and control, and (3) the challenge of allowing "wrong" ideas to linger. Presenting these challenges individually may lead one to incorrectly assume they are distinct, but they are, in fact, quite interrelated, and teasing them apart is merely an artifact of recording them on paper. For each challenge I provide the context surrounding the emergence of the challenge, a description of the tensions I encountered, a reflection on the decisions I made, and a discussion of the larger implications of each challenge for teachers. Most of the scenarios presented below describe events from the first week of the workshop because the challenges first emerged during that time; nevertheless, these challenges continued throughout the morning science talks during our second week.

Tensions and Challenges

Challenge 1: Fostering Mechanistic Reasoning

The context. I wanted workshop participants to begin thinking mechanistically about the process of decomposition as soon as possible. My goal for the opening day was to offer a few thought-provoking, open-ended questions that would intrigue participants and motivate them to begin considering what happens to things that decompose: How do they decompose? And where does the stuff go? By asking open-ended questions and eliciting and encouraging their thoughts and ideas, I hoped to create an environment in which possibilities and potentials became the focal point, as opposed to facts and correct ideas. Yet I also wanted to make sure that we shared a common understanding of what we meant by decomposition during our discourse, since it's not uncommon for an adult to have little if any experience with the product of decomposition. It seemed to me that we could not hypothesize about how things break down and decompose if we did not first reflect on what something looks like before and after it decomposes. Therefore, I chose to begin the workshop with a brief discussion about compost and composting.

Participants had been asked two weeks prior to the workshop to start small compost heaps of their own; no other directions were provided. Several of the teachers did in fact start composting in a bottle, or created a compost pile in their yard. By building on these experiences, the opening question was designed to ease the participants into a discussion, as well as to provide an opportunity for everyone to have a common understanding of composting and what the product of a compost pile looks like.

Day 1: The tension—observational versus mechanistic accounts. Tensions associated with the direction of the discussion surfaced within the

110 April Cordero Maskiewicz

first half hour of the science talk on Day 1. The science talk opened with the question: "Who has a compost heap? Tell us about it." Many of the participants had something to share: what they added to their compost pile, what the end product of the compost pile looked like, the color of the compost soil, the texture, smell, etc. After about 15 minutes of spirited sharing, a comment from a participant allowed me to propose a new question with the intent of shifting the group toward focusing on the mechanism of decomposition: "You said *it* [the stuff you placed in the compost pile] decomposes; how does that happen?"

The room became silent and, after what felt like an uncomfortably long time, one participant offered the idea that insects might be eating the composting materials. A flurry of suggestions followed for how to improve composting, including adding worms, providing air, and other ideas. With this one comment about insects, the participants immediately shifted the conversation back to what's needed to create a better compost heap (i.e. how to get things to decompose) as opposed to *what is happening* inside the compost heap.

At one point, Cindy offered an idea about the role of water and air in a compost heap and I capitalized on her idea in an attempt to once again shift the discussion towards *how* things decompose:

1. *Cindy:* . . . If you have an active compost—if I let mine go for a series of months and I turn it, clearly you can see almost a layering up through that compost heap where it's more dense and broken down at the bottom then at the top. There has to be water and air for those little critters to do what they do best.

2. *Instructor:* So, the water and air serves the purpose of providing an environment for [the critters] to do their thing?

3. *Cindy:* An environment for the stuff to break down and mix with each other.

4. *Instructor:* Is it coming apart and mixing in with each other as a result of these [critters] or as a result of air and water?

5. *Cindy:* I think it's both.

6. *Instructor:* Air and water—so it facilitates insects and it also breaks things down on its own?

7. *Cindy:* I have a neighbor who religiously adds water to their compost. I don't do that. I look at it; if it's dry I add water. If it doesn't need water I don't add water.

8. *Sam:* I haven't added water once to mine. I'm wondering, did I screw mine up because I didn't add water?

9. *Jill:* There was probably moisture in there at the beginning.

10. *Sam:* I have cantaloupe in there so maybe that's where the water is coming from.

11. *Sara:* What are you putting in there? (multiple voices at once)

The Challenges of Teaching Responsively **111**

By asking for clarification about the role of water and air, I hoped to shift the conversation away from observations about composting. However, Cindy's emphasis on the importance of water in the compost pile led Sam to wonder what she may have done wrong when creating her compost pile, and the conversation shifted back towards a description of what should be placed in a compost heap. Clearly the group was still thinking about and interested in the *what* of composting versus the *process* of decomposition. After several minutes, the discussion transitioned back towards various factors that affect decomposition: air, water, sun. Yet procedures and experiences continued to be the emphasis as the participants focused on what to do to create a productive compost pile.

An hour into the discussion I chose to verbalize with the group the tension I felt because I saw this as an opportunity to discuss one of the challenges of responsive teaching with teachers who were learning how to be responsive in the classroom. I explained that I did not know where to go next to move the discussion forward, and a fellow PD facilitator proposed the idea of focusing on the decomposition of one item. I then asked the group: "When you throw a banana peel into a compost heap, what happens?" This phenomenon-focused question successfully shifted the teachers away from discussing their own composting experiences and into discussing what happens during decomposition as they reasoned about the fate of the banana peel.

Reflecting on my decisions. These 80 minutes of the opening day discussion were unexpectedly challenging for me. The first 15 minutes went as planned, as several participants enthusiastically discussed their composting experiences, offering knowledge about how to compost or what their compost looked like. When one participant made the assertion that the "stuff in the compost decomposes," I took the opportunity to redirect the conversation towards a causal question. Yet this shift from thinking about their composting experiences to thinking about how decomposition works may have been too abrupt for participants, and the conversation immediately ceased. Or it may have been that the participants had a different expectation about what type of conversation we were engaging in. In either case, whenever I tried to guide the direction of the discussion towards the *process* of decomposition, participants became quiet and *I* had to sustain the conversation. Notice in the first half of the transcript that I prompted Cindy to think about the role water and air played in the breaking down of materials (lines 2, 4, and 6). By intervening in this way I was trying to shift the discussion towards *how* decomposition occurs, but because this focus was not compelling for the participants, it required continuous prompting on my part. Yet, when the discussion centered on *procedures* for composting, the participants sustained the conversation, and my role as the instructor was more of a record keeper recording ideas on the board.

Why were so many more interested in discussing observations and procedures (e.g. how to set up the conditions for decomposition) as opposed to underlying

112 April Cordero Maskiewicz

causes? One possible explanation is that it is easier to discuss personal experiences about composting than to think about the underlying invisible mechanisms of decomposition. Observations about phenomena relate directly to our own experiences. Mechanistic explanations are more challenging because they require formulating an explanatory model that we may not have direct experience with. As with most biological and physical phenomena, the mechanism of decomposition is abstract and invisible. Thus, participants might have been less confident about their explanatory ideas as compared with their physical and observational experiences. (Recall the silence that followed the first "how" question only 15 minutes into Day 1.)

I had not expected the strong attraction toward composting procedures, nor did I at the time consider it productive for promoting mechanistic reasoning. In hindsight, I recognize that there were implied mechanisms in the explanations for how to create a better compost heap; yet the participants were not eager to engage in a discussion about *why* water or air improves the rate of decomposition. In the moment I did not know the best way to get the conversation to shift to what was happening to the items in a compost heap in a responsive way. Asking the phenomenon-focused question about the banana finally shifted the discussion away from suggestions for how to compost, but only temporarily. Observational and procedural conversations prevailed for the first few days.

Reflecting on the challenge of promoting a mechanistic focus. Some may argue that the participants' focus on the act of composting was my fault, that I should not have begun the workshop by asking about personal experiences with composting. Yet I still believe it was important that as a group we shared a common understanding of what the product of decomposition looks like so as to create puzzlement about where all the "stuff" the items are made of disappears to. In addition, developing causal explanations usually involves reflecting on personal experiences and knowledge, and the teachers' experiences composting at home could help promote that way of thinking. Finally, discussing our composting experiences helped promote the establishment of our group as a community of inquiring scientists. Yet there were unexpected consequences to my opening the discussion with a focus on personal experiences. I wanted the participants to talk about the underlying mechanisms for why or how the variables they proposed affected decomposition. Thus on the first day, when a participant stated that the "stuff in the compost decomposes," it seemed obvious to ask about that process. However, this redirection was not something that emerged from the group; rather it was a conversation *I* wanted the participants to have. Participants were thinking differently about the purpose or intent of the conversation and seemed uninterested in switching focus.

Why not just tell the participants that we were no longer going to discuss the doing of composting? At any time I could have explained my objective and the norms or structure of scientific explanations. Then if the discussion shifted away from the mechanistic explanations and towards procedural ones, I could intervene by revealing how the explanations were different. I believed at the time, and still do, that this instructional move would undermine my goal that the participants develop expectations that scientific inquiry is about their *own* pursuit of an account for a phenomenon. I feared that asserting my authority in this way might shift the learners from thinking and reasoning about the phenomenon into the mode of trying to figure out what I wanted them to be saying or doing (Tang, Coffey, Elbin, & Levin, 2010; Coffey, Hammer, & Levin, 2011). As the instructor, I wanted to be careful not to make science about pleasing the teacher or pursuing the answer the teacher expects (Jimenez-Aleixandre, Rodriguez, & Duschl, 2000). The trade-off for not "telling" was that much class time was spent on sharing observations that were not mechanistic explanations. The payoff, however, was that the participants' ideas continued to be the focal point of the discussions. This preserved the participants' expectation that they were responsible for drawing on their *own* knowledge and experiences to make sense of decomposition and composting.

In summary, I endured the challenge of persistent procedural and observational explanations during the first three days of the workshop by prioritizing the learners' agency over their explanations. I tried to take participants' ideas seriously and value them as topics of discussion, thus passing down the responsibility to the participants to pursue their own explanations. This meant redefining my role in the classroom; I tried to become an explorer of the ideas along with the participants instead of an evaluator and provider of information. And over time, this shift in roles empowered the participants to share ideas and evaluate the merits of those ideas with each other. The tension that non-mechanistic explanations posed continued to persist for me, but by setting the learners' ownership of ideas as a priority over their type of explanation I allowed the generative conversations to continue. That does not mean, however, that I did not push for mechanistic explanations at every turn (e.g. trying to make their mechanism explicit by probing their procedural comments), but I was only willing to do so in ways that preserved the participants' agency in the activity.

Challenge 2: The Challenge of Balancing Facilitation and Control

The context. To authentically engage in the pursuit of a scientific explanation, students need the autonomy to pose their own questions, to have their own ideas heard, and to assess the quality of those ideas. Allowing student ideas to take center stage, however, requires a shift in classroom culture, new norms and practices, and a belief that students learn more when they do the intellectual work of making sense of phenomena (Michaels & O'Connor, 2012). This shift to give more power and authority to the students and their ideas can be complicated and comes with some unfamiliar and uncomfortable choices. If we are not cognizant of and intentional about the challenges of these new roles as listeners, co-explorers, and facilitators, then we may find that our agenda interferes with our ability to really listen and hear students' ideas.

114 April Cordero Maskiewicz

As I reflect on my pedagogical approach during the first few days of science talks, I question if I was as responsive as I could have been to participants' ideas. While navigating the conversations, I began filtering students' ideas through my own expectations of what I wanted them to be saying, and this created conflict for me. Supporting learners as they engage in scientific inquiry necessitated that I let go of my need to know exactly what ideas and content would be covered, including sacrificing my schedule for what the class should be doing at any particular moment.

Day 2: The tension—chaotic discussions versus fully developed mechanistic explanations. At the start of the second day, I posted at the front of the room two lists summarizing our work from the previous day's discussions. One list included the ideas the group proposed for possible causes for decomposition (animals, air, etc.), and the other was a list of phenomena we were familiar with or noticed about decomposition and composting:

List A (How decomposition occurs)

Living things eat items and produce waste

- Insects
- Worms
- Fungi
- Bacteria

Compost heaps

- May get warm
- Smell bad (sometimes)
- Layering items can improve smell
- If too cold, things don't decompose

List B (Observations we "know" of)

Natural elements do "something"

- Sun (light and heat)
- Moisture
- Air (or oxygen)
- Temperature
- Heavy items cause compression
- Turning compost speeds up decomposition
- Redwood deck doesn't decompose
- Bobcat in cavern fully preserved
- Mummies do not decompose

Participants were asked to break into small groups and consider how the causes for what is going on in the compost pile (List A) can explain phenomena that they observe about composting (List B). After 20 minutes, the whole group reassembled to share their conclusions. The subsequent conversation seemed disorganized and unfocused as participants discussed ideas about what it means for things to decompose (e.g. breaking apart, rotting), physical versus chemical changes, optimum conditions for decomposition, the molecular composition of things that decompose, comparisons of things that do and do not decompose, the role of organisms in decomposition, and the nutrient value of compost soil.

During this 54-minute conversation, ideas were tossed around, ignored, and almost always left unanswered. Consider, for example, the following excerpt:

1. *Paula:* My biggest one [question] is how do we KNOW it's finished. When is decomp- you know, the end product we are looking for. Are we looking for the [compost] tea? Are we looking for the mushy stuff? How do we know it's done?

2. *Sam:* And that came up both in terms of our compost pile but also in terms of what happens in the forest. When is THAT done? How do we know?

3. *Paula:* The other thing about the environment that has- is when it is void of living things.

4. *Susan:* There are some things that don't decompose, and so-

5. *Ericka:* McDonald's French fries.

6. *Susan:* Right. Or the bobcat. So, I'm wondering (pause)

7. *Instructor:* So I'm wondering, the bobcat didn't decompose. Some of you are posing- as a result of conditions. Are there some things that never decompose even in optimal conditions?

8. *Sara:* Are you guys saying moisture that breaks things apart is not really decomposition? But [instead] decomposition is what living organisms do? (pause)

9. *Ellen:* I don't know.

10. *Instructor:* Okay.

11. *Sara:* Are you guys saying, for your hypothesis, that moisture and heat breaks things apart? Are you saying that's not decomposition, and that what really is decomposition is what living organisms do?

12. *Susan:* That's what I'm saying. I don't know about my group.

13. *Cindy:* I mean, I think there is a whole range of things. That's why we are struggling with when is it finished. When does it start? I mean, it probably starts with exposure to air. And so, that's another big open discussion. I think of it more that that's just a phase or a stage of it.

14. *Instructor:* So stages of decomposition. So both are decomposition, but different stages of it? Breaking apart into [smaller] pieces of same stuff, and then you said a chemical change? Other questions?

15. *Audrey:* Marilyn was saying, if you had the right conditions, even Styrofoam and plastic would decompose. That's something that you have to think about, because I don't know.

16. *Linda:* And those conditions may not be here [on Earth], get it close to the sun and yeah

116 April Cordero Maskiewicz

17. *Audrey:*   It would have to be a chemical reaction
18. *Linda:*   But it wouldn't be the optimal conditions, if it's not decomposing.
19. *Ellen:*   But then you just said, close to sun, so melt. Melting is not decomposition.
20. *Linda:*   Burning up. Right.
21. *Ellen:*   Do you know what I'm saying? So it all goes back to the—
22. *Veronica:*   Wait, but don't they say it takes something like 2,000 years or something to decompose a diaper.
23. *Ellen:*   Yeah
24. *Veronica:*   So it *does* decompose.
25. *Ellen:*   But she is saying, the Styrofoam; if I put it up to the sun it'll decompose. But that's melting, not decomposing.
26. *Instructor:*   If I poured a chemical in there, . . . if I had some chemical and I poured it in my Styrofoam cup, is that decomposing?
27. *Belinda:*   No. That's a chemical change.
28. *Sara:*   But we just said, that's a chemical change.
29. *Jill:*   It goes back to the whole thing—what is [decomposition]?

In only four minutes, the participants questioned how to know when decomposition is finished, how it is that some things do not decompose such as French Fries and a bobcat found in an underground cavern, and what is and is not considered decomposition, including the role of water, the sun, and chemical changes. At this point the group had been discussing for 24 minutes, with more questions generated than answered. And only once did the conversation specifically focus on the initial question for the day—how causes of decomposition can explain our observations of phenomena. After allowing this discussion to continue for another 30 minutes, we ended the science talk for the day.

Reflecting on my decisions. As the instructor I experienced a lot of anxiety while facilitating what seemed to be a chaotic discussion that darted from topic to topic. Yet, as previously mentioned, I allowed this discussion to continue for 54 minutes. In my reflection notes for the day I recorded some thoughts:

> Should I stop the conversation and redirect towards the original question? Or do I allow the conversation to continue because many participants are sharing ideas and questioning others? The lack of direction in the conversation makes me question whether this is productive; yet, the participants are discussing both how things decompose and what happens to things that decompose.

In the moment I didn't recognize the scientific value of this discussion because I felt that I was not in control of the conversation, nor did I know where it might be going or when it might end. While I was clearly uncomfortable with the scattered nature of the conversation, I nevertheless chose to allow the conversation to continue for an extended period of time because the participants were

The Challenges of Teaching Responsively   **117**

enthusiastic, engaged, and invested in the topic (note that 12 of the 14 teachers were participating in the short four-minute excerpt included above). In other words, I recognized the participants' investment in the conversation and made that a priority above my own desire to make progress on the day's topic—to develop mechanistic explanations. Recall that my first objective for the workshop was for students to "take up (become intrigued by and discuss) the phenomena of what occurs in a compost pile." So although I was not at all sure in the moment that the discussion was a productive scientific discussion, I did appreciate the participants' ownership of the discussion.

When reviewing and analyzing this discussion after the fact, I realized that although the conversation diverged quite a bit from the original question posed, the group *was* clarifying their own understanding while discussing ideas related to the process of decomposition. Considering what it means for decomposition to be "finished" (lines 1–3) involves thinking about the process of decomposition—what is happening *during* decomposition. Clarifying what is and is not considered decomposition emerged from thinking about things that do not decompose (lines 4–7), and these ideas led Sara to question the proposal that water breaking things apart is not decomposition, whereas organism consumption is (line 8). In fact, as participants wrestled with deciding what constitutes decomposition (lines 9–29) they began to develop their own specific, plausible meaning for the term.

Productive nascent mechanistic reasoning can include identifying parameters that reproduce an outcome (e.g. "If I add water to my compost it decomposes faster"), exploring implications (e.g. "If this compost box has worms in it and this one does not, the food scraps in the box with worms will disappear faster"), creating representations of an idea (e.g. drawing a diagram), creating analogies (e.g. "The nutrients go up the roots like water goes up a paper towel"), and debating a point from different perspectives (Hammer et al., 2008; Russ et al., 2008). These aspects of mechanistic reasoning are the germ of scientific explanations, and it is important to recognize them as such.

Had I been carefully listening to the substance of the participants' ideas, I may have heard the incipient aspects of their mechanistic reasoning and been able to craft more specific, productive follow-up questions directly related to the underlying mechanisms in their ideas. Instead, I felt anxious about making progress towards my second objective—to have participants begin to develop mechanistic explanations early in the workshop—and this hindered my ability to listen. When I didn't hear micro-level explanations of the processes of decomposition, I became troubled because I felt that being responsive to the participants' ideas and interests conflicted with my second objective. Indeed, one of the challenges of responsive teaching is learning to listen to the substance of student ideas without filtering stated ideas through our own expectations about what *ought* to be brought forth and discussed. So, although I was not focusing on hearing scientifically accurate core concepts, I *was* evaluating their ideas through my "mechanistic explanation" filter and therefore didn't hear their budding mechanistic reasoning.

118 April Cordero Maskiewicz

Reflecting on the challenge of balancing facilitation and control. I have found that teaching responsively can create an anxiety about next moves that doesn't seem to exist with more traditional curricula, where the objective is focused on standards-based or textbook concepts. With a traditional structured curriculum, a set of content objectives guides the direction of activities and discussions, and the instructor continually redirects the participants to focus on the question or topic at hand, leading learners towards the intended scientific idea. Students learn to wait to be given the right answer, which, in effect, could lead them to devalue their own ideas and understandings. When teaching responsively, however, the instructor's role is to facilitate in a way that promotes the learners to take up the responsibility for making sense of and explaining a phenomenon.

Self-sustaining chaotic discussions, like those described in the episode above, are not uncommon when teaching responsively, and the challenges navigating these conversations persist (Gallas, 1995). (See also a video example here: http://www.studentsthinking.org/rtsm). I often struggled with my desire to redirect or gain control over what we were discussing and how we were discussing it. Added tensions arose for me as I grappled with when to intervene or allow continued discussion, and when to leave a topic for another topic without "closure." And only in retrospect did I discover that my desire to be in control led to an anxiety which inhibited me from hearing the learners' nascent mechanistic reasoning.

Adjusting to this challenge of balancing facilitation and control lies, once again, in establishing one's priorities. I found that if I kept returning to my primary objective—for students to have ownership of the ideas being generated and the explanations we arrived at—then I was able to become more comfortable with allowing students' conversations to run their course. As the instructor, I could have asserted my control at any time by stopping a conversation, restating my initial question, and redirecting the topic of discussion. Yet just because I have this option does not make it the best option. Being responsive means I had to be willing to pursue unexpected tangents and to follow up on unique solutions or disagreements in order for the learners to accept that the expectations of this learning environment were different from a traditional one. I was at times successful at this, but at the cost of feeling anxious about not being in control. Although we may feel that we've lost control in these situations, Lindfors (1999) explains that we have not lost *power*:

> I submit that what the teacher is giving up is control but not power. Indeed, in exploratory classroom genres, the measure of her loss of control may be precisely the measure of her gain in power, for if her goal in such events is to better understand the children's thinking, then the more that the thinking can reveal itself, the more fully she reaches her goal.
>
> (p. 174)

The Challenges of Teaching Responsively **119**

If we really mean to make the substance of our students' ideas and reasoning the focal point, then we have to accept that there will be times when we feel we have lost control, but it is at those times that we might rest assured that we are being responsive. Our new teacher role as participant/learner becomes realized in these instances.

For me, prioritizing learners' ownership of the conversation and its direction allowed me to make intentional—albeit challenging—decisions about when and how to intervene. I now recognize that engaging deeply with students' ideas helps to control your desire to interfere with their sense-making because you begin to see the value in those ideas and the productive directions they can take the class. Thus, surrendering control over the course content and timing is best practiced by sustained concentration on the ideas and not on our own goals.

Challenge 3: What to Do About "Wrong" Ideas

The context. Although we currently hear a lot about the importance of "process" in the science classroom, most teachers, parents, and administrators cringe if you say that you value process over content—that you would allow students to leave the classroom with an incorrect scientific idea because they were engaging so deeply in the practices of science. Yet, engaging in scientific inquiry responsively means that the learner—not the teacher—has the freedom, power, and responsibility to recognize a confusion, identify an inconsistency, and clarify one's understanding through argument with others. In a responsive classroom, when possible, it is the students' ideas, correct or incorrect, that are the ones under investigation. And it is the learners' engagement with the ideas that prompts them to reassess their understanding and, as such, their knowledge becomes increasingly sophisticated over time (Engle & Conant, 2002). By not immediately banishing incorrect ideas, the responsive teacher grants students the opportunity to identify the flaws in their initial understanding.

Day 6: The tension. There were numerous times throughout the 18 hours of science talks when ideas and explanations were proposed that were scientifically incorrect. Consider, for example, our discussion about what constitutes "decomposition" during the first few days. Decomposition is defined by scientists as the process of bacteria or fungi converting organic material into inorganic material. Yet early on in the first week, many incorrect ideas about what is and what is not considered decomposition were proposed: insect digestion or the effect of air or water on substances (by breaking them into smaller pieces), neither of which constitutes decomposition. During the first few days of the workshop, encouraging the participants to pursue these ideas as possible explanations was not as challenging for me because my focus was on trying to get the participants to discuss and explore the *process* of decomposition: to shift from procedures and observations to mechanistic accounts. Therefore any causal idea was encouraged.

120 April Cordero Maskiewicz

Listening past these incorrect ideas became more challenging as reasoning mechanistically became routine. By the end of the first week, most of the participants had taken up the pursuit of trying to understand and make sense of the process of decomposition, and by Day 5 they were proposing mechanistic accounts of what happens during decomposition. Because I no longer needed to listen as intensely for ways to cultivate mechanistic reasoning, the incorrect ideas became more obvious to me. As a result, I now found it more challenging to prompt the group to explore all ideas, including those that were less correct than others. A group's presentation from Day 6 exemplifies this difficulty.

I began Day 6 by posing the question, "Why compost?," which was a question a participant had posed on Day 1 and which resurfaced several times during the first week. What participants were really seeking was an understanding of the role or function of decomposition in nature. After posing this question, a participant rephrased it for the class in a way that made it more meaningful for her: "How is the stuff that got decomposed re-used again?" Small groups discussed their ideas for 25 minutes and then shared their explanations with the whole class. One group had begun by considering how plants obtained specific nutrients, such as a spinach plant with more iron or a banana plant with more calcium, and then inquiringly shared with us the issues they were wrestling with:

> How do the nutrients get from that compost selectively into different plants? . . . It doesn't come out of nowhere. So, it's not going to get into the plants through photosynthesis. So it's got to come up through those roots. How does one plant know to- how does a banana know that it needs to pull the potassium out of the ground? The spinach knows that it needs to pull the [iron] out.

They also discussed related agricultural practices: "And then we started talking about the need for crop rotation because if you have the same plants in same area, all the one nutrient is going to go [away]. But, those are very smart little roots to be able to- I'm assuming that they know what to suck out of the compost." They closed by sharing their model of how nutrients might cycle from a banana back to a tree: A gorilla eats a banana, digests and defecates. Then flies and worms consume that [product] and put it back into the ground through their defecation. A tree takes this product up as fertilizer.

Questions about how plants get nutrients were very interesting questions for this group to be pursuing, but I found it discouraging that the model this group settled on involved feces as the product of decomposition. I believed that as a class, we had come to a shared understanding the previous week that decomposition was distinct from insect digestion. Yet, that was the explanation this group proposed.

Reflecting on my decisions. When the class did not challenge the model associating digestion with decomposition, it was very uncomfortable for me to remain quiet, yet I did. I choose not to remind the group that we had concluded that digestion and decomposition were not the same because this would put me in the traditional role of evaluator of ideas. The questions this group had been wrestling with were interesting, generative questions, and I didn't want to diminish the value of the discussion they had engaged in by highlighting their incorrect description of decomposition. Further, my second objective for the workshop was for the participants to arrive at a "meaningful, mechanistic, mutually agreed upon, explanation of the phenomenon of decomposition, which might not necessarily be scientifically accurate." Being responsive meant allowing incorrect ideas to linger, but this was incredibly difficult.

Reflecting on the challenge of allowing "wrong" ideas to linger. Whenever I heard incorrect ideas, my first instinct was to gently correct them; or at least to intend to "fix" the incorrect ideas by at the end of the day. In most cases, however, I did not correct the participants' ideas. If the participants knew, that I, as the authority, would validate or invalidate the ideas proposed, than they would likely not see a need to engage in the process of developing an explanation other than to please the instructor. Several responsive practitioners have argued that it's important that learners take up a problem, question, or task as their own so that learning can occur; but often times the teacher intervenes and the learners perceive the situation as another instance of relying on the teacher for knowledge (Balacheff, 1991; Gallas, 1995; van Zee, 2000). Therefore, as the instructor, I did my best not to directly address these incorrect ideas because my goal was for participants to engage in scientific inquiry—to evaluate their own and others' competing ideas and thus to take responsibility for developing plausible explanations for phenomena. In fact, in most instances I tried to encourage the pursuit of all ideas as possible explanations. I wanted the participants to take responsibility for assessing the quality of their own ideas and understanding as scientists do. This meant allowing groups to pursue incorrect ideas in hopes that, over time, the scientific community we had created would challenge that thinking.

If my objective had been for learners to develop a set of specific text-based concepts, then all ideas and responses I heard would have been categorized as right or wrong as I listened for the correct idea to emerge. Instead, I had to listen carefully past the scientific "correctness" of the participants' ideas to determine if they were thinking and reasoning like scientists. My central objective was not for the participants to leave the workshop with a memorized definition of what does and does not constitute decomposition. Rather, it was to help participants reason about and refine their understanding of the process of decomposition by listening to each other's ideas, challenging those ideas, pressing for clarity and coherence among ideas, and drawing on their own experiences to determine the reasonableness of the ideas proposed. This means the scientific ideas may not always emerge. While the new national standards (i.e. Next Generation Science Standards) encourage a focus on scientific practices, they do not address how to manage this tension between content (disciplinary core ideas) and practices. In

122 April Cordero Maskiewicz

short, what is the instructor to do if students are engaging productively in scientific inquiry, yet come to incorrect conclusions? In Hammer's (1997) reflection of his high school physics class, he describes the tension associated with honoring students' nascent scientific reasoning while also helping students develop scientifically accepted knowledge. Although in theory Hammer's objectives should not conflict, in practice student explorations did not always lead to correct discoveries. For example, one group of students concluded Styrofoam conducted electricity.

If our goal is to foster scientific inquiry and mechanistic reasoning through responsive teaching, we need to learn to encourage all ideas, no matter their scientific validity, and allow the participants to be the evaluators of those ideas. If learners are to be the evaluators of ideas, they need to have this authority passed down to them from the teacher. Although it is not easy, resisting the urge to "fix" learners' ideas as they are being presented is vital for reaching that goal. In my situation, leading a professional development workshop, I could prioritize the groups' ownership of the ideas—correct or incorrect—ahead of ensuring that specific accurate scientific content is addressed. This tension between incorrect ideas and learners' ownership of ideas can be exacerbated, however, when an instructor has external pressures (e.g. state exams) to address specific disciplinary core content. Developing priorities ahead of time (i.e. ownership of ideas over correctness of ideas) and persistently foregrounding those priorities may help to shed light on how to begin to manage this tension in a K–16 classroom.

Conclusion

When teaching responsively, the carefully structured lesson plan is replaced with a handful of generative questions and an imaginative list of possible responses learners might offer. In my case, I had clear objectives for what I wanted learners to experience and be doing during the science talks: to become intrigued about the process of decomposition as they wrestled with their own ideas and those of their peers in pursuit of a coherent, mechanistic explanation. I wanted the participants' ideas to be the terrain for the discussions and explorations so that they viewed themselves as sense-makers and their ideas as valid for developing new knowledge. As I led the science talks for this professional development workshop, I intentionally tried to model consistent responsive teaching so participants could engage in scientific inquiry. Yet the sheer unpredictability of the direction and content of student-generated discussions created challenges for me when instructional decisions had to be made. This chapter tries to make explicit those challenges, because when we choose to be responsive to students' ideas, we as instructors need to learn to expect and adjust to the tensions these challenges pose (Lindfors, 1999).

Although there were many more challenges I experienced during the 18 hours of science talks, I presented these three challenges because they seemed to create the most discomfort for me as I tried to teach responsively. The challenge of

The Challenges of Teaching Responsively **123**

getting the participants to focus on and to sustain how and why explanations, instead of shifting back towards procedural explanations, created a tension because I didn't want to assert my authority and play a major role in guiding the discussions. Asserting my authority would have taken away the participants' agency and ownership of the content and the learning. This tension influenced the ideas I was able to hear and was influenced by the ideas I heard. As I listened to participants' ideas through my mechanistic explanation filter, I sometimes missed their budding mechanistic reasoning. The challenge of how much control to exert, and when, was further compounded by the types of ideas that students put forth (e.g. correct vs. incorrect). In many instances it would have been easier to redirect the discussions in ways that alleviated these tensions, but this would ultimately invalidate the participants' attempts at developing their own understanding. It would not have allowed the participants to listen to each other, take risks, or build complex explanations cooperatively.

I used a journal to record the ideas I heard, which helped me to stay focused and to prioritize the students' ideas over my desire to take back control. And as the participants engaged in the work of doing science during the two weeks of PD, they did, in the end, develop mechanistic explanations for what occurs during decomposition. The participants improved in their ability to hear ideas, ask for clarification, and challenge the explanations proposed by others without my overt intervention. In the responsive environment we created, the participants developed scientific inquiry skills that will help them facilitate their own classroom discussions.

Reflecting on and articulating my experiences and decisions as I confronted challenges during the PD teacher workshop generates insight and knowledge about the practice of teaching responsively for others (Lampert & Ball, 1998). Describing the tensions I felt and the choices I made more clearly illuminates the distinction between responsive teaching and more traditional instruction. In the traditional classroom, power and responsibility are held by teachers, and our role is to provide accurate information and to make decisions about curricular content and outcomes. In that environment, learners expect knowledge to come from the teacher, the authoritative evaluator of all ideas. When teaching responsively, the role of the teacher is quite different. The authority to evaluate ideas and to propose new directions emerges from the learners as they consider and critique each other's claims. National standards and documents (e.g. Achieve, Inc., 2013; NRC, 2012) state that students should use argumentation to listen to, compare, and evaluate competing scientific ideas and methods based on their merits, because the evidence from research shows that when learners' ideas and reasoning are made visible, public, and available to all participants, learning occurs (NRC, 2007, 2012). Yet these documents neglect to explain how difficult it can be to encourage and facilitate students' evaluation of their own and others' competing ideas, as well as to be silent and set aside the need to control every aspect of the learning.

124 April Cordero Maskiewicz

Through sustained professional development, teachers can gain first-hand experience learning in a responsive environment as well as engage in learning communities as they traverse the challenges of teaching responsively. As teachers learn to orchestrate the elicitation of students' productive resources and the generation of community-validated explanations of the natural world in their own classrooms, they will undoubtedly encounter the three challenges described here, as well as many others. As educators, we can help ease these challenges by anticipating the tensions inherent in following students' exploration of ideas and maintaining our prioritization of objectives.

Acknowledgments

I would like to thank the teachers and the professional development team, Dr. Janet Coffey for encouraging me to write this self-reflection paper, and Ms. Janice Yuwiler, Dr. Jennifer Lineback, Dr. Jessica Watkins, Ms. Lilianna Rumberger, and the editors for their substantive comments that helped improve this chapter.

Note

1 NSF grant 0732233, "Learning Progressions for Scientific Inquiry: A Model Implementation in the Context of Energy."

References

Achieve, Inc., (2013). Next Generation Science Standards (Appendix F). Achieve, Inc. on behalf of the twenty-six states and partners that collaborated on the NGSS. Accessed 5/1/13: www.nextgenscience.org

Balacheff, N. (1991). Benefits and limits of social interaction: The case of teaching mathematical proof. In A. Bishop, E. Mellin-Olsen, & J. van Dormolen (Eds.), *Mathematical knowledge: Its growth through teaching* (pp. 175–192). Dordrecht, The Netherlands: Kluwer Academic Publisher.

Ball, D.L. (1993). With an eye on the mathematical horizon: Dilemmas of teaching elementary school mathematics. *Elementary School Journal, 93,* 373–397.

Chinn, C.A., & Malhotra, B.A. (2002). Epistemologically authentic inquiry in schools: A theoretical framework for evaluating inquiry tasks. *Science Education, 86*(2), 175–218.

Coffey, J., Hammer, D., & Levin, D. (2011). The missing substance of formative assessment. *Journal of Research in Science Teaching, 48*(10), 1109–1136.

Engle, R.A., & Conant, F.R. (2002). Guiding principles for fostering productive disciplinary engagement: Explaining an emergent argument in a community of learners classroom. *Cognition and Instruction, 20*(4), 399–483.

Gallas, K. (1995). *Talking their way into science: Hearing children's questions and theories, responding with curriculum.* New York: Teachers College Press.

Hammer, D. (1997). Discovery learning and discovery teaching. *Cognition and Instruction, 15*(4), 485–529.

Hammer, D., Russ, R., Mikeska, J., & Scherr, R. (2008). Identifying inquiry and conceptualizing students' abilities. In R.A. Duschl & R.E. Grandy (Eds.), *Teaching scientific inquiry: Recommendations for research and Implementation* (pp. 138–156). Rotterdam, The Netherlands: Sense Publishers.

Jimenez-Aleixandre, M.P., Rodriguez, A.B., & Duschl, R.A. (2000). 'Doing the lesson' or 'doing science': Argument in high school genetics. *Science & Education, 84,* 757–792.

Lampert, M. (1985). How do teachers manage to teach? Perspectives on problems in practice. *Harvard Educational Review, 55*(2), 178–194.

Lampert, M., & Ball, D.L. (1998). *Teaching, multimedia, and mathematics: Investigations of real practice. The practitioner inquiry series.* New York: Teachers College Press.

Lindfors, J.W. (1999). *Children's inquiry: Using language to make sense of the world.* New York: Teachers College Press.

Michaels, S., & O'Connor, C. (2012). *Talk science primer.* Document from The Inquiry Project at TERC. Retrieved from http://inquiryproject.terc.edu/shared/pd/Talk-Science_Primer.pdf

National Research Council. (2007). *Taking science to school: Learning and teaching science in grades K–8.* Committee on Science Learning, Kindergarten Through Eighth Grade. Edited by Richard A. Duschl, Heidi A. Schweingruber, & Andrew W. Shouse. Board on Science Education, Center for Education. Division of Behavioral and Social Sciences and Education. Washington, DC: The National Academies Press.

National Research Council. (2012). *A framework for K–12 science education: Practices, crosscutting concepts, and core ideas.* Committee on a Conceptual Framework for New K–12 Science Education Standards. Board on Science Education, Division of Behavioral and Social Sciences and Education. Washington, DC: The National Academies Press.

Reiser, B., Tabak, I., Sandoval, W., Smith, B., Steinmuller, F., & Leone, A. (2001). BGuILE: Strategic and conceptual scaffolds for scientific inquiry in biology classrooms. In S.M. Carver & D. Klahr (Eds.), *Cognition and instruction: Twenty-five years of progress* (pp. 263–305). Mahwah, NJ: Erlbaum.

Russ, R., Scherr, R., Hammer, D. & Mikeska, J. (2008). Recognizing mechanistic reasoning in student scientific inquiry: A framework for discourse analysis developed from philosophy of science. *Science Education, 92,* 499–525.

Tang, X., Coffey, J., Elby, A., & Levin, D. (2010). The scientific method and scientific inquiry: Tensions in teaching and learning. *Science Education, 94,* 29–47.

van Zee, E.H. (2000). Analysis of a student-generated inquiry discussion. *International Journal of Science Education, 22*(2), 115–142.

van Zee, E., & Minstrell, J. (1997). Using questioning to guide student thinking. *Journal of the Learning Sciences, 6*(2), 227–269.

6

WHAT TEACHERS NOTICE WHEN THEY NOTICE STUDENT THINKING

Teacher-Identified Purposes for Attending to Students' Mathematical Thinking

Adam A. Colestock and Miriam Gamoran Sherin

Supporting student learning in mathematics requires a responsive stance on the part of teachers. Teachers must attend closely to what students say and do, make sense of their ideas, and respond in ways that move the lesson forward productively. Much remains to be understood, however, about the details of teachers' in-the-moment noticing of student mathematical thinking. In particular, we know little about what precisely teachers notice when they notice student thinking. As B. Sherin and Star (2011) suggest, knowing the "sensory data" available to the teacher at a given time does not necessarily tell us to what that teacher is attending. Here we claim that an account of teacher noticing is incomplete unless we understand the significance that a teacher ascribes to a particular student comment or method. For example, in one middle school lesson, students were comparing a ratio of 3 cups of water to 2 cups of lemonade mix with a ratio of 4 cups of water to 3 cups of lemonade mix. When asked which lemonade is "more lemony" a student replied "Well, I think they're the same 'cause it's just one more." The teacher might have noticed simply that the idea was incorrect. Alternatively, the teacher might have noticed that the student was using a different method to compare ratios than the other students at her table. Or the teacher might have noticed that the student was talking about "sameness" in a way that was novel to her. To us, these different approaches reflect important differences in teacher noticing.

The goal of this chapter is to identify specific approaches to noticing as demonstrated by teachers in the moment of instruction. To accomplish this we use digital video techniques that allowed teachers to document their attention to student thinking. In all, we present six approaches illustrated by four mathematics teachers and discuss similarities and differences in the teachers' use of these approaches. This work contributes to our theoretical understanding of teacher noticing and also has practical implications for the design of professional development intended to help teachers attend to student mathematical thinking.

Studying Teacher Noticing

Over the past decade, research on teacher noticing has received increased attention, particularly in the mathematics education community. There is general consensus that noticing is a key component of expertise in teaching, and, more specifically, that responsive and adaptive teaching hinges on a teacher's noticing abilities (Sherin, Jacobs, & Philipp, 2011).

Current research emphasizes that teacher noticing is an active process. A great deal happens in a classroom at the same time. Teachers must actively decide what to attend to (and what not to attend to) (Miller, 2011). Schoenfeld (2010) argues that noticing is largely driven by a teacher's goals for a lesson. That is, a teacher attends to those features of classroom interactions that are consequential for what the teacher wants to achieve in class that day (Erickson, 2011; Russ & Luna, 2013).

Extensive professional development efforts have focused on helping teachers learn to effectively attend to their students' thinking. Our own work in this area highlights the goals of (a) helping teachers notice substantive mathematical thinking on the part of students during instruction, (b) fostering teachers' interpretation of student math thinking, and (c) encouraging teachers to base their claims about student thinking in evidence (van Es & Sherin, 2008). Much of our work has taken place in the context of video clubs, in which teachers watch and discuss excerpts of videos from their classrooms.

The study of teacher noticing is not without challenges, however. Research on teacher noticing has primarily relied on retrospective accounts from teachers of their noticing. For example, Rosaen, Lundeberg, Cooper, Fritzen, and Terpstra (2008) asked teachers to comment on videos from their classroom and to describe their thinking at certain points in time. Yet removed from the demands of the classroom, teachers may not accurately describe their in-the-moment thinking. In other cases, teachers are asked to respond to videos of other teachers' instruction as a way to probe how they attend to classroom situations (Kersting, Givvin, Thompson, Santagata, & Stigler, 2012). This approach may also be problematic because teachers do not have all of the contextual information they usually draw on to notice interactions during instruction. In this study, we make use of novel digital video techniques in order to more effectively capture teachers' in-the-moment noticing.

Methods

The data for this study was collected as part of a larger project on the use of digital technologies to investigate teachers' in-the-moment noticing. Four mathematics teachers participated in the study. All four teachers taught in the same urban public school district in a large Midwestern city; three taught at the middle-school level and one taught at the high-school level. Each teacher had between five and nine years of teaching experience. The middle school teachers were using a standards-based curricula (either MathThematics, Connected Math, or CME) and had recently served as professional development facilitators for their peers around these curricula. All three curricula provide explicit information for teachers about students' mathematical thinking, with the intention that teachers use this information as a basis for instruction. The fact that these teachers had been selected by the district as professional development leaders suggested to us that they were likely accomplished in using the curricula and had developed teaching practices that included a focus on student thinking. We also had evidence that the high school teacher's practice centered on student thinking to some degree, having worked with him in a previous context. In sum, we anticipated that working with these teachers might be a productive way to explore teachers' attention to student thinking and, further, that the teachers would find the tasks in which we asked them to participate feasible to undertake.

The teachers volunteered to use a new digital video camera equipped with selective-archiving capability (see http://www.vio-pov.com for information on the POV 1.5). The camera videotaped continuously but allowed teachers to "tag" moments of video as they occurred. When reviewing the videotape on a computer, users could instantaneously move from tag to tag. The camera was quite small and was worn by the teacher on the brim of a hat. A separate unit that could be held or attached to a teacher's belt featured the "tagging button." Because the teachers essentially "wore" the camera, the video collected was from the teacher's own perspective; it showed classroom interactions from the teacher's point of view.

Each teacher used the camera between three and nine times. Teachers were asked to "tag important or interesting moments of student math thinking" as they taught the lesson. Prior research documented that teachers find this a reasonable task (Sherin, Russ & Colestock, 2011); for example, the effort to tag moments is not so burdensome that teachers do so only for the first few minutes of the class. Instead, teachers generally tag moments throughout a lesson and as the class makes use of different participant structures.

Shortly after using the camera, each teacher was interviewed by the first author. In these interviews the teacher and researcher viewed the 20–30 seconds prior to the tagged moment in order to remind the teacher of the particular moment. We chose not to show the teachers the entire tagged moment in order to limit ad hoc explanations of what took place. (For a further discussion of this issue, see Sherin, Russ, & Colestock, 2011). The teacher was then asked to explain the student thinking displayed in the tagged moment and why that moment had been interesting or important. In all, the teachers tagged and subsequently discussed a total of 204 moments. Table 6.1 lists the number of tagged moments per teacher.

Teacher-Identified Purposes for Attending 129

TABLE 6.1 Teacher camera use

Teacher	Number of lessons	Total number of tagged moments
Ms. Astor	7	56
Mr. Cooke	9	56
Ms. Mather	9	49
Mr. Larson	3	43

Analysis proceeded through several phases. First, we sought to identify the different types of significance that teachers attributed to the student thinking they noticed during instruction. To do so, a subset of tagged moments and corresponding comments by the teachers were reviewed in order to compile a list of potential categories. Several potential categories were drawn from prior research. For example, Schifter (2001) describes several analytic skills that teachers use when attending to student thinking, including assessing the validity of students' ideas and listening for the sense in students' thinking. Davis (1997) introduces the notion of "evaluative listening" and distinguishes this from "interpretive listening." Furthermore, Lampert (2001) presents a range of activities she draws on when discussing her own first-hand accounts of attending to student thinking, including "listening and watching," "interpreting written products," and "locating students' observed performances in an anticipated mathematical domain." These categories were used as important starting points in our analysis. Through an iterative cycle of analysis, we identified six approaches to attending to student thinking that the four teachers in our study used repeatedly.

We were not intending to identify a target number of categories in this analysis (and in fact, there were times in our analysis that we had as many as thirteen categories and as few as five). Rather, we settled on these six categories for two main reasons. First, we were able to consistently distinguish between teachers' use of these six approaches in our preliminary coding. With more than six, we began to see overlap in the categories. In contrast, with fewer than six, we felt that there were important distinctions among the approaches that remained hidden. Second, we found that all four teachers used each of the six categories. Furthermore, this particular collection of categories consisted of those that were used more frequently by each of the four teachers in our study. This suggested to us that these six categories likely held some significance for teachers.

The six categories are not intended to be comprehensive. There are certainly other approaches teachers use to attend to their students' thinking that we did not capture in our analysis. However, we believe exploring teachers' use of these six categories is a valuable step in investigating how teachers make sense of student thinking during instruction.

With these six categories in place, we then coded the entire data set. We decided to assign a single approach to each individual moment. While there were likely moments in which teachers applied more than one approach, we chose to code only the primary approach for each moment since our main focus was to simply identify and illustrate different ways in which teachers were attending to student thinking. In contrast, coding for more than one approach per moment would have been particularly interesting if, for example, we wanted to explore relationships among the six approaches. Because we identified only the primary approach used in each moment, our results likely underrepresent teachers' use of the six approaches in their instruction.

One researcher, the first author, coded all 204 tagged moments. A second researcher independently coded 20% of the data for each teacher. Inter-rater reliability, as calculated using Cohen's Kappa, was 85%, indicating a level of "very good." Disagreements were resolved through consensus.

The above analysis was quite useful in allowing us to see how the six approaches were used by the teachers in our study. Still, after having completed the coding, we suspected that the teachers did not always use a particular approach in precisely the same way. To explore this issue, we conducted a few additional analyses. First, we compared the frequencies with which each teacher applied the six approaches. Specifically, we examined the extent to which the six approaches were used across the four teachers, as well as whether each teacher's pattern of use was distinct in any specific ways. Second, we investigated two other dimensions of the tagged moments: (a) whether each moment represented teacher attention to an individual student or to a group of students; and (b) whether each moment represented noticing of a single point in time or of an extended period of time. Our definitions of the approaches did not take these characteristics into account, but based on prior research (Sherin, Russ, Sherin, & Colestock, 2008; Sherin et al., 2010; Sherin, Russ, & Colestock, 2011) we suspected that the teachers' use of the approaches might vary along these dimensions.

Results

The main result of this work is the introduction of six approaches teachers use when noticing student thinking during instruction. In particular, the approaches reflect different ways that teachers understand the significance of students' ideas. We believe that these approaches extend prior research in important ways. First, they go beyond distinguishing simply between teachers' attempts to evaluate versus teachers' attempt to interpret students' ideas, something that we, along with other researchers, have highlighted as an important distinction in the ways that teachers attend to students' thinking (e.g., Sherin & Han, 2004).

Second, the approaches are intended to reflect the ways that teachers understand the pedagogical significance of students' ideas. Our use of the word pedagogical here stems from the idea that teachers' attention to students' thinking is driven, at least in part, by the teachers' goals for instruction. Thus, we claim that often it is precisely because a teacher has a particular pedagogical goal in mind that the teacher will focus on a student's comment in a particular way. Of course, it can also be the case that when a teacher sees or hears a particular idea from a student, it can serve to trigger a particular goal on the teacher's part (Schoenfeld, 2010).

To be clear, the categories we introduce here are not focused on describing how a teacher unpacks the mathematical meaning of a student's idea. Thus, for example, the categories do not explain whether the teacher makes sense of a student's idea by locating the source of the idea or by posing additional questions to the student. Rather, the approaches illustrate different ways in which student thinking appears consequential to the teacher in the context of instruction.

Teacher Approaches to Noticing Student Thinking

In what follows, we describe each of the six approaches (Table 6.2). To begin we discuss two approaches that concern teachers noticing whether or not students have learned. In *indicator of learning*, student thinking stands out to the teacher precisely because it reveals that students have learned something. In contrast, moments coded as *problem to be addressed* are cases in which a teacher noticed that a student was not understanding a concept or idea.

TABLE 6.2 Approaches used by teachers for attending to student thinking

How student thinking is viewed by the teacher	Description	Related instructional goal
Indicator of learning	Teacher sees student ideas as illustrating understanding on the part of students	Track student learning
Problem to be addressed	Teacher sees student ideas as errors or misunderstandings that need to be addressed	Deal with obstacles to learning
Resources to be collected	Teacher sees student ideas as a set of actions or events to be observed	Monitor the range of ideas in the classroom
Foundations to build on	Teacher sees student ideas as strategies or concepts to develop	Connect and build on student ideas
Message to be deciphered	Teacher sees student idea as comment or methods that needs to be interpreted	Make sense of student thinking
Products of a process	Teacher sees student ideas as the outcome of lesson design	Reflect on lesson design

Approach 1: Student Thinking as an Indicator of Student Understanding

Across the data, teachers tagged moments of student thinking in order to document what students were learning. In these instances, student ideas served as indicators, for the teacher, of student understanding. Sometimes this involved the teacher noticing that a student's current way of thinking differed from the student's previous method. For example, Ms. Astor's class had been exploring ratios and proportions, and students were solving problems involving unit rates. Ms. Astor approached Carter to check on his solution to a problem that involved comparing the cost of CDs from different vendors. She tagged the moment and explained, "When I talked to Carter I noticed that he really had a better grasp today than he had in the past about how to calculate the total cost . . . I was like, 'What does that mean?' . . . and he said 'Well, it is the same number of CDs and I am looking for the lowest price.' And so that was a big jump for him. I mean that stood out to me as, okay, we are starting to see at least some connection going on." What stood out to Ms. Astor was that Carter's current thinking illustrated that he had learned—his thinking about units rates was more advanced than on the previous day.

In other cases, teachers compared an individual student's idea with the thinking of his or her classmates. In one instance, Ms. Mather identified a contrast between Alex's understanding and that of the rest of the class. She commented that while Alex "understood [the algebraic expression], not everyone else was understanding it." In this moment, what was significant to Ms. Mather was that Alex was able to represent a distance-rate-time situation algebraically, even though this was one of the first times the class had encountered this type of problem.

Regardless of the type of comparison made, when using this approach teachers attended to student thinking with the goal of tracking student learning. This focus on student learning seems somewhat related to what prior research has characterized as a focus on correctness. For example, Crespo (2000) describes a group of prospective teachers whose initial stance on student thinking involved considering correct answers as evidence of student learning. Similarly, in our own work on video clubs, we found that teachers typically focused on student thinking initially by simply evaluating whether or not an idea was correct (Sherin & van Es, 2009). In line with such work, here we find that teachers also attend to the correctness in a student's idea. Yet in addition, we found that the teachers frequently went beyond simply noting that a student's answer was accurate and also described what the student understood.

Approach 2: Student Thinking as a Problem to Be Addressed

The second approach involves teachers viewing student thinking as a problem that needed to be addressed. Here, student errors or misunderstandings stood out to the teachers as concerns and often as issues they needed to work with students to correct. For example, Ms. Astor noticed that Maria had set up her ratio incorrectly and solved for "boxes per dollar" rather than "dollars per box." Ms. Astor tagged the moment and explained "Maria thought she needed to do six over seven . . . She was trying to justify that . . . but ended up getting [boxes per dollar] as her result." At times teachers noted student errors and also discussed how they addressed the error or planned to address the error. For instance, Ms. Astor tagged a moment in which Tracy set up a proportion incorrectly and stated, "So after this, I told her [how] to set it up and then she was like 'Oh, okay' and then she knew what to multiply and divide. But we had to go through setting up the proportion step by step." Ms. Astor recognized a particular difficulty Tracy encountered and decided that she needed to walk her through the correct solution. There were also cases in which teachers recognized a student error and were explicit that they were unsure of how to address the error productively.

Interestingly, in a few cases, rather than recognize a specific student error, the teachers instead commented that they noticed a potential obstacle, that is, what seemed to them to be the warning signs of a difficulty that might be realized if action was not taken. For instance, one student in Ms. Astor's class used the terms "dollars per CD" and "dollars per student" interchangeably. In the given task, this did not pose a problem, as each student received only one CD—thus the ratios were the same. However, Ms. Astor recognized that in the future this could be problematic: if, for example, a problem involved students receiving more than one CD.

Evaluating student errors is seen as an important component of teaching expertise (Hill & Ball, 2009), therefore it is not surprising that this approach was used frequently by all four teachers. In fact, a number of professional development programs have as a key goal to introduce teachers to likely student errors in particular content areas (e.g., Goldenstein, Barnett-Clarke, & Jackson, 1994; Seago, Mumme, & Branca, 2004). Furthermore, it seems likely that as teachers work to move a lesson forward productively they may be watching for students errors that could divert the lesson's progress, whether at this moment or in the future (Leinhardt, Putnam, Stein, & Baxter, 1991).

To us, these first two approaches reflect what we might think is typical of the way that teacher attention to student thinking operates: teachers are watching for evidence of student learning or of students not learning. As we look at the remaining four approaches, however, we see that the ways in which teachers attend to student thinking is more nuanced, with student thinking having other possible relevance for the teacher.

Approach 3: Student Thinking as Resources to Be Collected

In a third approach, teachers viewed student thinking as resources that could be observed and that represented the range of ideas that were "in the air" in the classroom at that moment. When using this approach, teachers focused on the presence of particular mathematical ideas within their classroom, rather than on whether or not a student's idea was correct, as they did with the first two approaches. In some cases this took place as teachers intentionally monitored the room to get a sense of the different solution methods that students were using. In one lesson, students in Mr. Cooke's class had been asked to determine the perimeter for a rectangle whose area could be found using the equation $A = s(35-s)$, where s is the length of one side. Mr. Cooke tagged several moments in which he observed how particular students solved the problem. He explained, "So [we] got three methods essentially ... He was making rectangles, he did 35 times 2, and he took the maximum [from the graph] and worked backwards." The significance that Mr. Cooke ascribed to these students' thinking was simply to note the methods students had used to solve the problem.

In other instances, teachers noted important mathematical ideas or justifications. For example, students in Ms. Mather's class were exploring the least possible output for a quadratic equation. Ms. Mather captured a conversation with a student and explained, "I [tagged] that moment because ... that was the first evidence that I heard understanding how to make [the minimum possible output]." This student's thinking was significant to the teacher because she was the first to express a solid justification for her answer. In fact, we observed numerous occasions in which the first appearance of an idea or method proved to be particularly salient for a teacher. Still, teachers were not always looking for something particular in regards to student thinking. Sometimes teachers captured moments in which they simply noted what a student was thinking without discussing a potential pedagogical purpose for that idea.

This approach to attending to student thinking has similarities with the instructional practice described by Smith and Stein (2011) as "monitoring," in which teachers listen to and keep track of students' ideas. Our use of the term "resources to be collected" is intended to emphasize our sense that quite often we found that teachers used, or planned to use, the information they gathered to advance instruction.

Approach 4: Student Thinking as Foundations to Build On

Another approach that teachers demonstrated involved seeing student thinking as something that they could build upon to extend students' understanding. In the previous approach teachers primarily gathered information about their students' thinking. In contrast, here students' thinking represented ideas that teachers planned to develop further—often at that moment in time—in order to achieve their learning goals for students. In some cases, this involved the teacher realizing that a student's thinking could be enriched by connecting it to mathematical ideas previously explored. For example, students in Ms. Astor's class were working with proportions. Earlier they had used a scale factor method—identifying the scale factor between the numerators and applying it to the denominators, or vice versa. Currently students were using cross multiplication. Ms. Astor tagged a moment in which she spoke with a group about their method. "They were able to set it up pretty efficiently . . . I wanted them to be able to reason about how they could check it [so] I [reminded] them [about] the scale factor. 'Now that you've set up your proportion, you can check it using scale factor.'" Ms. Astor recognized students' proficiency with cross multiplication as an opportunity to reinforce another way of thinking about proportional relationships, that of scale factors.

At other times, student thinking was seen as a foundation to be extended by encouraging students to develop new understandings. For instance, Mr. Cooke's students were exploring how to create a graph to represent the relationship between the length of a side and the area of a rectangle with a fixed perimeter. Mr. Cooke found that one group finished the problem earlier than the others and seemed to have a solid grasp of what the graph represented. He challenged them to consider whether or not they would be justified in connecting the points that they had plotted on the graph. In describing the students' thinking Mr. Cooke explained, "They did a great job . . . I just wanted to keep them stretching so I asked them about, 'Can I connect the dots? Is this continuous?'" Although this was not necessarily part of his lesson plan for the day, Mr. Cooke recognized this moment as an opportunity to have students consider when it is appropriate to connect a set of points and what it means for a function to be continuous.

Lampert (2001) discusses the importance of mathematics teachers deliberately structuring opportunities to make connections among content during instruction. Here we find teachers making such connections in a more opportunistic way—when students' ideas were recognized by the teachers as having the potential to serve as the foundation for new understandings.

Approach 5: Student Thinking as Messages to Be Deciphered

In a fifth approach, teachers tagged moments of student thinking in which they were actively trying to understand what a student meant or how a student was thinking about a particular concept or problem. In such moments, the student thinking on display represented a message that the teacher wanted to decipher. Sometimes students have tentatively formed notions, discuss ideas in unconventional ways, or do not fully articulate their thinking. In those moments a teacher's noticing may be directed towards trying to unpack or figure out what a particular student might be thinking. For example, a group was graphing and analyzing a situation with three different CD vendors, and Ms. Astor tagged a moment in which she asked the group what they observed. She was puzzled by the ambiguity of the pronoun the student used. "They . . . told me . . . that it went down, and that's all they said, is 'it went down' for the website. And so I said 'What is it?' . . . So then we kind of looked at it and I said 'Do you mean that the amount that the cost is increasing by is what is going down?'" Ms. Astor considered the student thinking in this moment as something that was not transparent to her and that had to be clarified.

In other cases, the teachers worked to make sense of the source of a student's idea. For example, Mr. Cooke tagged a moment in which students were trying to calculate the perimeter of a rectangle in which two sides sum to 35. He saw that Cara had solved the problem incorrectly and asked her what she had done. "It was interesting to see her paper because it was like 8.75, 8.75, 8.75 and I was like 'Where did that come from?' And it was like really cool thinking. She was on the right track, she just didn't realize that she took half of the half." Mr. Cooke viewed Cara's solution as something that he did not initially understand and that required further investigation.

Much of the rhetoric around reform efforts in mathematics education emphasizes the importance of teachers making sense of the meaning of students' ideas and comments—deciphering what method a student followed and/or why that method made sense to the student. Despite the strong focus on this practice in the research literature (Ball, Lubienski, & Mewborn, 2001), we found that the frequency of this approach was quite low among the teachers in this study. We suspect, however, that this number underrepresents the degree to which teachers may have been interpreting students' ideas. Specifically, in cases where teachers honed in on an interpretation of student thinking relatively quickly, the sense-making act may not have been particularly salient to the teacher.

Approach 6: Student Thinking as Products of a Process

In the final approach, teachers viewed student thinking as evidence that could be used as a basis for assessing and reasoning about the design of lessons. Here, students' ideas were seen as the products of a learning process and as such provided teachers with a resource for reflecting on the outcome of a lesson. In some cases teachers had predictions about how student thinking would develop over a lesson, and observing students during instruction served as a way to check those predictions. For example, in one lesson Ms. Astor selected prices for CDs that were atypical, elaborating that she "purposely [chose] numbers that they don't normally associate with CDs so [students] would have to actually think about the process and not just the answer." When Ms. Astor questioned Melanie about how she solved the problem, Melanie momentarily doubted that the answer she had was correct and went back to check her work. Ms. Astor explained, "I was actually glad to see that, because it made her actually think about why her proportion was set up correctly." The student thinking that Ms. Astor observed in this moment was significant to her primarily because it affirmed that the numbers she had selected for the problem had the desired effect.

Another way that student thinking was seen as the outcome of a lesson design occurred when teachers observed students' difficulties and considered which elements of the lesson design or learning environment might have contributed to the confusion Alternatively, teachers might observe a student insight and consider which elements of the learning environment supported that thinking. For example, Mr. Cooke was pleasantly surprised when a student was able to successfully factor an expression during a warm-up exercise even though factoring had not yet been explicitly taught. "That was huge because we haven't talked about factoring, really at all . . . So for her to intuitively just get it was kind of interesting." The student's thinking led Mr. Cooke to realize that he had sequenced the warm-up so that the third and fourth problems were related, the third problem asking students to apply the distributive property, and the fourth problem asking students to simplify an expression quite similar to that of the answer to the third problem. The moment stood out to Mr. Cooke primarily as evidence that the structure of the lesson was effective. "I think that it helped that I put basically the same problem, just showed it a different way."

Interestingly, this approach indicated that teachers sometimes reflected on the design of a lesson as it unfolded in class. Prior research suggests that this approach can be quite valuable. Specifically, Choppin (2011) documents that teachers who use students' thinking to inform instructional design tend to adapt lessons in ways that enhance the complexity of the tasks and provide ongoing opportunities for students to explore substantive mathematical ideas.

Teachers' Use of the Six Approaches

In addition to identifying the six approaches teachers used when noticing students' thinking during instruction, we also compared the frequency with which the four teachers used the different approaches (Figure 6.1). While the data was limited to a few days of observation for each teacher, we nevertheless can see some patterns in their use of the six approaches.

First, it is worth noting again that all four teachers used each of the six approaches. This suggests to us that we have not identified an idiosyncratic set of approaches for attending to student thinking. If that were the case, we would expect to see some of the strategies used by only a subset of the teachers. Still, because this data reflects the practices of only four teachers, we suspect that there may be other approaches commonly used by teachers that would be revealed with a larger data set.

Second, we want to point out that the teachers used the six approaches with varying frequencies. Mr. Larson used the resources to be collected approach quite extensively, 44% of the time. This may reflect an instructional goal on the part of Mr. Larson to continuously monitor the mathematical methods being used by his students. In contrast, Mr. Cooke's primary approach was to consider student ideas as problems to be addressed. Mr. Cooke may therefore believe that his primary instructional role is to diagnose and correct student errors. Schoenfeld (2010) discusses the goal-based nature of teacher decision-making. It might be that these teachers have different overarching instructional goals and beliefs

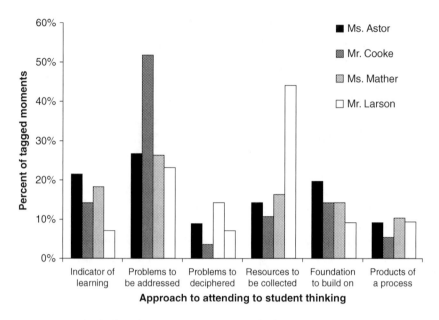

FIGURE 6.1 Individual teachers' attention to student thinking.

about teaching that promote distinct approaches for attending to students' mathematical thinking.

Finally, we find Ms. Astor's and Ms. Mather's data also quite interesting. They used all six approaches in a relatively balanced manner. That is, no one or two approaches seemed particularly prominent in the moments they tagged. Further, on closer examination of these teachers' tagged moments, we found that they switched back and forth among the six approaches throughout their observations. To us this reflects a degree of flexibility in their practice relative to attending to student thinking that the other teachers may not have shared. At the same time, it may be that the six approaches have become somewhat integrated in their practice, so that they draw on several of the practices regularly as they interact with the students in their classrooms.

Characteristics of the Six Approaches

For each approach we also investigated the extent to which the tagged moments primarily represented attention to individual student thinking or to the student thinking of a group of students. In the examples described earlier, Ms. Astor's attention to Carter's error in calculating the cost of CDs illustrates attention to an individual student, while Mr. Cooke's focus on the solutions of several different students reflected his focus on a group of students. In addition, we noted whether the teachers' attention reflected noticing of a particular moment in time or an extended event. Referring to the same two examples once more, we consider Ms. Astor's focus on Carter's error as a moment that relates to an extended time period—she compares Carter's current understanding with what he expressed the previous day. In contrast, we consider Mr. Cooke's attention to the three different student solutions as reflecting a single point in time because his focus is on three methods that were being used in class at that point in time. As shown in Figure 6.2 and Figure 6.3, the frequency of these features differed somewhat among the six approaches.

Teachers tended to tag moments in which they attended to an individual student's thinking rather than to a group of students' thinking (Figure 6.2). The one exception is the case of foundations to build on, in which 63% of the tagged moments related to the thinking of a group of students. This is evidence that when teachers identify moments in which they can connect or extend students' thinking they usually have the whole class in mind. In contrast, when they are noting a correct or incorrect answer, for example, it usually relates to an individual student. Prior research indicates that teachers, particularly novice teachers, tend to focus on the class as a whole rather than on individual students (Kagan, 1992). Thus the fact that so much of these teachers' attention to student thinking reflected attention to individual students suggests to us that perhaps these teachers were

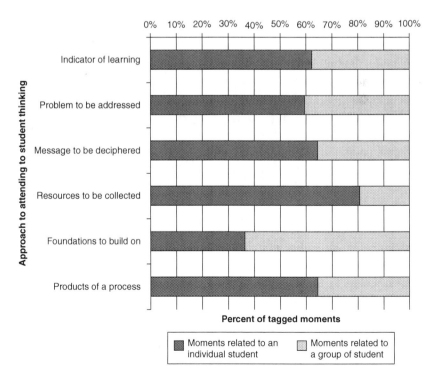

FIGURE 6.2 Frequency with which tagged moments related to individual vs. group of students.

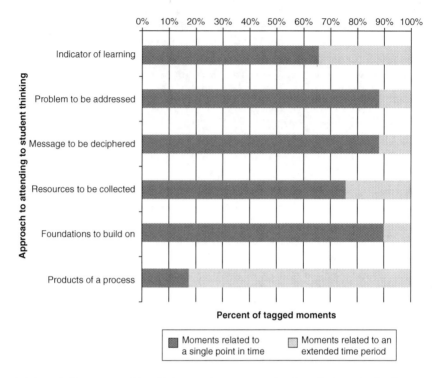

FIGURE 6.3 Frequency with which tagged moments related to single point in time vs. extended period of time.

particularly accomplished in their ability to notice student thinking. Recall that we selected these teachers as participants in part because of their likely focus on student thinking; thus this seems like a reasonable conclusion.

Furthermore, a great deal of professional development around teacher noticing of student thinking fosters attention to the details of individual student's comments and methods (e.g., Cohen, 2004). Because of the reliance on this skill during teaching, such professional development may play a particularly important role in helping teachers to learn to attend to student thinking in ways that may transfer productively from the professional development context to instruction.

In terms of whether teachers noticed events that related to a single point in time or to an event that occurred over a more extended period of time (as can be seen in Figure 6.3), we found that teachers predominantly attended to events at a single point in time. This was somewhat surprising to us, as we had suspected that approaches such as indicator of learning and resources to be collected would reflect the need for teachers to attend to student thinking over time as they kept track of what students were understanding, and where and how they wanted students' learning to progress. The focus on students thinking at a single point in time, even within these approaches, may therefore suggest potential areas in which teachers' noticing skills could be further developed. We note, however, that the majority of moments tagged as products of a process were coded as related to moments extended over time (84%). This likely reflects the fact that these moments concern the relationship between lesson design and lesson implementation—events that typically happen at different times.

Considering Teachers' Responsiveness

The focus of our chapter has been on the construct of teacher noticing, and in particular teachers' noticing of students' mathematical thinking. In previous work we have emphasized the idea that teacher noticing consists of identifying significant moments of instruction and interpreting those moments (Sherin & van Es, 2009). Other researchers, however, have made the claim that "responding" is also a key component of teacher noticing (Luna, 2013; Jacobs, Lamb, & Philipp, 2010). In particular, Jacobs et al. (2010) claim that attending, interpreting, and responding happen simultaneously during teachers' interactions with students in the classroom, and therefore it is important to consider these processes jointly. It is in that spirit that here we consider what we might learn about teacher responsiveness from our investigation of teachers' approaches to noticing student thinking.

First, as other researchers have argued, we believe that an important connection between noticing and responding stems from the observation that a teacher can only respond to what he or she notices (Erickson, 2011; Schoenfeld, 2010). In addition, we make the more specific claim that how a teacher responds to a student's thinking is dependent on what the teacher sees in that student's thinking. The six approaches that we present here provide one possible answer to the question, "What are teachers noticing when they notice student thinking?" Beyond just the semantic content of a student's idea, teachers may view the student's thinking as it relates to a variety of aspects of the ecology of the classroom, including their learning goals, their lesson plan, prior and future instruction, the design of the curriculum, etc. Each of these perspectives will likely guide the teacher's response in a particular way. In fact, in talking with the teachers in our study about what they noticed related to students' thinking, teachers often replied by not only commenting on what they noticed but also by stating how they responded to students. For instance, in discussing a group of students who had solved a proportion problem, Ms. Astor commented, "They were able to set it up pretty efficiently. And then, so I wanted them to be able to reason about how they could check it. And at this point I [reminded] them [about] the scale factor. 'Now that you've set up your proportion, you can check it using scale factor.'" Here Ms. Astor recognized that students' facility with the cross multiplication algorithm provided an opening to advance their understanding of why this methods works. And she chose to do so by connecting the work to scale factors, a topic studied previously. Had she seen their thinking as simply correct, for example, she might have responded very differently.

142 Adam A. Colestock and Miriam Gamoran Sherin

Second, it seems to us that those who study responsive teaching have taken up the challenge of defining this construct in part by identifying instances of responsive teaching in videos of instruction. For example, Pierson (2008) describes responsiveness as a quality of a teacher's interaction with a student based on the extent to which a teacher takes up the student's idea and incorporates it into the teacher's response. In doing so, Pierson and others (Levin, Hammer, & Coffey, 2009) note the extent to which a student's idea is highlighted in the discourse between a teacher and the student. This assumes that responsive teaching is constituted by overt engagement with student thinking. We contend that such an approach may be strengthened by acknowledging that a teacher can be deeply engaged in student thinking and focused on the development of that thinking in ways that are not immediately apparent in an open exchange between a student and teacher. The methodology that we used in this study revealed to us numerous instances of teacher attention to student thinking that would not have been immediately apparent to us in simply observing the lesson. For example, in an observation we might have recognized that Ms. Astor noticed student thinking when she asked Carter what his answer to the CD problem meant. Only the follow-up interview, however, enabled us to see that this moment was significant to Ms. Astor because she was using it as an indicator of learning, and that other moments were significant to her for very different reasons. Because some moments tagged by teachers were about internal reflections and had no outward manifestation, they might have been entirely missed in a classroom observation—for example, Mr. Cooke's products of a process moment in which he realized that putting two problems next to each other in a warm-up allowed a student to make a key connection.

Third, noticing appears to be an important leverage point for the development of responsive teaching practice. That is, attending to students' thinking seems to be a *sine qua non* for teachers to be able to be responsive to students' ideas (Jacobs, Lamb, Philipps, & Schapelle, 2011). Still, we argue that it is likely not enough to encourage teachers to "pay attention to students' ideas." Teachers need support in order to understand what that practice means. In this chapter we have endeavored to provide a starting point for such support by describing six specific ways in which teachers can attend to student thinking. Future work could benefit from examining whether some of these strategies afford more opportunities for student learning than others, and if so, whether these might be productively advanced in teachers.

References

Ball, D.L., Lubienski, S., & Mewborn, D. (2001). Research on teaching mathematics: The unsolved problem of teachers' mathematical knowledge. In V. Richardson (Ed.), *Handbook of research on teaching* (4th ed., pp. 433–456). New York: Macmillan.

Choppin, J. (2011). Learned adaptations: Teachers' understanding and use of curriculum resources. *Journal of Mathematics Teacher Education, 14,* 331–353.

Cohen, S. (2004). *Teachers' professional development and the elementary mathematics classroom: Bringing understandings to light*. New York: Routledge.

Crespo, S. (2000). Seeing more than right and wrong answers: Prospective teachers' interpretations of students' mathematical work. *Journal of Mathematics Teacher Education, 3*(2), 155–181.

Davis, B. (1997). Listening for differences: An evolving conception of mathematics teaching. *Journal for Research in Mathematics Education, 28*(3), 355–376.

Erickson, F. (2011). On noticing teacher noticing. In M.G. Sherin, V.R. Jacobs, & R.A. Philipp (Eds.), *Mathematics teacher noticing: Seeing through teachers' eyes* (pp. 17–34). New York: Routledge.

Goldenstein, D., Barnett-Clarke, C., & Jackson, B. (1994). *Mathematics teaching cases: Fractions, decimals, ratios and percents—Hard to teach and hard to learn?* Portsmouth, NH: Heinemann.

Hill, H., & Ball, D.L. (2009). The curious—and crucial—case of mathematical knowledge for teaching. *Phi Delta Kappan, 91*(2), 68–71.

Jacobs, V.R., Lamb, L.C., & Philipp, R.A. (2010). Professional noticing of children's mathematical thinking. *Journal for Research in Mathematics Education, 41,* 169–202.

Jacobs, V.R., Lamb, L.L.C., Philipp. R.A., & Schappelle, B.P. (2011). Deciding how to respond on the basis of children's understandings. In M.G. Sherin, V.R. Jacobs, & R.A. Philipp (Eds.), *Mathematics teacher noticing: Seeing through teachers' eyes* (pp. 97–116). New York: Routledge.

Kagan, D.M. (1992). Professional growth among preservice and beginning teachers. *Review of Educational Research, 62,* 129–169.

Kersting, N.B., Givvin, K.B., Thompson, B.J., Santagata, R., & Stigler, J.W. (2012). Measuring usable knowledge: Teachers' analyses of mathematics classroom videos predict teaching quality and student learning. *American Educational Research Journal, 49,* 568.

Lampert, M. (2001). *Teaching problems and the problems of teaching*. New Haven, CT: Yale University Press.

Leinhardt, G., Putnam, R.T., Stein, M., & Baxter, J. (1991). Where subject knowledge matters. In P. Peterson, E. Fennema, & T. Carpenter (Eds.), *Advances in research on teaching* (pp. 87–113). Greenwich, CT: JAI Press Inc.

Levin, D.M., Hammer, D., & Coffey, J.E. (2009). Novice teachers' attention to student thinking. *Journal of Teacher Education, 60*(2), 142–154.

Luna, M. (2013). *Investigating elementary teachers' thinking about and learning to notice students' science ideas*. Dissertation, Northwestern University, Evanston, IL.

Miller, K.F. (2011). Situation awareness in teaching. In M.G. Sherin, V.R. Jacobs, & R.A. Philipp (Eds.), *Mathematics teacher noticing: Seeing through teachers' eyes* (pp. 51–65). New York: Routledge.

Pierson, J. (2008) *The relationship between patterns of classroom discourse and mathematics learning*. Unpublished doctoral dissertation, University of Texas at Austin, Austin, TX.

Rosaen, C.L., Lundeberg, M., Cooper, M., Fritzen, A., & Terpstra, M. (2008). Noticing noticing: How does investigation of video records change how teachers reflect on their experiences? *Journal of Teacher Education, 59,* 347–360.

Russ, R.S., & Luna, M.J. (2013). Inferring teacher epistemological framing from local patterns in teacher noticing. *Journal of Research in Science Teaching, 50*(3), 284–314.

Schifter, D. (2001). Learning to see the invisible: What skills and knowledge are needed to engage with students' mathematical ideas? In T. Wood, B.S. Nelson, & J. Warfield (Eds.), *Beyond classical pedagogy: Teaching elementary school mathematics*. New York: Routledge.

Schoenfeld, A.H. (2010). *How we think: A theory of goal-oriented decision making and its educational applications*. New York: Routledge.

Seago, N., Mumme, J., & Branca, N. (2004). *Learning and teaching linear functions: Video cases for mathematics professional development, 6–10*. Portsmouth, NH: Heinemann.

Sherin, B.L., Sherin, M.G., Colestock, A.A., Russ, R.S., Luna, M.J., Mulligan, M., & Walkoe, J. (2010). Using digital video to investigate teachers' in-the-moment noticing. In K. Gomez, L. Lyons, & J. Radinsky (Eds.), *Learning in the disciplines: Proceedings of the 9th International Conference of the Learning Sciences* (ICLS 2010)—Volume 2, Short Papers, Symposia, and Selected Abstracts. Chicago: International Society of the Learning Sciences.

Sherin, B.L., & Star, J. (2011). Reflections on the study of teacher noticing. In M.G. Sherin, V.R. Jacobs, and R.A. Philipp (Eds.), *Mathematics teacher noticing: Seeing through teachers' eyes* (pp. 66–78). New York: Routledge.

Sherin, M.G., & Han, S. (2004). Teacher learning in the context of a video club. *Teaching and Teacher Education, 20,* 163–183.

Sherin, M.G., Jacobs, V.R., & Philipp, R.A (Eds.). (2011). *Mathematics teacher noticing: Seeing through teachers' eyes*. New York: Routledge.

Sherin, M.G., Russ, R.S., & Colestock, A.A. (2011). Accessing mathematics teachers' in-the-moment noticing. In M.G. Sherin, V.R. Jacobs, & R.A. Philipp (Eds.), *Mathematics teacher noticing: Seeing through teachers' eyes* (pp. 79–94). New York: Routledge.

Sherin, M.G., Russ, R., Sherin, B.L., & Colestock, A. (2008). Professional vision in action: An exploratory study. *Issues in Teacher Education, 17*(2), 27–46.

Sherin, M.G., & van Es., E.A. (2009). Effects of video club participation on teachers' professional vision. *Journal of Teacher Education, 60*(1), 20–37.

Smith, M.S., & Stein, M.K. (2011). *5 practices for orchestrating productive mathematics discussions*. Reston, VA: National Council of Teachers of Mathematics.

van Es, E.A., & Sherin, M.G. (2008). Mathematics teachers "learning to notice" in the context of a video club. *Teaching and Teacher Education, 24,* 244–276.

7

THE ROLE SUBJECT MATTER PLAYS IN PROSPECTIVE TEACHERS' RESPONSIVE TEACHING PRACTICES IN ELEMENTARY MATH AND SCIENCE

Janet E. Coffey and Ann R. Edwards

This chapter arose out of efforts to better understand the ways in which the content knowledge and subject matter background of elementary teacher candidates in a master's certification program were consequential for their learning to attend to student ideas and reasoning in mathematics and science. During the program the authors, who were the teacher candidates' mathematics and science methods course instructors, quickly noticed an interesting pattern: although the courses were designed with the same goals, similar activities, and parallel assignments, as the teacher candidates learned to attend to student thinking in science and mathematics, notable differences emerged in teacher candidates' practices of attending to student thinking across the two disciplines. This chapter presents analyses and findings from a study aimed at explaining the important differences that became apparent across subject matters.

Background Literature

It is well accepted that a teacher's content knowledge matters for teaching (Fishman, Marx, Best, & Tal, 2003; Hill, Rowan, & Ball, 2005; Shulman, 1986; Spillane, 2005; Stodolsky, 1988). An important aim of teacher education, then, is to help teachers to develop the pedagogical content knowledge and practices needed to support student learning (Putnam & Borko, 2000; Shulman, 1986; Singer-Gabella et al., 2009). This study builds on literature in teacher education that focuses on developing teachers' pedagogical content knowledge (Ball, 2000; Putnam & Borko, 2000; Shulman, 1986), specifically that which emphasizes the cultivation of practices of attending to student thinking (Ball, Thames, & Phelps, 2008; Levin, Hammer, & Coffey, 2009; Grossman et al., 2009; Sherin & Han, 2004; Windschitl, Thompson, & Braaten, 2011).

146 Janet E. Coffey and Ann R. Edwards

In efforts to develop an empirical foundation for the notion of pedagogical content knowledge (Shulman, 1986), some researchers and teacher educators have pushed towards more practice-based accounts of what teachers need to know in order to be effective (Ball & Bass, 2000; Ball et al., 2008; Ball, Hill, & Bass, 2005; Herbst & Chazan, 2011; Putnam & Borko, 2000; Windschitl et al., 2011). Ball and Forzani (2010, 2009) emphasize the need to identify the "high-leverage" practices that underlie effective discipline-based teaching and are most likely to affect student learning. Learning to attend and respond to students' ideas and reasoning are critical (Ball & Forzani, 2010; Ball et al., 2005; Ball et al., 2008). Several distinct, although reinforcing, lines of work have spawned from this vision. Important for situating our work are efforts to develop and support teachers' *responsive use* of pedagogical content knowledge by situating teacher education in the contingent complexities of teaching and learning. Kazemi, Franke, and Lampert (2009) establish "ambitious teaching"—where "teachers teach in response to what students do" (p. 11)—as a goal of their work with teacher candidates. This work shifts the focus from requisite teacher knowledge to the practices through which that knowledge is employed, and focuses the teacher education and research communities on the development, understanding, and implementation of pedagogies of practice that help support teacher candidates to learn how to engage in the complex practices of teaching in the often diverse and challenging settings in which they actually engage students.

The design of the methods courses and subsequent analytical focus align with this work and foreground practices of attending and responsiveness as essential to a coherent set of high leverage practices (Ball & Forzani, 2010; Franke, Kazemi, & Battey, 2007; Kazemi et al., 2009; Levin et al., 2009). This focus includes recognizing generative subject-matter specific ideas and disciplinary reasoning practices and using and building on these for instructional decision-making (Ball, 1993; Davis & Krajcik, 2005; Kazemi & Franke, 2004).

Whereas what teachers notice and attend to with respect to student thinking has been a focus of professional development with practicing teachers (Jacobs, Franke, Carpenter, Levi, & Battey, 2007; Sherin & Han, 2004; Sherin & van Es, 2009), less research has addressed the role that pre-service teacher education can play in facilitating the development of teachers' practices of attending to student thinking. The research that does exist has shown that teacher candidates' engagement in specific instructional activities that embody ambitious teaching through scaffolded opportunities for rehearsal, practice, and enactment can support development of practices that undergird high-quality mathematics teaching (Franke & Kazemi, 2001; Singer-Gabella et al., 2009; van Es, 2011) and science teaching (Windschitl et al., 2011). None of this work, however, examines practice across disciplinary contexts.

Science and mathematics teaching can present challenges for elementary teachers, who often lack strong foundations in these disciplines (Ball, 1990; Davis & Krajcik, 2005; Lewis et al., 1999; National Research Council, 2007).

Furthermore, while we know that the subject matters for instruction, the ways in which a subject matters for *learning to* teach—thus, learning to respond to student ideas—is less clear. Our study examines this issue with respect to learning to teach elementary mathematics and science, seeking insights specifically into the following research questions:

- In what ways is the process of learning to attend to student thinking similar or different across school subject matters, specifically mathematics and science?
- What factors influence such differences?

In this chapter, we focus primarily on the latter question, though in doing so we draw on examples illustrative of the first question.

Our Study

This study took place during the 2008–09 school year in the context of a one-year graduate-level elementary masters certification program at a large public university located in the mid-Atlantic United States. The study specifically focused on the mathematics and science methods courses and associated field experiences. The two authors were course instructors. The design of the program, and the mathematics and science methods courses in particular, were anchored in "high leverage practices" of eliciting, analyzing and interpreting, and responding to students' ideas and reasoning (Kazemi et al., 2009; Ball et al., 2008), which included centrally notions of formative assessment (e.g., Black & Wiliam, 1998; Erickson, 2007).

Coursework framed teaching as responsiveness to students' ideas and reasoning. Both the mathematics and science methods courses asked students to engage in case studies of student thinking and individual and collaborative reflection on student work, among other field-based assignments. Both courses also regularly engaged students as mathematics or science learners, participating in doing disciplinary reasoning and problem-solving tasks and reflecting on what that doing entailed. Parallel assignments were given in the two methods courses, including an initial positioning paper, a case study of student reasoning, curriculum analyses, lesson planning, and individual and collaborative reflection on artifacts of practice. Each course met weekly for three hours during the fall semester, and instructors met weekly to coordinate course emphases, in-class activities, and field-based experiences. In addition to university coursework, the teacher candidates spent three days each week in field placements in large public school districts with uniform curricular demands and diverse student populations.

Data was drawn from coursework, including artifacts generated in participants' field placements where they had teaching responsibilities. We analyzed audio and video records of course meetings as well as the course assignments,

148 Janet E. Coffey and Ann R. Edwards

which included written reflections and activities involving analyses of students' scientific and mathematical thinking; field-based assignments involving instructional design and implementation; an analytic case of their students' disciplinary thinking and leaning (for mathematics and science); and observations of teaching (video recordings and in-person observations).

In early observations and conversations, we noticed a variety of differences, including how the teacher candidates talked and wrote about each of the disciplines, their previous experiences as a learner in mathematics and science, and, especially, their teaching practices. We sought to systematically examine the nature of those differences, as well as to investigate cases of similarities. Analytic work across the 26 cases revealed several dimensions as salient for explaining patterns and contrasts across the broader group. The data presented below focuses primarily on one teacher candidate to illustrate the nature of distinctions we noted as individuals learned to teach science and mathematics. Kim, who was interning in third-grade classrooms at the time of this study, is just one of 26 consenting teachers from whom data was used to inform the broader analysis. We do not argue that the analyses presented here comprehensively capture all the dynamics at play in attending and responding to student thinking; however, across the teacher candidates the dimensions we discuss below appeared fundamental to understanding the variation in learning to teach in discipline domains within the broader cohort.

A Case Study of an Elementary Teacher Candidate's Engagement in Attending to Student Thinking in Mathematics and Science

Like many of her peers, Kim demonstrated differences in her practices of attending to student thinking across her mathematics and science methods courses. We include two snippets from her coursework and interactions with children that illustrate these differences. The subsequent section builds on this description to specify the nature of the differences—what she attends to, how she attends, and how that becomes consequential for students.

Practices of Attending to Disciplinary Thinking

Kim's Science Teaching

Over the course of the semester in her science methods coursework, the focus of Kim's analysis of classroom activity was on the substance—i.e., on the meaning behind what the student was trying to convey rather than solely on correctness—of students' ideas and reasoning. In her classroom teaching experiences, attending to student thinking served as a way for Kim to help her students clarify their reasoning and explore and engage with each other's ideas. Kim's written analyses of student thinking and reflection on her own teaching show that over the course of the semester she began to see her role as a science teacher as one of facilitating

The Role Subject Matter Plays   **149**

students' articulation of reasoning, and student engagement in reasoning as the primary bridge to conceptual understanding. The analysis below helps illuminate this positioning.

The following excerpt comes from Kim's transcript of her third-grade students discussing the question of why there were more hours of daylight in summer than in winter, a topic and format that Kim selected for her case study assignment. The goal of this assignment was to "elicit students' ideas and reasoning so that you can interpret and think about ways to respond to them" (Course assignment description). This transcript segment begins with an explanation set forth by one of the students early in the conversation that "the sun goes around the Earth slower and the Earth spins faster."

Kurt: I was thinking that the sun . . . that the sun goes around the Earth slower and the Earth spins faster. So, so, it's um, so the sun goes to the other side of the Earth, um it goes to the other side of the Earth cause because the Earth is rotating around . . . [*Gestures movement that he is describing with hands.*]

Kim: Can you draw me a picture of what you mean up here? Can you draw a picture? I'll erase some space. Can you draw a picture you think?

Kurt: Yup.

Kim: OK, draw us a picture. Let's see if we agree on understanding Kurt.

Kurt: So this (*drawing sun's orbit around Earth*), so the sun is going around and this the Earth is spinning fast. So this is the, hold on, this is the Northern Hemisphere and this is the Southern. So now it's so, so, and then it turns like it turns really fast like, and if you, its night time and the sun is here and . . .

Kim: Ok. Guys, look up here at what Kurt did. He said, here's the sun, he said the sun is going around the Earth like this. And the Earth is spinning like that. Does anyone agree or disagree with what Kurt is saying. Think about what we know about the Earth, and day and night, and the sun . . . Rye?

Rye: I agree.

Kim: You agree with him? Why do you agree with him?

Rye: Because the sun does go around fast, and the Earth, but I disagree a little bit because the Earth goes slow around.

Kim: Explain it, say it again. What do you mean the Earth goes faster and what do you mean it goes slower?

Rye: It goes slower because if it went faster it would be the year 3000 tomorrow.

Kim: So you're saying if it went too fast then time would pass?

On first consideration, what may jump out in the transcript are the inaccuracies of the students' ideas, for example that the sun is going around the Earth and that there is variability in the rate of rotation. Rather than immediately addressing these inaccuracies, Kim's treatment of those ideas—both in her immediate responses in the classroom discussion and in her written reflection—demonstrates a commitment to helping students clarify their reasoning and engage with each

150 Janet E. Coffey and Ann R. Edwards

other's ideas. Importantly, she wanted to understand her students' thinking. Despite the fact that Kurt's and Rye's ideas were wrong, Kim sought clarification (e.g., asking students to draw a picture, asking for more explanation, asking for clarification, rephrasing to check her interpretation) in a way that indicates she was trying to understand the reasoning behind the explanations. She also pulled the students' attention to the ideas (even the wrong ones) and asked them to respond to their classmates' ideas (e.g., referring to the diagram Kurt drew on the board, pulling out and restating the idea and asking if anybody agrees or disagrees).

In analysis of this conversation Kim wrote, "Some students said that the Earth can speed up and slow down, and that's why we have longer or shorter days . . . They do get that the Earth rotates on its axis and that is what causes day and night. So it must seem natural that the speed of the rotation must change to explain the change in the length of day. We can't feel the Earth moving anyway, so we probably wouldn't feel a change in speed." Implicit in her statement is an assumption that students are engaging in logical explanation. Following their reasoning and trying to understand where students may be coming from helps her support the students in developing more robust explanations. We see her pushing students to consider the ideas in light of other things they "know"—"think about what we already know about the Earth, and day, and night, and the sun." In her analysis and reflection, Kim also noted instances when she could have made different instructional moves: ". . . Looking back I could have followed up with asking them what causes the Earth to spin slower or faster." This analysis indicated that she was also able to identify instances where she could have pressed students on their reasoning in productive directions. Even though she did not necessarily recognize the opportunity in the moment in the midst of the real-time flow of teaching, she was able to see the opportunity in retrospect, after a closer review of the transcript.

Kim appeared to allow goals for conceptual understanding to emerge from the discussion. For example, although she expressed concern in her analysis about the inaccuracy of the statement that "the sun goes around the Earth slower and the Earth spins faster," Kim addressed students' conceptual understandings not by "correcting" their statements but by encouraging students to examine the logic of their reasoning—". . . Ok. Guys, look up here at what Kurt did. He said, here's the sun, he said the sun is going around the Earth like this. And the Earth is spinning like that. Does anyone agree or disagree with what Kurt is saying? Think about what we know about the Earth, and day and night, and the sun . . ." When the first student she called on agreed with this statement, she responded by asking for the grounds on which he agreed. In any given moment of interaction, Kim attended to students' ideas and reasoning in ways that propelled them to engage meaningfully with each other's ideas.

Following the exchange above, Kim offered students a globe and differently sized balls "to allow them to model what they knew." She explained, "I had hoped that if we established some things we all agreed to be true, we would be able to reason that the Earth always rotates on its axis at a constant speed once every twenty-four hours." After working with the globe and balls, a student challenged the idea that the sun orbits the Earth, offering as explanation that "the Earth spins so slow that the side facing the sun is in the summer and it stays that way until it moves out of the light, and then it becomes winter." Kim noted,

> Her response was right in so many ways . . . she knew that the Earth orbits around the sun and that the relationship somehow caused the different seasons to happen on different sides of the earth. She also knew that the Earth was rotating on its axis while it was orbiting. However, it was hard for me to let it go there because we just established that the day/night cycle happens every twenty-four hours . . .

Kim held students accountable for their reasoning. Recognizing the inconsistency in the student's reasoning, Kim explained:

> I brought the discussion back to that idea and sure enough a student was able to challenge her on her idea. Dan responded, 'I have to disagree with Verna because . . . if it was summer over here, if it was summer over here, then like how could it move because its [sic] summer over here and its winter over here. I don't get it. Because if it was summer over here, it would have to be summer there for, like, a season and if was, um, winter over here it would have to be winter for a season. And then they would never have day, well it would never be night.

As this brief snippet exemplifies, in science teaching Kim saw students' reasoning as the bridge to their understanding, and her role as teacher as one of facilitating this connection. We saw Kim attend to the nature and clarity of student's reasoning and ideas, largely so students could begin to attend to the same, which she began to see as the primary work for learners doing science. In the moment she does not appear to be concerned about the specific directionality of the reasoning, although in retrospective reflection she expected to see conceptual progress towards canonically accepted explanations. This differs from what we saw in her math teaching, which we turn to now.

Kim's Mathematics Teaching

Kim's attending practices looked quite different in the mathematics methods course. For Kim, successfully navigating and completing a mathematical task was essential for "getting it" or "making sense" of the mathematics—for herself as well as her students. Thus, in contrast to her attending practices in science instruction, where her primary instructional goals were revealing and supporting students' reasoning processes, attending in mathematics teaching was a means of assessing students' understandings relevant to the task at hand and determining the viability

152 Janet E. Coffey and Ann R. Edwards

of their approach for successfully completing the task. She then drew upon this information to pose questions that she felt would guide students toward successful solutions. Thus, while she attended to the substance of student mathematical thinking in her practice (and, as will be shown, valued conceptual reasoning), these practices were embedded within an instructional approach oriented to task completion rather than mathematical reasoning processes such as justifying and representing.

The following example comes from Kim's case study project where she is working with a small group in class, and is typical of her questioning practice as well as her perspective on "making sense." The goal of this assignment was to "create opportunities to reveal and respond to student mathematical thinking using problematic tasks in your teaching" and to "closely analyze the thinking of three selected students" (Assignment description). For this assignment, Kim chose the task: "Greg climbed 2,600 meters up the side of a mountain. His brother Harry climbed half as far. How far did Harry climb?"[1] Before launching the task, Kim focused the students on problem-solving strategies ("What are some important steps when you are problem solving?" "What are some possibilities for solving problems that maybe you've tried before, some strategies you used?"), as well as the multiplicity of strategies that could be used to solve a problem ("Are there different ways to solve problems?" "Do you agree that there are multiple ways to solve a problem not just one correct way?"). Though she began by soliciting students' ideas on problem-solving, her interactions with the students as they worked on the task reflect how she uses questions to reveal students' understandings in order to "guide" them towards "success" on the problem. Immediately prior to this start of the excerpt, Kim has looked over at Mish and sees that he is confused about how to begin.

Kim: What if we separate these two numbers [2000 and 600], Mish. What if we separate them by what their place value is?

Mish: What do you mean separate them?

Kim: What does the two really mean there?

Mish: Two thousand.

Kim: Ok, so if we do 2000, then what's the rest? Do you remember when we did expanded notation?

Mish: Yes. . .

Kim: So, how can we divide all these numbers in half? What is half of zero?

Mish: Zero.

Kim: Yup, half of zero is zero. What is half of 600?

Mish: 300.

Kim: You're right. How do you know that it's half of 600?

Mish: Because 300 plus 300 is 600. . .[Mish completes the problem, writing 1000, 300, 0, 0 and then 1300.]

Kim: You're right, now tell me why.

The Role Subject Matter Plays **153**

Mish: Because that's in the thousands [referring to 1000], that's in the hundreds [referring to 300], that's in the tens and ones [referring to the two zeroes], so and I don't have anything to add up to these so they stay in [referring to the 1 in the 1000s digit and the 3 in the hundreds digit], these two I don't change [referring to the zeroes].

Kim: And you're going to add these two numbers together?

Mish: Yes.

Kim: So we've figured out half and you're going to add the halves together. Does that make sense to you?

Mish: No.

Kim: No? Well why doesn't it make sense. Think about it. You know you're right and I just want you to think about why that's true.

The episode begins with Kim's using a "what if" question to suggest an approach to the problem involving the decomposition of 2,600 "by what their place value is," a reference to expanded notation. This suggestion, notably, is not a strategy for solving the problem, unlike "drawing a picture" or "figuring out what you have to find," which were suggestions raised by other students in the same discussion. Rather, Kim's question suggests a specific calculational move and provides a clue or guidepost for a solution path she has in mind. However, she is not explicit about her reasons for taking this first step, nor does she explain how it is related to the problem context. Mish asks her, "What do you mean separate them?," indicating that he is uncertain about what she is referring to. Kim responds with a question that focuses his attention on the value of the digit 2, "What does the two really mean here?" He answers correctly and in the next several turns, Kim's questions lead Mish through the procedures involved in decomposing 2,600 using expanded notation, dividing each of the resultant quantities in half, and then recomposing to get the final answer. She also asks questions along the way that check his knowledge at specific junctures of the process (e.g., "What is half of zero?" "What is half of 600?" "How do you know that it's half of 600?"), to which Mish gives brief correct responses.

Once he arrives at the correct answer, Kim first confirms that he is correct and then directs Mish to explain why. This move is Kim's first clear invitation for Mish to share his reasoning in this episode, and he proceeds to try to explain how he arrived at 1300 from 1000 + 300 + 0 + 0. However, Kim does not understand his explanation and, rather than asking for clarification, she revoices what she supposes he means—that adding 1300 and 1300 is 2600—with a question seeking his confirmation ("you're going to add these two numbers together?"). When he answers affirmatively (even though this was likely not what he meant), she then continues, "So we've figured out half and you're going to add the halves together," providing a kind of summary of her understanding of his process. However, he is talking about a different "two numbers" than she is. He is referring to how he arrives at 1300 from the decomposed 1000, 300, 0 and 0, while she is referring

154 Janet E. Coffey and Ann R. Edwards

to adding 1300 and 1300 as a way of checking his work. Thus, while she begins this exchange with an invitation for Mish to share his thinking, she closes with an inaccurate summary of what she thought he was thinking and what she thought he should do.

The episode ends with a final checking of his understanding ("Does that make sense to you?"). When Mish says "no," Kim responds by telling him to "think about" why his answer is correct. In contrast to how she uses similar questions such as "Does it make sense to you?" in her science instruction, in this mathematics episode, Kim poses the question almost rhetorically; that is, since he was able to successfully arrive at the solution ("you know you're right"), Kim's response implies that Mish simply needed to take the time to think through and articulate the procedures he undertook to complete the problem.

These closing turns reveal what "making sense" means to Kim in teaching mathematics. Rather than a process of exploration and meaning construction, "making sense" of mathematics is about arriving at the correct answer and understanding why a chosen solution strategy works. Kim's perspective on "making sense," however, despite the apparent similarity to a procedural focus in mathematics teaching, does not preclude attention to conceptual understanding and reasoning processes. Indeed, in her own mathematical activity in the math methods class, Kim demonstrates that she values deep understanding of mathematical concepts and processes, such as mathematical explanation and justification. Regardless, however, Kim's instructional focus is on helping students to get to the correct solution and to grasp the steps involved in getting there, including the concepts and processes involved in "making sense" of the solution.

Kim viewed her instructional approach as consistent with the mathematics methods course's goal of listening and responding to student thinking, in that her questions could elicit a student's reasoning and help her guide the students down solution paths. As Kim explained in her analysis of the interaction above, "By [this] task, I felt really comfortable with my questioning strategy and I think I was able to do less work and let the students do more work. Some of my favorite questions were: Where are you going next? How will you know when you have your answer? What does that mean? When I was watching [the] video, I think that these questions turned the work back on the students and made them think about what it was that they were doing and trying to accomplish. It also helped me understand them." Examination of the transcript excerpt, however, does not appear to support Kim's interpretation that she is doing "less work" and letting the student do "more work." Though she asks questions and directly requests student explanations with moves such as "How do you know?" and "Now tell me why," her attending moves in this case, as well as other mathematics teaching episodes, narrow the mathematical possibilities of the task. In contrast to her work in the science classroom, Kim's analyses of her students' mathematical thinking address conceptual and procedural understanding, though not mathematical processes such as explanation and justification.

The Role Subject Matter Plays **155**

Making Sense of Kim's Differences in Attending Practices

Since our study was trying to understand teacher candidates' emergent attending practices, we focused analyses on elements of mathematics and science that arose in ways that would support or hinder teacher candidates' attention. It is likely not surprising, then, that the teacher candidates' orientation to the specific discipline—mathematics or science—became one initial focus. Through analysis we saw that a teacher's visions for teaching not only were subject specific but also seemed to link to their subject matter teaching practices, and thus teachers' orientation toward discipline-specific teaching became another salient dimension. We also recognize that any attention is informed by a multitude of factors, including institutional demands, such as standards, learning objectives, and accountability measures (Apple, 2004; Darling-Hammond & Rustique-forrester, 2005; Popham, 2001; Resnick, 2001; Valli, Croninger, Chambliss, Graeber, & Buese, 2008); perceptions of students (Edwards, 2010; Rosenthal & Jacobson, 1968); one's own experience as a student (Lortie, 1975); as well as subject matter understandings and background (Ball, 1993; Cohen, 1990; Spillane, 2005; Stodolsky, 1988).

We identified two key factors that were salient for understanding how Kim and her peers were learning to teach in mathematics and science:

- **Orientation to the discipline:** Beliefs about nature of each discipline (mathematics and science), discipline-related experiences, epistemological issues, attitudes and dispositions, content area competency (self-described and demonstrated).
- **Orientation towards discipline-specific teaching:** Visions of discipline-specific teaching, role of the teacher, ideas about student learning, goals and priorities within the discipline.

We recognize that the influence is not unidirectional. For example, we have data to suggest that aspects of context, such as instructional materials, can focus teachers' attending practices (and attention) in such a way as to influence how teachers view the subject matter and subject matter teaching.

We now return to Kim to consider how her orientations to the disciplines and discipline-specific teaching influence and to help make sense of the ways in which she attended to student thinking and reflected on that practice. We could say that the differences primarily resided in the different formats and topics of the actual activities. In science, Kim is leading a whole-group discussion, whereas in mathematics she is working with one student during a small-group task. Further, the prompts are as different as the structures of pedagogical activity. While we do not want to rule these factors out as contributing influences, it is important to note that the teaching episodes came from very similar case study assignments, where the teacher education students were able to choose a task or activity that would elicit rich student thinking. That Kim selected such differing tasks for mathematics and science assignments suggests that she envisions eliciting student thinking differently in the disciplines and, perhaps, that she envisions the disciplines themselves very differently.

Such a difference in attending practices could also be a result of the very nature of the disciplines of mathematics and science, i.e., that inherent differences in the structures and practices of the disciplines result in different attending practices. This possibility is certainly worthy of further consideration. Here, however, disciplinary differences appear tightly coupled with teacher candidates' experiences and orientations towards disciplines, making a closer examination of the impact of the nature of the disciplines difficult to tease out.

The differences we saw in Kim's mathematics and science attending practices with students seem to coordinate with differences we see in her orientations to, and relationships with, the disciplines of science and mathematics and teaching in the disciplines. The section that follows takes up these dynamics and offers an illustration of how these dimensions can interplay in the presentation of two such different teaching practices. While we are not making causal claims and recognize that other factors are at play, we illustrate that there is a dynamic here worth further exploration.

Shedding Light on Kim's Attending Practices in Science

Orientation to the Discipline

Kim identified science as one of her favorite subjects growing up, in part because she said it was a "break" from other academic subject matters. She wrote of it as "a chance to explore, and have fun doing it." Not unlike some of her peers, she drew on experiences outside of the classroom to inform her views about science. When asked to describe a positive learning experience in science, she wrote of exploring the woods and streams around her house as a child, and about excursions with her father. The theme of exploration—of things and ideas—is echoed in her own science teaching.

Kim's practices of attending to student thinking further facilitated her own engagement and explorations in doing science. In the science methods course, discussion of video clips of elementary students doing science presented opportunities for engagement in reasoning about interesting phenomena. An example occurred during a conversation the teacher candidates were having about a transcript of second-graders talking about whether a cup full of water and ice will overflow when the ice melts. Two competing ideas were under consideration by the elementary-aged students: "Ice gets smaller when it melts so it would be less water;" and "So the water holds the ice up and then when it melts it sinks to the bottom and pushes the water out." Kim asked her classmates, "Why *does* ice expand when it freezes? What's happening?" Like this, on many occasions, Kim displayed an interest in investigating the children's question for her own scientific understanding, as well as to better understand the students'

The Role Subject Matter Plays **157**

reasoning. She appeared to move fluidly between thinking as a *science learner* and thinking as a *teacher*.

Orientation to Discipline-Specific Teaching

At the start of the semester, Kim articulated the importance of "student ownership" in science, which she saw achieved through the relevance of topics. Over the semester, Kim's focus shifted to creating opportunities for students to articulate and question their scientific reasoning. She still talked of "ownership," but that came through thinking deeply about something. Her primary goal involved helping students engage in questioning and sustained reasoning of everyday phenomena to which they may or may not bring prior knowledge, or even see as relevant. To help students engage with each other's ideas, Kim regularly asked, "Do you understand what she is saying?" and "Does that make sense?" We see some of those same questions—does that make sense?—in the interaction in her mathematics instruction; however, their context and function were quite different. In science, content goals became secondary in practice to her facilitation of and responsiveness to reasoning, although she did not drop them all together. One led to the other.

Shedding Light on Kim's Attending Practices in Mathematics

Orientation to the Discipline

During the semester in her math methods class, Kim's orientation to mathematics shifted from a belief that mathematics is primarily about getting a "right answer" and a focus on its instrumentality to the centrality of conceptual understanding and sense-making, though she held a particular view of "making sense" of mathematics that supported the instructional practices illustrated earlier. At the start of the semester, Kim reflected that her experiences learning mathematics fostered a view of school mathematics as concrete, straightforward exercises that "are either right or wrong," and a view of mathematics learning as primarily mastery through repetition and memorization. At the same time, she recognized the instrumentality of mathematics outside of school and felt that the usefulness of mathematics was a key motivation for students. Through the course of the semester, her own doing of mathematics became more about achieving deep conceptual understanding and the satisfaction of "getting it" through "successful" problem-solving. She approached mathematical explorations and problematic tasks in the methods class as puzzles to be pursued. As in the science methods class, she took up opportunities to analyze student thinking as invitations to engage deeply in the conceptual content. Despite her clear enthusiasm and competency in pursuing these personal mathematical challenges, her central goal, however, remained "getting" or mastering them. She tended not to view the processes of conjecturing or problem-solving, for example, as worthy mathematical goals in and of themselves and oriented strongly to task completion.

158 Janet E. Coffey and Ann R. Edwards

Orientation to Discipline-Specific Teaching

Teaching mathematics for Kim involved providing students with opportunities to explore and make sense of problems in order to achieve "success" on the problem. She reasoned that this mastery of tasks would help them to develop understandings of mathematical concepts. She also recognized that tasks in mathematics may be open to multiples strategies or solution paths. She saw her role as revealing students' strategies and reasoning by asking questions and then using that information to pose questions that supported students' movement toward correct solutions. During the mathematics methods course, she also began to value students' sharing of their strategies with one another to make multiple solutions available to students so they had other ways of successfully solving problems. In this way, she saw questioning and eliciting student thinking as strategies for supporting students' success with problems.

On many levels, we see notable differences in how Kim attended to her students' thinking in her mathematics and science teaching. As noted in the previous analysis, these differences can be understood, in part, in light of her distinct orientations to the disciplines and discipline-specific teaching. While Kim was typical among the group in the manifesting of significant differences across disciplines, the variation that emerged across the teacher candidates was also importantly illuminating. It is in explaining the variation where we begin to see the differences in dynamics of the dimensions, as well limitations of focusing on discipline-related dynamics alone.

Understanding Variation

Due to space, we chose to focus on the case of Kim; however, variation across teachers was informative. Other cases revealed that stronger disciplinary background and confidence alone were not enough to precipitate robust practices of attending to student thinking. We were also reminded that the dynamics of teaching cannot be considered apart from the institutional and social contexts in which they occur. Contrasts in science and mathematics teaching were also rooted in different contextual presses, such as high-stakes testing and prescription of adopted curriculum. Other cases highlight how views and expectations of students shade notions of attending.

Conclusion

This study began to explore the role of disciplines in learning to teach within and across math and science at the elementary grade levels. Data reveal that practices of attending to student thinking have disciplinary grounding and therefore should not be expected to share generic characteristics across disciplinary contexts, and analysis provided some insight into how we can account for those differences.

The role that subject matter plays in learning to attend to student thinking and learning to teach is particularly important to understand for work with elementary school teachers. To support teacher candidates' learning to conceptualize, and to enact attending to student thinking as central to teaching, we need to better understand how disciplinary understandings and orientations toward teaching specific to those disciplines interact with practices of attending to student thinking, including how, to what, and for what ends. We have begun to identify dimensions that seem salient and dynamic. Our work suggests that teacher education, particularly for elementary teacher candidates, should consider how the interactions among these dimensions of teacher knowledge and practice can be leveraged to foster deep reconsideration of discipline and disciplinary teaching. We see promise in better understanding these dynamics for informing teacher education.

We recognize limitations of our study. We considered teacher candidates only during semester-long methods courses, but see longer-term study work as necessary to better understand what travels with them from our coursework to their classroom teaching. We also know that disciplinary-related dynamics are just part of the constellation of influences on learning to attend and attending to student reasoning, as suggested above. Better understanding how factors such as institutional context and curriculum interplay with disciplinary-related dynamics, particularly for elementary school teachers, is worthy of further study.

We see promise in teacher education's capacity to help teacher candidates establish a stance towards practices of disciplinary attending that contribute to more robust notions of disciplinary learning and understanding and deeper conceptual understandings. We also see considerable value in teaching across multiple content areas and contexts. Knowing the student in multiple contexts, including across subject areas, may provide useful insights for identifying resources students bring to their subject matter learning. Elementary teacher education offers an opportunity to support teacher candidates' navigating across subject areas—including across the nature of the discipline and the disciplines as represented in school and text. We see these directions as additional generative next steps for study.

Note

1 Kim's choice of task would likely not meet the criterion of a "problematic task" for most mathematics educators. We discuss the potential significance of her choice later. We chose to present this particular episode because it clearly and concisely illustrates the predominant patterns in her mathematics teaching practices.

References

Apple, M. (2004). Creating difference: Neo-liberalism, neo-conservatism and the politics of educational reform. *Educational Policy, 18*(1), 12–44.

Ball, D. (1990). The mathematical understandings that prospective teachers bring to teacher education. *Elementary School Journal, 90*, 449–466.

Ball, D. (1993). With an eye on the mathematical horizon: Dilemmas of teaching elementary school mathematics. *Elementary School Journal, 93*(4), 373–397.

Ball, D. (2000). Bridging practices: Intertwining content and pedagogy in teaching and learning to teach. *Journal of Teacher Education, 51*, 241–247.

Ball, D., & Bass, H. (2000). Interweaving content and pedagogy in teaching and learning to teach: Knowing and using mathematics. In J. Boaler (Ed.), *Multiple perspectives on the teaching and learning of mathematics* (pp. 83–104). Westport, CT: Ablex.

Ball, D., & Forzani, F. (2009). The work of teaching and the challenge for teacher education. *Journal of Teacher Education, 60*(5), 497–511.

Ball, D., & Forzani, F. (2010). Teaching skillful teaching. *Educational Leadership, 68*(4), 40–45.

Ball, D., Hill, H., & Bass, H. (2005). Knowing mathematics for teaching: Who knows mathematics well enough to teach third grade, and how can we decide? *American Educator, 29*(1), 14–17, 20–22, 43–46.

Ball, D., Thames, M., & Phelps, G. (2008). Content knowledge for teaching: What makes it special? *Journal of Teacher Education, 59*(5), 389–407.

Black, P., & Wiliam, D. (1998). Assessment and classroom learning. *Assessment in Education, 5*(1), 7–74.

Cohen, D.K. (1990). A revolution in one classroom: The case of Mrs. Oublier. *Educational Evaluation and Policy Analysis, 12*, 327–345.

Darling-Hammond, L., & Rustique-forrester, E. (2005). The consequences of student testing for teaching and teacher quality. *Yearbook of the National Society for the Study of Education, 104*(2), 289–319.

Davis, E., & Krajcik, J. (2005). Designing educative curriculum materials to promote teacher learning. *Educational Researcher, 34*, 3–14.

Edwards, A.R. (2010). Pursuing problems of practice in collaborative reflection: Making sense of diversity as an issue of teaching practice. In M.Q. Foote (Ed.), *Mathematics teaching and learning in K-12: Equity and professional development* (pp. 59–76). New York: Palgrave.

Erickson, F. (2007). Some thoughts on "proximal" formative assessment of student learning. *Yearbook of the National Society for the Study of Education, 106*(1), 105–131.

Fishman, B.J., Marx, R.W., Best, S., & Tal, R.T. (2003). Linking teacher and student learning to improve professional development in systemic reform. *Teaching and Teacher Education, 19*, 643–658.

Franke, M.L., & Kazemi, E. (2001). Learning to teach mathematics: Developing a focus on students' mathematical thinking. *Theory into Practice, 40*, 102–109.

Franke, M.L., Kazemi, E., & Battey, D.S. (2007). Mathematics teaching and classroom practices. In F.K. Lester Jr. (Ed.), *The second handbook of research on mathematics teaching and learning* (pp. 225–256). Charlotte, NC: Information Age.

Grossman P., Compton, C., Igra, D., Ronfeldt, M., Shahan, E., & Williamson, P. (2009). Teaching practice: A cross-professional perspective. *Teachers College Record, 111*(9), 2055–2100.

Herbst, P., & Chazan, D. (2011). Research on practical rationality: Studying the justification of action in mathematics teaching. *The Mathematics Enthusiast, 8*(3), 405–462.

Hill, H., Rowan, B., & Ball, D. (2005). Effects of teachers' mathematical knowledge for teaching on student achievement. *American Educational Research Journal, 42*(2), 371–406.

Jacobs, V.R., Franke, M.L., Carpenter, T.P., Levi, L., & Battey, D. (2007). Professional development focused on children's algebraic reasoning in elementary school. *Journal for Research in Mathematics Education, 38*(3), 258–288.

The Role Subject Matter Plays **161**

Kazemi, E., & Franke, M.L. (2004). Teacher learning in mathematics: Using student work to promote collective inquiry. *Journal of Mathematics Teacher Education, 7*, 203–235.

Kazemi, E., Franke, M., & Lampert, M. (2009). Developing pedagogies in teacher education to support novice teachers' ability to enact ambitious instruction. In R. Hunter, B. Bicknell, & T. Burgess (Eds.), *Crossing divides, proceedings of the 32nd annual conference of The Mathematics Education Research Group of Australasia*, Vol. 1 (pp. 11–29). Palmerston North, New Zealand: Mathematics Education Research Group of Australasia.

Levin, D.M., Hammer, D., & Coffey, J.E. (2009). Novice teachers' attention to student thinking. *Journal of Teacher Education, 60*(2), 142–154.

Lewis, L. Parsad, B., Careym, N., Bartfai, N., Farris, E., & Smerdon, B. (1999). *Teacher quality: A report on the preparation and qualifications of public school teachers.* Washington, DC: National Center for Education Statistics.

Lortie, D. (1975). *Schoolteacher: A sociological study.* London: University of Chicago Press.

National Research Council. (2007). *Taking science to school: Learning and teaching science in grades K-8.* Washington, DC: National Academics Press.

Popham, W.J. (2001). Teaching to the test. *Educational Leadership, 58*(6), 16–20.

Putnam, R.T., & Borko, H. (2000). What do new views of knowledge and thinking have to say about research on teacher learning? *Educational Researcher, 29*(1), 4–15.

Resnick, L.B. (2001). The mismeasure of learning. *Education Next, 1*(3), 78–83.

Rosenthal, R., & Jacobson, L. (1968). *Pygmalion in the classroom.* New York: Holt, Rinehart & Winston.

Sherin, M.G., & Han, S.Y. (2004). Teacher learning in the context of a video club. *Teacher and Teacher Education, 20*, 163–183.

Sherin, M.G., & van Es, E.A. (2009). Effects of video club participation on teachers' professional vision. *Journal of Teacher Education, 60*(1), 20–37.

Shulman, L. (1986). Those who understand: Knowledge growth in teaching, *Educational Researcher, 15*(2), 4–14.

Singer-Gabella, M., Cartier, J., Forman, E., Knapp, N., Kannan, P., Shahan, E., Lancaster, L., & Barrick, N. (2009). Contextualizing learning progressions for prospective elementary teachers of mathematics and science. Paper presented at the annual meeting of the American Educational Research Association, San Diego, CA.

Spillane, J. (2005). Primary school leadership practice: How the subject matters. *School Leadership & Management, 25*(4), 383–397.

Stodolsky, S. (1988). *The subject matters: Classroom activity in math and social studies.* Chicago: University of Chicago Press.

Valli, L., Croninger, R., Chambliss, M., Graeber, A., & Buese, D. (2008). *Test driven: High-stakes accountability in elementary schools.* New York: Teachers College Press.

van Es, E. (2011). A framework for learning to notice student thinking. In M. Sherin, V. Jacobs, & R. Philipp (Eds.), *Mathematics teacher noticing: Seeing through teachers' eyes* (pp. 134–151). New York: Routledge.

Windschitl, M., Thompson, J., & Braaten, M. (2011). Fostering ambitious pedagogy in novice teachers: The new role of tool-supported analyses of student work. *Teachers College Record, 113*(7), 1311–1360.

8

ATTENDING TO STUDENTS' EPISTEMIC AFFECT

Lama Z. Jaber

It was the first day of the water cycle module when a group of fifth graders were grappling to explain what happens to rain water that evaporates from a puddle. Students suggested multiple ideas; however, it was not clear how all the ideas related to each other. At one point, Eric,[1] one of the students, was having a side conversation with others at his table. He looked frustrated and made intense facial expressions and emphatic statements about some of the ideas. Noticing these behaviors, Mr. James, the teacher, invited Eric to share his thinking with the class. Eric expressed confusion about the connections between the different ideas, and as he struggled to communicate his own idea, which concerned water "steaming" and "rising up," causing the water level to decrease, Eric looked uneasy and anxious. When Mr. James pressed him to clarify his reasoning, Eric became more and more hesitant and showed signs of frustration.

What could Mr. James do at this point? It was clear that Eric was in distress and Mr. James could relieve Eric from this uncomfortable situation simply by calling on another student. Mr. James could also give Eric a hint or two to alleviate some discomfort. But how about encouraging Eric to persist and articulate his idea? This way, Mr. James could help Eric and the rest of the students appreciate the value of struggle in intellectual work, and Eric could see himself as a significant contributor to the conversation.

This situation might resonate with many educators who find themselves in similar situations in the classroom and also wonder how to manage the tension between relieving students' frustration and supporting their disciplinary engagement. As I review here, teachers commonly report a challenge in being responsive to students' feelings and well-being while at the same time attending to students' disciplinary learning, a challenge that often leads them to compromise one goal over the other.

Attending to Students' Epistemic Affect **163**

In this chapter, I propose that by rethinking the nature and role of affect, educators can bridge these two goals. When affect is perceived as part and parcel of the epistemic experience, educators can recognize and respond to students' emotions, *not at the expense of* but *as integral to* their attention to the discipline. For instance, rather than seeking to shield students from discomfort and frustration, they can see these moments as opportunities for students to experience and appreciate the emotional complexity of intellectual pursuits. This perspective motivates my guiding questions, which I explore here in the context of Mr. James's and Eric's interaction:

- In what ways did Mr. James attend and respond to Eric's affect as integral to his disciplinary learning?
- Were these acts of attending and responding consequential to Eric's engagement and persistence in inquiry?

Using classroom video and interview data, I argue that Mr. James's intention for Eric to struggle at the intellectual level was part of his caring for him as an epistemic agent (Scardamalia & Bereiter, 2006). In this way, I illustrate how caring can be connected to, rather than separate from, attending to the discipline, and I discuss implications for instruction and teacher education.

Epistemic Affect

This work draws on a perspective on "epistemic affect" (Jaber & Hammer, in press), which refers to the feelings and emotions inherent in inquiry, and to the awareness and regulation of these feelings and emotions. Epistemic affect includes, for example, excitement for ideas, unease at inconsistencies, fascination with phenomena, thrill at facing intellectual challenges, empathy with the object of inquiry, and tensions within argumentation. These feelings are tightly connected to reasoning; they are, in other words, *epistemic*. Epistemic affect, Jaber and Hammer argue, is pervasive in accounts of scientists (e.g., Aldous, 2006, 2007; Gruber, 1974; Keller, 1983; Lorimer, 2008; Osbeck, Nersessian, Malone, & Newsletter, 2011; Thagard, 2008) and of learners engaged in inquiry. As students grapple with ideas and make sense of phenomena, their feelings might prompt the need to clarify a line of reasoning; they might tacitly signal a budding idea and further motivate its development. Part of learning science involves the refinement of such epistemic feelings to pursue questions and to persist in the face of challenges.

This perspective motivates careful attention to affect in responsive teaching, not as an "add-on" but as inherent in the intellectual work of science. However, as I review further on, the literature commonly treats affect and disciplinary learning as separate areas, focusing either on teacher attention to students' emotions or on their attention to student thinking in science. These two research lines rarely come into contact, which, as I argue later, often manifests as an instructional challenge for teachers.

Teachers as "Carers"

In educational psychology, school counseling, and elementary education research, much emphasis is placed on the importance of fostering a culture of care, warmth, and affection in the classroom (e.g., Burgess & Carter, 1992; Nias, 1989, 1999; Noddings, 1984). Teaching in this sense entails a commitment to enacting caring attitudes by attending and responding to students' affective and social needs. The focus is less on learning within a discipline and more on the social and psychological well-being of learners.

For instance, Noddings (1984, 2005) offered a notion of caring as about being engrossed in students' experiences to help them realize their potential and to develop a sense of belonging to an authentically caring community. Noddings described herself as a teacher as "first and foremost one-caring and, second, enactor of specialized functions" (1984, p. 176). She asserted that as "carers" teachers should be educators first and teachers of particular subject matter second. Arguing against the "traditional supremacy of the disciplines," she notes, "my contention is that such instruction is not [the teachers'] main task" (p. 10). Conversely, she called for what she terms "centers of care" or "relation" as "preced[ing] any engagement with subject matter" (p. 36). For Noddings, these caring relations are at the heart of teaching.

Noddings' caring theory has been applied to research on teaching in a variety of contexts (e.g., Cassidy & Bates, 2005; Goldstein & Lake, 2000; Rogers & Webb, 1991; Wentzel, 1997), and the findings suggest that an ethics of caring frames much of the interactions in elementary science classes. Teachers' attention is primarily on creating trusting environments that are sensitive and responsive to students' emotional and social needs (e.g., Beck & Kooser, 2004; Nias, 1999; Noddings, 1984; Rogers & Webb, 1991). In these accounts, caring for students' feelings occurs alongside the discipline, separately from the epistemic experience itself.

Teachers as Accountable to Disciplinary Learning

Current research in science education aims to promote student engagement in the practices and norms of the discipline (e.g., Driver, Newton, & Osborne, 2000; Engle & Conant, 2002; Ford, 2008; Hammer, 2004; Hammer, Goldberg, & Farguson, 2012; Lehrer, 2009; Minstrell & van Zee, 2000; NRC, 2011; Rosebery, Ogonowski, DiSchino, & Warren, 2010). Accordingly, teachers endeavor to elicit and interpret student thinking in order to identify disciplinary beginnings and to adapt instructional objectives in response to student-generated ideas and questions. In these spaces, students get to experience what it means to think and reason like a scientist; they get to see themselves as the creators and critics of knowledge claims (Coffey, Hammer, Levin, & Grant, 2011; Ford, 2008).

While this body of work provides evidence for the importance of attending and responding to students' sense-making in science, it also shows that research on disciplinary learning has primarily focused on the conceptual and epistemological dynamics of student inquiry. Meanwhile, in these meaning-making spaces teachers and students encounter a wide range of feelings and emotions, from tensions within argumentation to anxiety at formulating new and uncertain ideas. Teachers, particularly in elementary classrooms, are often not at ease with affectively charged moments that children experience within inquiry. As I review next, they might actually perceive them as a threat to safe spaces or a disruption to the flow of the lesson, especially when they themselves are not comfortable in these open-ended inquiry environments. These concerns might consequently lead teachers to recoil from engaging students in inquiry.

In sum, with respect to affective issues, the literature on caring and that on disciplinary learning do not seem to make contact with each other. As I show next, this separation can be experienced by teachers as a tension that manifests in their instructional decisions.

Affect Versus Substance—A Tension in Teaching

Teachers' accounts in various studies show that paying attention both to the cognitive demands of the discipline and to the affective dynamics in the classroom often creates a dilemma for teachers (e.g., Gellert, 2000; Hargreaves, 2000; Williams-Johnson et al., 2008). For instance, while interviewing teachers on how they managed emotional events in the classroom, Williams-Johnson et al. (2008) found that teachers felt they had to choose between allowing emotions in the classroom and maintaining learning goals by repressing them as they navigated their instructional agendas. Teachers who chose to restrict emotional transactions expressed their worry about emotions sabotaging learning goals. Williams-Johnson et al. (2008) explain:

> We [. . .] noticed a disconnect between what many of the teachers described as the desire to create a comfortable learning environment, and an unwillingness to discuss an individual student's emotions during instructional time. Although the teachers acknowledged these instances and the emotional impact of building relationships with the individual student, some felt that it was of great importance to continue instruction and asked the student to push the emotions aside and approach the situation at a later time.
>
> (p. 1601)

Looking across a set of studies, we find that the tension between attending to affect and learning goals plays out differently in elementary and secondary schools.

In secondary classrooms, affect seems to be pushed further to the background: Teachers tend to view themselves mostly as responsible for the cognitive aspects of the discipline they teach rather than for students' emotional needs. Hargreaves (2000) observed that by and large in secondary classrooms, "emotions are normalized or neutralized to make the pedagogical process as smooth and easy as possible" (p. 822). Emotions are addressed only when they threaten to disturb the order of the classroom. When asked about situations where "positive emotions like exhilaration and enjoyment" were promoted, teachers in Hargreaves's study mentioned events that "took place outside the core processes of teaching and learning" (p. 823), such as dances, competitions, school-wide awards, ceremonies, or the cafeteria.

Elementary classrooms, on the other hand, are primarily seen as spaces that cater to students' emotional well-being, at times at the expense of conceptual and epistemic learning goals. Gellert (2000) observed that teachers' concern with creating a "safe space" shifted their attention away from student substantive engagement as they attempted to "relieve" (p. 251) students from the anxiety associated with mathematics. One teacher stated that "mathematics should be wrapped up in a way that students do not become aware of the fact that mathematics is taught" (p. 259). Other teachers attempted to make mathematics less "deadly serious and rigorous" (p. 264) by having appealing pictures in the classroom or using games to teach math in playful ways. Gellert argued that teachers "wanted to shelter [children] from a mathematical shock" (p. 266) to protect them from feeling anxious or frustrated.

In the context of elementary science teaching, Zembylas's (2005) findings shed light on yet another tension. The author showed how conventions around "appropriate" emotions—or what he termed the institutionalized "emotional regime" (p. 474) in the school—created challenges for teachers in the classroom. The teacher Catherine, whose case will be revisited later in the chapter, saw students' excitement and frustration during scientific explorations as resources to capitalize on. However, she felt pressured by the school culture to tune down emotional transactions. Varelas, Becker, Luster, and Wenzel (2002) voice a related concern regarding the emotional and epistemic expectations of disagreeing and arguing over ideas in science, which creates dilemmas for teachers who worry about clashes in the classroom and struggle to equitably integrate students' preferences, girls in particular, for agreement rather than argumentation.

These findings point to a tension, widespread among educators, between attending to affect and attending to the discipline. These two goals are often perceived in friction, or at best, as isolated from one another. I argue that by viewing affect as part of the epistemic experience, educators could bridge those goals, and as such could relax their worry about negative feelings in the classroom. Next, I discuss research that begins to examine teachers' attention to affect as integral to disciplinary engagement, before I turn to my case study of Mr. James and Eric introduced at the outset of the chapter.

Attending to Affect as Integral to the Discipline

Building on Noddings's (2005) caring relations, Hackenberg (2005, 2010) studied the development of "mathematical caring relations" (or MCRs) as an evolving

Attending to Students' Epistemic Affect **167**

interaction "that conjoins affective and cognitive realms in the process of aiming for mathematical learning" (p. 237). To explore this idea, Hackenberg (2010) provided students with mathematical tasks that either aligned with or challenged current levels of students' understanding. She explained how she made "in-the-moment interpretations" (p. 242) and instructional decisions grounded in students' cognitive and affective responses by closely monitoring students' emotional reactions and using them as cues about their mathematical thinking. By interpreting their affect as part of their sense-making, Hackenberg explained how she cared for her students as mathematical thinkers, grounding her caring within the work and norms of the discipline.

In science education, Zembylas (2004, 2005) explored the role of emotional transactions in Catherine's classroom, the elementary science teacher whom I introduced earlier. Zembylas (2005) recounts how "[s]eeing the children being excited about their learning affected Catherine's emotional style as well as her decisions and actions" (p. 478). Catherine "built on how children felt to endorse and sustain feelings of excitement" (p. 478) and to nurture their curiosity about phenomena. She explained:

> One of the things that to me is really important is that children get a chance to experience and to feel the world around us. That just seems to be really important to give kids a chance to fool around with it and share how they feel for what they are doing. I encourage them to experience and feel science.
>
> (p. 479)

Catherine wanted her students to experience science as about exploring phenomena and "messing about" (Hawkins, 1965), and to experience the feelings that are part of that process of exploration. Zembylas (2004) described how Catherine reflected openly on the feelings in the science class as a way to promote her students' cognitive and emotional engagement with the world. This reflexive dynamic between talking science and talking about feelings in science, Zembylas (2005) argues, was at the basis of "Catherine's ability to create *affective alliances* with her students and with what was being studied" (p. 479, emphasis in original). This idea resonates with Hackenberg's MCRs, making possible, and perhaps indispensible, the integration of affect in responsive teaching to promote a meaningful engagement with the discipline.

These studies, in addition to others (e.g., Milne & Otieno, 2007; Richards, 2013; Olitsky, 2007), suggest the importance of teacher orchestrating affective and cognitive dynamics in their moment-to-moment instructional decisions. They also imply that student emotions, including their excitement, impatience, and anxiety, can be used as cues about the substance of their thinking. Building on these efforts, I now turn to my case study in Mr. James's classroom.

168 Lama Z. Jaber

Context and Analysis Methods

The data is from a three-year project on learning progressions,[2] also known as "Responsive Teaching in Science" (cipstrends.sdsu.edu/responsiveteaching/), which was designed to promote and study teaching practices centered on recognizing, interpreting, and responding to the substance of student thinking (Coffey, et al., 2011; Hammer, et al., 2012; Maskiewicz &Winters, 2012). As part of the program, teachers implemented responsive teaching modules designed to elicit rich student thinking and to help learners experience science as a pursuit by following their own lines of inquiry. The project staff collected videotapes from teachers' classrooms, as well as from meetings, interviews, and teachers' debriefs. In this chapter, I use qualitative video analysis (Derry, et al., 2010) with tools from discourse and interaction analysis (Jordan & Henderson, 1995) to explore the moment-to-moment affective, conceptual, and epistemological dynamics at play in a teacher-student interaction around water evaporation. I adopt a multi-modal approach (Sidnell & Stivers, 2005) to identify affective markers within the flow of activity. These might comprise explicit discursive markers as well as paralinguistic markers including prosody, intonation, hedging, gestures, posture, and facial expressions. I also draw on data from a stimulated recall interview with Mr. James, where he watched the clip and reflected on his interactions with Eric.

Situating the Episode

The episode I analyze is from the first day of the water cycle module in Mr. James's fifth grade science class. It began around thirty-five minutes into the discussion. At the beginning of class, Mr. James posed the following question: "One night it rains. When you arrive at school, you notice that there are puddles in the parking lot. When you go home, the puddles are gone. What happened to the rainwater?" Students grappled with the question and suggested various possibilities including that water goes into clouds, turns into vapor, and the sun evaporates it. Table 8.1 presents a timeline to situate the exchanges between Eric and Mr. James during the lesson.

TABLE 8.1 Timeline Situating the Episode

Time	*Description*
00:00–01:50	***Setting up the activity:*** Mr. James asks the puddle question.
	Discussion
10:09–11:09	***Confusion around use of terms:*** "What do you mean by 'sink down'?"
	Discussion
34:07–36:40	***Eric's episode- Part 1:*** "How are all these things connected?"
	Animated discussion
41:44–47:10	***Eric's episode- Part 2:*** "It would be steaming and the water might be sinking down."

Confusion Around Use of Terms: "What Do You Mean by 'Sink Down'?"

A salient feature of the conversation was students' use of particular terms, such as "sink down" and "rise up," without being specific about what the terms referred to. For instance, while some students used them to denote the sun rising and setting, others used them to describe water vapor rising, and others to signal that the level of water in a puddle increases or decreases. These terms were used across multiple topics, which created confusion, leading students to press for clarity on their meaning as evident in this exchange[3]:

1. *Daniel:*   It has to be sun, because if it's the afternoon, the water will just sink down.
2. *Dillon:*   What do you mean by "sink down"?
3. *Daniel:*   In the morning, the water rises. Then in the afternoon, it stays there.
4. *Mr. James:*   What water—what water stays there?
5. *Daniel:*   Let's say you're watering your plants. The water will quickly rise up in the morning. Then if you're watering it in the afternoon, it'll stay there, stay in the ground.
6. *Mr. James:*   Why?
7. *Daniel:*   Because the sun's not as strong as it is in the morning.
8. *Student:*   What?
9. *Mr. James:*   So Greg, what do you want to add? And I'll come back to you don't worry (addressing another student).
10. *Greg:*   I wanted to ask Daniel what he means by "rises"?
11. *Mr. James:*   I did, too, I like that question. Great job of coming up with that. (Addressing Daniel) What do you mean by "rise"?

While Daniel was using the terms "sinking down" and "rising up" to refer to the water level in the garden, other students seemed unclear about what he meant, as evident in Dillon's and Greg's explicit requests for clarification on lines 2 and 10. The teacher acknowledged the importance of clarifying these terms and further commented that "we need to be sort of in agreement in figuring out the sort of idea behind [them]." This confusion and the need for clarity will become relevant in understanding the subsequent interactions between Eric and Mr. James.

Eric's Episode—Part 1: "How Are All These Things Connected?"

As the conversation continued, students discussed different ideas and examples, including water evaporating from a cup, a swimming pool, and sauce drying up and leaving a stain. The role of the sun in evaporation became a point of contention. One student, Jimmy, described an instance where he left a glass of water in his kitchen at night and saw that the water level was lower in the morning; this, he claimed, supports the idea that water evaporates in the absence of the sun. Daniel questioned whether Jimmy's dog could have drunk the water, but Dillon challenged this possibility, saying that the dog would have dripped and left some evidence behind. Students then discussed how stains form on different surfaces as water evaporates from various liquids.

In the midst of this discussion, Eric and students at his table seemed to engage in a side conversation, looking around with confused faces and displaying signs of frustration (see Figure 8.1). Eric seemed the most expressive, hitting his hands together to emphasize points he was making. Mr. James explicitly directed the classroom's attention to Eric and his tablemates, inviting Eric to share with the rest of the class.

Mr. James: Eric, I'm hearing you guys having a little bit of a conversation. Can you share with us what you guys are thinking about? You've been sitting here real quiet, and I've heard you a couple of times—I've seen a couple of times a facial expression from you (Eric nods). Share with me what it is you've been thinking about when you hear them talk.

Attending to Eric's facial expressions and emotional displays, Mr. James inferred that Eric might have something to contribute or might be struggling to make sense of the conversation. In the interview, and without any probing on my behalf, Mr. James volunteered the following:

I did see in his face that sort of like—I call it a scrunchy face, and I try to bring that up with all of my students about the fact that "hey scrunchy face is a good thing because if you have scrunchy face, I know you're thinking about and you have been

FIGURE 8.1 Eric, on the right, and his tablemates.

listening to what other people were saying. So you're trying to, you know, figure out in your own head, what is it that you're hearing happening in the room or what is it that you wanna understand better." So scrunchy face to me is that sort of like "I don't get it" type of a thing or, you know, I—I'm thinking really really you know deeply about what is it that I wanna understand better.[4]

Interpreting Eric's emotional expressions as a sign of his cognitive engagement, Mr. James invited Eric to share his thinking, and Eric responded animatedly, with an assertive tone and with pronounced displays of emotions, gesturing and frowning (see Figure 8.2):

Eric:	Well, I'm kind of confused, like, you know, we were talking about the puddles (hits hands), and then the pool (hits hands), and then the glass of water (hits hands), and then the floor stain (gestures to floor, confused look [see Figure 8.2]).
Mr. James:	What's confusing?
Kevin:	How did they get to the floor stain? (Animated tone)
Students:	(Overlapping talk)
Mr. James:	You tell me.
Eric:	I don't know (shrugs), something—
Mr. James:	I want to hear—I want to hear what Eric has to say.

Eric seemed frustrated that the class was not staying on any one topic as implied by his emphasis when he enumerated the various topics (puddles, pool,

FIGURE 8.2 Eric mentions the floor stain.

172 Lama Z. Jaber

glass of water, and floor stain); his frustration might also be related to the fact that he was not following the logic and connectedness between the different ideas. While Eric originally raised a concern about a lack of coherence in the conversation, Mr. James pushed him to articulate what specifically was confusing.

Mr. James then revoiced Eric's initial concern in different ways (O'Connor & Michaels, 1993), checking to see if he understood Eric's question ("How are they related I think is what you're asking, right?"), and pushing Eric further to reason about the question:

Mr. James: With everything that you've been hearing them talk about (Eric nods), what keeps coming back up in your mind? That connection piece. How are they related I think is what you're asking, right? (Eric nods) How are they related? Do you see a connection? And if so, where do you see it? What sort of thing do you see in how we got to different places?

Being asked, on the spot, to formulate an idea, Eric became hesitant. Rather than taking up Mr. James's invitation to contribute an idea, Eric responded with a brief "Um, I don't really know." As Mr. James probed him one more time, Eric said:

Eric: I think it's, you know, like, the puddle, then, you know how it, like, evaporates? (Moves hands in circular motion) And then, you know, like, the next morning, it comes up higher? (Raises one hand up) And then it's like a big pool or something? (Shrugs and spreads hands)

Eric began to express a muddled idea about water evaporating and "coming up higher," but he was having difficulty articulating his thinking. Mr. James pressed him to clarify what he meant by "comes up higher." In response, Eric became increasingly hesitant and flustered: He started to hedge ("I don't remember, maybe"), speaking in an unsure tone and lower voice and avoiding eye contact. Eric was restlessly shifting his posture, hunching over and shaking his head, and displaying contorted facial expressions. After a while, as Mr. James asked him one more time to clarify, Eric seemed about to disengage:

Mr. James: What is it that's going up? What is it that's going down?
Eric: Well (scratches head), the sun? (Unsure tone, looking away)
Mr. James: The sun? So it's the sun that's coming up and going down?
Eric: Oh my God. (Covers eyes with hand [see Figure 8.3]) Yeees (Loud, exasperated tone).
Mr. James: Okay, all right. Greg,
Eric: (In a low voice and shaking his head) I'm confused.

Attending to Students' Epistemic Affect **173**

FIGURE 8.3 Eric gets frustrated.

FIGURE 8.4 Eric smiles at Mr. James' praise.

Eric covered his eyes and face (see Figure 8.3) as he uttered a prolonged and impatient "Yeeees," followed by a subdued and brief "I'm confused." Noticing Eric's heightened affect and noticing other students raising their hands, Mr. James made a move to transition to another student, explicitly praising Eric for his participation:

Mr. James: Greg, I saw your hand go up as soon as I said "how are all of these things connected?" Eric, you're doing a great job of participating (Eric smiles, see Figure 8.4), paying attention, and giving us some ideas to think about. Keep it up. (Eric nods)

174 Lama Z. Jaber

Eric responded positively to Mr. James's praise, looking up and smiling (see Figure 8.4). Reflecting on this moment, Mr. James said:

> *I think his anxiety had gotten up to that point where you know he'd been called upon, you know he tried to give an answer and his anxiety was starting to get the better of him [. . .], so I think that he had just, he had reached his saturation point in a sense on how much, how much I can push back and get from him.*

In this interview excerpt and throughout this initial exchange, we have evidence that Mr. James was monitoring and responding to Eric's affect. When he saw that Eric reached his "saturation point," he transitioned to another student while praising Eric precisely for attending to ideas, sharing his confusion, and contributing to the conversation. He also encouraged Eric to "keep it up," to help him be "a little bit more self confident in participating more in class," as he noted in the interview. As such, Mr. James's praise was at once an affective repair and an epistemological move to reaffirm the value of attending to and offering ideas and persisting in the face of an intellectual challenge. While this exchange might sound less than promising in terms of disciplinary progress, it will soon become clear that it formed a productive tension that seeded what came next.

Eric's Episode—Part 2: "It Would Be Steaming and the Water Might Be Sinking Down"

Right after Mr. James directed the conversation to Greg, various students complained about the flow of the ideas and questioned their coherence in an animated debate: "I don't really get what we're talking about"; "We went from DOG to stain!"; "No wait, but how does that connect to the water puddle?" Students experienced this lack of coherence with intense emotions, as evident by their loud voices, overlapping talk, and expressive faces and gestures. Almost five minutes later, Eric raised his hand and Mr. James called on him (see Figure 8.5).

1. *Mr. James:* Eric, did you get some help?
2. *Eric:* No, but I was thinking, I thought water—the sun, it hits the water. You know how it boils, if it's 300 degrees, and then the water sinks down. And then it turns, it's all bubbly and then it sinks down until it completely [inaud] (looking serious and assertive, and making various gestures [see Figure 8.6]).

Unsure about what Eric meant by the water "sinks down," and possibly given the contention that had already developed in class around that term, Mr. James asked Eric a few probing questions to clarify his idea. He asked his questions in the form of possible interpretations of Eric's idea (lines 3, 5, and 7). Eric responded with a "No" to each interpretation (lines 4, 6, and 8):

Attending to Students' Epistemic Affect   **175**

FIGURE 8.5 Eric raises his hand and Mr. James calls on him.

FIGURE 8.6 Eric explains his idea about the water sinking down.

3. *Mr. James:* The water sinks down. What do you mean by "the water sinks down"? The water that I have up here [in reference to the puddle] sinks down?
4. *Eric:* No, but if you have it 300 degrees, you know how it boils? And then you know how it stops boiling, the water sinks down?
5. *Mr. James:* So where does the water—so the water sinks here?
6. *Eric:* No, but.
7. *Mr. James:* In Zack's stove, the water sinks down? [referring to an idea brought up earlier by Zack]
8. *Eric:* No.
   With Mr. James's attempts to clarify Eric's idea proving unsuccessful, Eric tried once again to explain with an example:
9. *Eric:* But I just thought of it, and I've done it once. I just put some water, you know how you put eggs and you boil it, or something like that. But I just put water in it, and then I just turn it on for 300

degrees, and then when it's boiling, I just turn it off. I just watch it sinks down, until it's all used up completely (trails off).
10. *Mr. James:* What sinks down?
11. *Eric:* The heat.
12. *Mr. James:* The heat sinks down?
13. *Eric:* If it's 300 degrees.
14. *Mr. James:* The water stays the same though?
15. *Eric:* No.
16. *Mr. James:* What happens?
17. *Eric:* It's gone, completely. Not completely but just a little bit.
18. *Mr. James:* So the water, when you say "sinks down," I want to make sure that I'm real clear on what you mean by the water "sinks down." What do you mean by that?
19. *Eric:* Like, um—like—(Eric looks away, scratches his ear, and gestures in search for words [see Figure 8.7])
20. *Silence* (~6 seconds)

In essence, Eric's example concerns boiling water and noticing that the water level becomes lower. However, Eric had trouble stating his idea clearly, and Mr. James up to that point did not understand it, but was working patiently with Eric to make sense of his reasoning. Mr. James asked Eric multiple times to clarify what he meant by "sinking down" (lines 10, 12, and 18). Just like in the first exchange, Eric was having difficulty communicating his idea. However, unlike the first exchange, he remained engaged in this prolonged period of unsuccessful communication without showing signs of anxiety like he had before. He was more confident and determined to articulate his thinking, as evidenced by his assertive tone, serious look, and eye contact with Mr. James.

But there were indicators that this might change soon: After Mr. James asked him "What do you mean by that?" on line 18, Eric was at a loss for words. He became fidgety and looked away, scratched his ear with his left hand (see Figure 8.7, 1st frame) which he then flung back down, and gesturing as if he were

"It's like…"   "um…like…"   "Could you draw me a picture of it?"

FIGURE 8.7 Eric at a loss of words and Mr. James invites him to draw his idea on the board.

Attending to Students' Epistemic Affect **177**

looking for words (see Figure 8.7, 2nd frame); he was then silent for about 6 seconds. Eric's anxiety was obviously on the rise. However, rather than moving to another student like he did before, Mr. James proposed an alternative for Eric to express his thinking, by suggesting that he draws his idea on the Smart Board. As Eric moved to the board in front of the class, Mr. James moved to the back, which could possibly signal his deferring authority to Eric as the "expert" in that moment.

21. *Mr. James:* Could you draw me a picture of it? (Approaches Eric and hands him the Smart Board pen [see Figure 8.7, 3rd frame])

22. *Eric:* I could (takes the pen and prepares to walk to the board).

23. *Mr. James:* Try it. See if you can draw me a picture of what you mean by "sinks down." Remember how to change the page? It's that arrow at the very top? So show me what you mean by "sinks down."

In the interview, Mr. James explained that he felt Eric was comfortable enough to draw his idea. He also noted that "having him come forward" to draw and share his idea was something he felt Eric wanted:

> *It didn't seem as though he had as much anxiety about drawing it as he's had in other times, um, so but you know having him come forward to do that I thin- um, was was something he wanted to do [. . .] he did seem like he was more interested in doing it.*

One might wonder whether Mr. James's focus on the meaning of the word "sink down" merely reflects his concern with correct terminology rather than his attention to Eric's sense-making. I argue that it's not, for at least three reasons: First, part of Eric's challenge in this instance was to articulate a clear idea and make it visible to others. This is an essential and often challenging part of scientific argumentation. Students need opportunities to grapple with formulating and communicating ideas as they learn to participate in scientific discourse.

Second, as evident in the earlier examples from Dillon and Greg, the meanings of words, including "sink down," were not "taken-as-shared" (Yackel & Cobb, 1996) and were contested by students at multiple times. Situated in this classroom history, Mr. James's press for clarity seems to be part of his responsiveness to students' request to clarify meanings behind words.

Third, in this moment, Eric was using the term "sink down" while at the same time creating shifting meanings for it. He was, in other words, navigating a "semantic space" (Sfard, 2000), and by pressing him on what exactly he meant, Mr. James was encouraging these shifts and helping Eric gain greater clarity of the substance of his argument.

At the board, Eric drew a cup of water, and added a wiggled line to show the water boiling and a downward arrow on the outside to show the water level falling or "sinking down" (see Figure 8.8, 2nd frame).

24. *Eric:* Here's a cup of water, right? (draws cup of water) This is how much it has. So if something's 300 degrees Fahrenheit, it might boil or something like that or something (draws wiggled lines on top of water). And then the water just sinks down, like right here (draws arrow on outside of cup [see Figure 8.8])
25. *Mr. James:* The water, so is the water on the outside?
26. *Eric:* Noooo.

When done with his drawing, Eric twisted around to look at Mr. James (see Figure 8.8, 3rd frame) who asked if the water was on the outside of the cup, possibly in reference to a previous discussion on condensation. Eric responded with a strongly pronounced "Noooo," conveying his exasperation for being misinterpreted. But, instead of giving up, Eric turned to the board and immediately started a new drawing (see Figure 8.8, 4th frame). At this point, other students started raising their hands.

A visiting administrator who was not part of the research project interjected: "What happens when you boil water in a teapot, what do you see coming out of the spout?" Eric and others answered that "it will be steaming"; She continued: "so where does the steam go?" At this point, Mr. James approached her in a side conversation (off camera):

Mr. James: No you're giving him too much. Let him—let him work
Administrator: But I, [OK, and I want him to—
Mr. James: [I know I know and you gotta—
Administrator: [But now—
Mr. James: [You gotta let him— you've got to let him work (Louder, assertive tone).
Administrator: (Addressing Eric) Now, what's gonna happen?

We cannot tell for sure why the administrator decided to step in. It might be that she wanted to guide Eric toward the right answer, or that she wanted to relieve him from this moment of struggle, or perhaps a combination of both. As evident in the literature at the beginning of the chapter, the urge to "protect" Eric

FIGURE 8.8 Eric's first attempt to explain his idea with a drawing.

Attending to Students' Epistemic Affect **179**

is an understandable and often common teacher reaction in such tense moments. Mr. James, however, did not seem alarmed by Eric's affective displays; and rather than shying away from this challenging moment that both he and Eric were experiencing, he acted to protect Eric's agency and his right to experience the uncertainty and struggle to work out his ideas. In interrupting the administrator, Mr. James took a strongly oppositional stance, as implied by the use of "no" and "but," the imperative form ("let him work," "you gotta let him"), and the assertive tone of voice that became louder as the exchange unfolded. While both Mr. James and the administrator were attending to Eric's affective experience, they clearly responded to it differently and probably for different purposes.

Mr. James then shifted the conversation to Eric and asked him once more to explain what he meant by "sinking down."

27. *Mr. James:* (Addressing Eric) I'm curious what you meant by "sinking down," that's really where I want to get to. Can you explain for me what you mean by "sinking down"? Because your arrow is on the outside of—
28. *Eric:* Yeah I know.
29. *Mr. James:* What was that again? [The cup?
30. *Eric:* [A cup. Yeah
31. *Mr. James:* So is the water on the outside of the cup?
32. *Eric:* No.
33. *Mr. James:* Okay, so explain.
34. *Eric:* Alright. If it's right here (points to the water level in his second drawing), and then if it's 300 degrees, it might be boiling right here (adds bubbles). And then it would be steaming (draws an upward wiggled line), and after—
35. *Mr. James:* Give him a chance [here/Sarah]
36. *Eric:* After 20 or half an hour, the water might be sinking down right here, and it will be right here (draws same arrow but inside the cup, pointing to a lower water level [see Figure 8.9])
37. *Mr. James:* OOHH, oh, oh oh oh okay, wait wait wait wait. Daniel, pay attention, because I want to make sure that I and—that everybody here understands. Could somebody tell me, Addison, could you tell me what he means by "sinking down"? Do you understand his word for sinking down?

On line 32, Mr. James said: "Okay, so explain." This move marks a shift from previous ones where Mr. James was either asking clarifying questions or revoicing what he took Eric to be saying. By asking him very directly to explain, Mr. James was sending a message to Eric that he indeed *had* something important to explain; he was also encouraging Eric to persist and not to give into his exasperation. In response, Eric adjusted his drawing by adding an arrow inside the cup, pointing downward to a lower level of water. As Eric was explaining his diagram (line 33), some students tried to help him out. Mr. James immediately interjected to "give

"It might be boiling…"   "the water might be sinking down…"   "…and it will be right here"

FIGURE 8.9 Eric's second drawing attempt.

[Eric] a chance" (line 34) to finish his idea. In the end, Eric succeeded in explaining his idea that the water first is boiling and then it "would be steaming" (line 33), as represented by the wiggled line, causing the water level to "sink down."

When Mr. James finally understood Eric's idea, he excitedly exclaimed, "OOHH! Oh oh oh oh okay!" But he did not stop there; he asked students to "pay attention" to make sure "everybody understands" Eric's thinking (line 36), conveying as such the worth of Eric's contribution. By inviting Addison and others to explain Eric's "word for sinking down," the teacher positioned Eric's idea at the center of the discussion. Students rephrased Eric's idea, asked him questions about it, proposed hypothetical scenarios such as what happens to the water level if the cup were covered with a lid or if it were placed in a microwave, and wondered whether the water level of a swimming pool decreases like that of the cup.

To sum up this second exchange, Eric raised his hand to offer an idea—that water "rises up" in the form of steam, which decreases the water level in the cup. After many unsuccessful attempts to communicate his idea, Eric was at a loss for words. Mr. James, rather than being dissuaded by Eric's discomfort, pressed him to pursue his idea and invited him to draw it on the board. Despite various challenges, Eric was able to persist without becoming overly frustrated and eventually succeeded in explaining his thinking. In what follows I revisit the questions I set out to explore regarding Mr. James's attention and responsiveness to Eric's epistemic affect.

In What Ways Were Mr. James's Attention and Responsiveness to Affect Part of His Attention to Eric's Thinking?

Rather than unpacking how Eric's affect was entangled with his reasoning—a task that might require additional evidence—in this section I show how Mr. James oriented to Eric's affect as integral to his reasoning.

First, Mr. James interpreted Eric's facial expressions and behaviors as indicators that Eric was either not following the conversation or that he had something to

Attending to Students' Epistemic Affect **181**

contribute. Accordingly, Mr. James provided Eric an extended period of time to share what he was thinking about (two and a half minutes in the first exchange and five minutes in the second). This implicitly conveys that Mr. James was confident that Eric *had* something valuable to contribute, and that articulating one's thinking takes time and effort.

Perhaps Mr. James could have guessed Eric's idea as referring to water evaporating and causing the water level to decrease, thus he could have easily saved precious instructional time and relieved Eric from uncomfortable feelings. If he did guess, he chose not to express that. Mr. James wanted Eric to linger in this difficult space as part of his right to experience the struggle of developing and communicating ideas, a challenging but central part of science. This, I argue, reflects Mr. James's attention to Eric's affect as part of his epistemic experience. Intending for his students to struggle at the intellectual level does not mean, however, that Mr. James doesn't care for how they feel; on the contrary, it means that the ways in which he cares for students' feelings are connected to and in service of their engagement in the discipline. By considering Eric's affect as part of his doing of science, Mr. James was able to relax his worry about hurting Eric and was able to care for him as a disciplinary thinker.

Additionally, Mr. James was protective of Eric's agency and what that agency entailed affectively, including the navigation of uncertainty, the persistence in the face of challenges, and the anticipation of pleasure at formulating clear ideas. When the administrator stepped in to help Eric, Mr. James immediately asked her to step back. He also made sure that other students didn't jeopardize Eric's right to have and contribute ideas (Duckworth, 2006). Mr. James deferred his authority to Eric by moving to the back of the class and giving Eric the resources and the space (Engle & Conant, 2002) to experience himself as a valuable epistemic agent (Scardamalia, 2000) in the classroom.

In What Ways Were Mr. James's Attention and Responsiveness to Affect Consequential to Eric's Engagement?

To illustrate how Mr. James's attention and responsiveness to Eric's affect were consequential to Eric's engagement, I show how the teacher's moves, Eric's reactions, and Mr. James's subsequent responses were linked up in a chain of events that possibly hints to a causal sequence between the teacher's responsiveness to affect and Eric's engagement.

At the beginning of this episode, there were signs that Eric and his peers were irritated by what was going on. Their side conversation could have potentially disengaged them from the discussion. By noticing and responding to their frustration at the right time, Mr. James brought the boys back into the discussion.

Mr. James patiently elicited Eric's thinking while closely monitoring his affective responses. When Eric showed signs of increased frustration at the end of the first episode, Mr. James moved to another student, making sure to praise Eric for his attempt. In response to his praise, Eric raised his head and smiled. Five minutes later, he raised his hand enthusiastically to contribute an idea. As soon as Eric raised his hand, Mr. James called on him, providing ample space for him to express his thinking. When he noticed Eric's anxiety rising as he was at a loss for words, Mr. James suggested that he draw his idea. Eric again responded positively and was able to pursue his reasoning with less distress.

In these ways Mr. James's dynamic attention to affect was consequential to Eric's engagement and persistence in inquiry. Throughout the exchange Mr. James made moves to encourage Eric to persevere, validating Eric's struggle and allowing him to openly express how he felt. Despite having experienced a significantly difficult moment, Eric was thus willing to come back to the discussion and remain engaged.

Conclusions and Implications

This chapter argues for attending to students' affect as integral to attending to their reasoning in science. I showed how this took place in the context of a teacher-student interaction in a fifth grade science class. Rather than hindering his attention to disciplinary learning, Mr. James's attention and responsiveness to Eric's feelings was part and parcel of his attention to Eric's thinking and engagement. This work thus challenges the false dichotomy that positions teachers either as "carers" or as "accountable to disciplinary learning."

This perspective invites questions for teachers and teacher educators: How might teacher education programs help teachers attend and respond to students' affect as part of their epistemic experiences? How might they promote teachers' awareness of and openness to a range of affective dynamics that arise within inquiry? How might teachers' natural attunement to affect be leveraged to cultivate students' epistemic feelings and epistemic motivations? These questions have implications for instruction and for teacher education, as I discuss below.

Implications for Instruction

In terms of instruction, I am suggesting that part of interpreting, recognizing, and cultivating the beginnings of science in children's thinking involves attention to their affect. When students approach a novel situation or present ideas at odds with the classroom consensus, they often experience and express discomfort and vulnerability. When they are fascinated by a question or annoyed at an inconsistency, they might display excitement and eagerness. These affective displays are not merely a reflection of engagement; they are evidence of substantive disciplinary work, and both teachers and students need to recognize them as such.

Moreover, affect is part of what students should learn in science. To take up science as a pursuit, students need to develop disciplinary dispositions (Gresalfi, 2009; Lehrer, 2009) such as tolerance for disagreement, acceptance of uncertainty, inclination to seek criticism, appreciation of the tentative nature of knowledge, and a drive to work through challenges. Learning science is in part becoming familiar with the feelings and emotions inherent in intellectual work. It involves learning to regulate and productively leverage affective dynamics within inquiry. By encouraging students to linger in inquiry, teachers create opportunities for students to experience and reflect on the emotional complexity that permeates scientific pursuits and help students perceive intellectual challenges as motivating and valuable.

However, as I have reviewed at the outset of the paper, teachers, particularly at the elementary level, are especially "concerned to fend off and manage negative emotion that threatens" (Hargreaves, 2000, p. 823) students' comfort and safe spaces in the classroom. Like the visiting administrator in this case, educators might be inclined to shelter students from struggles, especially when they themselves are unfamiliar and uncomfortable with affective dynamics in inquiry. They might feel the weight of what Swadner (1992) termed "the hegemony of nice" (as cited by Goldstein & Lake, 2000, p. 861) to fit popular expectations of elementary classrooms as warm spaces devoid of negative feelings. This raises important implications for teacher education, as I discuss next, especially that affect is typically relegated to a minor status in teacher training programs (William et al., 2008; Zembylas, 2007).

Another aspect to consider in attending and responding to affect in the classroom are the personal and cultural differences in how different people experience, perceive, and express feelings and emotions (e.g., Briggs, 1970; Goetz, Spencer-Rodge, & Peng, 2008; Shweder, Haidt, Horton, & Joseph, 2008). For instance, whereas some cultures normalize heightened displays of emotionality, others underscore reservation. Moreover, individual differences play a role in how people experience and engage issues of affect. Within the same household, one person might feel stimulated by vibrant discussions, and another could feel intimidated and overwhelmed. Such variability in how people experience and express emotions highlights the importance of teachers' awareness and sensitivity to nuances within affective dynamics and the diverse emotional symbols and lexicons in the classroom.

Implications for Teacher Education

I propose at least two ways in which affect could be more substantively integrated in teacher education and professional development (PD). First, teachers should be supported to experience for themselves the feelings and emotions that come up in the doing of science. This could happen in PD spaces that provide a space for teachers to experience science as a pursuit, where they can grapple with ideas and questions for extended periods of time and reflect on their feelings and emotions along the way. Teachers then develop for themselves a taste for what it feels like to engage in inquiry and become familiar with confusion, frustration, and tensions within argumentation (see Watkins, Coffey, Maskiewicz, & Hammer, in press). As they experience their own epistemic feelings in science, teachers can come to recognize their students' feelings as part of the epistemic experience of the discipline.

Second, teacher education programs should prepare teachers to navigate the emotional complexity of inquiry in the classroom. Teachers face tensions in making moment-to-moment decisions as they respond to affect—for example, to press students to persist without intimidating them, or to relieve students from the discomfort of a challenging moment. They also face tensions when a single idea provokes different affective reactions among students, and at times between them and their students. One way to help teachers navigate these tensions is through discussions and reflections on their practice using classroom videos of affectively challenging moments. For instance, teachers and PD staff could watch classroom interactions, such as the one discussed here between Mr. James and Eric, and reflect on possible teaching moves to respond to and leverage Eric's and other students' affect in productive ways. These discussions might help teachers become less worried about the need to shelter students from anxiety and frustration.

Teaching responsively entails developing facility at orchestrating, harmonizing, and coordinating attention across various aspects of classroom dynamics at any moment in time. Teachers are constantly making in-the-moment instructional decisions and adjustments to create spaces that are conducive to student engagement and agency. This is complex and hard work. I do not mean to pile another layer of complexity by arguing for the need to attend to affect; I am rather pointing out that affect is inherent to those dynamics of attention and responsiveness. Attending and responding to affect is an organic aspect of teacher's interaction with students and happens naturally within the flow of activities. What I am proposing is to ground our attention to affect *in* the discipline. Increased attention to affective issues, Gresalfi (2009) warns us, can defeat its own purpose if misunderstood as a separate conversation from other aspects of disciplinary engagement. I agree, and I further caution against a view of affect as just one more item on the list of teachers' attention. Affect, I emphasize, is substantive to the epistemic experience of learning science, and teachers must attend and respond to it accordingly.

Acknowledgments

I would like to thank the teacher and his wonderful students for their time and collaboration. Special thanks to David Hammer for the rich discussions and ongoing support leading to the formulation of the ideas in this manuscript. Special thanks as well to Jennifer Richards and Luke Conlin for their contributions on a previous version of this work and on their thoughtful insights on data. Also, I would like to thank Amy Robertson, Rachel Scherr, Jessica Pierson Bishop, Jim Minstrell, Chandra Turpen, Bárbara M. Brizuela, Michelle Wilkerson-Jerde, Jessica Watkins, Ayush Gupta, Orit Parnafes, and Dana Vedder-Weiss for their insights and thorough comments on versions of this work. This work was supported by the National Science Foundation under grant # DRL 0732233, Learning Progressions for Scientific Inquiry: A Model Implementation in the Context of Energy. The views expressed here are those of the author and are not necessarily endorsed by the foundation.

Notes

1 The names used in this chapter are pseudonyms.
2 Goldberg, F., Hammer, D., Bendall, S., Coffey, J., & Maskiewicz, A. Learning Progressions for Scientific Inquiry: A Model Implementation in the Context of Energy. National Science Foundation Grant # 0732233, Washington, DC, 2007.
3 Transcript notation: Capitalized words refer to emphasis in speech; Two open brackets on different turns refers to overlapping speech; [text] refers to inaudible words or meanings; (text) describes paralinguistic aspects of the interaction.
4 Interview excerpts are italicized to distinguish them from classroom transcripts.

References

Aldous, C.R. (2006). Attending to feeling: Productive benefit to novel mathematics problem-solving. *International Education Journal, 7*(4), 410–422.

Aldous, C.R. (2007). Creativity, problem solving and innovative science: Insights from history, cognitive psychology and neuroscience. *International Education Journal, 8*(2), 176–186.

Beck, L.G., & Kooser, J. (2004, April). *Caring across cultures.* Paper presented at the annual meeting of the American Educational Research Association, San Diego, CA.

Briggs, J.L. (1970). *Never in anger: Portrait of an Eskimo family.* Cambridge: Harvard University Press.

Burgess, H., & Carter, B. (1992). "Bringing out the best in people": Teacher training and the "real" teacher. *British Journal of Sociology of Education, 13*(3), 349–359.

Cassidy, W., & Bates, A. (2005). "Drop-outs" and "push-outs": Finding hope at a school that actualizes the ethic of care. *American Journal of Education, 112,* 66–102.

Coffey, J.E., Hammer, D., Levin, D.M., & Grant, T. (2011). The missing disciplinary substance of formative assessment. *Journal of Research in Science Teaching, 48*(10), 1109–1136.

Derry, S.J., Pea, R.D., Barron, B., Engle, R.A., Erickson, F., Goldman, R., Hall, R., Koschmann, T., Lemke, J., Sherin, M., & Sherin, B.L. (2010). Conducting video research in the learning sciences: Guidance on selection, analysis, technology, and ethics. *The Journal of the Learning Sciences, 19*(1), 3–53.

Driver, R., Newton, P., & Osborne, J. (2000). Establishing the norms of scientific argumentation in classrooms. *Science Education, 84*(3), 287–312.

Duckworth, E. (2006). *"The having of wonderful ideas" and other essays on teaching and learning* (3rd edition). New York: Teachers College Press.

Engle, R.A., & Conant, F.R. (2002). Guiding principles for fostering productive disciplinary engagement: Explaining an emergent argument in a community of learners classroom. *Cognition and Instruction, 20*(4), 399–483.

Ford, M.J. (2008). "Grasp of practice" as a reasoning resource for inquiry and nature of science understanding. *Science & Education, 17*(2&3), 147–177.

Gellert, U. (2000). Mathematics instruction in safe space: Prospective elementary teachers' views of mathematics education. *Journal of Mathematics Teacher Education, 3,* 251–270.

Goetz, J., Spencer-Rodgers, J., & Peng, K. (2008). Dialectical emotions: How cultural epistemologies influence the experience and regulation of emotional complexity. In R. Sorrentino & S. Yamguchi, (Eds.), *Handbook of motivation and cognition across cultures* (pp. 517–593). Amsterdam: Elsevier Science.

Goldstein, L.S., & Lake, V.E. (2000). "Love, love, and more love for children:" Exploring preservice teachers' understandings of caring. *Teaching and Teacher Education, 16*(7), 861–872.

Gresalfi, M.S. (2009). Taking up opportunities to learn: Constructing dispositions in mathematics classrooms. *Journal of the Learning Sciences, 18*(3), 327–369.

Gruber, H.E. (1974). *Darwin on man: A psychological study of scientific creativity.* Chicago: University of Chicago Press.

Hackenberg, A.J. (2005). Mathematical caring relations as a framework for supporting research and learning. In G.M. Lloyd, M. Wilson, J.L.M. Wilkins, & S.L. Behm (Eds.), *Proceedings of the twenty-seventh annual meeting of the North American chapter of the International Group for the Psychology of Mathematics Education* (pp. 639–646). Roanoke, VA: Virginia Polytechnic Institute and State University.

Hackenberg, A.J. (2010). Mathematical caring relations in action. *Journal for Research in Mathematics Education, 41*(3), 236–273.

Hammer, D. (2004). The variability of student reasoning, lectures 1–3. In E. Redish & M. Vicentini (Eds.), *Proceedings of the Enrico Fermi summer school, course CLVI* (pp. 279–340). Bologna: Italian Physical Society.

Hammer, D., Goldberg, F., & Fargason, S. (2012). Responsive teaching and the beginnings of energy in a third grade classroom. *Review of Science, Mathematics and ICT Education, 6*(1), 51–72.

Hargreaves, A. (2000). Mixed emotions: Teachers' perceptions of their interactions with students. *Teaching and Teacher Education, 16,* 811–826.

Hawkins, D. (1965). Messing about in science. *Science and Children, 2*(5), 5–9.

Jaber, L.Z., & Hammer, D. (in press). Learning to feel like a scientist. *Science Education.*

Jordan, B., & Henderson, A. (1995). Interaction analysis: Foundations and practice. *Journal of the Learning Sciences, 4*(1), 39–103.

Keller, E.F. (1983). *A feeling for the organism: The life and work of Barbara McClintock.* New York: W.H. Freeman and Company.

Lehrer, R. (2009). Designing to develop disciplinary dispositions: Modeling natural systems. *American Psychologist, 64*(8), 759–771.

Lorimer, J. (2008). Counting corncrakes: The affective science of corncrake surveillance. *Social Studies of Science, 38,* 377–405.

Maskiewicz, A.C., & Winters, V.A. (2012). Understanding the co-construction of inquiry practices: A case study of a responsive teaching environment. *Journal of Research in Science Teaching, 49*(4), 429–464.

Milne, C., & Otieno T. (2007). Understanding engagement: Science demonstrations and emotional energy. *Science Education, 91,* 523–553.

Minstrell, J., & van Zee, E.H. (2000). *Inquiring into inquiry learning and teaching in science.* Washington, DC: American Association for the Advancement of Science.

National Research Council (2011). *A framework for K–12 science education: Practices, crosscutting concepts, and core ideas.* Washington, DC: The National Academies Press.

Nias, J. (1989). *Primary teachers talking.* London: Routledge and Kegan Paul.

Nias, J. (1999). Primary teaching as a culture of care. In J. Prosser (Ed.), *School culture* (pp. 66–81). London: Paul Chapman.

Noddings, N. (1984). *Caring: A feminine approach to ethics and moral education.* Berkeley, CA: University of California Press.

Noddings, N. (2005). *The challenge to care in schools: An alternative approach to education* (2nd edition). New York: Teachers College Press.

O'Connor, M.C., & Michaels, S. (1993). Aligning academic task and participation status through revoicing: Analysis of a classroom discourse strategy. *Anthropology & Education Quarterly, 24*(4), 318–335.

Olitsky, S. (2007). Promoting student engagement in science: Interaction rituals and the pursuit of a community of practice. *Journal of Research in Science Teaching, 44,* 33–56.

Osbeck, L., Nersessian, N.J., Malone, K., & Newstetter, W. (2011). *Science as psychology: Sense-making and identity in science practice.* Cambridge: Cambridge University Press.

Richards, J. (2013). *Exploring what stabilizes teachers' attention and responsiveness to the substance of student' scientific thinking in the classroom.* Unpublished doctoral dissertation. University of Maryland, College Park, MD.

Rogers, D.L., & Webb, J. (1991). The ethic of caring in teacher education. *Journal of Teacher Education, 42*(3), 173–181.

Rosebery, A.S., Ogonowski, M., DiSchino, M., & Warren, B. (2010). "The coat traps all your body heat": Heterogeneity as fundamental to learning. *The Journal of the Learning Sciences, 19*(3), 322–357.

Scardamalia, M. (2000). Can schools enter a Knowledge Society? In M. Selinger & J. Wynn (Eds.), *Educational technology and the impact on teaching and learning* (pp. 6–10). Abingdon: RM Education.

Scardamalia, M., & Bereiter, C. (2006). Knowledge building: Theory, pedagogy, and technology. In K. Sawyer (Ed.), *Cambridge handbook of the learning sciences* (pp. 97–118). New York: Cambridge University Press.

Sfard, A. (2000). Symbolizing mathematical reality into being: How mathematical discourse and mathematical objects create each other. In P. Cobb, K.E. Yackel, & K. McClain (Eds.), *Symbolizing and communicating: perspectives on mathematical discourse, tools, and instructional design* (pp. 37–98). Mahwah, NJ: Erlbaum.

Shweder, R.A., Haidt, J., Horton, R., & Joseph, C. (2008). The cultural psychology of emotions: Ancient and renewed. In M. Lewis, J. Haviland-Jones, and L. Barrett (Eds.), *Handbook of emotions* (3rd edition, pp. 397–414). New York: Guilford Press.

Sidnell, J. & Stivers, T. (2005). Multimodal interaction. Special Issue of *Semiotica, 156*(1/4), 1–20.

Thagard, P. (2008). *Hot thought.* Cambridge: MIT Press.

Varelas, M., Becker, J., Luster, B., & Wenzel, S. (2002). When genres meet: Inquiry into a sixth-grade urban science class. *Journal of Research in Science Teaching, 39*(7), 579–605.

Watkins, J., Coffey, J., Maskiewicz, A., & Hammer, D. (in press). An account of progress in teachers' epistemological framing of science inquiry. In G. Schraw, J. Brownlee, L. Olafson, & M. Vanderveldt (Eds.), *Teachers' personal epistemologies: Evolving models for transforming practice.* Charlotte, NC: Information Age Publishing.

Wentzel, K.R. (1997). Student motivation in middle school: The role of perceived pedagogical caring. *Journal of Educational Psychology, 89,* 411–419.

Williams-Johnson, M.W., Cross, D.I., Hong, J.Y., Aultman, L.P., Osbon, J.N., & Schutz, P.A. (2008). "There is no emotion in math": How teachers approach emotions in the classroom. *Teachers College Record, 110*(8), 1574–1612.

188 Lama Z. Jaber

Yackel, E., & Cobb, P. (1996). Sociomathematical norms, argumentation, and autonomy in mathematics. *Journal for Research in Mathematics Education, 27,* 458–477.

Zembylas, M. (2004). Young children's emotional practices while engaged in long-term science investigation. *Journal of Research in Science Teaching, 41,* 693–719.

Zembylas, M. (2005). Beyond teacher cognition and teacher beliefs: The value of the ethnography of emotions in teaching. *International Journal of Qualitative Studies in Education, 18*(4), 465–487.

Zembylas, M. (2007). Emotional ecology: The intersection of emotional knowledge and pedagogical content knowledge in teaching. *Teaching and Teacher Education, 23,* 355–367.

9

ATTENTION TO STUDENT FRAMING IN RESPONSIVE TEACHING

Jennifer Radoff and David Hammer

Among the challenges of responsive teaching is deciding where and how to focus one's attention. Teaching involves many choices, mostly tacit, that influence what the teacher notices and what aspects of students' thinking he or she pursues.

In this chapter, we present a case study from a third-grade class studying motion. We present two episodes from their work, one from the second day and one from the fourteenth day. We claim the evidence shows a change from the first episode to the second in the scope of the teacher's attention. She shifts from a wider consideration of the class's sense of what they are doing—their epistemological framing—to a more narrow consideration of the conceptual substance of particular ideas. We suggest this shift is itself responsive to the students' thinking: the class is more stably doing science on day 14, which lets the teacher relax her attention at that level to focus more attention on students' particular ideas within their inquiry.

Attending to Students' Thinking

Human attention is limited (Simons & Chabris, 1999). It is not possible for anyone to notice, let alone focus on, all aspects of the classroom dynamics. Teachers must constantly decide, explicitly or tacitly, how to distribute their attention. Prior analyses have focused on when and how teachers direct their attention to the substance of student thinking, arguing that it is context-sensitive and influenced by many factors, including the teacher's long- and short-term instructional goals, (pedagogical) content knowledge, epistemologies, local classroom dynamics, and institutional expectations and time constraints (Lau, 2010; Levin, 2008; Maskiewicz & Winters, 2012; Richards, 2013).

190 Jennifer Radoff and David Hammer

Much of the discussion has addressed attention to the substance of student thinking as opposed to, for example, student behavior, logistics, or canonically correct vocabulary (Coffey, Hammer, Levin, & Grant, 2011). But "attention to substance" is quite broad itself. Robertson, Richards, Elby, and Walkoe (Chapter 11 of this volume), for example, show a teacher shifting among several foci of attention, all aspects of the substance of students' thinking.

In this chapter, we study the choices that one teacher, Sharon Fargason, makes while attending and responding to student thinking. In particular, we identify her tacit choice between focusing more "widely" on students' epistemological framing and more "narrowly" on specific conceptual substance.

Attending to Students' Epistemological Framing

Sharon's "wider" attention is to which activity students think they are engaged in, or which "game" they think they are playing (Ford, 2005; Lemke, 1990). Students are beginning scientific inquiry, for example, when they are in pursuit of coherent, mechanistic accounts of natural phenomena. For teachers, much of the challenge is in recognizing and supporting students beginning that pursuit (Hammer, Goldberg, & Fargason, 2012; Radoff, Goldberg, Hammer, & Fargason, 2010). It is difficult in part because students' sense of what is taking place can vary, from student to student as well as from moment to moment. In this analysis, we are interested in students' sense of what is taking place with respect to knowledge, which we will discuss in terms of their epistemological framing (Redish, 2004; Scherr & Hammer, 2009).

Redish (2004) proposed the construct of epistemological framing to connect research on epistemological resources (Hammer & Elby, 2002) with research on framing (Goffman, 1974; Tannen, 1993). The former describes people as having rich collections of resources for understanding knowledge and epistemic activities, which they draw on in various ways in different contexts. The latter concerns how people form their sense of what is taking place, in different contexts and dynamically moment to moment.

It is an aspect of learning, starting as young children become familiar with various kinds of epistemic activities—storytelling, guessing games, pretending, and so on—each with various rules or heuristics for engagement, values and assumptions, and goals and criteria. Learning science, in this respect, means becoming familiar with science as a kind of epistemic activity, including its aims, values, and disciplined ways of constructing and assessing knowledge (Chinn, Buckland, & Samarapungavan, 2011; Ford & Forman, 2006; NGSS, 2013).

Thus, responsive teaching should include attention to framing—to how students are approaching and understanding the activity—which is a wider scope of attention than to their particular ideas and questions within the activity. The dynamics of framing makes attending at this wider scope more complex than simply assessing whether or not students are doing science. For young children in particular—who are learning many kinds of epistemic activity—how they frame what they are doing in one moment may not be the same as in another moment, and part of their becoming familiar with science is their developing stability in their framing.

The Reflexive Relationship Between Conceptual Substance and Epistemological Framing

Sharon's "narrower" attention is to details within the conceptual substance of student thinking. Here, for instance, students consider whether a car will catch on fire. Hearing them raise the idea, Sharon could focus on it, eliciting further and more detailed thinking about fire and cars and motion, or she could keep her attention wider in scope, a broader survey of the kinds of ideas students are offering.

The two levels interact: there is a "reflexive relationship" (Yackel & Cobb, 1996) between interpreting the conceptual substance of what students are trying to say and interpreting their epistemological framing. Teachers can infer the kind of epistemic activity in which students are engaged from the kinds of conceptual substance they offer, and they understand that substance based on their sense of what students are doing.

Imagine, for example, a student telling a story about her family's trip to the theme park. She says it was raining, and so the bumper cars were closed. She asked a park attendant why she couldn't ride the bumper cars in the rain, and he told her that the tires might slip around on the wet road and the driver could lose control of the car. The student might be trying to explain what she knows about tires and traction, or she might be trying to convey her disappointment at missing the ride. The teacher and other students listening would be influenced in their sense of her meaning by the epistemic context: whether it has been a discussion about friction or a discussion about what she did over the weekend.

At the same time, the teacher's and other students' responses would help to shape that context. The conversation could go one way if the teacher presses the student to unpack the connection between the slippery surface and the possibility of losing control of the car, and it could go another way if a student responds with a comment about his trip to that same park.

If there are multiple ways for students to interpret what is happening, a teacher might zoom out to a wide view in order to help students come to some stability around what they're doing. Instead of deeply pursuing the conceptual substance of an idea, she might serve as the gatekeeper to allow or deny entry for certain kinds of ideas, hoping to affect students' expectations around what kind of conceptual substance is appropriate. Once the students are more stably engaged in a particular kind of epistemic activity (in this case, doing science), the teacher can

192 Jennifer Radoff and David Hammer

zoom in to a narrower view where she delves deeply into particular aspects of students' thinking.

In this chapter, we focus on Sharon Fargason, who was part of the Responsive Teaching in Science project (Goldberg, Hammer, Bendall, Coffey, & Maskiewicz, 2007, NSF DRL-0732233, 2007). Sharon's teaching is featured on the project website cipstrends.sdsu.edu/responsiveteaching/, as well as in several published accounts (Bresser & Fargason, 2013; Hammer, Goldberg, & Fargason, 2012; Radoff, Goldberg, Hammer, & Fargason, 2010). In what follows, we examine two focal episodes to argue that when students showed more stability in doing science, Sharon focused her attention more narrowly on the ideas within their inquiry than she did when students showed less stability in doing science.

Methodological Considerations

Episode Selection

The episodes we present took place in the second and fifth weeks of the Toy Car unit (cipstrends.sdsu.edu/responsiveteaching/carmodule/), which began with a launching question about how to make a toy car move.

In the first episode, the students and teacher were in the throes of co-constructing expectations of what they were doing, both socially and scientifically. In the second episode, the students were evidently framing what they were doing as a pursuit of coherent, mechanistic accounts of (a toy car's) motion.

We selected these episodes for evidence of a contrast in how Sharon chose to pursue ideas. In the first, she was selective, actively discouraging lines of reasoning and frequently refocusing the discussion. In the second, she took up a student's idea that on its own would not seem scientific, and her choice led to a productive discussion.

Evidence of Student Framing

To build this argument, we begin with evidence of student framing. In essence, we are making conjectures about Sharon's thinking on the presumption that in the moment she noticed at least some of this evidence too. There are some indications of Sharon's attention in what she says and does, and we have checked our interpretations with her own memory and sense, but our argument depends on plausible inferences.

There is evidence of students' framing in their discourse, as Tannen (1993) described in several studies. In one, she examined interview data of women talking about a short movie they had seen to show how "surface evidence" can give insight into framing. For example, many subjects noted things that did not occur in the movie, evidence suggesting they expected those things were possible. There was evidence as well in linguistic markers that indicated attitudes such as surprise and judgment. Still other evidence included linguistic registers, shifting in ways that indicated, for participants in the conversation, how to interpret the meaning of an utterance.

In another study, Tannen and Wallat (1993) analyzed video data of a doctor examining a child. Similar sorts of evidence—of vocal register and language—signaled shifts in the doctor's framing of what she was doing, in particular whether she was speaking to clinicians, to the mother, or to the child. These markers helped the mother and child to recognize which audience the doctor was addressing. In effect, Tannen and Wallat made explicit the tacit channels of communication among participants in the conversation.

In what follows, we similarly study students' discourse for evidence of their framing—evidence that was available to them and their teacher. We invite readers to watch the video and assess our interpretations themselves. The videos and transcripts of both episodes are available online at http://www.studentsthinking. org/rtsm.

Data and Analysis

We begin with our analysis of an early episode, which reflected instability of student framing. That is, the class had yet to settle on the kind of conversation they were having, and this influenced how Sharon attended and responded to the framing. We then turn to a later episode, which took place approximately five weeks after the first.

Early Episode Overview

On the first day of a unit on motion and energy, Sharon held up a toy car in front of her third-grade class and asked the launching question, "How would you get this toy car to move?" The students spent some time in small-group discussion and then shared with the class how they might get the toy car to move. On the second day of the unit, the students worked in small groups, recording and illustrating their ideas on butcher paper to share with the entire class. Isaac and Jimmy were the first to share their idea: a large and complex roller coaster, equipped with fiery loop-the-loops and terrifying jumps over shark-infested waters (see Figure 9.1).

As Isaac and Jimmy presented their idea, the students attended to many different aspects of it. Some picked up on the sensational features of the roller coaster, while others held Isaac and Jimmy accountable to whether the idea would actually work to make a toy car move. Several students switched between talking about a toy car that lacks a power source, and thus relies only on the roller coaster's design to move, and a real car that has an internal energy source, which allows it to move independently.

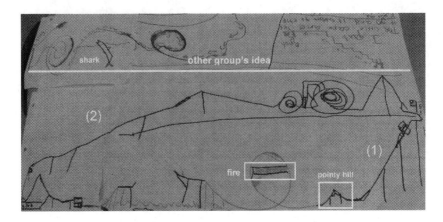

FIGURE 9.1 Isaac and Jimmy's roller coaster.

Throughout the episode, there was evidence of variation in how students framed their participation. While there were glimmers of proto-scientific engagement in students' attention to plausible mechanisms for the motion of a toy car, the students were not stable in it. Sharon, we show, attended and responded largely at the level of the students' framings, apparently picking up on and trying to draw out the glimmers of plausible mechanisms for the toy car's motion. For example, she asked students to clarify or repeat contributions that suggested attention to mechanism, and she disregarded or deferred those that focused on other things, such as fantastical design features. At times, she was explicitly directive, such as telling students that they should think of a toy car, not a real car with an engine.

We turn now to the analysis, to show (1) students' unsettled framings, and (2) Sharon's attention and responsiveness.

Early Episode Analysis: Student Contributions and Teacher Response

In analyzing this episode, we looked for stability in students' tangible reasoning about the motion of a toy car. Our purpose is to articulate evidence of students' framing that were available for Sharon during class. We consider how Sharon responded to students' contributions as evidence of her interpretations and local intentions. For example, her persistence in driving the conversation away from real cars indicates that she noticed that students kept returning to the topic. Her multiple attempts to shift the conversation indicate her effort to disrupt what she saw as a local stability around discussing real cars.

Throughout the Early Episode, Sharon promoted students' tangible reasoning about the motion of a toy car. For example, at the start of the episode Priscilla asked, "Is there something that pushes [the car] up here (referring to the stretch of incline labeled (2) in Figure 9.1), because I cannot believe them that it goes

Attention to Student Framing **195**

by itself" [line 2]. Her question is about causal mechanism, and is evidence of her expectation that there must be one. Her critique is about the physical viability of Isaac's and Jimmy's idea. Sharon tried several times to make Priscilla's question a focus of student attention by asking Priscilla to repeat it [4], by asking other students if they heard her question [4, 6], and by revoicing it [8].

Another example is Gustavo's concern that the car might fall at the top of the loop-the-loop [11, 15], and Jimmy's response that because of the initial drop (labeled (1) in Figure 9.1), the car will be going fast enough to make it around [42, 47]. Sharon repeated Gustavo's idea twice [16, 38] and then pursued Jimmy's response, "It'd have to go really fast," [42] even though she already called on another student [41, 46].

A third example is Jamir's concern about how the car would move when it gets to the "pointy hill" [82, 84]: "Won't the car jump and crash into the [loop-the-loop]. . . ?" Again, Sharon supported the question, asking Jamir to repeat it and commenting that she "was kind of wondering that too" [83].

In other moments, however, students' contributions suggest that they were not thinking about the physical plausibility of the phenomena but about the drama of the roller coaster ride and fantastical design features.

For example, Isaac's response to Jamir's question about the pointy hill was to describe an implausible device—"a thing right there that knows if it's gonna crash . . . and opens up a spot" to let the car through without crashing [89]. Sharon pointedly discouraged this response, laughing and articulating a tacit rule that she had in mind: "You're making stuff up as you go along! You can't do that!" [90].

In some moments, students focused on flashy aspects of the design that were not relevant to how the roller coaster made the toy car move. For example, early in the episode Jourdan asked, "What is that part with the big fish right there on the other paper?" [60]. Sharon deferred his question [62, 64, 66], asking for further conversation about an idea she had heard about the car's motion.

When Scarlett kicked off a conversation about whether the car will get burned by the fire on the loop-the-loop, Sharon initially supported this conversation, especially highlighting Ray's contribution that incorporated speed into the explanation, but shut it down when it moved too far away from issues concerning the car's movement, and quickly dismissed Kyleigh's suggestion to reposition the fire to the top of the roller coaster [67–81].

In addition to discussing the dramatic design elements of the roller coaster, students frequently shifted to thinking of "real" cars—cars that have engines and drivers. That framing of the topic would obviate questions such as Priscilla's, of what pushes the car up the hill. Sharon tried repeatedly to keep students thinking about a toy car.

One example is when Jamir and Isaac considered how the point of the pointy hill could get caught on "the bottom engines" and "materials" on the underside of a "real car" [103–125]. Sharon asked, "Can we talk about toy cars just to make this easier?" [126].

196 Jennifer Radoff and David Hammer

Another example is when Jose and Jimmy discussed how many times the car would go around the loop-the-loop [127–130]. Presumably because they did not seem to be discussing plausible toy car behavior, Sharon asked if they were talking about a toy car [131], and then followed up by insisting, "Make sure you're talking about a toy car. There's no driver in this car" [133]. When Jourdan suggested that perhaps the car is automatic [134] and Gustavo suggested that a remote control car is still a toy car [136], Sharon responded, "Just to be clear, we all need to be talking about toy cars today, not cars that people drive. All right?" [138].

Early Episode Discussion

In the Early Episode, when students showed instability in their framing, the game was about getting students to recognize what kind of conversation she wanted them to have—one about tangible mechanisms for a toy car's motion. Sharon did this by selecting and promoting certain kinds of contributions and discouraging others. Each time Sharon discovered that students weren't discussing the motion of a toy car, she changed the direction of the discussion, often quite abruptly.

It is important to note that even in moments where students were discussing the toy car's motion, Sharon did not focus much on the particular substance within those ideas. Most of her interaction with students' ideas involved revoicing or clarifying, rather than delving deeper into students' meaning or asking follow-up questions about the ideas.

The only instance in which she delved into a student's idea was in line 85, when she asked Jamir what would make the car jump. Certainly there were other opportunities. There were several places, for example, when students focused on the car's motion in the loop-the-loop. Jourdan remarked that the car would not fall at the top of the loop "because it goes down really fast" [60]; later, Jimmy focused on the car's motion in the loop [128, 130]. Sharon could have asked Jourdan why going fast would keep the car from falling at the top of the loop-the-loop, or asked Jimmy what would make the car loop around multiple times. However, her response to Jourdan was to deflect his closing question about "the big fish" [62]; her response to Jimmy was to check that he was "talking about a toy car" [131].

Our conjecture is that Sharon was aware of the variation in students' framing of what they were doing, and for this reason she continued to attend and respond at a wider view for the entire episode.

Late Episode Overview

By day 14 of the toy car unit, the students had discussed various factors that could affect a toy car's speed as it moves down a ramp, including the weight and shape of the car and the slickness of the ramp's surface.

At the beginning of class on day 14, Jamir shared something he had discovered the day before: when he put a rubber doorstop on a steep ramp, the doorstop

Attention to Student Framing **197**

didn't move at all. Jamir suggested that the doorstop's shape kept it from rolling down the hill. When he tried to demonstrate the phenomenon for the class, however, the doorstop slowly slipped down the ramp. Attempting to make sense of the discrepant results, some students argued that the ramp wasn't steep enough, and others argued that the doorstop wasn't slippery enough. After about fifteen minutes of discussing why the doorstop sometimes moved and sometimes did not, Ray said, "It's free will."

We chose this episode because of Sharon's response to the idea of "free will": She delved into it for an extended discussion. Free will hardly seems, in itself, a likely topic in the pursuit of mechanistic understanding. By this point in the lesson, however, the students seemed to have established a shared framing of what they are doing together—making sense of different things that impact a toy car's motion—and Sharon had seldom needed to intervene to promote mechanistic sense-making. Here, we propose, her sense of the students' stability in what they've been doing impacted her interpretation of an idea that, on the face of it, wouldn't belong in a conversation about the motion of toy cars.

Late Episode Analysis: Student Contributions and Teacher Response

The episode began with the puzzling observation that the doorstop would sometimes slide and sometimes just sit still at the top of the ramp. Sharon asked Jamir if he pushed it down the ramp, and Jose said, "He let it go." Then she asked whether "pushing it" and "letting it go" were the same.

Sharon's question prompted Ray to say, "It's free will." In response to Ray's comment, Sharon first asked the class whether the car or the doorstop had free will, and then she asked Ray what he meant [149]. Ray responded that free will is when "you just let it go, because you're not pushing it, that's all" [150].

Sharon tried three more times to elicit a definition [151, 153, 155] before she offered one herself, appropriating Jourdan's example of "letting a dog go for a walk by itself" [157]: "Free will means you get to choose what you want to do" [151]. She then asked, "Does the car or the doorstop have free will?" [158], to which several students responded, "No." Sharon seemed to expect this response, because she quickly followed up with what seems to be the central question, "What makes the car and the doorstop go down that ramp then?" [160].

It would be reasonable to expect the students to start working on other explanations, but Jourdan responded, "The car had free will" [161]. Sharon's exclamation, "Wait, a car has free will?" [163], is evidence she was not expecting that response. Again, she chose to pursue the topic.

Throughout the rest of the episode, Sharon attempted to understand what students meant by "free will." Jourdan suggested that the car has free will because its wheels allow it to slip freely down slippery things, but the doorstop does not have free will because it gets stuck going down the ramp [165, 172]. Alexis responded

198 Jennifer Radoff and David Hammer

to Jourdan's comment, noting that free will is about moving without a push, not about being able to slip freely on a slippery surface [174]. Gustavo added that a remote control car doesn't have free will because "you're controlling it" [176].

At this point, it seemed clear to Sharon that students considered a car not to have free will if a person controls its movement [175]. But then what do they think it means for a car to have free will? To narrow down the students' meaning, Sharon asked a clarifying question, "Ok so is that free will if a car goes down a slide by itself?" [179], to which some students replied, "Yes." Rather than thinking about anthropomorphized cars, some students were using free will as a way to distinguish the car's motion on a ramp (where you can just let it go) and the car's motion on a flat surface (where it requires a push), and Jourdan was using it to describe the state of non-impeded motion.

In response, Sharon clarified her definition of free will to involve only matters of choice: "Ok so free will means that you get to make a choice. So Jourdan, did that car make a choice to go down that hill?" [181]. Jourdan responded, "I don't think, because cars can't go alive" [183], and Gustavo added, "Yeah, they can't go alive only persons can" [184]. Kyleigh added that a real car does not have free will either "[b]ecause the person's driving the car" [189]. Following Sharon's clarified definition, Alexis concluded, "It didn't have free will because it didn't have another choice of staying or going, it had to go down . . . Because like if you're on top of a hill and the car goes down a slippery thing, like it has to go down because like there's nothing that could hold it. Unless if it was a real car, then the brakes" [204].

For much of the rest of the day, the students' framing was more clearly stable around coherent, mechanistic reasoning. Later, for example, the class sustained a 20-minute conversation about how wheels work to make a toy car move. The conversation focused deeply on mechanism, the students listened and responded to each other, and they held each other accountable to the larger framing so that Sharon didn't need to do much to maintain those boundaries. As a result, Sharon was able to focus her attention on eliciting the substance of a student's particularly complex idea that involved comparing rolling wheels to gears (More about that episode, "Isaac's Wheels," is available online. See http://www.studentsthinking.org/rtsm).

Late Episode Discussion

Our core contention about the Late Episode is that it shows a different pattern in Sharon's attention and responsiveness to student thinking from her attention and responsiveness in the Early Episode.

At the outset of the episode, the students' participation was at least consistent with, if not indicative of, mechanistic sense-making: They were focused on making sense of an inconsistency in the doorstop's behavior, citing evidence to support their arguments for what might account for that inconsistency. Ray's suggestion of free will as an explanation could easily be seen as a move to a different kind of conversation. But Sharon chose to take it up, asking him to clarify and guiding the class to think about the idea.

There was another decision point for her a moment later, when Jourdan said, "The car has free will," after many students had already agreed that it did not. Sharon could have shut down further consideration of free will, but again she chose to pursue it.

Jourdan's response indicated a need for Sharon to stop and reassess what she had previously taken for granted as shared understanding. On the face of it, the notion of free will has no place in a discussion about causal mechanisms, and it would be natural to see it as disruptive to that framing. Accordingly, had it come up in the Early Episode, Sharon would have been more likely to interpret it as a matter of epistemology—a shift, perhaps, to ideas about anthropomorphized cars—and so been more assertive in closing the topic. Recall how she quickly closed discussions about whether the car would get burned in the loop and discussions about "real cars."

On the few occasions when Sharon put considerable effort into understanding students' ideas in the Early Episode, the ideas ended up falling outside the epistemological boundaries of the conversation. For example, when Jamir claimed that the car might get stuck if it doesn't jump off the pointy-hill, it took about 40 turns for Sharon to realize that he was considering some sort of toy-car/real-car hybrid. The difference Jamir's idea, although it ended up being epistemologically out of bounds, seemed relevant on the surface. Free will, on the other hand, did not seem epistemologically appropriate on the surface, yet Sharon still pursued it.

In the latter case, Sharon saw the students as more stably framing their activity in ways that would exclude ideas about living cars from the landscape of acceptable knowledge. With reason to be more confident about the students' epistemological framing, Sharon could feel more free to draw out the conceptual substance of students' thinking and consider the possibility that what she meant by free will might not be the same as what the students meant by it.

Discussion and Implications

We have argued that the scope of Sharon's attention and responsiveness changed in response to the stability of students' epistemological framing. In the Early Episode, there was evidence of the students' varying, unstable sense of what they were doing together, and there was evidence that Sharon's attention was mainly at that level: rather than delve into students' ideas, she focused more on the kinds of ideas students were offering. In the Late Episode, by contrast, students were relatively stable in their sense-making, and Sharon responded to student thinking by probing into specific ideas. She did so even with an idea, free will, that on its own seems like the wrong kind of idea for a discussion about physical mechanism.

This claim of variation in Sharon's attention to students' thinking dovetails with Robertson et al.'s (Chapter 11, this volume) case that a teacher's attention can shift "between multiple foci within the substance of student thinking." Similarly, Maskiewicz and Winters (2012) compared across two successive years in "Mrs. Charles's" class, showing connected differences in the students' inquiry and the teacher's attention. They showed that the epistemic norms were different between the two classes for the same teacher, and they argued that it would be a mistake to attribute the difference simply to Mrs. Charles having made progress in responsive teaching.

Like these authors, we are arguing that there are interesting, important dynamics of attention within a focus on the substance of student thinking. Whereas Maskiewicz and Winters compared across successive years with different groups of students, we have compared across episodes within a single 14-day unit. Whereas Robertson et al. identified multiple foci of conceptual substance, we have characterized a shift between a wider view of the kind of activity the class is engaged in and a narrower view of the particularities within conceptual substance. Sharon, we claim, dynamically shifted between these views in response to the stability of students' epistemological framing.

On a larger scale, we are interested in understanding how a class makes progress toward establishing shared expectations around epistemic activities, in particular, progress toward disciplinary practices. We suspect that Sharon's skillful attending and responding played a large role in this progress. Even in the limited context of these two episodes, we can see the beneficial consequences of Sharon's attending to students' epistemological framing.

For Making Sense of the Substance of Student Thinking

Student thinking takes on different meaning according to the epistemological context. As we have discussed, whether a contribution is epistemologically appropriate depends largely on why the student is offering it. An awareness of epistemological framing can help teachers engage more meaningfully with students' ideas. As we have shown, Sharon's treatment of "free will" in the Late Episode differed from her treatment of "real cars" in the Early Episode. Although on the surface the topic of "real cars" seems more tightly linked to a toy car's motion than the topic of "free will" does, Sharon's attention to the epistemological context helped her decide which ideas to pursue further and which ones to hold off.

For Helping Students Refine Their Disciplinary Expectations

If learning science means becoming familiar with it as a kind of epistemic activity, then teaching science means, in part, helping students develop a sense of the epistemic norms and values of the discipline. Research shows that how teachers engage with the substance of student thinking impacts what students come to see as valued and valuable forms of knowledge in the classroom (Coffey et al., 2011; Cobb, Stephan, McClain, & Gravemeijer, 2001; Cobb, Wood, Yackel, & McNeal,

1992; Yackel & Cobb, 1996). In light of this research, how a teacher responds to student thinking impacts how students come to understand what it means to do science.

In Sharon's case, she responded to students' varied epistemological framings by acting as a gatekeeper, winnowing kinds of ideas, supporting some and suppressing others. She discovered, recognized, and supported productive aspects of students' contributions, which in turn signaled to the students what kind of contributions are valued, leading to further contributions to discover. In this way she supported the emergence, development, and stability of students' sense of the discipline. When the class was more stable in their epistemological framing, she focused less attention on forming shared expectations and more on delving into the substance of particular ideas, which in turn may have helped students to refine their framing. Moving forward, we plan to analyze more of the data from the 14 days of the Toy Car investigations in order to better understand the reflexive dynamics of how Sharon's attending and responding to students' framing contributes to their progress in scientific engagement.

Acknowledgments

This work was supported by the National Science Foundation under grant # DRL 0732233, Learning Progressions for Scientific Inquiry: A Model Implementation in the Context of Energy, and by the Gordon and Betty Moore Foundation, Grant #3475, The Dynamics of Learners' Persistence and Engagement in Science. The views expressed here are those of the authors and may not be shared by either foundation.

References

Bresser, R., & Fargason, S. (2013). *Becoming scientists: Inquiry-based teaching in diverse classrooms, grades 3–5.* Portland, ME: Stenhouse Publishers.

Chinn, C.A., Buckland, L.A., & Samarapungavan, A. (2011). Expanding the dimensions of epistemic cognition: Arguments from philosophy and psychology. *Educational Psychologist, 46*(3), 141–167.

Cobb, P., Stephan, M., McClain, K., & Gravemeijer, K. (2001). Participating in classroom mathematical practices. *Journal of the Learning Sciences, 10,* 113–164.

Cobb, P., Wood, T., Yackel, E., & McNeal, B. (1992). Characteristics of classroom mathematics traditions: An interactional analysis. *American Educational Research Journal, 29,* 573–604.

Coffey, J.E., Hammer, D., Levin, D.M., & Grant, T. (2011). The missing disciplinary substance of formative assessment. *Journal of Research in Science Teaching, 48*(10), 1109–1136.

Ford, M.J. (2005). The Game, the pieces, and the players: Generative resources from two instructional portrayals of experimentation. *The Journal of the Learning Sciences, 14*(4), 449–487.

Ford, M.J., & Forman, E.A. (2006). Redefining disciplinary learning in classroom contexts. *Review of Research in Education, 30,* 1–32.

Goffman, E. (1974). *Frame analysis: An essay on the organization of experience*. Boston: Northeastern University Press.

Goldberg, F., Hammer, D., Bendall, S., Coffey, J. and Maskiewicz, A. (2007). *Learning progressions for scientific inquiry: A model implementation in the context of energy*. Washington, DC: National Science Foundation Grant 0732233.

Hammer, D., & Elby, A. (2002). On the form of a personal epistemology. In B.K. Hofer & P.R. Pintrich (Eds.), *Personal epistemology: The psychology of beliefs about knowledge and knowing* (pp. 169–190). Mahwah, NJ: Erlbaum.

Hammer, D., Goldberg, F., & Fargason, S. (2012). Responsive teaching and the beginnings of energy in a third grade classroom. *Review of Science, Mathematics and ICT Education, 6*(1), 51–72.

Lau, M. (2010). Understanding the dynamics of teacher attention: Examples of how high school physics and physical science teachers attend to student ideas (Doctoral dissertation). University of Maryland, College Park.

Lemke, J. (1990). *Talking science: language, learning and values*. Ablex Publishing Corporation.

Levin, D.M. (2008). What secondary science teachers pay attention to in the classroom: Situating teaching in institutional and social systems (Doctoral dissertation). University of Maryland, College Park.

Maskiewicz, A.C., & Winters, V.A. (2012). Understanding the co-construction of inquiry practices: A case study of a responsive teaching environment. *Journal of Research in Science Teaching, 49*(4), 429–464.

NGSS (2013). The Next Generation Science Standards. Retrieved October 1, 2013, from http://www.nextgenscience.org/next-generation-science-standards.

Radoff, J., Goldberg, F., Hammer, D., & Fargason, S. (2010). The beginnings of energy in third graders' reasoning. In C. Singh, M. Sabella, & S. Rebello (Eds.), *2010 Physics Education Research Conference*, Vol. 1289 (pp. 269–272). Portland OR: American Institute of Physics.

Redish, E.F. (2004). A theoretical framework for physics education research: Modeling student thinking. In E. Redish, C. Tarsitani, & M. Vicentini (Eds.), *Proceedings of the Enrico Fermi summer school, Course CLVI* (pp. 1–63). Bologna: Italian Physical Society.

Richards, J. (2013). Exploring what stabilizes teachers' attention and responsiveness to the substance of students' scientific thinking in the classroom (Doctoral dissertation). University of Maryland, College Park.

Scherr, R.E., & Hammer, D. (2009). Student behavior and epistemological framing: Examples from collaborative active-learning activities in physics. *Cognition and Instruction, 27*(2), 147–174.

Simons, D.J., & Chabris, C.F. (1999). Gorillas in our midst: Sustained inattentional blindness for dynamic events. *Perception, 28,* 1059–1074.

Tannen, D. (1993). What's in a frame? Surface evidence for underlying expectations. In D. Tannen (Ed.) *Framing in discourse* (pp. 14–56). New York: Oxford University Press.

Tannen, D., & Wallat, C. (1993). Interactive frames and knowledge schemas in interaction: Examples from a medical examination/interview. In D. Tannen (Ed.), *Framing in discourse* (pp. 57–76). New York: Oxford University Press.

Yackel, E., & Cobb, P. (1996). Sociomathematical norms, argumentation, and autonomy in mathematics. *Journal for Research in Mathematics Education, 27,* 458–477.

10

METHODS TO ASSESS TEACHER RESPONSIVENESS *IN SITU*

Jennifer Evarts Lineback

Responsive teaching, where teachers respond to the *essence* of students' ideas during instruction and allow those ideas to direct future class activity, is a dimension of teacher practice that has been gaining attention in the literature (Ball, 1993; Hammer, 1997; Lampert, 1990; Levin, 2008; Pierson, 2008; Ruiz-Primo & Furtak, 2007). Teaching responsively has been correlated with deeper student understanding and increased student performance in both mathematics (Carpenter, Fennema, Peterson, Chiang, & Loef, 1989; Pierson, 2008) and science (Ruiz-Primo & Furtak, 2007). Thus, there is support for mathematics and science educators to teach this way.

To date, there have been few empirical studies that have assessed responsive teaching in the classroom. Part of the scarcity is due to the challenges inherent in characterizing nuances in teacher responsiveness *in situ*. Related research in areas such as "teacher noticing" and "teacher attention" have accumulated valuable teacher data in situations external to the classroom, such as professional development settings and preservice courses (see Sherin, Jacobs, & Philipp, 2011, for an excellent overview). In addition, there have been teacher-researchers who have provided insights into the dilemmas faced while teaching responsively (e.g. Ball, 1993; Hammer, 1997; Lampert, 1990; Maskiewicz, this volume). However, as responsive teaching gains recognition as a powerful means of encouraging student understanding in mathematics and science, it becomes increasingly important for the community to elaborate methods of assessing teacher responsiveness in the classroom. The purpose of this chapter is to present and exemplify three approaches for assessing responsive teaching: (1) exploring a teacher's follow-up questions, (2) examining a teacher's redirections, and (3) identifying classroom events that speak directly to a teacher's responsiveness. The intended results of this chapter are for the reader to (1) gain familiarity with these methods, (2)

204 Jennifer Evarts Lineback

understand their affordances and limitations, and (3) be informed if/when select-ing an appropriate method for research purposes.

All of the classroom examples included in this chapter are taken from the longitudinal case study of an elementary school teacher, Mrs. Miller[1], who par-ticipated in a extended professional development/research project known as the Learning Progressions for Scientific Inquiry Project[2] ("LP project"). This project (see Responsive Teaching in Science, 2013, for more information) had among its goals to develop elementary and middle school teachers' ability to teach scien-tific inquiry. Inquiry, for the purposes of the project, was taken to be "the pursuit of coherent, mechanistic accounts of phenomena" (Hammer, Russ, Mikeska, & Scherr, 2008, p. 150). To promote this kind of inquiry, the LP project staff pro-duced curricular "modules" that provided context for teachers to engage stu-dents in the consideration of natural phenomena. These modules contained no prescribed lesson plans. Rather, they were designed with a generative "launching question" (see following example) and some suggestions for potential teacher "next moves" that built upon emergent student ideas.

Mrs. Miller had taught science for over twenty years. During that time, her instructional tendency had been to guide students through organized lesson plans to predetermined learning outcomes. The water cycle module that Mrs. Miller implemented as part of the LP project differed dramatically from the structured curricular materials she had enacted previously. To illustrate, she initiated each iteration of the module with a similar version of the following question:

> Suppose that one night it rains. When you arrive at school, you notice that there are puddles of rainwater in the parking lot. When you go home, you notice that the puddles are gone. What happened to the rainwater?

Based upon student responses, Mrs. Miller then decided where to go next. Except for slight phrasing alterations, the launching question was identical for each implementation; yet the trajectory traversed during the three fifteen-hour "units" was substantively different. Each time, however, the participants held lively discussions, conducted investigations, and gained an appreciation for water cycle phenomena.

It is important to mention that although all three methods of assessing respon-siveness described in this chapter are exemplified with Mrs. Miller's classroom sessions, the purpose in selecting these segments is to illustrate each method's application to classroom teaching. It is not the intension of this author to praise, criticize and/or suggest improvements in this teacher's instructional practice.

Method I: Exploring a Teacher's Follow-Up Questions/Comments

A "hallmark" of responsive teaching is a teacher taking up student ideas. Some researchers have explored class sessions broadly, examining teacher talk for confirming and/or disconfirming evidence that they are attending to/noticing student thinking (Levin, Hammer, & Coffey, 2009; Sherin & van Es, 2009). While this approach can provide a basis for making general claims about the presence/absence of responsiveness, it is arguably less capable of capturing nuances in this dimension of teacher practice. To this end, other researchers have engaged in detailed discourse analyses to determine *how* teachers' individual comments and/or questions respond to student ideas (Franke et al., 2009; Pierson, 2008). It are these latter, more sensitive types of analyses that are pursued further here.

Pierson (2008) coded the utterances of middle school math teachers according to the degree to which they took up their students' ideas:

- *Low* (limited responsiveness to student thinking),
- *Medium* (some responsiveness to student thinking),
- *High I* (highly responsive to the student but emphasizing *teacher* thinking),
- *High II* (highly responsive to the student and emphasizing *student* thinking).

Consistent with this scheme, she considered teacher follow-up questions that responded to and/or openly displayed *student thinking* to be evidence of the highest level of teacher responsiveness.

To illustrate this approach, suppose a teacher asks her students a question about a graph and a student answers, "Only straight lines." If the teacher follows-up with "Incorrect," her response would be coded as **Low** because it is *evaluative* and displays no evidence of taking up the student's idea. If the teacher responds with, "They would be straight only if the cars were at a constant speed," her statement would be coded as **High I**, since it displays some level of taking up the student's idea, but foregrounds the *teacher's* thinking rather than *the student's*. If the teacher responds with, "Can you say more about that?" or if she asks the class, "What do you think of his statement?" her questions would constitute **High II** responsiveness, since the *student's thinking* is emphasized.

In a separate study, Franke and her colleagues (2009) investigated how various kinds of teacher follow-up questions elicited mathematics thinking in students. The researchers categorized the questions as (1) general, (2) specific, (3) leading, and (4) "other." General questions were non-specific invitations for a student to make further comment, whereas specific questions took up aspects of students' comments and requested specific clarification and/or elaboration. For example, "Can you say more about that?" would constitute a general question, while "Can you say more about what you mean by, 'Only straight lines'?" would be specific. Leading questions, in contrast to the others, appeared to guide students toward a specific response without really incorporating the student's thinking. Questions that couldn't be categorized (of which there were few in Franke et al.'s study) were labeled as "other." The researchers found that teachers' specific questions encouraged students to "make sense of their ideas in relation to the mathematics" (p. 390). The authors also found that *probing sequences* of two or more specific

206 Jennifer Evarts Lineback

questions directed to the same student were most likely to be linked with correct and complete mathematical explanations.

Both Franke et al. (2009) and Pierson (2008) outline methodologies that are capable of assessing responsiveness via coding teacher follow-up questions/comments. To demonstrate their application to classroom data, I now provide two excerpts. The first is taken from a discussion concerning the formation of liquid water on a bag of ice. Prior to this particular segment, the class had been debating a student (Jasper's) idea to place a cold/frozen bottle inside a sealed clear, plastic bag as a way to test the origin of dripping water. In the table provided (Table 10.1), both Pierson's and Franke et al.'s codes are shown to the right of the transcript text.

TABLE 10.1 Classroom Excerpt A

	Transcript	*Pierson (2008) code*	*Franke et al. (2009) code*
1	Jack: If he [filled the bottle] with a different drink, it would work.		
2	Mrs. Miller: Why would you want to use a different drink, other than water?	**High II**	**Specific question**
3	Jack: Because then you would have no clue whether it was leaking or not. You don't know if it was water from a leak or water from condensation.		
4	Mrs. Miller: Like, what would you want to freeze?	**High II**	**Specific question**
5	Jack: If you use soda and then water in the bag, if you drink it and you found out it wasn't soda.		
6	Jasper: Ohh. I hear what you're trying to say!		
7	Mrs. Miller: [looks to Jack, then nods at Jasper] Go ahead, finish what you're saying. What are you saying?	**High II**	**General question**
8	Jasper: I get what Jack's saying. If you use a different drink, orange juice or soda, if it was leaking- If you use a colored drink- If it was leaking- You would know it was from the colored water. If you thought it was leaking water- You would know it from the condensation, because the orange juice is yellow. It's not all clear like the water.		

In this excerpt, Mrs. Miller issues three follow-up questions: the first two are directed to Jack (lines 2 and 4), while the third is directed to Jasper (line 7). According to Pierson's (2008) scheme, all three of these questions would be categorized at the High II level of responsiveness since they emphasize student ideas above the teacher's thinking. For example, in line 1 Jack posits that if a different drink is used (i.e. a liquid *other than* water), then Jasper's design would work. Mrs. Miller immediately invites Jack to elaborate with the question, "*Why would you want to use a different drink?*" Since Mrs. Miller is asking Jack for more information about his *own* extension of Jasper's protocol, her question is coded "High II." The reasoning/questioning behind this designation is as follows:

1. Is the teacher's follow-up responsive to the student comment? **Yes** (Mrs. Miller inquires further into Jack's statement, "If he [filled the bottle] with a different drink, it would work.")
2. Whose idea is the focus of the follow-up comment? **Student's idea** (Mrs. Miller is pursuing Jack's idea of using a different drink.)
3. Whose reasoning is on display in the follow-up comment? **Student's reasoning** (Mrs. Miller is not trying to lead the discussion in a specific direction; she is questioning Jack about his own idea.)
4. Conclusion: **HIGH II responsiveness**

Mrs. Miller's other questions in this excerpt similarly emphasize student thinking and thus are coded as High II.

According to Franke et al. (2009), Mrs. Miller's first two follow-up questions (lines 2 and 4) would constitute "specific" questions, as they take up specific aspects of Jack's statements. Taken together, they also represent a "probing sequence," since the two consecutive questions are directed to a single student (Jack). Mrs. Miller's final question is coded as "general," since she invites Jasper to complete his thoughts (line 7) with the non-specific question, "What are you saying?"

Classroom Excerpt B (Table 10.2) is taken from a class session focused on clouds. Prior to this excerpt, Mrs. Miller had asked students whether clouds look differently in different locations, to which students were responding with several observations. The excerpt begins with one student's (Tommy's) contribution.

In this excerpt, Mrs. Miller makes six utterances, all of which can be characterized under Pierson's (2008) coding scheme. Three of Mrs. Miller's responses are coded as Low (lines 2, 4, and 12), while the other three are coded as High II (lines 6, 8, and 10). Her first response, "But are they- What's the altitude, I guess is what I'm asking. . ." (line 2) seems to indicate that Tommy's offering was not aligned with what she was hoping for. This type of question represents "low responsiveness." The reasoning/questioning behind this designation is as follows:

TABLE 10.2 Classroom Excerpt B

	Transcript	Pierson (2008) code	Franke et al. (2009) code
1	Tommy: Um, I was thinking that, when you're at the, like the, um, ocean? To the west, and early- You get dark clouds. Usually, it would be marine layer, and it- um, most of it would be moving in, and then when it gets in enough, it will just come into a cloud. I don't know-		
2	Mrs. Miller: But- Are they high or low? What's the altitude, I guess is what I'm asking. What's the altitude of the clouds?	**Low**	**Leading question**
3	Tommy: Well, when they're by the ocean, they're gonna be low. And then, when- When they're going on land- They're just going to drift a little higher and higher.		
4	Mrs. Miller: 'K, so they're gonna get higher. Is there someway we can connect how high they are with what they look like?	**Low**	
5	Jack: Ah, maybe they look different from different heights?		
6	Mrs. Miller: Can you- (4 sec pause) give an example?	**High II**	**General question**
7	Jack: Well- (10 sec pause)		
8	Mrs. Miller: Who can help him? Who can help him out? Jack made- he made a good comment, Jasper. He said clouds look different. Maybe, clouds look different at different heights. So, what does that mean? Cam?	**High II**	
9	Cam: Um, like, maybe when, like, there's storm rainy clouds, way high, maybe that means it just gonna drizzle or something. But, when they're (Mrs. Miller flips sheet) lower, they're gonna- it's gonna like pour and rain really hard.		

Transcript	Pierson (2008) code	Franke et al. (2009) code
10 Mrs. Miller: (writes) Lower. Clouds. Heavy rain. Higher clouds. Drizzle. What does anyone else think about that? About clouds and their altitude as to how they look. Michael?	**High II**	
11 Michael: Well, like, when you're in an airplane, and you look out the window, the clouds look like you could just, like, step on top of 'em and just walk across them.		
12 Mrs. Miller: 'K. I'm gonna add that back over here (flips sheet back a few pages).	**Low**	

1. Is the teacher's follow-up responsive to the student comment? *No* (Mrs. Miller does not take up the *essence* of Tommy's thoughts about the dark clouds and/ or marine layer. Instead, she asks him a question about their *altitude*.)
2. Conclusion: *Low responsiveness* (NOTE: The other questions in the reasoning pathway shown previously do not apply when the first answer is "No.")

Her utterances in lines 4 and 12 are also Low, as again she does not emphasize student thinking on these occasions. Rather, she highlights content correctness or her own thinking. In lines 6, 8, and 10, however, Mrs. Miller foregrounds her students' ideas. For example, in line 6 she asks Jack for an example, and in line 8 she asks the rest of her students to help make sense of Jack's "good comment." These remarks, according to Pierson (2008), represent "high responsiveness."

Only two of Mrs. Miller's questions can be coded according to the Franke et al. (2009) scheme in Excerpt B, since the majority of her responses are directed to the whole class and not to specific students, a requirement in the application of this coding scheme. The first is directed to Tommy (line 2) and is coded as a "leading" question. This designation is due to the fact that Mrs. Miller asks Tommy first if the clouds are "high or low" and then states, "What's the altitude, I guess is what I'm asking." This clearly puts *Mrs. Miller's agenda* on display. The second coded question is directed to Jack (line 6) and is characterized as a "general" question, since Mrs. Miller invites Jack to provide an example.

The results of applying these coding schemes to Classroom Excerpt A seem to indicate that Mrs. Miller is teaching responsively even in this briefest of segments. She uses a probing sequence of specific questions (Franke et al.'s (2009) scheme) and several High II responses (Pierson's (2008) scheme), all of which serve to extend her students' thinking. Further, by inviting both Jack and Jasper to elaborate their thinking she establishes a means for additional class discussion. Thus, evidence from both coding schemes seems to converge upon the same conclusion: Mrs. Miller is being highly responsive to her students' thinking.

The application of the same coding schemes to Excerpt B provides a slightly different interpretation of Mrs. Miller's responsiveness. Coding six utterances using Pierson's (2008) scheme yields three coded at low-level responsiveness and three coded at high-level responsiveness. Thus, Mrs. Miller varied in how she took up her students' ideas during the short segment. Franke et al.'s (2009) coding scheme is somewhat less informative when applied to Excerpt B. There are only two teacher questions that can be coded in this segment: one leading, one general. Thus, coding this segment by itself with Franke et al.'s scheme is limited in terms of supporting claims regarding Mrs. Miller's responsiveness.

Considering both schemes across the two excerpts, it is interesting to note that Mrs. Miller's "general" and "specific" questions (Franke et al.'s (2009) scheme) were consistently coded as "High" responsiveness (Pierson (2008) scheme). This can be explained by the fact that these types of questions invite students to provide clarification or elaboration of their ideas. In contrast, Mrs. Miller's leading question was coded as "Low" responsiveness (line 2 of Excerpt B, where she asked Tommy about the altitude of the "dark clouds"). Despite the fact that Mrs. Miller took up a component of Tommy's idea, she was clearly displaying her own agenda when asking the follow-up question. Such a cross-comparison of the two schemes reinforces that teachers' general and specific follow-up questions reflect higher levels of responsiveness to their students' thinking than do leading questions.

Affordances and Limitations of This Method

Affordances. Focusing on teacher follow-up questions and/or responses allows researchers to reduce classroom data to one teacher move for assessing responsiveness. This affords a means to conduct quantitative and/or qualitative analyses across multiple teachers and/or multiple instructional sessions over time (Franke et al. 2009; Pierson, 2008; Sherin & van Es, 2009). In addition, more than one *a priori* coding scheme is available (i.e. Franke et al., 2009, Pierson, 2008) to choose from when applying this method to classroom data. Selecting one method over the other might depend on whether a researcher opts to focus on teacher follow-up probes (Franke et al.'s (2009) scheme) or decides to characterize all teacher responses to assess responsiveness.

Limitations. Discourse analysis takes considerable time and effort on the part of the researcher(s). The application of Pierson's coding scheme requires researchers to analyze nearly every teacher utterance. While Franke et al.'s (2009) scheme does not characterize every teacher utterance (only probes directed to specific students), fine-grained discourse analysis is still required on the part of the researcher. Furthermore, in addition to taking time to code classroom data, researchers must recognize that it will take time to acclimate to the scheme itself.

Some teachers may elicit student thinking and invite students to provide clarification and/or elaboration on a regular basis, especially if they have participated

Methods to Assess Teacher Responsiveness **211**

in professional development and/or preservice training focused on responsive teaching strategies. Such teachers may offer little variation in their practice and, consequently, demonstrate a "highly responsive" ceiling effect. In such cases, the Pierson (2008) and/or Franke et al. (2009) methods may afford limited potential for detecting nuances in responsiveness and/or exploring teacher change.

Method II: Examining Teacher Redirections

Teachers regularly exhibiting high or low levels of responsiveness are less amenable to being assessed using the schemes above; thus a method more sensitive to detecting nuances in responsiveness would be more appropriate. Coding teachers' "redirections" (Lineback, 2012, 2014) represents such a method. A redirection is a teacher's question or comment that *interrupts* the ongoing flow of the classroom activity and *attempts to shift* the students' attention to either an alternate scientific locus for discussion or a new scientific activity.

Redirections are useful for researchers, since they can reflect subtle shifts in teacher responsiveness. Careful analysis of a teacher's verbal "bid" and its accompanying nonverbal behavior (e.g. gesture, eye gaze, body orientation) determine whether the teacher is responding to student thinking idea and, if so, *how*. Through redirection characterization, researchers can detect variations in responsive teaching in single teaching episodes and over time. It is beyond the scope of this chapter to provide a detailed description of the redirection coding scheme, to exemplify its application, or to demonstrate its inter-rater reliability; those elements are available elsewhere (Lineback, 2014). However, a brief overview of the different types of redirections is included here.

There are two broad types of redirections (see Figure 10.1): *focus redirections*, where a teacher bids to shift the focus of discussion, and *activity redirections*, where a teacher bids to shift classroom activity. Activity redirections are further characterized in terms of whether they are (A) *responsive* to a student's idea or (B) *non-responsive* to a student's idea. Focus redirections reflect subtler distinctions in teacher responsiveness; hence the coding scheme associated with focus redirections is more complex (see Figure 10.2). In addition to being classified as either (A) *responsive* or (B) *non-responsive*, focus redirections can exhibit (C) *delayed responsiveness* on the part of the teacher if he or she attempts to revisit a topic previously discussed. Furthermore, *responsive focus redirections* can be categorized depending on whether a bid (A_1) relates to a scientific *term*, (A_2) invites a student to *repeat* a previous explanation, (A_3) is *minimally* responsive to a student idea, (A_4) *elaborates* a student idea, or (A_5) invites students to *consider*, evaluate, or make sense of a student idea.

Consider the responsiveness reflected by the redirections shown in "Classroom Excerpt C" (Table 10.3). [NOTE: Please see video clip entitled "SameCupExperiment" at http://www.studentsthinking.org/rtsm.] Mrs. Miller and her students have been considering one student's home experiment: Allen had left a cup for which he was monitoring evaporation out in the rain. Mrs. Miller then makes a bid to shift the class in a different direction. The redirections are italicized and

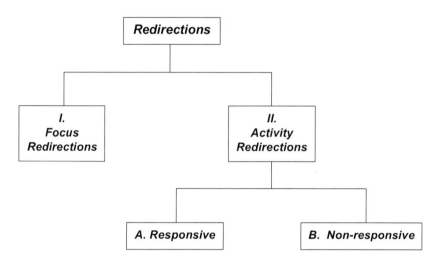

FIGURE 10.1 Redirection primary category codes.

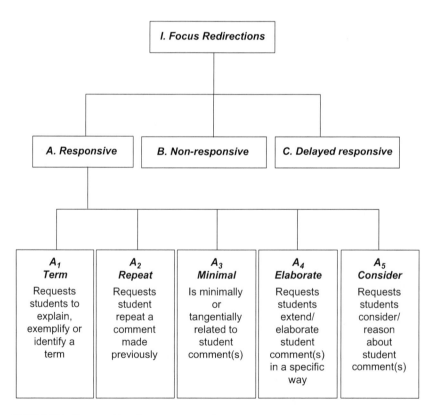

FIGURE 10.2 Focus redirection category codes.

TABLE 10.3 Classroom Excerpt C

	Transcript	Redirection Code
1	Mrs. Miller: So Allen, when you go home today, is that cup still there? Is it covered, or could it have gotten water in it from the rain today, or is it covered?	
2	Allen: It's not covered, it's just some plastic cup I grabbed.	
3	Mrs. Miller: Out on the driveway, or under a patio or?	
4	Allen: It's on my deck.	
5	Mrs. Miller: So is your deck covered or uncovered?	
6	Allen: Uncovered.	
7	Mrs. Miller: Alright, so.	
8	Sam: Even though it was in the rain!	
9	Mrs. Miller: So there's probably going to be more water in it.	
10	Allen: There was an umbrella on it.	
11	Mrs. Miller: So did you put your cup under the umbrella or not?	
12	Allen: No.	
13	Mrs. Miller: Alright, so it could be out. So let me bring you guys back together, because we're getting stuck on something. *So we want to come, let's go all the way back to Tyrella. Taking a cup, measuring out an amount of water, marking the water line.* (points at board) *How much water evaporates from the cup in 1 day? Let's go back to that, could everybody envision that happening?* . . . Can everybody envision a cup, marking a line on the cup, a water line on the cup. And 24 hours later, you're going to measure how much water is left on the cup. Can we do that? What problems- what complications do we eliminate by putting that water in a cup, instead of having it in a puddle? What does that do for us? What does it do for us to put the water in a cup? Everybody has the same cup, we put the same amount of water in the cup. And 24 hours later, we measure it again. *How does that help us?* Sol?	*Focus C Delayed responsive*
14	Sol: Because 24 hours you fill the cup and measure it. I don't think that it would, it would probably all be gone by that time.	

(Continued)

214 Jennifer Evarts Lineback

TABLE 10.3 Continued

Transcript	Redirection Code
15 Mrs. Miller: You think it'll all be gone by that time? *What do you think, Tyrella? Do you think all the water will be gone in the cup? In a 24-hour period?*	*Focus A_5 Consider*
16 Tyrella: It depends on how much water.	
17 Mrs. Miller: It depends on how much water, right? Sol?	
18 Sol: I would put it a couple of centimeters below the top.	
19 Mrs. Miller: A cup of centimeters below the top. So let's just say this is our cup, we're going to fill it up to this line right here. *We're going to put it over somewhere– Where do you want to put it? Where are we going to put it?*	*Focus B Non-responsive*
20 Student: [overlapping talk] Next to the window.	
21 Mrs. Miller: So we're going to put one next to the window. *Inside or outside?*	*Focus A_3 Minimal*

indicated in bold font for convenience purposes. The specific redirection codes are identified in the right column (see Figure 10.2 for brief descriptions of codes).

This segment of discussion took three and a half minutes of class time. In that interval, Mrs. Miller issued four focus redirections. The first one illustrates a lengthy "delayed responsive redirection," beginning when she tries to shift her students' attention "all the way back" to a experimental design proposed earlier (line 13). She then describes Tyrella's prior suggestion and concludes by asking, "How does that [experimental protocol] help us?" Following Sol's response to her inquiry, Mrs. Miller issues her second redirection, asking Tyrella what she thinks of Sol's suggestion that "the water will be all gone . . . in a 24 hour period?" (line 15). Since Mrs. Miller is inviting Tyrella to consider a student's (Sol's) idea, this represents a responsive focus redirection, specifically that of "consider."

The third redirection takes place after an exchange between Tyrella, Sol, and Mrs. Miller. Ascertaining from Sol the approximate volume of water to place in "our cup," Mrs. Miller then asks the class where she should place the cup. "We're going to put it over somewhere– Where do you want to put it?" (line 19). This bid to shift the students' attention from the volume of water in the cup to its prospective location is *not responsive* to student thinking. Rather, it appears to respond to a pre-planned learning objective: experimental design. [NOTE: This objective was confirmed in a debriefing interview with Mrs. Miller.] This represents a "non-responsive" focus redirection.

Methods to Assess Teacher Responsiveness **215**

The final redirection in this segment follows the students' overlapping responses to Mrs. Miller's inquiry as to where she should place "our cup." Since many of the students shouted that she should place the cup "next to the window" (line 20), Mrs. Miller asks, "Inside or outside [of the window]?" (line 21). This question, which responds to the students' collective idea "next to the window," represents a responsive focus redirection, as it does take up the students' idea about the window. However, it exemplifies a "minimally" responsive redirection, since it is superficially responsive to that idea. She uses the students' idea as a stepping-stone to move closer to the apparent learning objective—designing (and executing) an experimental protocol.

Now consider "Classroom Excerpt D" (Table 10.4). In this particular class segment, the students are debating how evaporation differs between cups and puddles. [NOTE: Please see video clip entitled "LayerModel_CLIP" at http://www.studentsthinking.org/rtsm.]

This dialogue takes approximately two and a half minutes of class time. In that interval, Mrs. Miller issues a single redirection where she invites students to subtly

TABLE 10.4 Classroom Excerpt D

	Transcript	*Redirection code*
1	Mrs. Miller: You're saying because the puddle is more spread out, what happens?	
2	Henrietta: You have more room to evaporate.	
3	Mrs. Miller: It has more room to evaporate. *What do you suppose she means by that, Larry?* (pause) *'The puddle had more room to evaporate.' What does that mean? What do you think it means?*	*Focus A_5 Consider*
4	Larry: That when the puddle is thinner, so it's like layers in the water, so it evaporates more. And the cup has the water higher and smaller layers, the water didn't evaporate.	
5	Mrs. Miller: What do you mean by a layer, what does that mean?	
6	Larry: The water that's evaporating in a layer.	
7	Mrs. Miller: So the water evaporating in a layer, do you think? [Larry: Yeah.] Oh, I never thought about-	
8	Barry: (nodding) Yeah.	
9	Mrs. Miller: You said yeah. Why are you saying yeah to Larry? Does that make sense to you, that the water can evaporate in a layer (raises hand horizontally)? Why does that make sense?	
10	Barry: Because the water is going to evaporate in a layer. So if you have water and it always stays straight like that (gestures horizontally). Then it's going to stay like this all the time, so it's (inaud) same amount.	

(Continued)

216 Jennifer Evarts Lineback

TABLE 10.4 Continued

Transcript	Redirection code
11 Mrs. Miller: Oh, interesting. Xander? . . .	
12 Xander: I was going to share what I did.	
13 Mrs. Miller: Can we hold off on yours for a second, because I want to follow up on what he's saying? Does anybody else want to comment about this whole idea that evaporation happens in layers?	
14 Jonah: In the puddle, what happens, when the water's gone, you still see a brown spot there, but not much water there. Then because it first went up the top layer, then it gets down to the cement, because that's where the water is down there.	
15 Mrs. Miller: So you think like Larry does. Wow. Henrietta?	

shift from one discussion topic (comparison of evaporation in cups/puddles) to another (a student's idea). In line 2, Henrietta explains that a puddle, as opposed to a cup, has "more room [for the water] to evaporate." Mrs. Miller then invites Larry to *consider* Henrietta's statement, redirecting his (and, by extension, the rest of the class's) attention to focus directly on Henrietta's thinking in line 3 with her question, "What do you suppose she means by that, Larry? The puddle had more room to evaporate. . ." This "consider" redirection reflects Mrs. Miller action of taking up Henrietta's idea and placing that idea for further examination by a different member of the classroom community.

At no other time during this classroom segment does Mrs. Miller attempt to shift her students' attention to another topic for consideration; on the contrary, she acts to *sustain* her students' focus on this topic. When Xander attempts to share something he tried at home (line 12), Mrs. Miller asks him to "hold off" so that she can "follow up on what [Larry's] saying" (line 13). Thus, Mrs. Miller's actions allow for additional development of Larry's "layer" model. Ultimately the discussion continues for six more minutes, partly as a result of an additional delayed responsive focus redirection (not shown here), where Mrs. Miller invites students to *revisit* Larry's model (after another student had meandered for a bit), asking, "Does anybody else want to make a comment about . . . water evaporating in layers, or the comparison of the puddle to the cup?"

In Classroom Excerpt D, Mrs. Miller's "consider" redirection, in conjunction to the (not shown) delayed responsive redirection issued a few minutes later, provides evidence that she is highly responsive to her students' thinking. She allows student thinking to be elaborated and developed by her students. In Classroom Excerpt C, the first two redirections similarly suggest that she is being highly responsive to her students' ideas. Mrs. Miller's delayed responsive redirection (line 13) shifts the students' attention to Tyrella's previously suggested experimental set-up, and

Methods to Assess Teacher Responsiveness **217**

her consider redirection (line 15) asks Tyrella what she thinks of Sol's suggestion. In contrast, the non-responsive redirection (line 19) and the minimally responsive redirection (line 21) provide evidence that she is being less responsive to her students' thinking. Such mixed findings, with both confirming and disconfirming evidence of responsiveness, could be used as partial evidence to support different kinds of claims: responsiveness varies within instruction, being responsive to students' thinking is complex, and/or teachers balance concurrent goals of reaching content objectives and producing scientific thinkers. Both segments, as mentioned previously, occupied less than five minutes of class time. Hence, additional data would be required in order to draw substantive conclusions regarding Mrs. Miller's responsiveness.

Affordances and Limitations of This Method

Affordances. Employing a construct like the redirection elaborates and extends previous coding schemes like Pierson (2008) and Franke et al. (2009). This construct provides researchers a means of exploring varying degrees of responsiveness (i.e. responsive, non-responsive, delayed responsive) and is sensitive enough to distinguish between different *types* of responsiveness (A_1, A_2 etc.), a nuance that the two previous coding schemes were less able to achieve. In addition to teasing apart high levels of responsiveness (and thus minimizing the ceiling affect), this coding scheme can also characterize differences in low levels of responsiveness. For example, a difference could be detected when a teacher question is non-responsive (C) as opposed to minimally responsive (A_3). According to Pierson's (2008) coding scheme, however, both types of teacher responses would be coded as "Low." Thus, the redirection scheme offers researchers a more sensitive approach to assessing responsive teaching across a range of responsiveness levels.

As was the case for the other *a priori* schemes, the redirection scheme allows for quantification, permitting the detection of changes in responsiveness across time and/or across teachers. For example, redirection frequencies were used to investigate Mrs. Miller's change in responsiveness over three implementations of the water cycle. Table 10.5 displays the distribution of her focus and activity redirections, as well as her total number of redirections for each implementation. Table 10.6 displays the distribution of the different kinds of *focus responsive* redirections over the three implementations. Results showed that while there was a significant difference in the total number of redirections issued by Mrs. Miller [$X^2_{(2)} = 49.17, p < 0.01$], there was no significant difference found for how those redirections were distributed among focus and activity varieties [$X^2_{(2)} = 5.120, p > 0.05$]. Furthermore, while there was a significant difference found in the pattern of different kinds of responsive redirections issued by Mrs. Miller [$X^2_{(6)} = 15.10, p < 0.05$], there was no significant difference found for the total number of responsive redirections [$X^2_{(2)} = 4.339, p > 0.05$]. These findings spur additional questions: what might account for the decrease in the

218 Jennifer Evarts Lineback

TABLE 10.5 Mrs. Miller's Redirections Across Three Implementations of the Water Cycle Module

Year	Activity Redirections	Focus Redirections	Total Redirections
1	13	287	300
2	14	180	194
3	11	348	348

TABLE 10.6 Mrs. Miller's Focus Responsive Redirections Across Three Implementations of the Water Cycle Module

Year	Focus Responsive / hr discussion[a]	Term redirections	Repeat[b] redirections	Minimal redirections	Elaborate redirections	Consider redirections
1	20.24	9	9	77	32	52
2	10.13	12	0	36	10	34
3	21.11	5	6	118	37	58

[a] Total focus redirections have been standardized per hour of whole class discussion.
[b] Repeat responsive redirections not included in the chi-square analysis, since none were recorded during the second year.

number of focus redirections in year 2 and the subsequent increase in year 3? Do the similar frequencies of specific focus redirections observed in years 1 and 3 reflect similar teacher behavior or is there a difference if one looks beyond the numerical data? These questions demonstrate how the redirection construct can provide a productive vehicle to investigate teacher change in responsiveness (see Lineback, 2012, for further exemplification).

Limitations. Adopting any reductionist approach, like investigating teacher follow-up questions (Method I) or redirections (Method II), narrows the researchers' scope to only *one dimension* of teacher practice. While this method makes the data more manageable, it is entirely possible—indeed likely—that other indicators of teacher responsiveness will be overlooked. For example, if a teacher's redirections are analyzed, his or her follow-up questions may not be explored. Thus, this potential avenue to assess a teacher's responsiveness will be bypassed. Additionally, redirection analysis demands a considerable amount of time and effort on the part of the researcher to gain familiarity with the complex coding scheme and, similar to the coding schemes mentioned in Method I, requires detailed discourse analyses to code teacher utterances.

Method III: Identifying Classroom Events That Speak Directly to a Teacher's Responsiveness

The previous two methods of assessing teacher responsiveness require a researcher to be familiar with specific coding schemes prior to analyzing classroom data (i.e.

Franke et al., 2009; Lineback, 2014; Pierson, 2008). In addition, the grain-size of analysis is comparably small, for every utterance must be evaluated for a potential code. While these methods afford researchers many benefits, they also demand a lot of time and effort. The third method of assessing teacher responsiveness contrasts with the first two in that there is no *a priori* coding scheme to apply to the data. Rather, the researcher observes the teacher during instruction and allows instances of responsiveness to emerge from the data itself. Thus, the researcher must *identify* and subsequently *characterize* specific events that speak to a teacher's responsiveness to student thinking. To do so, a researcher should ask these questions: are there moments in the classroom session(s) where the teacher took up students' ideas in particularly interesting ways? If so, when, how, and to what end did the teacher take up student thinking? What evidence exists to support this claim?

Below I present two examples from Mrs. Miller's case study that illustrate how this type of analysis might transpire. Both of these examples involve characterizing unplanned classroom events that *emerged* from paying close attention to Mrs. Miller's data and that speak directly to her responsiveness. In the first example, Mrs. Miller spontaneously abandons her teaching agenda. In the second, Mrs. Miller spontaneously enacts a student's idea.

Example 1: Mrs. Miller's Spontaneous Abandonment of Her Teaching Agenda

Mrs. Miller approached her class sessions, like most teachers, having specific learning outcomes for her students. These lesson objectives included helping her students achieve deeper conceptual understandings about science and encouraging her students to develop better scientific practices. Although her students were not held accountable to specific content objectives during her participation with the LP program (i.e. they did not have to take the district mandated standardized tests in the area of the water cycle), Mrs. Miller still wanted her students to develop a more scientifically correct understanding about evaporation and condensation. For example, she hoped her students would realize that the water appearing on the outside of a bag of ice came from the water vapor in the air and not from the ice water inside the bag. The open-ended water cycle module provided opportunities for Mrs. Miller to allow her students' ideas to establish the foundation for scientific reasoning and argumentation while simultaneously making room for scientific content to emerge.

Mrs. Miller had tended to design structured lesson plans and, thus, was consistent with what Clark and Peterson (1986) would characterize as a so-called "comprehensive planner." Although Mrs. Miller often elicited student ideas and engaged her students in participating in discussions, she regularly guided her students through heavily scripted lessons. As such, evidence of Mrs. Miller abandoning her plans, even temporarily or in minor increments, could be considered noteworthy. This would especially be the case if classroom evidence suggested

220 Jennifer Evarts Lineback

such abandonment was in response to Mrs. Miller opting instead to nourish, elaborate, and/or develop her students' own ideas.

Classroom Excerpt E (Table 10.7) is a relatively brief classroom excerpt taken from the "Ice Bag" discussion, the same discussion that from which Classroom Excerpt A was taken. In this new excerpt, Mrs. Miller is quite explicit in indicating her intention to move in a different direction. However, she states that she first would like to hear from *one more student* as to how it would be possible to determine the origin of water dripping off an ice bag.

TABLE 10.7 Classroom Excerpt E

Transcript
1   Mrs. Miller: Okay, who's got an idea that they want to share, because I really want to wrap this up, because I really want the time to go off in a different area if possible. Reina? Did you and Jasper come up with an idea?
2   Jasper: You get a cold water bottle, then wipe it off, the water vapor, that was on it from before. And get a plastic bag that's hole-less.
3   Mrs. Miller: Hole-less? I think we're creating new vocabulary here, too. All right.
4   Jasper: Then you put the water bottle in the plastic bag, and then you see if the water, if the condensation, the water vapor condenses on the water bottle or the plastic bag. (4 sec. pause)
5   Mrs. Miller: (scans the rest of the class) Does anybody have a question for Jasper about that idea? (Nods to Mack.) What's your question?

In line 1 of Classroom Excerpt E, Mrs. Miller explicitly articulates her initial intent to move her students in a different direction by informing them that she "really want[s] to wrap this [discussion] up," and stating that she'd like "the time to go off in a different area if possible." Jasper then introduces his group's idea for an experiment, which consists of placing a cold water bottle into a hole-less, plastic bag and sealing it up. Rather than moving on, however, Mrs. Miller then extends an invitation to the rest of the class: "Does anybody have a question for Jasper about that idea?" (line 5). For the next fifteen minutes, the classroom community, including Mrs. Miller, discusses, elaborates, and extends Jasper's experimental protocol. This discussion includes the consideration of various modifications to the experimental design and enacting a spontaneous prototype. The conversation even resumes briefly the following day, when a few ambitious students describe their findings after trying something at home. What had begun as a simple elicitation for one more student to share an idea prior to "going off in a different area" became an extended discussion about a student's idea. The fact that Mrs. Miller abandons her agenda in order to pursue Jasper's idea illustrates that she was highly responsive to her students *in the moment*. Mrs. Miller's debriefing interview confirmed that she indeed had planned to move in a different direction with her students. However, once she heard the students enthusiastically sharing their ideas about Jasper's design, she decided to "just go" with the students. Thus, Mrs. Miller opted to suspend her lesson plan to pursue her students' ideas.

Methods to Assess Teacher Responsiveness **221**

Example 2: Mrs. Miller's Spontaneous Enactment of a Student Idea

A second classroom event that speaks directly to Mrs. Miller's responsiveness involves her creating a model of a student's idea, arguably in order to better enable her and her students to visualize that idea. This kind of enactment moves beyond a simple gesture; rather, it reflects Mrs. Miller's intentional attempt to physically *represent* a students' idea to the rest of the class. Thus, the occurrence of such an event serves as evidence that she is being highly responsive to her student thinking.

To illustrate, I return to the ice bag discussion in Mrs. Miller's classroom and Jasper's water bottle protocol just after Mrs. Miller announces her desire to "go off in a different area" (see Classroom Excerpt E, line 1). Once Jasper introduces his experimental design, it is soon apparent that *no one* truly seems to grasp what he is describing. I now present an extended version of the previous excerpt (now called Excerpt F—Table 10.8), which includes Mrs. Miller's eventual *enactment* of Jasper's experimental set-up.

TABLE 10.8 Classroom Excerpt F

	Transcript
1	Mrs. Miller: Okay, who's got an idea that they want to share, because I really want to wrap this up, because I really want the time to go off in a different area if possible. Reina? Did you and Jasper come up with an idea?
2	Jasper: You get a cold water bottle, then wipe it off, the water vapor, that was on it from before. And get a plastic bag that's hole-less.
3	Mrs. Miller: Hole-less? I think we're creating new vocabulary here, too. All right.
4	Jasper: Then you put the water bottle in the plastic bag, and then you see if the water, if the condensation, the water vapor condenses on the water bottle or the plastic bag.
5	Mrs. Miller: (4 second pause, while scans the rest of the class) Does anybody have a question for Jasper about that idea? (nods to Mack) What's your question?
6	Mack: Can you repeat the middle, beginning and the end?
7	Jasper: (smiling) Okay! (Mrs. Miller begins to create an experimental set-up similar to that described by Jack—see Figure 10.3.) You get a cold water bottle in a plastic bag, the water vapor that was on it from before, you wipe it off, so it doesn't have any water vapor on it. And then you put the water bottle in the plastic bag
8	Mack: That's hole-less.
9	Jasper: (smiles) Yeah. And then you wait to see if the water vapors condense on the- (points towards Mrs. Miller's set-up) plastic bag or the water bottle.
10	Mrs. Miller: So this (taps finger at her set-up), only the water inside-? Would you have it cold or frozen?
11	Jasper: Cold.
12	Mrs. Miller: You think just cold would work? (Looks to her class) What do you guys think about that?
13	Students: Frozen.

(Continued)

TABLE 10.8 Continued

Transcript
14 Mrs. Miller: So we're going to freeze (seals the baggie) the water in the bottle, wipe off all the condensation (gestures wiping), make sure it's dry, put it in a plastic bag like this (holds up the plastic baggie), then what?
15 Jasper: Then you wait to see if the water condenses on the plastic bag or the water bottle.

FIGURE 10.3 Mrs. Miller enacts a student's idea for an experimental design. The visual model includes an unopened water bottle placed into a clear plastic bag (quart-sized), which would then be sealed above the water bottle.

Mack's question to Jasper in line 6 to repeat the "middle, the beginning, and the end" of Jasper's protocol clearly demonstrate that he (Mack) is having difficulty visualizing exactly what experimental set-up Jasper is trying to describe. Mrs. Miller's spontaneous move to construct Jasper's set-up (line 7 and Figure 10.3) can be viewed as being responsive to both Mack and Jasper. Her action is responsive to Mack in that she is potentially helping Mack (and the rest of the class) see what

Jasper's describing. She is being responsive to Jasper by highlighting his idea as a focus for the entire class's attention. Her spontaneous construction of the set-up allows the classroom community to have something to which they can (and do) refer from that point onwards. Ultimately, the class continues to consider, expand upon, and elaborate Jasper's experimental design for nearly fifteen minutes, leading some members of the class to try out some experimentation at home.

Affordances and Limitations of This Method

Affordances. Unlike the first two methods discussed in this chapter (characterizing teacher follow-up questions and redirections), the method of identifying and describing classroom events that speak to a teacher's responsiveness to students does *not* require detailed discourse analysis on the part of the researcher, nor does it require familiarization with an *a priori* coding scheme. While transcripts and classroom excerpts may be used to support claims regarding a teacher's practice, individual teacher utterances are not subjected to the application of specific codes or categories. Instead, larger chunks of transcripts, photos, and other classroom artifacts are used to provide evidence that a teacher was responsive to student thinking. In addition, teacher reflections and/or interview data may be used, if available, to support claims of this kind. This lessens the fine-grained analysis demands that the first two methods place upon the researcher.

Limitations. These are unplanned events. A researcher must be able to recognize the event(s) during the examination of the data set and support its existence with evidence (i.e. from the video/transcript). If and when such an occurrence *does* happen, it represents an opportunity for the researcher to carefully examine the teacher's activity and document the interactions/discussions that happen surrounding its occurrence. Such an event potentially provides the researcher with data to use as evidence for teacher responsiveness. However, such events may or may not occur on the day a given researcher is video recording an instructional session. If an event does not happen, it doesn't mean the teacher is not responsive to his or her students' thinking. If an event does happen (i.e. the teacher abandons his or her agenda.), it does not necessarily mean the teacher is responsive to his or her students' thinking (i.e. The teacher spontaneously decides to dismiss his or her lesson plans because he or she recalls seeing a deer in the woods on the way to work. This spurs an idea for a new discussion topic.). Rather, this type of event represents an opportunity for the researcher to look closely at the data to determine whether or not the teacher is indeed being responsive to his or her students' thinking.

Considerations: How to Select a Particular Method

Each of the three methods described in the sections above has affordances and limitations, some of which have been briefly discussed. In selecting a method of analysis, interested individuals should (of course) consider the particulars of the intended study. For example, researchers focused on comparing the responsiveness of several teachers during single class sessions (a "snap shot" study) may consider applying an *a priori* coding scheme (Methods I and/or II). In particular, Pierson's (2008) or Franke et al.'s (2009) coding scheme that characterize teacher follow-up responses to student talk might be most appropriate. If researchers are conducting in-depth case studies concerning *how* teacher responsiveness changes within and/or across class sessions, then an analysis using the redirection coding scheme (Lineback, 2014) may be the best method, since this method affords a more *sensitive* means to describe nuances regarding how teachers respond to students' thinking.

In contrast, some researchers may wish to investigate responsiveness from alternative angles or at larger grain sizes. A fine-grained discourse analysis associated with Methods I and II may be less appropriate or undesirable. In such cases, a method that allows for evidence of responsiveness to emerge from the data set, such as assessing for evidence that a teacher abandoned his or her agenda or enacted a student's idea during one or more class sessions, would likely be preferable. Regardless of the methodology ultimately selected, researchers should acknowledge the affordances and limitations inherent in the various analysis approaches considered and eventually applied in the research setting.

Each of the three methods described in this chapter are capable of capturing evidence of responsiveness. While admittedly few research studies would have the time and manpower to devote to concurrent analyses using a combination of two or three of the methods, the methods described in this chapter have the potential to complement one another nicely. A study that is able to code a teacher's redirections and his or her follow-up questions, and that allows for the characterization of responsive teaching events, for example, could generate a rich case study of a teacher's responsiveness. Such a study would have the benefit of "casting a wider net," since researchers could capture dimensions of responsive teaching possibly lost when only one method of analysis is applied.

In my own assessment of Mrs. Miller's practice, I was fortunate enough to be able to conduct analyses that allowed for such triangulation (Lineback, 2012). Quantitative and qualitative analyses of Mrs. Miller's redirections (i.e. analysis Method II) over three implementations of the water module showed that Mrs. Miller was more likely to hear, take up, and nourish her students' potentially productive ideas in later implementations. Additional analyses, which included investigating her follow-up questions (Method I) and characterizing emergent responsive events (Method III), revealed Mrs. Miller was more likely to (1) encourage students to entertain and develop alternative scientific explanations and (2) utilize student ideas as the basis for additional discussion and activity in later implementations. Integrating across these analyses converged on a general claim of *increased* responsiveness to student ideas in Mrs. Miller's teaching practice over the course of the three implementations of the water cycle module. Thus, conducting parallel studies using all three methods of analysis allowed for a richer and more elaborated view of Mrs. Miller's responsiveness, one more substantiated than if only one analysis method had been applied to the classroom data.

Conclusion

When teachers take up the essence of their student's ideas during class time, they are empowering their students to take an active role in helping to shape the academic contours of the classroom community. As such, the educational research community stands to benefit from the continued exploration into *how, when, where,* and *to what end* teachers attend and respond to students' thinking in those classrooms. This chapter has presented various methodological approaches to assessing teacher responsiveness in the classroom. With further research in the area of responsive teaching in the years to come, it is likely that additional methods will be developed and be added to those described here. This list represents an initial foundation from which researchers can methodologically build.

Acknowledgments

I would like to thank the LP professional development team and teachers (especially Mrs. Miller), Dr. Fred Goldberg and Dr. April Maskiewicz for their invaluable help and encouragement, and Dr. Miriam Sherin, Dr. Paul Hutchinson, Dr. Sam McKagan, and the editors for their constructive feedback that helped improve this chapter.

Notes

1 All teacher and student names presented in this chapter are pseudonyms.
2 The "Learning Progressions for Scientific Inquiry project" or "LP" is the shortened name of the NSF funded project (#0732233) officially entitled "Learning Progressions for Scientific Inquiry: A Model Implementation in the Context of Energy."

References

Ball, D.L. (1993). With an eye on the mathematical horizon: Dilemmas of teaching elementary school mathematics. *Elementary School Journal, 93*(4), 373–397.

Carpenter, T.P., Fennema, E., Peterson, P.L., Chiang, C.P., & Loef, M. (1989). Using knowledge of children's mathematics thinking in classroom teaching: An experimental study. *American Educational Research Journal, 26*(4), 499–531.

Clark, C.M., & Peterson, P.L. (1986). Teachers' thought processes. In M.C. Wittrock (Ed.), *Handbook of research on teaching*, 3rd ed. (pp. 255–296). New York: Macmillan Publishing Company.

Franke, M.L., Webb, N.M., Chan, A.G., Ing, M., Freund, D., & Battey, D. (2009). Teacher questioning to elicit students' mathematical thinking in elementary school classrooms. *Journal of Teacher Education, 60*(4), 380–392.

Hammer, D. (1997). Discovery learning and discovery teaching. *Cognition and Instruction, 15*(4), 485–529.

Hammer, D., Russ, R., Mikeska, J., & Scherr, R. (2008). Identifying inquiry and conceptualizing abilities. In R.A. Duschl & R.E. Grandy (Eds.), *Teaching scientific inquiry* (pp. 138–156). Netherlands: Sense Publishers.

Lampert, M. (1990). When the problem is not the question and the solution is not the answer: Mathematical knowing and teaching. *American Educational Research Journal, 27*(1), 29–63.

Levin, D.M. (2008). *What secondary science teachers pay attention to in the classroom: Situating teaching in institutional and social systems.* Unpublished doctoral dissertation, University of Maryland, College Park, MD.

Levin, D.M., Hammer, D. & Coffey, J.E. (2009). Novice teachers' attention to student thinking. *Journal of Teacher Education, 60,* 142–154.

Lineback, J.E. (2012). *Mrs. Miller's evolution in teaching science as inquiry: A case study of a teacher's change in responsiveness.* Unpublished doctoral dissertation, University of California–San Diego & San Diego State University, San Diego, CA.

Lineback, J.E. (2014). The redirection: An indicator of how teachers respond to student thinking. *Journal of the Learning Sciences,* 1–42. DOI: 10.1080/10508406.2014.930707

Pierson, J.L. (2008). *The relationship between patterns of classroom discourse and mathematics learning.* Unpublished doctoral dissertation, University of Texas–Austin, Austin, TX.

Responsive Teaching in Science. (2013). Retrieved from: http://cipstrends.sdsu.edu/responsiveteaching/index.html. Date accessed: February 14, 2015.

Ruiz-Primo, M.A., & Furtak, E.M. (2007). Exploring teachers' informal formative assessment practices and students' understanding in the context of scientific inquiry. *Journal of Research in Science Teaching, 44*(1), 57–84.

Sherin, M.G., Jacobs, V.R., & Philipp, R.A. (Eds.). (2011). *Mathematics teacher noticing: Seeing through teachers' eyes.* New York: Routledge.

Sherin, M.G. & van Es, E.A. (2009). Effects of video club participation on teachers' professional vision. *Journal of Teacher Education, 60*(1), 20–37.

11

DOCUMENTING VARIABILITY WITHIN TEACHER ATTENTION AND RESPONSIVENESS TO THE SUBSTANCE OF STUDENT THINKING

Amy D. Robertson, Jennifer Richards, Andrew Elby, and Janet Walkoe

The education research community is trying to figure out how to foster and assess responsive teaching, which in turn requires us to conceptualize what counts as progress toward greater responsiveness. As we discuss below in our literature review, much of the existing work on teacher noticing/attention/responsiveness describes responsive teaching in terms of levels (or a spectrum), with greater responsiveness consisting of more attention to the substance of student thinking and more responses that interpret rather than correct students' ideas. These accounts often treat a teaching episode as "more" vs. "less" responsive or as "responsive" vs. "not responsive."

In this chapter, using our analysis of a middle school teacher's attention during an extended classroom episode, we seek to refine—and in some ways challenge—these senses of what counts as progress toward greater responsiveness. We show that one teacher's attention shifts not between substance and correctness, but rather between multiple facets of the substance of student thinking. These shifts occur over timescales of minutes or even seconds. Further, we argue that a given focus of attention plays different roles in advancing the teacher's goals and the students' engagement in scientific practices at different points during the episode. Our illustration of the layered, multi-faceted nature of the substance of student thinking—and of teacher attention to that substance—adds to the literature on responsive teaching by:

- challenging developmental accounts of responsive teaching that assume teachers pass fairly predictably though stages of responsiveness.
- problematizing levels-based conceptions of—and assessment schemes for—responsiveness that associate a given de-contextualized focus of attention or kind of response with the teacher's degree of responsiveness.

228 Amy D. Robertson et al.

- arguing that expert responsive teaching is defined in part by the teacher's meta-level responsiveness about which focus of attention to foreground in the moment, in concert with both the teacher's goals and the students' activities.

Situating Our Case Study in the Literature

Since Chapter 2 of this volume comprehensively reviews the literature on responsive teaching, here we briefly describe how our analysis fits into and adds to prior work.

Our Work Highlights the Multi-Faceted Nature of the Substance of Student Thinking and of Teacher Attention to Substance

Researchers studying teacher responsiveness rarely distinguish among the various facets of disciplinary substance within student thinking. Attention and responsiveness to the substance of student thinking is instead defined in opposition to other foci of attention, usually canonical correctness. Such analyses treat teacher attention to substance as "on" or "off," or as "more" or "less." This becomes apparent in:

- **Evidentiary distinctions between attention and inattention** (Crespo, 2000; Davis, 1997; Goldsmith & Seago, 2011; Levin, Hammer, & Coffey, 2009; Levin & Richards, 2011; Sherin & van Es, 2009; van Es, 2011; van Es & Sherin, 2008, 2010). For instance, Levin, Hammer, and Coffey contrast attention and inattention, saying that in order to count as responsive to the substance of student thinking, "the [teacher's] response or report must focus on the sense of the [student's] idea from the student's perspective"; it cannot "notic[e] and respon[d] only to correctness" (p. 147). Paralleling this distinction, researchers generally characterize interpretive teacher moves as responsive and evaluative moves as not responsive (or as less so).
- **Characterizations of teachers' moves as more or less responsive** (Brodie, 2011; Empson & Jacobs, 2008; Lineback, 2014; Pierson, 2008). Brodie and Pierson both categorize teachers' follow-up moves into levels of responsiveness. For instance, in Brodie's scheme, pressing a student for more information about his or her idea is categorized as more responsive than eliciting something specific from a student, because targeted elicitation may narrow the student's contributions. Empson and Jacobs (2008) formalized shifts toward greater responsiveness into a progression in which teachers move from directive listening (focusing on alignment between a student's idea and an expected response, and seeking to elicit the expected response), to observational listening (passively listening to students' ideas without seeking to extend them), to responsive listening (probing students' ideas to understand and build on them).

These distinctions and coding schemes enable researchers and practitioners to decide to what extent a teacher is attending and responding to the substance of student thinking. However, they do not address the multi-facetedness of "substance" or of teacher attention to it.

In articulating multiple facets of the substance of students' thinking to which a teacher, Sam, attends at different moments, and by situating shifts in Sam's attention within coarser-grained instructional foci, we complement existing practitioner accounts (Ball, 1993; Chazan & Ball, 1999; Hammer, 1997; Lampert, 1990; Rosebery & Warren, 1998) and case studies (Maskiewicz & Winters, 2012; Richards, Elby, & Gupta, 2014; Schifter, 1996; Schifter, 2011) that depict teachers' attention to numerous—and at times, conflicting—aspects of what students are saying and doing. For example, Ball (1993) describes her attention to three different "components of mathematical practice [within the flow of her classroom activity] . . . : the content, the discourse, and the community in which content and discourse are intertwined" (p. 376). She highlights the dilemmas she faced when choosing among them, particularly when they seemed to conflict, such as when a community-negotiated consensus was canonically incorrect. Likewise, Hammer (1997) attends to multiple different facets of the substance of student thinking, including the content of students' ideas, students' participation in scientific practices such as experimentation and argumentation, etc. Although these case studies focused on other arguments, we draw on them to make our case that *substance*—and teacher attention to it—is multi-faceted.

Our Work Informs Notions of Progress and Assessment of Responsive Teaching

One challenge to assessing responsive teaching is that shifts in responsiveness may represent fluctuations rather than stable progress. Research has noted the variability of teacher responsiveness over multiple timescales (Lau, 2010; Levin et al., 2009; Russ & Luna, 2013), with teachers shifting into and out of attending to student thinking even over the course of minutes in the classroom. Other researchers highlight trends in teacher responsiveness over time (e.g., Fennema et al., 1996; Sherin & van Es, 2009), but they also note fluctuations worth exploring and understanding. For instance, in describing the classroom practice of teachers in their video clubs, Sherin and van Es (2009) note that "attending to student ideas had become more established, though they continued to either directly dismiss an idea raised by a student or to simply not probe the idea in class" (p. 31).

Furthermore, it is not obvious to us what *should* count as progress or expertise. As described above, researchers tend to define certain approaches or moves as more or less responsive than others, and to assess progress largely by frequency counts, averages, or proportions—how much the teacher is *pressing* versus *eliciting*,

230 Amy D. Robertson et al.

to use an example from Brodie (2011). In addition to noting that averaging might mask important fluctuations in teacher attention, we echo a call from Chazan and Ball (1999):

> Rather than taking a prescriptive view of appropriate teacher moves and style, we argue for a more pragmatic approach in which teacher moves are selected and invented in response to the situation at hand, to the particulars of the child, group or class and to the needs of the mathematics (p. 7).

For example, *press* might not always be preferable to *elicit*. It depends on the particulars of the context.

We urge the research community toward detailed empirical case studies as a means of continuing to flesh out our intuitions about what constitutes progress in responsive teaching before we decide how to assess it. This chapter contributes one such case study that informs notions of progress and assessment by showing that (i) a teacher's attention can shift over short timescales, (ii) the focus of attention can shift among multiple facets *of* the substance of student thinking, and (iii) these finer-grained shifts in teacher attention are embedded in coarser-grained coherences of attention and response. We use these results, along with practitioner accounts from the literature, to propose an additional component of progress toward expert responsive teaching: the teacher's flexibility and meta-level responsiveness about *which* facets of the substance of student thinking to attend and respond to in the moment.

Research Methods

Classroom Context

In the episode featured in this chapter, Sam's seventh-grade students discuss the question, "If you're walking with keys, and you want to drop the keys into a small trash can sitting on the floor, should you release the keys before the container, over the container, or after the container?" Sam had set aside the entire class period for discussion. He organized the students into a "fishbowl," in which an inner circle of eight students initially discussed the question while the rest of the students listened. The part of the discussion we analyzed lasted for approximately sixteen minutes; we provide the full transcript online (http://www.studentsthinking.org/rtsm).

In her dissertation, Richards (2013) classifies this episode as an exemplar of relatively stable attention/responsiveness to student thinking over time, using tools and warrants from studies reviewed above (Brodie, 2011; Lau, 2010; Levin, 2008; O'Connor & Michaels, 1993; Pierson, 2008; van Zee & Minstrell, 1997). Richards argues that Sam's attention is primarily focused on students' causal

Variability Within Teacher Attention **231**

storytelling—the extent to which students offer mechanistic explanations for *why* the dropped keys would behave as predicted—and the substance of those stories.

Episode Selection

We initially chose this episode because we expected it would help us to flesh out our intuitions about assessing responsive teaching, the original goal of our collaboration. Richards argued in her dissertation that Sam's responsiveness in this episode differed from his responsiveness a year earlier when teaching a similar lesson, making it plausible that characterizing these differences would help flesh out notions of progress and/or expertise.

Watching the episode, we noticed a relatively abrupt and significant shift in Sam's attention in the middle of his conversation with his students. Looking more closely, we came to believe that Sam's attention shifted repeatedly on short timescales among different aspects of the substance of student thinking. These finer-grained foci of attention and the shifts among them quickly became the target of our analysis. Admittedly, we were primed to notice and focus on shifts in attention because of our original interest in figuring out ways to assess responsive teaching that take into account such shifts. At the same time, we felt that the number of shifts in Sam's attention was not idiosyncratic; looking at other classroom examples of teacher attention generated similar discussions of variability. Thus, we expected our analysis to yield theory-building insights about teacher responsiveness more generally.

Analytic Flow

In the spirit of interaction analysis (Derry et al., 2010; Erickson, 1986; Jordan & Henderson, 1995), we watched segments of the episode together and debated the focus of Sam's attention at different moments. After several hours of this group analysis, we systematically analyzed the transcript as individuals, highlighting and characterizing natural shifts in the discussion as defined by discourse analytical markers (Schegloff & Sacks, 1999; Stivers & Sidnell, 2005; van Dijk, 1997)—places where a new conversational segment began. Comparing notes, we noticed that (1) often the shifts we identified reflected different timescales, but (2) there was significant overlap in how we segmented the episode and characterized Sam's attention. Notably, we all saw the fine-grained foci of attention as nested within coarser-grained foci of attention. Through further discussion, we reached an initial consensus about how to segment the transcript. Further refinements to the timing of the shifts and the characterization of the segments grew out of the writing of each subsection of this chapter by different authors. Although we strove to stay open to different interpretations of the data, our sense of Sam's overarching, coarse-grained focus of attention in the episode as a whole (on the practice and substance of students' causal storytelling) undoubtedly influenced our analysis.

After drafting the analysis sections, we looked at video of stimulated recall interviews (Lyle, 2003) that Jen Richards conducted with Sam for her dissertation research. In these interviews, Jen and Sam watched and discussed video of the key-drop episode, pausing the video regularly for Sam to discuss students' thinking and his own actions. As we briefly discuss, Sam's reconstruction of his rationale for the lesson as a whole and for particular teaching moves aligned well with our own analyses.

Analysis, Part 1: Sam's Attention Shifts Among Multiple Foci Within the Substance of Student Thinking, on Short Timescales

Collectively, we identified four primary foci of Sam's attention. He shifted among these foci on short timescales, sometimes even within a given speech turn. Figure 11.1 illustrates our breakdown of the episode and highlights the variability within Sam's attention and responsiveness to student thinking.

In what follows, we provide examples of each of these foci of attention and highlight in what ways each is attentive and responsive to the substance of student thinking.

Focus A: Students' Interpretation of the Scenario Under Discussion

Periodically throughout the episode, Sam attended to the meaning students were making of the key-drop scenario, and he clarified the scenario by (re)explaining it, bounding it, and/or attempting to show its plausibility and relevance. For instance, when Kendra asked, "Are you tossing it or just dropping it?" (line 39), Sam re-explained that "you're just dropping it" (40). At times, he bounded the scenario when he sensed students were talking about variations, like when Chavez suggested that the keys were dropped by someone running instead of walking (211–212). Such clarifications, especially when not responding to a direct question, demonstrated Sam's attentiveness to which question the students thought they were addressing (as opposed to just their answers to the question). Sam strove to keep students on the same page throughout the discussion.

Sam also faced several challenges to the scenario's validity. For example, Sam defended the realism of the scenario by elaborating on it: in line 84, Drake asked why the person throwing away the keys did not just stop and put the keys in the

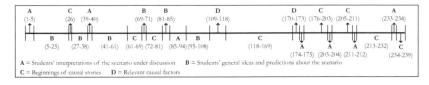

FIGURE 11.1 Fine-grained breakdown of the focal episode. Numbers in parentheses refer to line numbers in transcript.

trash can instead of dropping them in while walking. Sam responded that the person did not want to stop because he was in a hurry (86). Drake challenged the scenario again by asking why the person didn't just keep the keys in his pocket until the next day (89). In response, Sam created a scenario in which, because the person's job was to throw away trash all day, he did not want to stop at each trash can (90). As evidenced by this exchange, Sam elaborated upon the original key-drop scenario multiple times in an effort to make it more psychologically and socially realistic in response to confusion or resistance from students.

Focus B: Students' General Ideas and Predictions About the Scenario

Sam also attended to students' general ideas about the scenario and what they predicted would happen, asking for further clarification and predictions even when students were not offering the kinds of causal stories he sought to draw out. For instance, in response to Tim's idea that the keys won't make it into the container if they're dropped before or after (line 27), Sam did not ask Tim why, but rather for an additional prediction:

Sam: Where will it go if we drop it before the container? (28)
Tim: On the ground. (29)
Sam: On the ground in front of the container, or on the side of the container, or behind the container? (30)

Neither Tim nor Sam oriented to explaining the predictions in subsequent turns.

In another example in lines 50–61, Teresa initially talked not about where to drop the keys, but about the fact that some people have bad aim, miss the trash can, and then abandon their mess (50 and 53). Sam initially encouraged her participation by revoicing her idea ("So some people don't play basketball very well . . . ," line 52) and requesting clarification ("They might need to be guided to the location, is that what you mean?", line 54). After Teresa restated her ideas (55), Sam elicited her prediction about the original key-drop question in a way that connected to her ideas: "So Teresa, you said some people have bad aim, so those people who have bad aim, should they drop it before they get to the container, or above, or after?" (56). Thus, Sam sometimes focused on general ideas and predictions that students had about the scenario without trying to press for further explanation.

Focus C: Beginnings of Causal Stories

Sam also noticed the beginnings of causal stories in students' ideas and tried to draw them out. For instance, after Sam's exchange with Teresa in lines 50–61, he reoriented the class to Cooper's explanation from earlier: "So now let's, we want to get back to—why, why above? Cooper, you had some explanation why, what's the

234 Amy D. Robertson et al.

reason for it?" (61). By asking "why" and "what's the reason for it," Sam requested more than a restatement of where Cooper thinks the keys should be dropped; he asked for an explanation. Cooper responded, "Because the gravity, like, because of its weight, the gravity will push it down, it'll like fall directly in" (62). Sam then asked the rest of the class, "Is there any *other* reason why it will—why we should drop it above?" (63, emphasis added), indicating that he both attended to and accepted Cooper's explanation as a *reason*, and wanted students to offer other reasons, not just answers.

Teresa responded that dropping it before or after reaching the can will create litter, and hence dropping it directly above the can contributes to "saving the world" (73). She took up Sam's "why" question with an appeal to social utility, not causal mechanism. Unlike in his previous interaction with Teresa in lines 50–61, where he did not press for mechanism, Sam elicited a physical justification for why the object will miss the can unless dropped from directly above:

Sam: So . . . what you're saying, Teresa, is that the, the (pause) that there's a stronger likelihood if I don't drop it above the container, it's gonna fall on the ground, right? ((Teresa nods)) So . . . Why is it strongly likely that it's gonna fall outside the container if I don't drop it above? (pause) What's making you more certain of it, of it falling out of the container if I don't drop here ((holds keys above)), as opposed to here ((holds keys before)) or there ((holds keys after))? (74)

Focus D: Relevant Causal Factors

At times, Sam noticed and highlighted relevant causal factors in students' ideas. In line 109, for instance, Sam highlighted the weight of the keys, a factor cited previously by students as affecting the keys' motion (e.g., Cooper's statement in line 62). He altered the scenario so that the keys were made of plastic or paper (111), and students began to offer ideas about falling slowly and floating (114–115). Then Kendra asked a question:

Kendra: Is it windy outside? (117)
Sam: Oh, so we're throwing in other variables. Windy, how would the- (118)

Sam's answer here contrasts with one he gave to an earlier question from Kendra. In lines 39–40, Kendra asked, "Are you tossing it or just dropping it?" (39), and Sam clarified that "you're just dropping it" (40). So, in this earlier exchange, Kendra's question about the scenario was taken as such and answered. In lines 117–118, by contrast, he took up Kendra's question about wind as a suggestion of another causal factor (variable) to consider.

In summary, we documented four different foci of Sam's attention within this classroom episode, each one a facet of the substance of students' thinking. He noticed and responded to (A) how students were interpreting the task at hand, (B) students' general ideas and predictions about the scenario, (C) whether students were fleshing out causal stories about how the keys would behave, and (D) particular causal factors students introduced. Further, we show in Figure 11.1 that his attention to A, B, C, and D varied on short timescales, on the order of minutes or even seconds.

Analysis Part II: We Infer Coarser-Grained, Local Coherences in Sam's Attention and Responsiveness to the Substance of Student Thinking

We also identified two broader coherences within Sam's attention and responsiveness to student thinking:

1. *(Re)framing students' activity toward causal storytelling about the key-drop (1–109)*: Sam attends to the nature of students' epistemic activity and their interpretations of the key-drop problem, and he tailors his responses to gently nudge students toward causal storytelling about the key-drop scenario, in such a way that takes up and responds to what students are asking and offering.
2. *Unpacking students' causal stories (118–239)*: Sam attends to the substance of students' causal stories and tailors his responses toward encouraging students to flesh out their causal stories.

Figure 11.2 depicts these broader coherences and how they relate to the foci described previously. Note that lines 109–118 are in neither coherence; this transitional segment corresponds to the abrupt shift that first caught our attention in the episode.

Although *(re)framing students' activity toward causal storytelling about the key-drop* and *unpacking students' causal stories* are both foci of attention and response, like A through D above, we call them "coherences" to underscore the following claims:

- The finer-grained foci of attention (A through D) embedded within each of the larger-scale foci of Sam's attention and responsiveness (see Figure 11.2) are consistent with—and cohere to form the substance of—the larger-scale foci.

FIGURE 11.2 Coarse-grained coherences in the focal episode.

236 Amy D. Robertson et al.

- Each coherence helps to explain the **shifts** between the finer-grained foci of attention embedded within the coherence.
- Each coherence helps to define and explain the **role** played by the embedded finer-grained foci in the classroom discourse.

In brief, we claim that attributing these coarser-grained coherences of attention and responsiveness to Sam provides additional descriptive and explanatory power beyond that provided by describing the finer-grained foci of attention A through D. Indeed, our sense that these finer-grained foci of attention *cohere with*—and function in the service of—coarser-grained foci of attention and responsiveness problematizes the association of specific, turn-by-turn discourse moves with "high" or "low" responsiveness, as we discuss in the "Findings and Implications for Research and Assessment" section.

In deciding on the substance and boundaries of the two coherences, we attended to (i) the consistency between the proposed coherence and the finer-grained foci of attention—and shifts between them—subsumed by the coherence, and (ii) the proportions of foci A through D within the broader coherences. Later, using the stimulated recall interview, we checked our attribution of coherences against Sam's reconstructions of his goals and interpretations of students' thinking.

Coherence 1: (Re)Framing Students' Activity Toward Causal Storytelling About The Key-Drop

Consistency Between the Finer-Grained Foci and the Coherence

In lines 1–109, Sam's attention shifted between foci A, B, and C, with most emphasis on focus B (Figure 11.2). Sam's instantiation of focus B is consistent with an overarching focus on helping students frame their activity as causal storytelling. Especially at the start of a discussion, pursuing students' general ideas and predictions can establish a safe space where students begin to feel comfortable offering their own accounts of what they think is going on. Sam's emphasis on students' predictions also sets the stage for deeper exploration of the reasoning behind the predictions.

Sam's focus on clarifying the scenario under discussion (Focus A) and on pursuing causal stories (Focus C) were also consistent with *(re)framing students' activity toward causal storytelling about the key-drop*. Focus A occurred when students asked clarification questions about the scenario (39–40) or questioned its validity. The longest exchange of this type stemmed from Drake asking why you would not just stop and put the keys in the trash can (85). As described above, Sam generated a scenario about someone picking up trash for a living (90–92). Striving to make the scenario realistic is consistent with Coherence 1 and might be particularly important for getting students to substantively engage with the question. Sam also began to gently push students toward telling causal stories (Focus C), repeatedly drawing the class' attention back to Cooper's idea that gravity pulls the keys down, which could signal to students that he sought this kind of explanation (see lines 61 and 72). Although Sam was primarily focused on getting students to share their ideas and predictions at all, he started to probe for deeper explanations of why the keys would behave as the students predicted, attempting to draw them into causal storytelling.

Consistency Between the Coherences and the Shifts Among Finer-Grained Foci

The shifts in Sam's attention from one focus to another also cohered with an overarching emphasis on (re)framing student activity. Shifts from Focus B to Focus A occurred when students asked questions that required clarification of the key-drop scenario. For instance, Sam shifted from Focus B to Focus A when Drake asked why you would not just stop and put the keys in the trash can (85), and Sam strove to make the scenario more realistic for Drake. The subsequent transition from Focus A back to Focus B occurred when Drake accepted Sam's response and proposed an experiment (93). Although Sam initially hesitated (94, "Well not (holds hands toward Drake), maybe not, maybe-"), he quickly switched to pursuing Drake's idea (96, "What will that, what will that show us?"). In each case, once Sam addressed the questions or concerns (A), he transitioned back to focusing on students' ideas (B), including those heading in directions he did not want to pursue, such as Drake's experimentation suggestion—perhaps because he wanted to promote student agency as a first step toward promoting causal storytelling (see next subsection).

Shifts from Focus B into Focus C occurred when Sam prompted students to articulate *why* they would drop the keys before, over, or after the trash can, attempting to nudge students into causal storytelling. As the conversation progressed, he emphasized Cooper's explanation that gravity would pull the keys straight down (61 and 72) and pressed students who offered ideas to articulate "why"—e.g., line 67 ("Why would a toss make it more likely to go in as opposed to me just dropping it?"), line 74 ("But what, what, why, why will it fall on the ground if I drop it before or after?"), and so on. However, when Sam's bids to articulate "why" were not taken up by students, Sam tended to encourage the non-mechanistic thinking that arose rather than press for mechanism. This delicate balance between valuing students' ideas and pressing for deeper mechanistic explanations is consistent with gently nudging students toward causal storytelling.

Consistency With the Teacher's View, as Expressed During Stimulated Recall Interview

In the stimulated recall interview, Sam articulated a distinction between his actions at the beginning and end of the episode. Jen and Sam paused the video shortly

238 Amy D. Robertson et al.

after Teresa talked about bad aim (50–60). Sam described what he wanted in the classroom dialogue, but noted that he was not pushing students too hard:

Sam: I didn't really press them too hard to, to give explanations at this point. It may have come up a little, a little more, um, but I didn't really—I was basically trying to get them to, to, to, to weigh in all the potential factors and also to, um, to come up with some kind of causal story as to how and where the, the item should be dropped. What are those factors, and uh, trying to get them to think more deeply about the movement of the, of the keys as related to the container . . . I just thought that they were struggling with, with, um, making sense of the whole thing . . . but they had some great ideas . . .

In Sam's reflection, we see signals of each of the fine-grained foci of attention described above and also of *(re)framing students' activity toward causal storytelling about the key-drop.* He talked about how students were struggling to make sense of the scenario or task at hand, which relates to Focus A. He noted students' "great ideas" (Focus B) and indicated that he pressed students a bit for explanations (Focus C), but not "too hard . . . at this point." His sense that students "were struggling with . . . making sense of the whole thing" and his reticence in pressing students *too* hard for explanations coheres with our sense that he was easing students into offering their own ideas and predictions in order to create a safe space for the more mechanistic discussion he was after.

Coherence 2: Unpacking Students' Causal Stories

Around line 118, a different coherence of attention and responsiveness emerges. As students began voicing mechanistic ideas more consistently, Sam shifted from *(re)framing students' activity toward causal storytelling about the key-drop* to *unpacking students' causal stories.*

Consistency Between the Finer-Grained Foci and the Coherence

In contrast to the previous coherence, the predominant finer-grained focus in lines 118–239 was Focus C, *causal stories.* When Evan offered, "If it was made out of paper, it would float over the container and just go outside" (114), Sam pursued Evan's line of reasoning through line 147 in the face of numerous distractions (e.g., lines 119–120, 129–131). For example, in line 118, Sam shifted his focus in mid-sentence from Kendra's question about its being windy outside (117). He begins, "Oh, so we're throwing in other variables. Windy, how would the- okay, so now, if the, if the keys are light, let's say they're wooden keys, okay? Um, Evan-." Although Sam temporarily focused on the variable introduced in Kendra's question, he quickly returned to Evan and pursued the beginnings of a causal story in Evan's answer. Similar extended exchanges occurred with Tim (176–208) and

Chavez (209–232) as Sam pursued their causal stories. This attention to mechanistic detail characterizes much of the discussion in lines 118–239 and epitomizes *unpacking students' causal stories.*

The other two foci of attention in lines 118–239 were Focus A (students' interpretation of the scenario under discussion) and Focus D (relevant causal factors). In line 118, Sam took up Kendra's question about its being windy outside (117) as another variable to consider (Focus D)—"Oh, so we're throwing in other variables. Windy, how would the-". Interestingly, "Is it windy outside?" was similar in nature to a question she asked earlier, "Are you tossing it or just dropping it?" (39). In both questions, Kendra requested clarification of the physical scenario. Yet Sam took the questions up differently. Within the broader coherence of *(re)framing students' activity*, Sam answered her question, "You're just dropping it." (40). Here, by contrast, he does *not* answer the question but instead takes it up as proposing a causal factor to consider (118), reflective of a broader coherence of *unpacking students' causal stories.* To be clear, helping students articulate causal factors could be an end in itself, different from helping them tell causal stories (Richards, 2013). But in lines 118–239, Focus D occurs only once, and only briefly (170–173), consistent with our argument that the focus on causal factors was in the service of students' causal storytelling.

In lines 118–239, Sam also clarified the relevant scenario under consideration (Focus A) four times. Two of these instances, in lines 174–175 and 233–234, resembled previous instantiations of Focus A in which students asked clarification questions and Sam re-explained the scenario at hand. In contrast, the other two instances of Focus A, in lines 203–204 and 211–214, seemed to serve a different purpose. As students articulated their reasoning, Sam was sensitive to moments when students abruptly started talking about scenarios different than the one under discussion. In lines 190–200, a debate arose about whether air causes the keys to "move backwards" (199) or to "move forward" (200) when dropped while walking "kind of fast." In line 203, Tim appeared to suddenly change the scenario:

Tim:　　Like, if somebody goes hunting and they're shooting a deer, and the deer's running fast, you have to shoot before so that it hits- (203)

Sam:　　So but we're not talking about running now, we're just talking about walking fast, not running, but walking fast (204).

Here, Sam focused on the words "running fast" and jumped in to clarify that we're "not running, but walking fast." Similarly, Sam interjected when Chavez discussed running in line 211:

Chavez:　Because, because if you run, and- (211).

Sam:　　Now, we're walking now, we're not running (212).

Note that these clarifications occurred as interruptions to students' statements, unlike the Focus A statements earlier in the discussion. The forceful, directive

240 Amy D. Robertson et al.

nature of these clarifications is consistent with the broader coherence of *unpacking students' causal stories*. Other students were in the middle of debating causal stories about the effect of air on the keys while walking when Tim, and then Chavez, started discussing scenarios involving running. These shifts interrupted rather than added to unpacking the competing causal stories under discussion at line 200. Therefore, attributing to Sam a broader coherence of attention and responsiveness to *unpacking students' causal stories* is consistent with and could even help explain Sam's forcefulness in clarifying the scenario to Tim and Chavez, given his generally gentler touch throughout the episode.

We did not note any pure examples of Focus B (students' general ideas and predictions) in lines 118–239. On the one hand, students more frequently offered clear beginnings of causal stories (unlike before line 118), and on the other hand, Sam pressed more in that direction.

Consistency Between the Coherence and the Shifts Among Finer-Grained Foci

The shifts between foci also cohered with an emphasis on *unpacking students' causal stories*. Shifts from Focus C (the predominant focus in lines 118–239) into Focus A occurred either when a student asked for clarification or interrupted an unfolding causal story by proposing a change to the scenario; by (re)focusing students, Sam enabled students to keep explaining a single, shared scenario. Once the scenario was clarified, Sam returned to Focus C, pursuing students' causal stories. For example, after Sam clarified to Chavez that "we're walking now, we're not running" (212), Chavez paused and said, "Oh never mind, I thought you were running, that's why" (213). Sam further clarified that "we're walking fast" (214) and asked "what do we have to do?" (214), inviting Chavez to share his thinking and pressing Chavez for mechanism in line 216: "What's the causal reason? What causes us to have to [drop] it before [the can]?"

The shift from Focus C to Focus D in line 170 was more difficult for us to understand. At this point in the discussion, both Evan and Drake had provided different causal stories that drew on distinct factors, gravity and wind. So Sam may have been looking to summarize the stories in play in order to open space for others. Evidence for this interpretation comes from his repetition of "So" at the beginning of line 170 ("So, so I've heard people talk about gravity, um, someone-now we're into wind, what other factor is it? The weight would have an effect?"), indicating that he's restating or tracing a consequence of previous ideas, and the plural in "I've heard people talk about" indicates that he's referring to multiple people's ideas. But this evidence is thin and hence our conclusion is speculative.

We found more grounds on which to interpret the shifts from Focus D to other foci. In the shift from Focus D to Focus A in lines 172–175, Sam responded to a clarification question from Tim and then pursued his line of reasoning about the scenario, turning the conversation back to unpacking a student's causal story. The shift from Focus D to Focus C in line 118, on the other hand, seemed to involve Sam monitoring himself. Recall that Sam said, "Oh, so we're throwing in other variables. Windy, how would the- okay, so now, if the, if the keys are light, let's say they're wooden keys, okay? Um, Evan-" (118). A critical signal in this line is the false start in the second sentence, represented by the short dash. Sam started to ask a question about the "wind" variable Kendra mentioned, then cut himself off and redirected his attention back to the scenario Evan had been discussing just before Kendra's question. This suggests that Sam realized he was going in a different direction without letting Evan complete his thoughts, so Sam diverted back to Evan and the causal story he was starting to tell—consistent with *unpacking students' causal stories*.

Consistency With the Teacher's View, as Expressed During Stimulated Recall Interview

In the interview, Sam indicated, "I'm trying to get at a causal story . . . but I don't always say what's your causal story? But I will say, well, can you explain it, can you give a little more detail?" At a meeting of teachers approximately two months before the key-drop discussion, Sam indicated that both the fishbowl and inquiry Monday structures—in which Mondays were devoted to students' explanation-building and argumentation unfettered by content coverage requirements—were put in place to make space for "possible causes, causal stories" from students. Within these structures, Sam was able to press students for extended explanations.

Sam's earlier statement from the interview also provides evidence of this coherence. He said that he wanted students "to come up with some kind of causal story as to how and where the, the item should be dropped." Even though he delayed pursuing this objective at first, noting that he "didn't really press them too hard to . . . give explanations" early on, his sense that he was headed toward pursuit of causal stories is consistent with the shift we are proposing, from a broader coherence of *(re)framing students' activity toward causal storytelling about the key-drop* to *unpacking students' causal stories*.

Findings and Implications for Research and Assessment

Our analysis, like expert practitioner accounts of their own teaching (e.g., Ball, 1993; Hammer, 1997), illustrates that teacher responsiveness is more complex than just "attending to the substance of student thinking." It involves choosing between multiple, competing foci of attention both within and outside the substance of student thinking—choices that depend on both the unfolding conversation and the teacher's coarser-grained instructional foci and goals. In this section, we discuss implications of our work for conceptualizations and assessment of responsive teaching.

242 Amy D. Robertson et al.

Our Findings Inform Conceptualizations and Assessment of Progress Toward Responsive Teaching

Our research community has not yet reached consensus about what constitutes expert responsive teaching or how to measure progress in a teacher's responsiveness. Researchers have begun to address this challenge by describing shifts in the ways that teachers listen to and take up their students' ideas in the classroom (e.g., Davis, 1997; Empson & Jacobs, 2008; Sherin & van Es, 2009). These studies describe as "favorable" shifts away from attention to correctness and associated evaluative responses and toward attention to the mathematical sense-making within student thinking and associated responses aimed at interpreting student ideas.

The variability we document in Sam's attention and responsiveness *within* the substance of student thinking, at multiple grain sizes, adds three distinct layers of complexity to the challenge of conceptualizing and measuring progress toward more responsive teaching. The first is multi-facetedness: as Sam illustrates, a teacher might vary not only between attending and not attending to substance, but also between attending to multiple facets *within* the substance of students' thinking. The second is variation: Sam's attention shifts between these foci of attention on short timescales, minutes, or even seconds. The third is multiple grain sizes of attentional foci: the finer-grained foci in Sam's attention and the shifts between them appear to function in the service of broader-scale foci of attention and responsiveness (the two coherences discussed above). These layers of complexity problematize (1) accounts of developmental trajectories toward greater responsiveness and (2) existing observational rubrics for characterizing and assessing responsive teaching.

1. Problematizing developmental trajectories toward responsiveness. As described previously, Empson and Jacobs (2008) characterize teacher responsiveness as developing along a trajectory from "directive listening" (stage 1) to "observational listening" (stage 2) to "responsive listening" (stage 3).[1] They specifically describe this trajectory as "a pathway by which children's mathematics becomes progressively more central as teachers move from *directive* to *observational* to *responsive* listening" (p. 267). In describing the stages, these authors note that the shift from observational to responsive listening "appears to constitute a fundamental and irreversible change in how [teachers] conceptualize their work" (p. 270), although the transition from observational to responsive listening may be rocky and even directive at times as teachers struggle to pursue students' ideas. In the key-drop episode, Sam problematizes these characterizations by showing evidence of occupying all three of Empson's and Jacobs's stages, and not always in order. When Sam attends to students' interpretations of the scenario (Focus A), he often responds by providing direct answers to students' questions and pushing them toward a particular "correct" view of the scenario—evidence of directive listening. When he focuses on whether students are offering their own ideas and even pursues "off-topic" lines of reasoning (Focus B), many of Sam's moves could be characterized as observational listening. When he pursues students' causal stories (Focus C), Sam exhibits responsive listening, pressing students to flesh out their thinking in particular, discipline-related directions. It's implausible that Sam "developed" from directive to responsive listening over sixteen minutes. Furthermore, as Figure 11.1 shows, Sam frequently "reverts" from higher to lower stages of Empson's and Jacobs's scheme as the episode proceeds.

Maskiewicz and Winters (2012) also challenge developmental schemes for responsiveness, highlighting the idea of working flexibly with what students offer. Given the variability in what students offer and in what teachers attend and respond to over a wide range of timescales, from minutes in our example to years in Maskiewicz's and Winters's study, more predictive and explanatory power should emerge from modeling the complex dynamics of teachers' attention than from assigning them to stages that might characterize a minority of their actual behavior.

2. Challenging levels-based observational rubrics for responsive teaching. Using a predetermined observational rubric to code teachers' responses as "better" or "worse" is problematic because teachers' responsiveness is tied in part to the context in which their actions are embedded—including the meaning they make of their context—not just to their actions or to the ways in which students take those actions up. This characteristic of teacher responsiveness is an explicit part of the dynamics in practitioner accounts of responsive teaching (e.g., Chazan & Ball, 1999; Lampert, 1990).

To illustrate this point, consider Sam's elicitation and encouragement of general ideas the students offered, even if tied only loosely to the targeted physics (Focus B). A researcher might code this responsiveness as worse than when he tries to elicit causal stories in particular (Focus C). For instance, as discussed above, Empson and Jacobs (2008) would likely code certain Focus B responses as "observational listening," a lower level than the "responsive listening" in Focus C. However, if Sam's intent in lines 1–109 was to (re)frame the activity for the students, and if we see him as responsively deciding how best to draw in individual students—supporting some students in offering their ideas *at all*, while pressing harder on others—then his responsiveness within Focus B might seem just as good as his responsiveness within Focus C. Our point is that Sam's responsiveness is not made up solely of the actions he takes; it is located in the complex interplay among the actions he takes, in specific contexts, toward specific ends.

Our Findings Suggest the Importance of "Meta-Responsiveness," the Teacher's Intentional Flexibility About Which Facets of Student Thinking to Foreground

Since responsive teaching is a social phenomenon, the actions and perspectives of the participants evolve as they continually make sense of (and shape) their contexts

244 Amy D. Robertson et al.

and respond to other participants who are simultaneously making sense of (and shaping) the context (Anderson-Levitt, 2006; Becker, 1966; Bredo, 2006; Erickson, 1986; Guba & Lincoln, 2005; Maxwell, 2004; Moss et al., 2009).[2] Yet the result is not a free-for-all; classroom norms and self-organization lead to coherences in the participants' attention and actions. It is no surprise, therefore, that Sam's attention displayed coherences and variability at multiple timescales. The complexity of these dynamics, we claim, stemmed partly from Sam's meta-responsiveness, by which we mean his responsiveness about which facets of the substance of student thinking to attend and respond to. For instance, in the first coherence Sam showed evidence of monitoring whether a given student needed to be encouraged in sharing her own thoughts and predictions at all (leading to Focus B) or if the student was ready to be pushed toward causal stories in particular (leading to Focus C). In other words, he was responsive about *which* facets of the substance of student thinking to foreground, in addition to being responsive to the substance of students' thinking in the first place.

Ball's (1993) practitioner account offers additional support for our claim that expert responsiveness involves being responsive about which facets of the substance of student reasoning to respond to in a given moment. Ball recounts a series of classroom events in which her students debate and discuss a student's— Sean's—proposal that six is both even and odd, since it is comprised of three (an odd number) groups of two (an even number). Ball articulates the tension she faced when deciding whether to pursue Sean's idea. The lesson was intended to support students in defining even and odd numbers, and pursuing Sean's proposal might "confuse [the students] since it's nonstandard knowledge" or "interfere with the required 'conventional' understandings of even and odd numbers" (p. 387). At the same time, Ball acknowledged the idea's "potential to enhance what kids are thinking about 'definition' and its role, nature, and purpose in mathematical activity and discourse . . ." (p. 387). Ultimately, she chose to encourage Sean's pursuit, pointing out to the class that he had invented a new kind of number and pressing him and others to define and explore the properties of "Sean numbers." In this account, Ball is meta-responsive about which aspect of the substance of Sean's thinking to foreground in her response: the content of his argument about why six is both odd and even versus the mathematical practices of argumentation and definition-building.

To be clear, we (and Ball) are not advocating unlimited flexibility; a teacher should not give every student idea equivalent status or airtime. For example, Sam did not sustain his pursuit of Teresa's ideas about littering for nearly as long as he strove to pull out Evan's causal reasoning connected to gravity. Our point is that expert responsiveness includes not only responsiveness toward a variety of facets of the substance of student thinking, but also responsiveness toward *which* of those facets to foreground. "Progress" in responsive teaching could therefore be manifested in more nuanced, perceptive, intentional flexibility or in broadening the scope or sophistication of the disciplinary practices noticed within student thinking, rather than in greater percentages of particular behaviors or foci of attention.

Conclusion

In this chapter, we used a case of responsive teaching to demonstrate that a teacher's attention varies on short timescales as he focuses on multiple facets of the substance of his students' thinking. Our analysis empirically establishes that (i) teachers' attention can shift not only between the substance of student thinking and other things, but also between multiple foci within the substance of student thinking; and (ii) these foci sometimes cohere into coarser-grained coherences of attention and responsiveness. We used these results to challenge notions of expertise in responsive teaching and associated assessment schemes that equate levels of responsiveness with particular foci of attention or types of response, without analyzing the teacher's intent or the broader flow and context of the classroom discourse. Based on our analysis, we recommend that researchers attend to this multi-layered complexity in their accounts and assessment of responsive teaching.

We feel that we are at the *beginning* of a much-needed dialogue about expertise in and assessment of responsive teaching. Our analysis contributes a number of preliminary suggestions, such as conceptualizing expertise partly in terms of "meta-responsiveness" or responsive flexibility.

Acknowledgments

The authors gratefully acknowledge the support of the National Science Foundation under Grant Nos. DRL-0822342, DUE-0831975, and DRL-0733613; as well as the support of a Physics Education Research Leadership Organizing Committee Scholar-in-Residence Grant. We appreciate the substantive feedback offered by Luke Conlin, Abigail Daane, Lezlie DeWater, Kara Gray, Ayush Gupta, David Hammer, Daniel Levin, Sarah McKagan, Rachel Scherr, Lane Seeley, Jessica Watkins, Michael Wittmann, and Stamatis Vokos.

Notes

1 Other researchers, such as Davis (1997) and van Es (2011), describe similar schemes but take a less firm stance on their developmental nature.
2 Erickson (2007) has aptly written that "...face-to-face social interaction is a process akin to that of climbing a tree that is climbing you back at the same time" (p. 194).

References

Anderson-Levitt, K.M. (2006). Ethnography. In J.L. Green, P.B. Elmore, A. Skukauskait, & E. Grace (Eds.), *Handbook of complementary methods in education research* (pp. 279–295). Mahwah, NJ: Lawrence Erlbaum Associates.

Ball, D.L. (1993). With an eye on the mathematical horizon: Dilemmas of teaching elementary school mathematics. *The Elementary School Journal, 93,* 373–397.

Becker, H.S. (1966). The life history and the scientific mosaic. In J.C. Shaw (Ed.), *The Jack-roller.* Chicago, IL: University of Chicago Press.

246 Amy D. Robertson et al.

Bredo, E. (2006). Philosophies of educational research. In J.L. Green, P.B. Elmore, A. Skukauskait , & E. Grace (Eds.), *Handbook of complementary methods in education research* (pp. 3–31). Mahwah, NJ: Lawrence Erlbaum Associates.

Brodie, K. (2011). Working with learners' mathematical thinking: Towards a language of description for changing pedagogy. *Teaching and Teacher Education, 27,* 174–186.

Chazan, D., & Ball, D.L. (1999). Beyond being told not to tell. *For the Learning of Mathematics, 19,* 2–10.

Crespo, S. (2000). Seeing more than right and wrong answers: Prospective teachers' interpretations of students' mathematical work. *Journal of Mathematics Teacher Education, 3,* 155–181.

Davis, B. (1997). Listening for differences: An evolving conception of mathematics teaching. *Journal for Research in Mathematics Education, 28,* 355–376.

Derry, S.J., Pea, R.D., Engle, R.A., Erickson, F., Goldman, R., Hall, R., . . . Sherin, B.L. (2010). Conducting video research in the learning sciences: Guidance on selection, analysis, technology, and ethics. *Journal of the Learning Sciences, 19,* 3–53.

Empson, S.B., & Jacobs, V.R. (2008). Learning to listen to children's mathematics. In D. Tirosh & T. Wood (Eds.), *Tools and processes in mathematics teacher education* (pp. 257–281). The Netherlands: Sense Publishers.

Erickson, F. (1986). Qualitative methods in research on teaching. In M.C. Wittrock (Ed.), *Handbook of research on teaching* (pp. 119–161). New York, NY: Macmillan.

Erickson, F. (2007). Some thoughts on "proximal" formative assessment of student learning. *Yearbook of the National Society for the Study of Education, 106,* 186–216.

Fennema, E., Carpenter, T.P., Franke, M.L., Levi, L., Jacobs, V.R., & Empson, S.B. (1996). A longitudinal study of learning to use children's thinking in mathematics instruction. *Journal for Research in Mathematics Education, 27,* 403–434.

Goldsmith, L.T., & Seago, N. (2011). Using classroom artifacts to focus teachers' noticing: Affordances and opportunities. In M.G. Sherin, V.R. Jacobs, & R.A. Philipp (Eds.), *Mathematics teacher noticing: Seeing through teachers' eyes* (pp. 169–187). New York, NY: Routledge.

Guba, E.G., & Lincoln, Y.S. (2005). Paradigmatic controversies, contradictions, and emerging confluences. In N.K. Denzin & Y.S. Lincoln (Eds.), *The Sage handbook of qualitative research* (pp. 191–215). USA: Sage Publications, Inc.

Hammer, D. (1997). Discovery learning and discovery teaching. *Cognition and Instruction, 15,* 485–529.

Jordan, B., & Henderson, A. (1995). Interaction analysis: Foundations and practice. *The Journal of the Learning Sciences, 4,* 39–103.

Lampert, M. (1990). When the problem is not the question and the solution is not the answer: Mathematical knowing and teaching. *American Educational Research Journal, 27,* 29–63.

Lau, M. (2010). *Understanding the dynamics of teacher attention: Examples of how high school physics and physical science teachers attend to student ideas* (Unpublished doctoral dissertation). University of Maryland, College Park, MD.

Levin, D.M. (2008). *What secondary science teachers pay attention to in the classroom: Situating teaching in institutional and social systems* (Unpublished doctoral dissertation). University of Maryland, College Park, MD.

Levin, D.M., Hammer, D., & Coffey, J.E. (2009). Novice teachers' attention to student thinking. *Journal of Teacher Education, 60,* 142–154.

Levin, D.M., & Richards, J. (2011). Learning to attend to the substance of student thinking in science. *Science Educator, 20,* 1–11.

Lineback, J.E. (2014). The redirection: An indicator of how teachers respond to student thinking. *Journal of the Learning Sciences,* 1–42.

Lyle, J. (2003). Stimulated recall: A report on its use in naturalistic research. *British Educational Research Journal, 29,* 861–878.

Maskiewicz, A.C., & Winters, V.A. (2012). Understanding the co-construction of inquiry practices: A case study of a responsive teaching environment. *Journal of Research in Science Teaching, 49,* 429–464.

Maxwell, J.A. (2004). Using qualitative methods for causal explanation. *Field Methods, 16,* 243–264.

Moss, P.A., Phillips, D.C., Erickson, F.D., Floden, R.E., Lather, P.A., & Schneider, B.L. (2009). Learning from our differences: A dialogue across perspectives on quality in education research. *Educational Researcher, 38,* 501–517.

O'Connor, M.C., & Michaels, S. (1993). Aligning academic task and participation status through revoicing: Analysis of a classroom discourse strategy. *Anthropology & Education Quarterly, 24,* 318–335.

Pierson, J.L. (2008). *The relationship between patterns of classroom discourse and mathematics learning* (Unpublished doctoral dissertation). University of Texas at Austin, Austin, TX.

Richards, J. (2013). *Exploring what stabilizes teachers' attention and responsiveness to the substance of students' scientific thinking in the classroom* (Unpublished doctoral dissertation). University of Maryland, College Park, MD.

Richards, J., Elby, A., & Gupta, A. (2014). Characterizing a new dimension of change in attending and responding to the substance of student thinking. In J. L. Polman, E. A. Kyza, D. K. O'Neill, I. Tabak, W. R. Penuel, A. S. Jurow, K. O'Connor, T. Lee, & L. D'Amico (Eds.), *Learning and becoming in practice: The International Conference of the Learning Sciences (ICLS) 2014, Volume 1* (pp. 286–293). Boulder, CO: International Society of the Learning Sciences.

Rosebery, A.S., & Warren, B. (Eds.). (1998). *Boats, balloons, and classroom video: Science teaching as inquiry.* Portsmouth, NH: Heinemann.

Russ, R.S., & Luna, M.J. (2013). Inferring teacher epistemological framing from local patterns in teacher noticing. *Journal of Research in Science Teaching, 50,* 284–314.

Schegloff, E.A., & Sacks, H. (1999). Opening up closings. In A. Jaworski & N. Coupland (Eds.), *The discourse reader* (pp. 263–274). London, England: Routledge.

Schifter, D. (1996). *What's happening in math class?: Envisioning new practices through teacher narratives.* New York, NY: Teachers College Press.

Schifter, D. (2011). Examining the behavior of operations: Noticing early algebraic ideas. In M.G. Sherin, V.R. Jacobs, & R.A. Philipp (Eds.), *Mathematics teacher noticing: Seeing through teachers' eyes* (pp. 204–220). New York, NY: Routledge.

Sherin, M.G., & van Es, E.A. (2009). Effects of video club participation on teachers' professional vision. *Journal of Teacher Education, 60,* 20–37.

Stivers, T., & Sidnell, J. (2005). Introduction: Multimodal interaction. *Semiotica, 156,* 1–20.

van Dijk, T. (Ed.). (1997). *Discourse as structure and process.* London, England: Sage Publications.

van Es, E. (2011). A framework for learning to notice student thinking. In M.G. Sherin, V.R. Jacobs, & R.A. Philipp (Eds.), *Mathematics teacher noticing: Seeing through teachers' eyes* (pp. 134–151). New York, NY: Routledge.

van Es, E.A., & Sherin, M.G. (2008). Mathematics teachers' "learning to notice" in the context of a video club. *Teaching and Teacher Education, 24,* 244–276.

van Es, E.A., & Sherin, M.G. (2010). The influence of video clubs on teachers' thinking and practice. *Journal of Mathematics Teacher Education, 13,* 155–176.

van Zee, E.H., & Minstrell, J. (1997). Reflective discourse: Developing shared understandings in a physics classroom. *International Journal of Science Education, 19,* 209–228.

EPILOGUE

David Hammer

I'm writing this in March 2015, with our book manuscript due to Routledge in just a few weeks. It's hard to believe it was only three years ago last month that Amy and Rachel first approached me with the thought of a conference on responsive teaching, maybe to become a book. (I can remember where the three of us were sitting in Rachel's house; she was hosting a wonderful dinner.) They wanted to bring folks together with similar interests and perspectives, to create an opportunity for us to interact among ourselves.

We all spend so much of our time and energy engaging with the "real world" of ongoing instructional practices—at our institutions, in K–12 schools, with standards and states and "stakeholders." It's rare to be able to dig into our scholarship, driven by our curiosities and interests. We should do more of this; there should be more room for and expectations of scholarship in education. It's been awesome—and Amy and Rachel, thank you. And thank you, too, for giving me the honor of having the last word.

In January, when I was starting to think about what to write for this epilogue, I heard about "Teacher Preparation Issues," a proposal by the US Department of Education for "new regulations to implement requirements for the teacher preparation program accountability system under title II of the Higher Education Act [HEA] of 1965." The preamble reminds readers that "Section 200(23) of the HEA defines the term 'teaching skills' as those skills that enable a teacher, among other competencies, to effectively convey and explain academic content."

The regulations are designed to hold teacher education programs accountable to that definition, and they may be in effect by the time this book is in print. Even if they aren't, the HEA has been in effect for 50 years, and the conceptualization of teaching that it encodes as law has driven education for much longer than that: To teach is to "convey and explain."

250 David Hammer

The Department of Education was soliciting comments, and I submitted some. I didn't spend much time; it seemed the main point was to register an objection. But it got me thinking about what I or any of us ought to be saying in response to that conceptualization. So what I'd like to do in this epilogue is think through how we might respond, starting, of course, by appreciating the sense of the notion that teaching means explaining.

It's common sense: If you know something someone else doesn't, and he or she wants to learn it, you should explain it. Like all common sense, it's useful in many situations—say if you're teaching how to change a tire or to use a microwave oven or to get to the science museum. Tell them! And try to be clear about it: demonstrate, use a diagram, give step-by-step directions.

The authors and editors of this volume expect most of our readers have moved past that common sense, or refined it, when it comes to teaching science. That's for two overarching reasons.

(1) We've seen that explaining is not effective for teaching concepts in science.

We've seen the well-established, all-too-reproducible findings that teachers' explanations, however clear and compelling they may seem, are neither necessary nor sufficient for students' learning. We're also familiar with theoretical accounts of learning that explain why that is, why it's not possible to "convey" concepts in science. I wonder if it can accomplish anything to explain why explaining doesn't work, but here's a try.

Learning in science means "modifying your common sense," as a student once put it to me; Einstein said it's a "refinement of everyday thinking." But modifying common sense isn't easy to do, nor is it easy to recognize that one should do so: Why question obvious truths?

The answer to that question is at the heart of why we call science a "discipline": Successful students, as nascent scientists, learn to be *disciplined* about assessing what they accept and understand as true. They learn the need for discipline from their experiences being wrong, wrong even about ideas that seem obvious; they learn strategies for assessing their ideas—habits of checking themselves, looking for what they might be missing. They also learn from the history of ideas in science: Over and over, ideas that seem obvious —forces make things move, blankets make things warm, dead flesh produces maggots, and so on—end up needing modification.

All of these ideas are useful in many situations, which is how they came to be part of common sense. If you're cold, you grab a blanket, because a blanket will make you warm. In another, less typical moment, you might need to protect your leg from a hot radiator, and you grab that blanket, this time to keep your leg cool. (The experience of using a potholder to protect your hand may be much more familiar, but who thinks of a potholder as a little blanket?)

That's how common sense works: It says different things in different contexts. Ask students whether an ice cube will melt more or less quickly if you wrap it in a

Epilogue **251**

blanket, and they're more likely to draw on their more typical experience of using blankets for warmth—that part of common sense is more available for immediate access. They may not have a habit—the discipline of mind—to look for and consider other parts of common sense, less available because they're less typical.

It takes effort and attention to connect and compare across different kinds of situations, to modify your common sense, and it isn't easy. In any context, ideas are entangled with other ideas, perceptions, and habits of mind. In other words, the cognitive dynamics that make the idea that "blankets make things warm" obvious in some contexts are different from those that make the idea that "blankets keep things cool" obvious in others. Disentangling general ideas from particular dynamics is hard work.

Part of the problem, again, is recognizing the need to do that work, the work of connecting and comparing, of finding and reconciling inconsistencies, of disentangling ideas and synthesizing new ones. That's what learning in *science* entails; that's what science entails: Scientists are professional learners.

So there it is, our first reason to dispute the HEA's definition of "teaching skills" as those "that enable a teacher, among other competencies, to effectively convey and explain academic content." It comes from our scholarship, from our own disciplined practices of learning, which led us to modify our understanding of learning and, from there, of teaching: Learning science isn't the same as learning to change a tire or to work a microwave, because understanding concepts in science requires synthesizing across seemingly disparate experiences. Students don't learn to do that work by hearing others' explanations.

For the authors of the HEA and the new regulations, and for the leader and staff of the Department of Education, the idea that "teaching is explaining" is still common sense. As common sense, it is entangled with many other ideas, habits, and attitudes, just like "blankets keep things warm"—plus, in this case, laws and institutional structures. For that very reason, I suppose it's probably not effective to "convey and explain" that explanations do not cause learning, any more than it is effective to convey and explain that forces do not cause motion.

What we need at the societal level is a grand shift to disciplined thinking about education, which involves questioning assumptions and holding unmodified common sense accountable to evidence and reasoning. We need society to learn how to learn about education.

But we have another reason to dispute the notion that teaching is explaining, and it might be an easier place to start. The first reason is, in essence, students have *to do science* in order to learn the concepts. The second reason is that doing science is an important objective in its own right.

(2) We're trying to teach the doing of science.

Doing science is a different instructional target from the concepts of science, that is, from "academic content." It's about students learning to have and pursue their own ideas, to recognize and question hidden assumptions, to come up with new possibilities, and to test and revise their ideas, looking backward and forward:

Can they account for existing evidence? What do their new ideas predict, and is that what happens? What new questions do they raise?

As a target of instruction, doing science aligns with goals of "Education for Innovation" and "meeting the needs of a 21st century workforce," which have become a focus of attention in politics and the popular press. For reasons largely deriving from technological advancement, there is growing societal interest in students learning to think for themselves, having and developing their own ideas, and being creative.

And, I believe, thinking about those interests taps into different parts of common sense about learning and teaching. Like "blankets make things warm," "explanation causes learning" fits with many everyday situations of teaching and learning—how to use a microwave and so on. But there are also situations when it's obvious explanations won't do it, when learning requires learners to work things out for themselves. In these situations, common sense epistemology aligns with research on learning.

I'll just mention one study. Bonawitz et al. (2011) designed an experiment in which an adult showed preschool children a toy that had many features. For about half the children, the adult gave "direct instruction," demonstrating one of the toy's features. For the other children, the adult acted as though she was just learning about the toy herself, "discovering" that same feature. The results were clear: Children who got an explanation spent much less time exploring the toy on their own and discovered fewer of its other features.

I suspect most people would see that finding as no surprise. Like moments when "blankets keep things cool" is obvious, there are moments when common sense says that "experience causes learning," and that explanations can interfere. And in such moments, the skills "to effectively convey and explain academic content" don't seem as relevant as the skills to recruit students to join the pursuit, and to attend, assess, and respond to their ideas and reasoning as they do. There are examples throughout this book.

I'm suggesting that as we engage with the "real world" we appreciate how common sense about teaching and learning is as varied and contextual as it is about natural phenomena. Some of our reasoning about responsive teaching in science and mathematics applies to the ways we reach out beyond our community. Ultimately, it does come back to that need for more disciplined thinking about education, and lasting progress will demand that grand shift. It may help to call out and consider these multiple ways people think about teaching.

We should also bear in mind how this cognition is distributed across institutional structures, materials, laws, and regulations. The stability of the notion that teaching is explaining goes beyond its quick availability in our individual experiences. It's a societal stability entangled with the economics of staffing schools, which is much easier if there are limited expectations of teacher preparation; with academia's established practices and policies that distinguish "teaching" from "scholarship"; with needs, expectations, and practices of large-scale, efficient, and standardized testing, which is much easier with respect to assessing the correctness of students' knowledge than to their becoming inventive, independent thinkers.

Bearing that in mind, I see I'm drifting into matters I don't know much about, of political science and critical theory. But I'll say just a little more: We in this community may contribute to that stability in the ways we talk, such as calling it the "real world," as if it's a fixed thing, and in describing responsive teaching as "ambitious."

We understand responsive teaching as subtle, sophisticated, intellectually demanding work, and for many that means we shouldn't expect it of most teachers. But across our projects, we keep finding reasons to believe we can. It's been great progress, how society has started to demand high expectations and rigorous education for all students. Maybe we should argue the point for all teachers too, even in the millions.

Reference

Bonawitz, E., Shafto, P., Gweon, H., Goodman, N.D., Spelke, E., & Schulz, L. (2011). The double-edged sword of pedagogy: Instruction limits spontaneous exploration and discovery. *Cognition, 120*(3), 322–330.

CONTRIBUTORS

Leslie J. Atkins (ljatkins@csuchico.edu) is an Associate Professor of Science Education & Physics at California State University, Chico. Her research focuses on how students and scientists create rigorous, creative, scientific theories about the world, and how we might construct learning environments and curricular materials that support such creativity. As an instructor, she focuses on the pre-service science content preparation of K–8 teachers.

Janet E. Coffey (janet.coffey@moore.org) is currently a Program Officer at the Gordon & Betty Moore Foundation, where she oversees the Foundation's science learning portfolio within the Science Program. Her research interests sit at the intersection of learning, assessment, and teaching, and she is particularly interested in meaningful student engagement in assessment. She has taught science at the elementary, middle, and secondary levels, and has worked in K–12 science teacher education and professional development.

Adam A. Colestock (acolestock@fwparker.org) is a middle school STEM teacher at the Francis W. Parker School in Chicago. He received a B.A. in Mathematics from Williams College and an M.A. in the Learning Sciences from Northwestern University. He has worked as a mathematics teacher, robotics coach, technology coordinator, and coding teacher at the middle school level. As both a teacher and researcher, he is interested in understanding how attending to student thinking can contribute to the design of learning environments that foster agency, autonomy, and mastery as students pursue personally meaningful and ambitious learning goals.

Ann R. Edwards (edwards@carnegiefoundation.org) is the Director of Learning and Teaching at the Carnegie Foundation for the Advancement of Teaching.

256 Contributors

She directs curriculum, instruction, and professional development in the Community College Pathways, a systemic reform initiative aimed at improving developmental mathematics outcomes nationwide. She is the co-PI of an NSF-funded project employing improvement science in the design and implementation of professional development for developmental mathematics faculty at scale. Her research interests include mathematics teacher learning and professional development and issues of equity in mathematics education. She has taught secondary and post-secondary mathematics and worked in K–16 mathematics teacher education and professional development.

Andrew Elby (elby@umd.edu), Associate Professor in the Department of Teaching & Learning, Policy & Leadership at the University of Maryland, focuses on science student and teacher epistemologies and their relation to enactment of scientific practices in the classroom, in physics and in the sciences more generally. Much of his work involves documenting and theorizing about context dependence in the conceptual ideas and epistemological stances displayed by teachers and learners.

Brian W. Frank (brian.frank@mtsu.edu) is an Assistant Professor of Physics and Astronomy at Middle Tennessee State University. His research focuses on how students see and make use of science content in their everyday lives. As an educator, he is dedicated to the preparation of physics teachers.

David Hammer (david.hammer@tufts.edu) has studied the learning and teaching of science (mostly physics) from elementary school through university, with particular emphases on students' intuitive epistemologies, how instructors attend and respond to student thinking, and resource-based models of knowledge and reasoning. From 1998 to 2010 he was a professor of Physics and Curriculum & Instruction at the University of Maryland, College Park. In 2010 he moved to Tufts University, where he is a professor of Education and Physics and, currently, chair of Education and co-director of the Center for Engineering Education and Outreach.

Lama Z. Jaber (lamazjaber@gmail.com) is an assistant professor at Florida State University in the School of Teacher Education. She is interested in studying the dynamics of students' disciplinary engagement in science in various contexts. More specifically, her research examines the interplay of affect and epistemology in these dynamics and the design of learning environments that empower students as epistemic agents in their learning.

Daniel M. Levin (dlevin2@umd.edu) is a Clinical Assistant Professor in science and mathematics education at the University of Maryland, College Park. Prior to his career in higher education, Dan worked for several years as a laboratory biologist, followed by a decade as a middle and high school science teacher. His research interests include responsive teaching, science and mathematics teacher education, students' participation in scientific practices, and integrated STEM teaching and learning. His current research in responsive teaching involves exploring the role of disciplinary writing as an aspect of teachers' efforts to attend and respond to students' participation in scientific practices.

Jennifer Evarts Lineback (JenLineback@pointloma.edu) is a former high school biology teacher and current Associate Professor in the Biology Department and the School of Education at Point Loma Nazarene University. She teaches a range of classes at PLNU, including those for upper-level biology majors, pre-service elementary teachers, and MAT students. Her research interests concern how science and mathematics teachers across all levels (elementary through college) implement novel instructional practices in their classrooms.

April Cordero Maskiewicz (AprilMaskiewicz@pointloma.edu) is an Associate Professor of biology and Director of the University NOW program at Point Loma Nazarene University in San Diego, California. Her current research focuses on developing more effective approaches for teaching ecology and evolution that are grounded in the learning sciences research so that students will develop not only content knowledge but also biological ways of thinking and reasoning about the living world. She is also active in several professional development projects with K–12 teachers, as well as with university biology faculty.

Jennifer Radoff (jennifer.radoff@tufts.edu) is a doctoral student in science education at Tufts University. Her research focuses on studying the dynamics of teaching and learning science, specifically with respect to understanding how classroom disciplinary norms get established and refined. She is currently a graduate research assistant for the Gordon and Betty Moore Foundation–funded project, The Dynamics of Learners' Persistence and Engagement in Science.

Jennifer Richards (jrich14@uw.edu) is a Research Associate in the College of Education at the University of Washington. She works with science teachers in educational and professional development settings to engage and support all students in participating in scientific practices and inquiry in the classroom. Her research centers on understanding how teachers learn and choose to teach responsively in K–12 classrooms in ways that attend and respond to students' developing ideas about scientific phenomena.

Amy D. Robertson (robertsona2@spu.edu) is a Research Assistant Professor in the Department of Physics at Seattle Pacific University. She works with undergraduate learning assistants as they interact with students in a teaching role for the first time. She is broadly interested in research that has the potential to build community or to empower students and teachers of science. This interest fleshes itself out in her research on responsive teaching and on the resources that students and teachers use to make sense of science or science teaching.

Rachel E. Scherr (scherr@spu.edu) is a Senior Research Scientist in the Department of Physics at Seattle Pacific University. Her research focuses on what people do to learn together. Scherr is a leader in video microanalysis methodologies for physics education research, conducting theoretically driven qualitative investigations into how learners construct understanding. She leads projects to support elementary and secondary teachers' teaching and learning of energy and is the editor of *Periscope*, a set of materials for university physics educator development based on classroom video of best-practices university physics instruction.

Miriam Gamoran Sherin (msherin@northwestern.edu) is Professor of Learning Sciences at Northwestern University in the School of Education and Social Policy, where she also serves as Director of Undergraduate Education. Her research interests include mathematics teaching and learning, teacher cognition, and the role of video in supporting teacher learning. Sherin investigates the nature and dynamics of teachers' professional vision, and the ways in which teachers identify and interpret significant interactions during instruction. *Mathematics Teacher Noticing: Seeing Through Teachers' Eyes*, edited by Sherin, V. Jacobs, and R. Philipp, received the AERA Division K 2013 Excellence in Research in Teaching and Teacher Education award.

Tiffany-Rose Sikorski (tsikorski@gwu.edu) is Assistant Professor of Secondary Science Education at George Washington University. Her research explores how learners of all ages seek coherence as they make sense of natural phenomena. Dr. Sikorski is co-PI of the National Science Foundation–funded project Building Capacity for Disciplinary Experts in Math and Science Teaching. A licensed physics educator, she continues to refine her responsiveness in secondary, post-secondary, and informal settings.

Janet Walkoe (jwalkoe@umd.edu) is an Assistant Professor at the University of Maryland, College Park. She earned her doctorate from Northwestern University in the Learning Sciences in 2012. She also holds an M.S. in Mathematics from the University of Illinois at Chicago and a B.A. in Mathematics from the University of Chicago. Before enrolling in graduate school, Janet taught high school mathematics (from 1996–2006), earning National Board Certification in 2003. Janet's research interests include teacher responsiveness in the mathematics classroom. In particular, she is interested in how teachers attend to and make sense of student thinking.

AUTHOR INDEX

Achieve, Inc. 86, 123
Aldous, C. R. 163
Alvarado, C. 48
Anderson-Levitt, K. M. 244
Anderson, R. 50
Ansell, E. 37
Apple, M. 155
Arsenault, A. 92
Atkins, L. J. 1, 56, 58, 60
Aultman, L. P. 165
Azevedo, F. S. 57

Bagrodia, R. 100
Balacheff, N. 121
Ball, D. viii, 1, 2, 3, 4–8, 28, 29, 30, 41,
    42, 43, 44, 46, 47, 48, 49, 81, 86,
    106, 107, 123, 133, 136, 145, 146,
    147, 155, 203, 229, 230, 241,
    243, 244
Ballenger, C. viii, 45, 90
Bang, M. 81
Barnett-Clarke, C. 133
Barrick, N. 145, 146
Barron, B. 168, 231
Bartfai, M. 159
Bartlett, F. C. 99
Bass, H. 146
Bates, A. 164
Battey, D. 2, 39, 146
Baxter, J. 133
Beasley, H. viii, 47

Beck, L. G. 164
Becker, H. S. 244
Becker, J. 166
Behrend, J. 37, 38, 58
Bell, M. 90, 101, 102
Bendall, S. 185, 192
Bereiter, C. 163
Best, S. 145
Black, P. 45, 147
Bonawitz, E. 252
Borko, H. 145, 146
Braaten, M. viii, 47, 145
Branca, N. 133
Bredo, E. 244
Bresser, R. 30, 192
Briggs, J. L. 183
Brodie, K. 1, 41, 228, 230
Bruner, J. B. 36
Buckland, L. A. 190
Buese, D. 155
Burgess, H. 164

California State Bureau of Education 18
Carey, D. A. viii, 2, 37, 38, 45
Careym, N. 146
Carpenter, T. P. viii, 1, 2, 37, 38, 39, 44, 45,
    46, 146, 203, 229
Carter, B. 164
Cartier, J. 145, 146
Cassidy, W. 164
Chabris, C. F. 189

260 Author Index

Chambliss, M. 155
Chan, A. G. 205, 206, 207, 208, 209, 210, 211, 217, 219, 224
Chazan, D. 2, 28, 41, 42, 43, 47, 48, 146, 229, 230, 243
Chiang, C.-P. viii, 2, 37, 38, 45, 46, 203
Chinn, C. A. 106, 190
Choppin, J. 137
Clark, C. M. 219
Clement, L. 46
Close, E. W. 56, 70, 71
Close, H. G. 56, 70, 71
Coates, J. 92
Cobb, P. 177, 191, 200, 201
Coffey, J. viii, 1, 2, 16, 28, 31, 43, 44, 45, 46, 49, 50, 81, 86, 87, 90, 105, 113, 142, 145, 146, 164, 168, 184, 185, 190, 192, 200, 205, 228, 229
Cohen, D. K. 155
Cohen, S. 140
Colestock, A. 1, 39, 40, 49, 126, 130
Compton, C. 145
Conant, F. 86, 87, 102, 119, 164, 181
Cook-Sather, A. 100
Cooper, M. 127
Cowan, B. 92
Crespo, S. 132, 228
Croninger, R. 155
Cross, D. I. 165
Czikszenthmihalyi, M. 100, 102

Daane, A. R. 48, 71
Darling-Hammond, L. 155
Davis, B. 129, 228, 242, 245
Davis, E. 146
Dennis, E. 90
Derry, S. J. 168, 231
DeWater, L. S. 56, 70
Dewey, J. 36
DiSchino, M. viii, 45, 164
diSessa, A. 2, 57
Driver, R. 164
Duckworth, E. 1, 44, 86, 87, 88, 90, 181
Dufresne, R. J. 24
Duschl, R. A. 113

Edwards, A. R. 50, 145, 155
Elby, A. 1, 2, 31, 44, 45, 49, 86, 87, 90, 190, 227, 229
Empson, S. B. viii, 1, 2, 37, 38, 45, 46, 228, 229, 242, 243
Engeström, Y. 69, 81
Engle, R. 50, 86, 87, 102, 119, 164, 168, 181, 231

Eppard, E. P. 48
Erickson, F. 45, 100, 127, 141, 147, 168, 231, 244, 245
Erstad, C. 56
Espinoza, M. 100
Even, R. 1, 43, 44

Fargason, S. vii, 1, 30, 44, 56, 79, 87, 190, 192
Farris, E. 146
Fennema, E. viii, 1, 2, 37, 38, 45, 46, 203, 229
Festinger, L. 100
Fishman, B. J. 145
Floden, R. E. 244
Flood, V. J. 2, 56
Ford, M. J. 14, 164, 190
Forman, E. 145, 190
Fortus, D. 101
Forzani, F. viii, 146
Fraivillig, J. L. 50
Frank, B. W. 56
Franke, M. viii, 1, 2, 37, 38, 39, 45, 46, 47, 146, 205, 206, 207, 209, 210, 211, 217, 219, 224, 229
Freund, D. 205, 206, 207, 208, 209, 210, 211, 217, 219, 224
Fritzen, A. 127
Furtak, E. M. 203
Fuson, K. C. 50

Gallas, K. viii, 1, 2, 45, 46, 86, 87, 107, 118, 121
Gearhart, M. viii, 45
Gellert, U. 165, 166
Gerace, W. J. 24
Ghousseini, H. viii, 47
Givvin, K. viii, 45, 89, 100, 127
Goetz, J. 183
Goffman, E. 190
Goldberg, F. vii, viii, 1, 44, 45, 56, 57, 66, 79, 87, 164, 185, 190, 192
Goldenstein, D. 133
Goldman, R. 168, 231
Goldsmith, L. T. 2, 39, 228
Goldstein, L. S. 164, 183
Goodhew, L. M. 48
Goodman, N. D. 252
Goodwin, C. viii
Graber, A. 155
Grant, T. viii, 1, 45, 46, 87, 164, 168, 190, 200
Gravemeijer, K. 200
Gresalfi, M. S. 182, 184
Grossman, P. 145
Gruber, H. E. 163

Author Index 261

Guba, E. G. 244
Gudeman, P. 56
Gupta, A. 229
Gweon, H. 252

Hackenberg, A. J. 166, 167
Haidt, J. 183
Hall, R. 168, 231
Hammer, D. iii, vii, viii, 1, 2, 3, 4, 8–11, 16, 27, 28, 30, 31, 41, 42, 43, 44, 45, 46, 47, 48, 49, 50, 56, 57, 79, 81, 86, 87, 89, 90, 101, 102, 105, 106, 107, 113, 117, 122, 142, 145, 146, 163, 164, 168, 184, 185, 189, 190, 192, 200, 203, 204, 205, 228, 229, 241, 249
Han, S. Y. 39, 130, 145, 146
Hankes, J. 92
Hargreaves, A. 165, 166, 183
Harrer, B. W. 2
Henderson, A. 168, 231
Hennessey, M. G. 101
Herbst, P. 146
Hiebert, J. viii, 45
Hill, H. 133, 145, 146
Hong, J. Y. 165
Horton, R. 183
Houghton, C. 101
Hudicourt-Barnes, J. viii, 45
Hughes, E. K. 50
Hutchison, P. 2, 16, 31, 41, 42, 46, 47, 87, 89

Ing, M. 205, 206, 207, 208, 209, 210, 211, 217, 219, 224
Igra, D. 145
Irby, D. 102

Jaber, L. Z. 48, 50, 87, 88, 162, 163
Jackson, B. 133
Jacobs, V. R. viii, 1, 2, 37, 39, 40, 45, 46, 50, 51, 127, 141, 142, 146, 203, 228, 229, 242, 243
Jacobson, L. 155
Jain, S. 102
Jiménez-Aleixandre, M. P. 113
Johnson, A. 14
Jordan, B. 168, 231
Joseph, C. 183
Jurow, S. 100

Kagan, D. M. 139
Kane, J. 92
Kannan, P. 145, 146
Kazemi, E. viii, 37, 46, 47, 146, 147

Keller, E. F. 163
Kersting, N. B. viii, 45, 127
Knapp, N. 145, 146
Kooser, J. 164
Koschmann, T. 168
Krajcik, J. 101, 146
Kruse, R. 66
Kuipers, J. 89, 99

Lake, V. E. 164, 183
Lamb, L. L. C. 1, 2, 39, 40, 50, 51, 141, 142
Lampert, M. viii, 41, 42, 47, 48, 49, 107, 123, 129, 135, 146, 147, 203, 229, 243
Lancaster, L. 145, 146
Lather, P. A. 244
Lau, M. 1, 2, 41, 43, 48, 50, 189, 229, 230
Lee, V. 99
Lehrer, R. 164, 182
Leinhardt, G. 133
Lemke, J. viii, 168, 190
Leonard, W. J. 24
Leone, A. 106
Levi, L. 1, 2, 37, 38, 39, 45, 46, 146, 229
Levin, D. M. viii, 1, 2, 28, 31, 43, 44, 45, 46, 49, 50, 81, 86, 87, 90, 105, 113, 142, 145, 146, 164, 168, 189, 190, 200, 203, 205, 228, 229, 230
Lewis, L. 146
Li, M. 50
Lincoln, Y. S. 244
Lindfors, J. W. 87, 105, 118, 122
Lineback, J. E. 2, 40, 41, 47, 48, 203, 211, 218, 219, 224, 228
Linnenbringer, T. 2, 39, 40
Loef, M. viii, 2, 37, 38, 45, 46, 203
Loesser, H. 102
Lorimer, J. 163
Lortie, D. 155
Lubienski, S. 136
Luna, M. 43, 50, 127, 130, 141, 229
Lundeberg, M. 127
Luster, B. 166
Lyle, J. 232

Maaske, E. L. 48
Maclin, D. 101
Malhotra, B. A. 106
Malone, K. 163
Marx, R. W. 145
Maskiewicz, A. 2, 28, 43, 47, 48, 50, 57, 91, 105, 168, 184, 185, 192, 200, 203, 229, 243
Massoud, L. A. 89, 99
Maxwell, J. A. 244
May, D. B. 2, 81

262 Author Index

Mazur, E. 24
McClain, K. 200
McGowan, J. 56
McKagan, S. B. 56, 70
McNeal, B. 200
Medin, D. 81
Mehan, H. 48
MeHeut, M. 101
Mestre, J. P. 24
Mewborn, D. 136
Michaels, S. viii, 40, 45, 50, 113, 172, 230
Mikeska, J. 106, 117, 204
Miller, K. F. 127
Milne, C. 167
Minstrell, J. 40, 50, 106, 164, 230
Moss, P. A. 244
Mulhern, K. 56
Muller, J. 102
Mulligan, M. 130
Mumme, J. 133
Murphy, L. A. 50

National Committee on Science
    Education Standards and Assessment vii
National Council of Teachers of
    Mathematics (NCTM) vii
National Research Council (NRC) 123,
    146, 164
Nersessian, N. J. 163
Newstetter, W. 163
Newton, P. 164
Next Generation Science Standards/NGSS
    Lead States vii, 17, 47, 106, 190
NGA Center and CCSSO 47
Nias, J. 164
Noddings, N. 164, 166
Nyeggen, C. G. 14

O'Connor, M. C. 40, 50, 113, 172, 230
Ogonowski, M. viii, 45, 164
Olitsky, S. 167
Osbeck, L. 163
Osbon, J. N. 165
Osborne, J. 164
Otero, V. 66
Otieno, T. 167

Paley, V. G. 49
Pappas, C. 92
Parsad, B. 146
Pea, R. D. 168, 231
Peng, K. 183
Peter, J. 90, 101, 102
Peterson, P. L. viii, 2, 37, 38, 45, 46, 203, 219
Phelps, G. 145

Philipp, R. A. 1, 2, 39, 40, 46, 50, 51, 127,
    141, 142, 203
Phillips, D.C. 244
Pierson, J. L. viii, 1, 2, 40, 41, 44, 45, 48,
    142, 203, 205, 206, 207, 208, 209, 210,
    211, 217, 219, 224, 228, 230
Popham, W. J. 155
Pothier, S. viii, 45
Prader, K. 56
Putnam, R. T. 133, 145, 146

Radoff, J. 50, 189, 190, 192
Redish, E. F. 2, 190
Reiser, B. 106
Resnick, L. B. 155
Richards, J. 1, 14, 36, 41, 43, 44, 46, 49,
    167, 189, 190, 227, 228, 230, 239
Robertson, A.D. iii, 1, 36, 48, 56, 190, 199,
    200, 227
Robinson, S. 66
Rodgers, C. R. 49
Rodriguez, A. B. 113
Rogers, D. L. 164
Ronfeldt, M. 145
Rosaen, C. L. 127
Roschelle, J. 2
Rosebery, A. S. viii, 41, 43, 44, 46, 49, 81,
    90, 164, 229
Rosenthal, R. 155
Roth, K. 89, 100
Rowan, B. 145
Roy, P. 2, 81, 90, 101, 102
Ruiz-Primo, M. A. 203
Russ, R. 2, 16, 31, 39, 40, 43, 50, 99, 106,
    117, 127, 128, 130, 204, 229
Rustique-forrester, E. 155

Sabo, H. C. 48
Sacks, H. 231
Salter, I. Y. 56, 58, 60
Samarapungavan, A. 190
Sandoval, W. 106
Sannino, A. 69, 81
Saxe, G. B. viii, 45
Scardamalia, M. 88, 163, 181
Schegloff, E. A. 231
Scherr, R. iii, 2, 48, 56, 70, 71, 106, 117,
    190, 204
Schifter, D. 1, 2, 39, 46, 129, 229
Schneider, B. L. 244
Schnepp, M. 28, 41, 42, 43
Schoenfeld, A. H. 127, 131, 141
Schulz, L. 252
Schutz, P. A. 165
Seago, N. 2, 39, 133, 228

Seeley, L. 56, 70
Seltzer, M. viii, 45
Sfard, A. 177
Shafto, P. 252
Shahan, E. 145, 146
Shappelle, B. P. 2, 39, 40, 51
Sherin, B. 39, 57, 99, 126, 130, 168, 231
Sherin, M. 1, 2, 39, 40, 46, 48, 49, 50, 126,
    127, 128, 130, 132, 141, 145, 146, 168,
    203, 205, 210, 228, 229, 231, 242
Shulman, L. 145, 146
Shultz, J. 100
Shweder, R. A. 183
Sidnell, J. 168, 231
Sikorski, T. R. J. 48, 85, 91, 98, 102
Simons, D. J. 189
Singer-Gabella, M. 145, 146
Smerdon, B. 146
Smith III, J. P. 2
Smith, B. 106
Smith, C. L. 101
Smith, M. S. 50, 134
Sotelo, F. L. viii, 45
Spelke, E. 252
Spencer, J. 100
Spencer-Rodgers, J. 183
Spillane, J. 145, 155
Star, J. R. 39, 126
Stein, M. 50, 134
Steinmuller, F. 106
Stephan, M. 200
Stevens, R. 98
Stewart, F. C. 48
Stigler, J. W. viii, 45, 127
Stivers, T. 168, 231
Stodolsky, S. 145, 155
Stroupe, D. viii, 47, 50

Tabak, I. 106
Tal, R. T. 145
Tang, X. 113
Tannen, D. 190, 192, 193
Terpstra, M. 127
Thagard, P. 163
Thames, M. 145

Thanheiser, E. 46
Thompson, J. viii, 47, 50, 145, 146
Thompson, N. 66
Timmons, A. 56
Turrou, A. C. viii, 47

Valli, L. 155
van Dijk, T. 231
van Es, E. 1, 2, 39, 40, 46, 48, 127, 132, 141,
    146, 205, 210, 228, 229, 242, 245
van Zee, E. viii, 1, 2, 40, 44, 49, 56, 86, 90,
    101, 102, 106, 107, 121, 164, 230
Varelas, M. 92, 166
Viechnicki, G. B. 89, 99
Vokos, S. 56, 70, 71

Walkoe, J. 39, 130, 190, 227
Wallach, T. 1, 43, 44
Wallat, C. 193
Warren, B. viii, 41, 43, 44, 45, 46, 49, 81,
    86, 164, 229
Watkins, J. 184
Wearne, D. viii, 45
Webb, J. 164
Webb, N. M. 205, 206, 207, 208, 209, 210,
    211, 217, 219, 224
Wells, L. 71
Wenk, L. 24
Wentzel, K. R. 164
Wenzel, S. 166
Wenzinger, S. W. 48
Wiliam, D. 45, 147
Williams, M. W. 165
Williamson, P. 145
Windschitl, M. viii, 47, 50, 145, 146
Winters, V. 2, 43, 48, 50, 57, 91, 168, 189,
    200, 229, 243
Wittmann, M. C. 2, 56, 70
Wood, T. 200
Wright, L. J. 89, 99

Yackel, E. 177, 191, 200, 201

Zavala, G. 48
Zembylas, M. 166, 167, 18

SUBJECT INDEX

affect: affective displays, facial expressions, and body language 168, 170–80; anxiety 165–7, 182, 184; attention and responsiveness to affect 166–7, 180–3; confusion 162, 168–9, 174, 183; emotional complexity of inquiry 165; emotional transactions in the classroom 165–7; epistemic affect 163, 180–1; excitement 163, 166–7, 182; feelings and emotions 162–7, 181–4; frustration 162–3, 166, 170, 172, 181, 183–4; teacher 49; tension 163, 165, 174, 183
affordances of responsive teaching 44–6
ambitious practices viii
assessment 78–80, 147, 200–1; assessing teacher responsiveness 203, 225, 227, 243–4

biology: composting and decomposition 108; diffusion and osmosis 14–18

caring: Noddings' caring theory 164, 166–7; teachers as "carers" 164
case studies of responsive teaching 41–4, 168, 189, 192, 204, 224–5, 231
challenges of responsive teaching 105, 109, 113, 119
characteristics of responsive teaching 1–2, 27, 42–3, 47, 189–92, 204, 219–23
Cognitively Guided Instruction 37–8
competing instructional goals 14, 28–9, 119, 166, 219; false dichotomy between affect and disciplinary substance 165, 182, 184

conceptual substance 191–2, 232–5
conceptual understanding viii, 45, 56, 219
content knowledge 30, 44, 145

disciplinary orientation 155–8
disciplinary practices 46
disciplinary teaching practices 155–6
discursive studies of responsive teaching 40–1, 192–3, 204–5; discourse and interaction analysis 168; using Franke et al. (2009) coding scheme 205–11, 224; using Lineback (2014) coding scheme 211–18, 224; moment-to-moment multimodel analysis 168; using Pierson (2008) coding scheme 205–11, 224

Earth science: clouds 207–9; condensation 206–7, 220–3; evaporation 168–80, 211, 213–16; seasons 149; water cycle 85
elementary students 4–8, 12–14, 85, 189–201
elementary teachers 166, 204
elementary teaching 159; challenges 146
equitable participation viii, 44–5

flow 89–91; *see also* storyline
foci of teacher attention 131–8, 189, 232–5
formative assessment 45
framing 43, 50, 189–201
further reading ix–x, 203
future directions for work on responsive teaching 47–51

266 Subject Index

high leverage practices viii
high school students 8–11, 14–18
high school teachers 127–8, 165
Higher Education Act 249

inquiry 56, 58, 106, 163, 165, 183–5
in-service teachers 70–80, 107
instructional goals 130–1, 137–8
intellectual demands of responsive teaching 30, 167, 184
interpreting student thinking 135–6

mathematics 4–8, 126, 151
mathematics teacher noticing 38–40, 126–7, 141–2, 203
middle school students 230
middle school teachers 127–8, 227

narrative coherence 99
Next Generation Science Standards 190

pedagogical content knowledge 146
peer responsiveness 5–6, 30, 48, 198
physics: electrostatics 8–11; forces 23–7, 70–8; magnetism 12–14; motion and energy 66–70, 70–8, 193–9, 230; optics 18–23; reflection 58–66
practitioner accounts of responsive teaching 4–11, 41–3, 105, 107
pre-service teachers 18–23, 58–66, 66–70, 146, 159
progress in responsive teaching 48, 229–30, 242–3

reflexivity 191–2, 200–1
responsive teaching practices 148–54
revoicing 172, 179

selective-archiving camera 128–9
storyline 89, 97, 99–100; *see also* flow
student agency viii, 87, 91, 98, 179, 181, 184; *see also* student voice
student engagement 190; disciplinary engagement 162, 164; engagement and persistence 163; formulating and communicating ideas 177, 180–1
student errors 132–3
student experience of responsive teaching 48, 85
student thinking as resourceful 2–3, 44–5, 190
student understanding 131–2
student voice viii, 87; *see also* student agency
supporting teacher learning 46, 145–6, 159, 183–4; of responsive teaching 48–50

time-scales for responsiveness 28, 235–41

University students 23–7
US Department of Education 249

variability in responsive teaching 3, 27, 48, 155, 199–200, 211–12, 217–18, 227
video clubs 127

Printed in the United States
by Baker & Taylor Publisher Services